HOW
TO PLAY
VIDEO GAMES

HOW
TO PLAY
VIDEO GAMES

EDITED BY

MATTHEW THOMAS PAYNE
AND NINA B. HUNTEMANN

New York University Press

NEW YORK

NEW YORK UNIVERSITY PRESS
New York
www.nyupress.org

References to Internet websites (URLs) were accurate at the time of writing.
Neither the author nor New York University Press is responsible for URLs
that may have expired or changed since the manuscript was prepared.

Library of Congress Cataloging-in-Publication Data
Names: Payne, Matthew Thomas, editor. | Huntemann, Nina, editor.
Title: How to play video games /
Edited by Matthew Thomas Payne and Nina B. Huntemann.
Description: New York : New York University Press, [2019] |
Includes bibliographical references and index.
Identifiers: LCCN 2018052609| ISBN 9781479802142 (cl : alk. paper) |
ISBN 9781479827985 (pb : alk. paper)
Subjects: LCSH: Video games—Social aspects. | Video games—Design. | Video games—
Moral and ethical aspects. | Popular culture.
Classification: LCC GV1469.34.S52 H68 2019 | DDC 794.8—dc23
LC record available at https://lccn.loc.gov/2018052609

New York University Press books are printed on acid-free paper, and their
binding materials are chosen for strength and durability. We strive to use
environmentally responsible suppliers and materials to the
greatest extent possible in publishing our books.

Manufactured in the United States of America

10 9 8 7 6 5 4 3 2 1

Also available as an ebook

For our students.

Contents

III. Industry: Industrial Practices and Structures

IV. Game Practices: Medium, Technology, and Everyday Life

    IAN BOGOST

32. NES D-pad: Interface   269
    DAVID O'GRADY

33. *Minecraft*: User-Generated Content   277
    JAMES NEWMAN

34. *Quake*: Movies   285
    HENRY LOWOOD

35. *Counter-Strike*: Spectatorship   293
    EMMA WITKOWSKI

36. *EVE Online*: Cheating   301
    KELLY BERGSTROM

37. *Night Trap*: Moral Panic   309
    CARLY A. KOCUREK

38. *Shovel Knight*: Nostalgia   317
    JOHN VANDERHOEF

39. *Tempest*: Archive   325
    JUDD ETHAN RUGGILL AND KEN S. MCALLISTER

40. *Walden, a game*: Reflection   333
    TRACY FULLERTON

    Acknowledgments   341

    Appendix: Video Games Discussed in this Volume   343

    Contributors   351

    Index   359

Foreword

ETHAN THOMPSON AND JASON MITTELL

To avoid confusion, we, the writers of the foreword, wish to clarify one thing up front: the title of this book, *How to Play Video Games*, is a joke.

We know because the format of this book is modeled on our own book, *How to Watch Television*. The title of that book was the same kind of joke. That is, our book didn't teach people how to watch television (who needs a book for that?), and these essays do not teach you how to play video games. Look elsewhere for walkthroughs, cheats, and speedruns.

Instead, *How to Play Video Games* features 40 essays, each focusing on a particular video game and modeling a critical approach to understanding video games as popular culture. The premise behind both of these books is to assemble essays written by very smart people with very smart things to say about popular culture, such as television and video games. Most of these authors are academics, who typically publish their work as 25-plus-page essays in journals or 200-plus-page monographs, often with hundreds of citations, detailed sections on methodology, and commentary on insider debates within the field. Although that may be all well and good for academics to share their insights with one another, who else wants to read that? We believe that the vast majority of people who watch television or play video games, whether they are students in a course or inquisitive everyday readers, have something to learn about popular culture from us media scholars if only we presented our ideas in a style designed to be more broadly read and understood. That's what these books are for.

This book is not a collection of instructions; video games stopped coming with detailed user manuals years ago, embedding their directions within tutorial levels and progressive design. It is also not a collection of reviews because these writers are not primarily reviewers. They don't write about video games to assign a number of stars—or whatever it is video game reviewers assign to video games so that you can decide whether to go out and buy them. They instead write to offer insight on how video games work as a distinctive medium, how people do things with them, how they are meaningful to individuals and society at large, and why they matter beyond "just fun."

Those are the kinds of issues about media culture that academics are interested in, and this book presents them in an accessible format by focusing on a particular game, and a particular approach, and by writing in a language that doesn't assume everyone reading it already has a PhD. Although the people who wrote these essays are not reviewers, they are also not just researchers. One of the key reasons they have been selected for this book is because they write well. The format of this book allows for a kind of middle ground between the academic journal article and the video game review—an area that is fertile terrain for those who study popular culture to loosen their style and share their insights more popularly.

Back to that "joke" of the book title. Truth be known, it is only "sort of" a joke.

Although these essays don't explicitly give you instructions for how to play video games, they do provide different ways to think about how video games work as culture and what you might be doing when you play them. Thus, by changing how you think about video games and what you notice while you're leveling up, it might just change how you play them. Have fun!

Introduction

A Game Genie for Game Studies

MATTHEW THOMAS PAYNE AND NINA B. HUNTEMANN

When we think of games we often think of words like play, and fun, and pleasure. But to play games is to willingly invite frustration into our lives. The feeling is a common one. You stare blankly at a weekend crossword puzzle convinced that the missing word is just out of reach. You restart a boss fight in the hope that it will be less menacing this time. You leap to your death again, and again, and again, barely missing a ledge in pursuit of a hard-to-reach collectible item. The scenarios differ, but the feeling is the same. So too is the solution to these problems. Indeed, once we've become sufficiently exasperated, many of us will turn to the internet for help. There, resources abound. A thesaurus, online videos, walk-throughs, how-to guides, and arcane button sequences promise to aid our analog and digital struggles. We quickly become online sleuths because we want to win; we want to finish what we have started. Of course, a less charitable interpretation is that this is not resourcefulness—this is cheating. In the spirit of play, permit us a quick indulgence—a side story that will frame our goals for this collection.

Beginning in 1990, Lewis Galoob Toys produced a series of pass-through devices for home game consoles called "Game Genies" that allowed players to manipulate data stored on cartridges to gain some gameplay advantage; usually this meant scoring extra lives, enjoying temporary invulnerability, accessing potent weapons, and so on. Galoob produced its Genies for a number of popular systems in the early to mid-1990s, including the Nintendo Entertainment System (NES), the Super NES, and the Sega Genesis, as well as the Nintendo Gameboy and Sega Game Gear handheld systems (see figure I.1). It was called a "pass-through" device because the Genie would be inserted into the system as any cartridge would, and a game would then be plugged into the top of the Genie. Upon powering up the system, the user would enter a series of codes that would temporarily "patch" the game data to create some desired effect. It was a fairly ingenious and popular means of manipulating the programming that had been black boxed in the cartridges' plastic housing.[1]

FIGURE I.1
A Game Genie for
the Super Nintendo
Entertainment System.

In addition to extra lives and ammunition, the Game Genie also gave us a land-mark court case: *Lewis Galoob Toys, Inc. v. Nintendo of America, Inc.* Nintendo ac-cused Galoob of manufacturing a device that altered the code and created a deriv-ative work, thus constituting copyright infringement. But in a 1992 ruling by the US Ninth Circuit Court of Appeals, it was determined that owners of copyrighted goods could manipulate those items for their personal use and that temporarily altering and experimenting with game code was a legally acceptable form of play.

How to Play Video Games is an analytic Game Genie for game studies and me-dia studies courses. It aims to give its readers—students and instructors alike—an analytical pass-through device for making sense of video games and gaming cul-ture. The "how-to" in the anthology's title is an admittedly audacious one. How-ever, this collection is not intended to operate in the same prescriptive manner as a walkthrough guide. The "how-to" is closer in spirit to a "how-about"—it is an intellectual provocation, not a preordained solution. The anthology's chapters present a range of pithy, accessible ways of thinking about games, their stories, play mechanics, characters, and creators, as well as the technologies and practices that bring these experiences to life.

This anthology foregrounds the utility of *play* as a means and as a method for reflecting on, thinking about, and researching video games. Framing this col-lection as a veritable Game Genie is offered in the hope that these chapters will open new pathways for appreciating how and why games might be taken seri-ously as objects of study. Furthermore, we'd like for the book's underlying design conceit—the pairing of a keyword with a game title, gaming artifact, or gaming practice—to encourage readers to crack open the cultural code of games to assess why they matter in the ways that they do.

Despite its description as a cheating tool (or "video game enhancer" as its label advertises), the Game Genie was always more than a device for altering code or a technology that challenged beliefs about copyright and notions of fair play. The Genie amplified one of the most salient experiential elements of gameplay, namely, boundary exploration. When players search for hidden items, when speedrunners exploit glitches to find faster paths through levels, or when hackers modify titles to reimagine how they might look or play, they are engaged in forms of boundary exploration. Sometimes that exploration is highly instrumental, as when a defensive end in American football uses split-second timing to anticipate the snapping of the football without being caught offsides; sometimes that boundary exploration is far more playful, as when the reptilian heads atop the menacing dragons of *The Elder Scrolls V: Skyrim* (Bethesda Game Studios, 2011) are replaced via a texture modification (mod) with the bearded visages of famed wrestler "Macho Man" Randy Savage (and with it, the dragon's roar is substituted with Savage's signature "Yeah!").[2]

Boundary exploration is, in effect, informal playtesting (i.e., the testing of play). Moreover, these actions run the spectrum from being hegemonically functionalist on the one end, with actions that support the game's underlying goals and ideological disposition, to free-form play on the other, including actions that may subvert or ignore a game's rules and its goals. We wish for this collection to serve as a catalyst for pedagogical boundary exploration, as something that might encourage instructors who are building syllabi, creating assignments, and fostering classroom discussions to *think playfully* when it comes to teaching about and through video games.

In a similar fashion, we wish for this collection to encourage students to *act playfully* when learning about video games. We are particularly interested in connecting with those students who may not think of themselves as gamers or game players for any number of reasons.[3] Acting playfully means exploring, wandering, wondering, failing often, and trying again. When learning is playful, obstacles are recast as opportunities for trying a different approach, making adjustments, questioning assumptions, taking stock of what is visible, and considering what is hidden. In short, play-as-method means a willingness to test new ideas in ludic (or playful) spaces where failure is permitted because it is a means of learning winning strategies.

Our aspiration that this collection inspires readers to be playful comes, in part, from our own experiences enjoying games in our youth as playthings and, later, as students of media and cultural studies, interrogating the social and cultural impact of games. Our intellectual development as media and cultural studies scholars has influenced our scholarly orientation toward games and game criticism—a critical disposition reflected in the humanist focus of this anthology.

Broadly speaking, game studies is divided into two dominant perspectives that shape the questions and methods that scholars apply to the study of games. Social scientists are largely concerned with the effects of games on players, asking, "What do video games do to people?" These researchers employ empirical methods drawn from behavioral, cognitive, and neuropsychology. Research about the influence of playing violent video games on the behavior of young people or assessing the cognitive benefits of playing puzzle games for older adults are examples of a social science approach to game studies. In contrast, humanists are mainly concerned with how players create meaning with and through games. This approach asks, "What do people do with video games?" Humanists employ a range of interpretive methods drawn from anthropology, philosophy, political economy, and literary and cultural studies, among others. Further theoretical and methodological developments in the field include platform and code studies, discourse analysis of game culture, and ethnographic accounts of live gaming events. These are only some of the approaches that have been used to understand how making meaning happens in virtual spaces and how identities, narratives, and communities are forged through acts of play. Readers will find the richness of humanistic game studies and criticism—its questions, issues, and approaches—represented in the 40 chapters included here.

It is perhaps an inevitable result of a 40-chapter anthology that different scholarly voices, originating from different countries, informed by different critical commitments, and analyzing gaming objects pulled from different platforms across decades, would produce a diversity of commentary. We've attempted to give readers some direction by organizing the chapters into four thematic units: formal properties, representational issues, industrial concerns, and gaming practices. Yet, given how frequently we reshuffled these chapters during the editorial process, we will be the first to admit that these boundaries are porous at best and that the groupings are ultimately a subjective matter. Yet we don't see this inherent flexibility as a liability. Rather, just as we played (and replayed) with the book's organization, we believe readers will chart their own paths based on their needs and interests. Digital and analog games are often pleasurable precisely because they cede to players the agency to make their own choices. We hope that readers will "choose their own adventure" when it comes to exploring this collection. Furthermore, it was never our goal to curate a canonical list of game titles or establish a critical vocabulary for game studies. Others have attempted those projects; see, for instance, *100 Greatest Video Game Franchises*,[4] *Debugging Game History*,[5] and *The Routledge Companion to Video Game Studies*.[6] Instead, we see our chapters' syntheses of concepts and gaming objects as being an instructional and conversational beginning.

When we first embarked on this project, we had confidence that uniting 40 game and media studies concepts with an equal number of gaming artifacts would result in something useful for classroom instruction. Much of our optimism was owed to this collection's spiritual predecessor: *How to Watch Television*,[7] edited by Ethan Thompson and Jason Mittell. As media professors, we were impressed with their anthology's versatility as a teaching tool. The modular design of Thompson and Mittell's collection made it easy to integrate into our course syllabi. Moreover, because of our universities' media collections and access to streaming services, it was easy to complement their chapters with televisual fare. Rare indeed is the academic anthology where one can assign students multiple chapters a week. Yet we discovered that students engaged with *How to Watch Television* because the essays clearly demonstrated how various key terms could reveal the layered complexities (e.g., narrative, cultural, industrial) of TV programming across genres and eras.

Yet one of the foremost challenges of iterating on *How to Watch Television* for game studies is the variability of the video game itself. Gameplay—understood for our purposes as the dynamic interactions between a person at play and a rules-based gaming platform—is a medium-specific experience that introduces unique logistical and pedagogical considerations. First, games don't always scale well in the classroom. Screening a film or TV show for a dozen students or for several hundred is easy. This is not the case if we're asking students to actually play the games being analyzed.

Second, some games take only a few minutes to play, while others require dozens of hours to master. The rules structuring arcade classics like *Pac-Man* (Namco, 1980) and *Space Invaders* (Taito, 1978) or mobile hits such as *Candy Crush Saga* (King, 2012) and *Crossy Road* (Hipster Whale, 2014) are relatively easy to comprehend. Contrast this to strategy games such as *Sid Meier's Civilization VI* (Firaxis Games, 2016) and sandbox games such as *Minecraft* (Mojang, 2011), where complexly layered rule sets and item-crafting systems invite players to invest countless hours designing their personalized approaches to running a nation for more than a millennium or to designing a sturdy fortress from basic resources.

There are also genres that are built around multiplayer competition and collaboration. Multiplayer online battle arena (or MOBA) titles like *Defense of the Ancients 2* (Valve Corporation, 2013) and *League of Legends* (Riot Games, 2009)—which are exceedingly popular in esports leagues—or massively multiplayer online (MMO) games such as *World of Warcraft* (Blizzard, 2004) and *EVE Online* (CCP Games, 2003)—which contain vibrant in-game marketplaces—are predicated on the collective activity of thousands of players. Similarly, there is no escalating drama in battle royale games like *PlayerUnknown's Battlegrounds*

(PUBG Corporation, 2017) and *Fortnite* (Epic Games, 2017) if there aren't dozens of players hunting one another while thousands spectate live on streaming sites.

Furthermore, watching fixed media such as film and television requires a relatively simple technical proficiency that is nearly universal: turning on a TV and pressing (or clicking) play on a DVR system or streaming service. Although many teachers have encountered ornery audiovisual systems in unfamiliar classrooms that required an emergency call to media support services, the anxiety of turning on a digital projector and setting the correct source pales in comparison to the performance anxiety of demonstrating to a lecture hall filled with undergraduates the game mechanics of a two-dimensional (2D) platformer like *Super Meat Boy* (Team Meat, 2010). When a speaker stands at a podium, audiences assume a level of expertise about the subject under discussion. Yet with video games, more so we would argue than with film or television, to be an expert *about* video games assumes an expertise at *playing* video games. At least for one of us (Nina) this is far from the case. She still aspires, after four decades of playing games, to complete a game above a "normal" difficulty setting. Moreover, even when gameplay skill isn't an issue, playing with and, especially, against students in a formal learning environment like a university classroom has the potential to trouble established boundaries. The other editor (Matthew) has faced off against students in frenetic combat games and sports titles. Although this kind of experience has the potential to affirm and grow interpersonal bonds, the passion of competition also stands to upset relationships. Gameplay is an undeniably messy thing.

If the anxiety of playing in front of students introduces a precarious state for instructors, this same concern is no less the case and is perhaps even more acute for students. We rarely hear "I don't watch TV" as a reason for not watching a show as part of a class. Yet students are frequently quick to declare, "I don't play video games," in an effort to avoid picking up a controller. One need only roll out a media cart equipped with a cathode-ray-tube (CRT) television connected to an NES console or Sega Genesis to paralyze normally tech-savvy students.

There are likewise financial and technological considerations when playing games in the service of media and game studies. Video games can be expensive. Gaming platforms and their operating systems change over time. Certain titles, like casual, mobile, and flash games, have a way of disappearing if not supported by their publishers. Collecting older systems requires more and more physical storage space (and an increasing array of adaptors). In short, there are numerous challenges when it comes to introducing games and gameplay into classrooms.

And, yet, there are also solutions. For the aforementioned reasons, we encouraged our contributors to select games for analysis that could be easily accessed. This concerted effort resulted in a table of contents that features games that can overwhelmingly be played across desktop computers and mobile devices.

Moreover, many of these games are either free or are fairly inexpensive. The mobile games can be downloaded for play on iOS and Android devices through their respective app stores. And many of the other games explored in this collection are available through popular digital distribution sites including "Steam" (http://store .steampowered.com), "Good Old Games" (https://www.gog.com), and "itch.io" (https://itch.io).[8]

Of course, not all topics lent themselves to this goal. For those games and gaming experiences that might be prohibitive—be it because of price, technological access, or skill—streaming sites such as YouTube Gaming and Twitch.tv host scores of "Let's Play" videos. Watching others play is no substitute for one's own virtual exploration, but it can give inquisitive readers a vicarious sense of a game's rules, mechanics, art design, and so on.

Despite the challenges of integrating gameplay into course curricula, we strongly believe that the educational benefits of play—as boundary exploration, as the iterative testing of ideas, as the adoption of new identities and the collaborative cultivation of narratives and magic circles—are simply too great to ignore. If games are engines for play, then play is the experiential Geist that fuels lifelong learning processes. *How to Play Video Games* is less about *playing* video games than it is about the *doing* of game studies. To that end, we humbly suggest that readers consider experimenting with the collection's combination of game titles and keywords. One might mix and match the chapters' pieces to create new combinations.

For example, Shira Chess analyzes *Kim Kardashian: Hollywood* through the lens of intersectional feminism, but how might we think about this game through the lens of gamification, the keyword of Sebastian Deterding's chapter about *Cookie Clicker*? Or swap the keyword and game pairing of Mark J. P. Wolf's world-building look at *Bioshock Infinite* with Soraya Murray's focus on masculinity in *The Last of Us*. One could just as easily scrutinize *BioShock Infinite*'s rescue narrative through the lens of masculinity while assessing the bleak world-building choices on display in the post-apocalyptic *The Last of Us*. Of course, not all chapters are amenable to easy substitutions. Yet the fact that so many are underscores the collection's implicit invitation to readers to craft compelling game-keyword combinations and quick-start their own game criticism.

The table of contents may also be "modded" for different ends. Some readers may want to approach the chapters in a chronological order that foregrounds changes over time—changes affecting the medium's form, industrial concerns, and its cultural discourse. Alternatively, one might rejigger the table of contents by genre, an approach which could reveal how prevailing textual properties and play mechanics structure our thinking about gaming experiences. Finally, one could easily introduce new words and games not explored in this collection. Forty chapters is a good start, but there are many more useful keywords and thousands of video games that could be analyzed. Ours is merely a beginning point.

It is an exciting time to play games, as gaming technologies such as virtual reality become affordable consumer products, as game designers innovate genres and modes of storytelling, as indie studios redefine commercial success, and as the gaming population continues to expand well beyond traditional markets. It is also an exciting time to study video games.

The vibrancy of the field is reflected, in part, by the rapid emergence of series and anthologies that are pushing game studies in new directions. These projects offer sustained attention to subjects including individual games, designers, technologies, cultural histories, and gaming identities. The following is merely a handful of recent examples that readers of this anthology might consider exploring: the "Influential Video Game Designers" series, co-edited by Carly Kocurek and Jennifer deWinter for Bloomsbury; the "Landmark Video Games" series, co-edited by Mark J. P. Wolf and Bernard Perron for University of Michigan Press; and from MIT Press, the "Platform Studies" series, co-edited by Ian Bogost and Nick Montfort, and "Game Histories," co-edited by Raiford Guins and Henry Lowood.

Finally, theoretical and critical approaches adjacent to game and media studies are advancing our understanding of gaming's identity politics. For example, Adrienne Shaw and Bonnie Ruberg's edited collection *Queer Game Studies*[9] uses queerness to challenge heteronormative ideas that have long-dominated gaming discussions. In a similar intellectual spirit, Jennifer Malkowski and TreaAndrea Russworm's *Gaming Representation*[10] connects questions of race, gender, and sexuality with how we make sense of game design, interactive narratives, and contested sites of play. We are humbled that *How to Play Video Games* features contributions from many of these scholars.

Let's return to the beginning. If playing video games invites frustration into our lives, these experiences carry with them an implicit promise that there are solutions to be found. In his masterful *The Grasshopper: Games, Life and Utopia*, philosopher Bernard Suits defines gameplay as "the voluntary attempt to overcome unnecessary obstacles."[11] Analog and digital games are often powerful experiences *precisely* because we willingly subject ourselves to rules and to situations not of our choosing. The pleasures of gameplay emerge from the productive tension between freely giving ourselves over to a set of temporary restrictions while exercising choice in navigating those unnecessary obstacles. Suits identified this embrace of game rules to facilitate a state of play as the "lusory attitude."

As you explore the following chapters, keep in mind that our contributors' insights are the dynamic result of bringing a diversity of critical commitments and personal experiences to bear on a range of playful experiences. The vagaries of gameplay and the idiosyncratic craft of scholarly interpretation mean that no two readings of a single game or ludic experience would necessarily be the same. Nor should it be. Although *How to Play Video Games* is intended to introduce readers to the craft of game studies, it is also an invitation to embrace the lusory attitude as a player and as a critic. It is a call to study games and gaming culture, playfully.

NOTES

1 This line of cheat systems is partly responsible for Galoob's corporate success in the 1990s and is a major reason why toy giant Hasbro acquired the firm in 1998 for $220 million. See Dan Fost, "Hasbro Adds Galoob to its Toy Chest," *San Francisco Chronicle*, September 29, 1998, www.sfgate.com.

2 To watch a gameplay video of this texture mod, see Ross Mahon, "Skyrim—'Macho Man' Randy Savage—Dragon Mod," YouTube video, 4:44, published November 18, 2014, https://www.youtube.com/watch?v=QlJULkof9xA.

3 People who play video games often reject self-identifying as a "gamer" because the term is frequently associated with an exclusionary and toxic subculture that is hostile to women, people of color, and lesbian, gay, bisexual, transgender, and queer people. It is also curious that engaging with games has inspired a classification of people (i.e., "the gamer") that other mediums, such as television and books have not. As Ian Bogost observes elsewhere, we do not think of people who watch television or read books as a group set apart from the rest of us. Why, then, do this for "gamers"? We encourage instructors and students to interrogate the "gamer" identity directly, unpacking the history of sexist, racist, and homophobic discourse often universally attributed to people who play games. For Bogost's reflections on the gamer, see *How to Do Things with Videogames* (Minneapolis: University of Minnesota Press, 2011). For those looking for more on this topic, we recommend the work by a number of this collection's contributors; specifically, Adrienne Shaw, John Vanderhoef, Carly Kocurek, Bonnie Ruberg, TreaAndrea Russworm, and Shira Chess have written elsewhere about the intersectional complexities of gamer identity.

4 Robert Mejia, Jaime Banks, and Aubrie Adams, eds., *100 Greatest Video Game Franchises* (Lanham, MD: Roman & Littlefield, 2017).

5 Henry Lowood and Raiford Guins, eds., *Debugging Game History: A Critical Lexicon* (Cambridge, MA: MIT Press, 2016).

6 Mark J. P. Wolf, ed., *The Routledge Companion to Video Game Studies* (New York: Routledge, 2014).

7 Ethan Thompson and Jason Mittell, eds., *How to Watch Television* (New York: NYU Press, 2013).

8 Another potentially useful resource is the Internet Arcade at the Internet Archive; see https://archive.org/details/internetarcade.

9 Adrienne Shaw and Bonnie Ruberg, eds., *Queer Game Studies* (Minneapolis: University of Minnesota Press, 2017).

10 Jennifer Malkowski and TreaAndrea Russworm, eds., *Gaming Representation: Race, Gender, and Sexuality in Video Games* (Bloomington: Indiana University Press, 2017).

11 Bernard Suits, *The Grasshopper: Games, Life and Utopia* (Peterborough, Ontario: Broadview Press, 2005), 55.

FURTHER READING

Kline, Stephen, Nick Dyer-Witheford, and Greig De Peuter, eds. *Digital Play: The Interaction of Technology, Culture, and Marketing.* Montreal: McGill-Queen's University Press, 2003.

Taylor, T. L. *Play Between Worlds: Exploring Online Game Culture.* Cambridge, MA: MIT Press, 2006.

Wolf, Mark J. P., and Bernard Perron, eds. *The Video Game Theory Reader.* New York: Routledge, 2003.

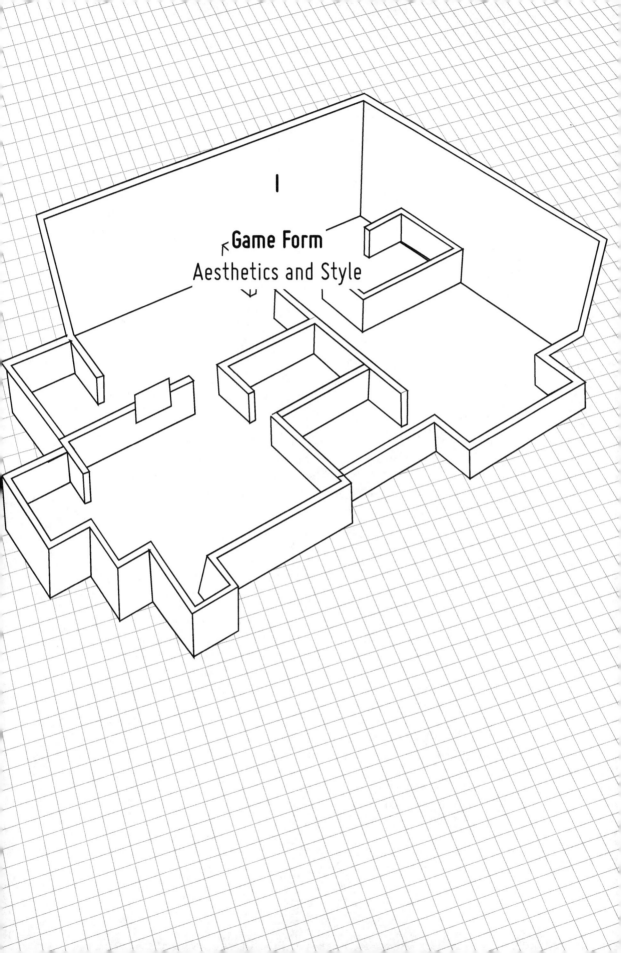

I

Game Form

Aesthetics and Style

1

FIFA
Magic Circle

STEVEN CONWAY

Abstract: Huizinga's concept of the magic circle is often discussed as the starting point of modern game studies, despite having been roundly critiqued and largely dismissed. Steven Conway uses the example of soccer and EA Sports' *FIFA* series to argue that the magic circle persists as a foundational concept because it conveys something fundamental about games and play: they are magic.

What happens when you play?[1] What happens to your perception, your movement, your body, your social relationships, your understanding of your immediate world? What comes into existence? What changes? What disappears? These are the kinds of questions that concerned Dutch historian Johan Huizinga (pronounced "how-zing-ha") in writing his book *Homo Ludens* (Man of Play) in 1938, now seen as foundational to modern game studies.

Huizinga did not anticipate digital games, yet the same questions apply equally well to soccer as to its digital incarnations, such as EA Sports' *FIFA* and Konami's *Pro Evolution Soccer* series. When we kick a ball, when we pick up a game controller, when we turn on a console, when we perceive a soccer field (whether made of grass or pixels), we understand and attach value to a bundle of things in a way different to our "everyday" lives. Although Huizinga argues playful behavior occurs across species, he sees something unique in human play, and he thinks it's something to do with the phenomenon of meaning.

On the first page of the first chapter of *Homo Ludens*, he offers an initial assessment: "It is a *significant* function . . . All play means something,"[2] and goes on to declare an essential link between play and imagination: play is primarily mind, *not* matter. Such an assertion positions Huizinga as an idealist (as opposed to materialist). He believes that ideas generate our interactions with the material world rather than the material world generating our interactions with ideas.

This hierarchy of mind over matter has enormous ramifications for Huizinga's view of play and games (this intermingling is a problem we'll come back to). He introduces what would become the famous "magic circle" thesis on play:

> All play moves and has its being within a play-ground marked off beforehand either materially or ideally, deliberately or as a matter of course. Just as there is no formal difference between play and ritual, so the "consecrated spot" cannot be formally distinguished from the play-ground. The arena, the card-table, the magic circle, the temple, the stage, the screen, the tennis court, the court of justice, etc., are all in form and function play-grounds, i.e. forbidden spots, isolated, hedged round, hallowed, within which special rules obtain. All are temporary worlds within the ordinary world, dedicated to the performance of an act apart.[3]

Importantly, Huizinga adds at the start of the next paragraph that "[i]nside the play-ground an absolute and peculiar order reigns . . . play . . . creates order, *is* order. Into an imperfect world and into the confusion of life it brings a temporary, a limited perfection."[4] Play is, in some "peculiar" way, vacuum-sealed from the wider world. To bring the "real" world, "ordinary life," into the game world is, for Huizinga, to be a "spoil-sport" who "breaks the magic."[5]

In soccer, there are a few interlocking "play-grounds" to consider: not only the soccer field and players but also the stadium, broader sports culture, and fans. When supporters speak of their team in terms of *we*, they are certainly placing themselves within the game. "Spoilsports" here range from cheats to streakers, racist chants from the crowd, bad weather, and everything between. In the *FIFA* series we must also think of bugs, glitches, crashes, broadband infrastructure, and electricity as spoilsports that may potentially puncture that thin membrane between play and the everyday.[6]

Huizinga offers a set of criteria for identifying the primary qualities of play: freedom (voluntary, autonomous), disinterestedness (external to biological needs or material gains), limitedness (in time and space), and repetition (within the moment of play, as technique and structure, and beyond the moment of play, becoming tradition, recognized game format, and community). If we trace Huizinga's account of the way play is different, we might be better served using the term *mana*. Otherwise mundane things are imbued with an extraordinary significance during the act of play. Why is a leather ball filled with compressed air the most important thing in the world to a person during a moment of play? Not because of its material value. Why do we defer authority to a line of chalk on grass? Certainly, it is nothing to do with its pH number or color. In *FIFA*, why do we find significance in a bunch of binary code transmogrified into light-emitting diodes flashing on a flat rectangular screen?

Simply, to play is to pledge oneself to an illusion. Indeed, one *should* commit so fully that one does not even see it as illusion (for to call something an illusion is to acknowledge its falsity and undermine its importance). A leap of faith is required, and this is why Huizinga places idealism above materialism: he believes it begins as an idea one pledges and has less to do with the material value of anything within that world.

One acts *as if* things specified by the game rules have value, without acknowledging the fantasy implied by the *as if*. Crucially, it is this moment of commitment that many of Huizinga's criteria find validation. Freedom is felt. It is the freedom to choose, to voluntarily commit oneself to the fantasy, the *as-if*. To be disinterested is to care about nothing but the objective of the play event. To be limited is to freely commit, and to remain disinterested in anything else, for this time and in this space. To fail to commit entirely, to fail to be disinterested in anything but the moment of play, is to fail to become a player. One is instead a trifler, someone who follows the rules (and is therefore not a cheat) but has not committed to believing in the goal of the game as significant. This is enormously frustrating for those pledged to play. The trifler is therefore a more passive type of spoilsport.

The emotion and excitement of soccer is founded upon commitment to a set of primordial *as-if* statements: behave *as if* the soccer ball is valuable, indeed *the most* valuable entity in this world at the moment of play; behave *as if* my arms and hands do not exist unless I am in one particular area of the field; behave *as if* the ball moving between two posts is a moment of intense significance, and so the statements continue, extending beyond the playing field into the spectatorship and so on. In *FIFA* we behave *as if* the game controller, console, pixels, and television *are* the game of football, are Cristiano Ronaldo, Old Trafford, and the World Cup. Never question the *as-if*, never even acknowledge it or, worse yet, treat it cynically or ironically. To do so is once more to risk becoming the "spoilsport" Huizinga admonishes.

What of Huizinga's circle then? Simply, a circle happens when play becomes a shared activity: when a girl joins her idea of lava with the floor and behaves *as if* the floor is lava and when a boy joins his idea of an airplane with his physicality and behaves *as if* he is an airplane. Huizinga is correct that play can certainly happen in a realm of pure imagination ("playing with ideas"), but if the circle is to achieve any solidity, any longevity, it must come down to earth and evidence itself in our material realm. This is the moment of repetition: a body, a rulebook, a football field, a stadium, a club, a video game allows for repeated performance by oneself and by others.

Shared enough—across people and over time—a magic circle transmogrifies into a more permanent entity: it becomes a *thing*, a game, a part of a culture. It gains solidity, a material existence, evidenced by the rubber of a pair of Puma Kings shoes, the polyester of a team shirt, the sound waves of a vuvuzela horn. It is in this moment that the circle is complete—binding, rigid, and, importantly, breakable. To wit, in the exact moment rules are set, they can be subverted, manipulated, and broken (by Huizinga's spoilsport).

Although Huizinga's thinking about play is useful, his movement between examples from both moments of play and *game*play as if they were unproblematic synonyms requires unpacking. Game and play do not have too much in common, either in what they are (ontology) or in how we understand them (epistemology). Indeed, one could argue, as Roger Caillois[7] (pronounced "kail-wah") later did, that play and game are, in many senses, diametrically opposed. Related they may be, but this relationship is antagonistic at best, fraught with disagreement and acrimony.

Stated bluntly, game does not care much about play, nor does play about game, if we follow Huizinga's definition. Although designers, players, and spectators may care about the play in and of a game, game as a thing could not care less. This is because the essence of a game is rules, and rules are (as a rule) always more concerned with adherence and procedure than with interpretation and style (which is the player's share of the circle). A game is binary; it is black and white. On the other hand, play is spectral, with lots of gray between perfect whites and the deepest blacks. If *play* says the striker scored a beautiful volley, the center back fumbled the ball across the line, or the goalie knocked the ball into his own net, the *game* simply responds 1–0.

Although this positions game as a rather dry, boring figure as opposed to its fun-loving sibling, play, let us consider the positive implications of such a binary imposition essential to games (but, to correct Huizinga, *not* play). As discussed earlier, Huizinga was explicit about the benefits: such structure brings a "limited perfection" into the "confusion of life."[8] As such the ontology of game brings clarity, vitality, and concision to counterpose the opacity, dreariness, and diffusion of everyday existence. There is no vagueness in a game's ontological structure (i.e., its rules), only that which the player brings through interpretation (i.e., play): this is one of the game–play antinomies.

As discussed earlier, all play is founded on an initial *as-if*. In competitive games, players then build on this with more *as-if* gestures meant to fool the opposition: one may "bluff" in poker, "take a dive" in soccer, or "pump fake" in basketball, but this is a consequence of the player's creative interpretation of a rule (or rule set), not the rule-in-itself. Erving Goffman called such actions *fabrications*[9] that, in the case of games, offer an impression of the situation (to others: the referee, opposition, spectators) that the player knows is false but hopes to benefit from. For example, in the soccer scenario, I fall over *as if* physically obstructed to convince the referee to award a penalty when, in fact, I know no contact occurred. Playing *FIFA*, I hit the pause button as my opponent nears my goal; I unplug the broadband connection when close to a loss to nullify the result.[10] Games (and indeed computers), as rule-bound systems, find such actions hard to judge as they sit within the grey area of play, obstinately refusing the binary black-and-white that rules demand.

Indeed, the very notion of a fabrication is muddied in certain games where deception is expected. For example, bluffing in poker is often presumed as the medium of paper card affords deceptive activity. It is much easier to hide a card's information from your opposition than the presence of a soccer ball, and the rules do not state a necessity to show one's hand unless final bets have been placed and more than one player is still active. To summarize, if game is the lawmaker, then play(er) is often the lawbreaker.

Let us now think about how the medium of video games deals with game and play, something Huizinga didn't have to concern himself with at the time of writing *Homo Ludens*. The medium relies on a computer, essentially a thing that calculates. No matter how sophisticated its hardware, the modern computer is at its core a binary processor. Until we achieve quantum computing, all processes are ultimately 1/0, yes/no.

As one might expect considering our discussion thus far, this kind of design fits very well with the ontological figure of game while leaving play out in the cold. A game is a set of rules, and computers are extraordinarily good at following rules as long as they are given clear yes/no conditions. Whereas for Huizinga, play in its purest form is irrational (fantasist, based on pretense statements, *as if*), free and unruly, computers are infamously rational (literalist, based on factual statements, *if–then–else*), rigid and rule-bound.

Once again, we must come back to the *experience* of the moment of play: Do you *feel* free to act? Are you *only* interested in the goal of the game? Is this sense of being *in* the game limited: temporally, spatially, ideationally, materially? These are all questions still worth pondering today, perhaps especially so with the expansion of games into all kinds of domains, formats, and devices, not least of all the computer.

How then does computation represent a game as open and emergent as soccer? As one would expect from a medium predicated on calculation, numbers are immensely important in the *FIFA* series, not simply in terms of what happens "behind the scenes" (the software program's execution) but ultimately for the player experience as well. This is because the soccer avatar is represented as a set of numbers tied to epistemic principles we hold for sport: power, speed, physicality, stamina, and so on. Therefore, setting training regimes to improve a soccer

FIGURE 1.1 The emergent, magic circle of play unfolds in *FIFA 16*.

avatar's numbers; trading squad members for ones with better statistics; designing strategies, formations, and tactics that take advantage of each avatar's numerical disposition; and so on are core aspects of the user's activity. In other words, the user experience is founded on data management, on a knowledge economy.

Yet such laborious, otherwise banal calculation and planning is wrapped up in a representational style that mimics, as closely as possible, the televisual portrayal of soccer (see figure 1.1): the broadcast angle, camera distortion, commentary team, and action replays are all present and correct in *FIFA 16* (EA Canada, 2015). One is not playing soccer but managing assets. One is not perceiving soccer but a televisual spectacle. The circle here is not only present; its rigidity is also palpable: constructed and policed by the *if–then–else* statements of the computer program, the design of which is informed by larger interlocking circles, such as our society's understanding of information, television, sport, masculinity, rationality, and so on. Yet this, too, is where freedom emerges. Freedom comes from a limitation of choice. To acknowledge the impossibility of doing everything, to decide on a course of action, is the moment of autonomy. As games and computers set rules, they generate freedom: new acknowledgments, new decisions, new possibilities for play. The more choices the player makes, the more complex, emergent, and free the play becomes.

Dare we venture so far as to speak of magic? Yes, indeed it is inevitable if we follow the preceding argument. Remember that play emerges through much of what is left unsaid by the rules, by the player's freedom to commit to an *as-if.*

This *as-if* is the player's projection of meaning and significance onto the activity, so much so that everything else is of disinterest. To perform otherwise, to sense a lack of freedom, to place interest beyond the activity itself is, for Huizinga, to be sinful in the eyes of play: in not giving belief freely, in using play for other interests (such as wanting to earn a wage or getting exercise), is to risk turning the phenomenon into something else entirely—namely, work.

Video games are successful by making magic *perceptible*: literally providing an abundance of meaning that is understandable and seizable. The medium accomplishes this by basing its design upon the historical, social, cultural, technological, economic, and political prejudices of its user. In contemporary Western society this hyper-rational approach to soccer, embedded within an overarching masculine rhetoric, conveyed through televisual convention, is in perfect alignment: it is no coincidence that the actions one takes within the game perfectly coincides with the labor practices of a postindustrial white-collar economy, where one's working life is focused on the gathering, interpreting, monitoring, and crafting of data into actionable information (and once more, the computer is essential to such tasks). In *FIFA 16* we therefore find a powerful example of a magic circle, and this magic will persist as long as our society places computation, rationality, and masculinity at the center of our sense-making as a civilization. *Homo Ludens* is then something of a misnomer: we are no longer man of play but of game, and there is a vast difference between the two.

NOTES

1 The author wishes to acknowledge the generous feedback from Daniel Golding, Tony Mills, and Andrew Trevillian on earlier iterations of this chapter.

2 Johan Huizinga, *Homo Ludens: A Study of the Play-Element in Culture* (London: Routledge & Kegan Paul Ltd, 1949), 1, original emphasis.

3 Huizinga, *Homo Ludens*, 10.

4 Huizinga, *Homo Ludens*.

5 Huizinga, *Homo Ludens*, 11.

6 As Garry Crawford ("Is It in the Game? Reconsidering Play Spaces, Game Definitions, Theming, and Sports Videogames," *Games and Culture* 10, no. 6 [2015]: 571–592), Jean-Marie Brohm (*Sport: A Prison of Measured Time* [London: Pluto Press, 1989]) and others have argued, this membrane is perhaps not only thin; it is perhaps not even best conceived as circular or separate; indeed, it might be a phenomenon that reinforces, rather than departs from, our everyday existence.

7 Roger Caillois, *Man, Play and Games* (Urbana and Chicago: University of Illinois Press, 2001).

8 Huizinga, *Homo Ludens*, 10.

9 Erving Goffman, *Frame Analysis: An Essay on the Organization of Experience* (Boston: Northeastern University Press, 1986).

10 This tactic, known as "plugging," has since been remedied by EA Sports so that any drop in connection results in a loss for the player whose data packets stop transmitting.

FURTHER READING

Brohm, Jean-Marie. *Sport: A Prison of Measured Time.* London: Pluto Press, 1989.

Consalvo, Mia. "There Is No Magic Circle." *Games and Culture* 4, no. 4 (2009): 408–417.

Conway, Steven, and Andrew Trevillian. "'Blackout!' Unpacking the Black Box of the Game Event." *ToDIGRA: Transactions of the Digital Games Research Association* 2, no. 1 (2015): 67–100.

Crawford, Garry. "Is It in the Game? Reconsidering Play Spaces, Game Definitions, Theming, and Sports Videogames." *Games and Culture* 10, no. 6 (2015): 571–592.

2

Tetris
Rules

ROLF F. NOHR

Abstract: Rules are integral to the functioning of game systems and to the experiences they create; for the puzzle game *Tetris*, this means aligning blocks into rows before they fill the screen. But to fully understand how rules breathe life into interactive experiences, Rolf F. Nohr contends that we must analyze both explicit, internal rules *and* all those implicit, external regulations that color gaming experiences; playing *Tetris* is, thus, more than the sum of its blocks.

Certain "classic" video games appear to be characterized by simple, elegant rules. The success of these titles can often be traced back to a design philosophy that might be summarized as "less is more." However, such an assertion is less useful than it might seem for the way it elides historically specific technological limitations and industrial design practices. Similarly, aphorisms that a game is "easy to learn, hard to master" or "easy to pick up, hard to put down" reflect a commonly held view that better games are those with fewer formal rules and regulations. This design maxim of "less is more" could also help explain the enduring success of the puzzle game *Tetris*. First developed in 1984 by Alexey Pajitnov at the Dorodnicyn Computing Centre of the Academy of Science of the USSR in Moscow, *Tetris* is a video game marked by aesthetic simplicity and an elegant rule set. However, a closer look at this popular game reveals layers of rules—internal and external—that determine how it is played and explain its continued success across platforms and decades.

It may seem strange to use *Tetris* to explore the concept of rules. This particular game, after all, gives players relatively limited options when it comes to managing their falling tetrominoes (shapes consisting of four squares) within its fixed, two-dimensional playfield. The player can move descending puzzle pieces left or right and perform quick drops, and the shapes may also be rotated clockwise and counterclockwise. The pleasures of *Tetris* are borne out of dealing expeditiously with these limited options in a limited timeframe. Level after level, the game increases in difficulty as the falling tetrominoes descend ever more rapidly. Complete the lines by moving shapes left, right, down, and around. What else is there to know? This is a true but incomplete picture. Indeed, there are additional layers of significance hidden in the on- and off-screen regulations that engender its gripping gameplay.

The initial spread of *Tetris* in the West is owed to its inclusion in the first Microsoft Windows Entertainment Pack and to its popularity on the Nintendo Game Boy handheld system, both released in 1989 (see figure 2.1).[1] On the back cover of the Nintendo Game Boy packaging, the following instructions appear: "Beams, boxes, zig-zags and L-shaped blocks drop down a narrow passage. Feel your pulse quicken as you spin, shift and align the shapes for a perfect fit. It's challenging and demands split second decision!"[2] Simplifying this marketing jargon we might say, "Avoid gap in line for high score." If this sounds familiar, it is because it is a variation of the well-known inscription appearing on Atari's first *PONG* arcade machine of 1972: "Avoid missing ball for high score." One could argue that it isn't necessary to know more than this single rule to play *Tetris* or *PONG* before it. Of course, such a functionalist view of rules reduces a game to those parameters that determine a win condition. But games are more than winning and losing, as the chapters in this anthology attest. Moreover, a game's manifest rules of play are accompanied by a number of other, often far less obvious regulations and expectations that shape that experience, a myriad of internalized (and not-so-obvious) social and cultural codes that orient a player to mediated rule sets, shaping their gameplay and that of others. Analyzing the rules that give rise to gameplay reveals a host of cultural values, design beliefs, and social mores.

The word *rule* possesses at least three definitional inflections: (1) a guideline, convention, standard, or regulation ("Whoever cheats, is out"), (2) a social regularity ("Don't go to school naked"), and (3) a predictable phenomenon ("When you let go of this crate, it will fall to the ground"). Although game rules are most frequently associated with the first meaning—that of a guideline or standard—analyzing game rules should also include a consideration of the latter understandings. For the moment, let us define game rules as a "set of socially agreed-upon instructions."

The idea of the rule-as-instruction is closely intertwined with notions of play.[3] Indeed, differing understandings of play invariably affect the relative value of rules. For instance, the free play of little kids playing "Cowboys and Indians" or "Princess Teatime" is perceived as possessing an emancipatory ethos because young people are able to interact playfully with the world through so-called trial actions. Young creatures of many species—humans and animals alike—develop valuable life skills through playful trial actions without fear of consequences. Just because play is recreational doesn't mean that it's not educational.

The concept of liberating play—which is typical of children's emergent games such as "tag"—stands in opposition to the procedurally and mechanistic nature of strict game rules. The idealized play of children presumes that gamic actions are free from worldly consequences. Or, as cultural sociologist Johan Huizinga puts it, "[a]ll play moves and has its being within a play-ground marked off beforehand either materially or ideally, deliberately or as a matter of course. The arena, the card-table, the magic circle . . . , are all in form and function play-grounds, i.e. forbidden spots, isolated, hedged round, hallowed, within which special rules obtain. All are temporary worlds within the ordinary world, dedicated to the performance of an act apart."[4] The "bang-you-are-dead" of children's play does not end in someone actually dropping dead. This emergent and dynamic "rule" is, in actuality, the communicative management of the play situation itself, one that is integral to the open-endedness of a game's variability. *Tetris*, therefore, can be understood as a liberating game insofar as playing *Tetris* has no consequences in real life.

But the seemingly borderless horizons of free play are colonized by rules so as to codify reliable and reproducible game structures: chess uses the same board; basketball uses the same size hoop; poker depends on the standard 52-card deck. Game rules serve as a foundational shorthand for justifying and legitimizing player actions. One who plays *Tetris* to create beautifully complex patterns as an expression of free play and not to clear the screen of its multishaped tetrominoes is no longer playing *Tetris* according to the stated rules.[5] Thus, rules are closely associated with ethical, communicative, and psychosocial processes dealing with what is deemed to be socially proper and improper behaviors. This negotiation is already practiced in children's play. Children do not just play "Cowboys and Indians." They spend a significant amount of time discussing the interpretation or exegesis of rules: "I've hit you; you're dead; you have to fall over!" and "No, I've got this super magic coat protecting me from your bullets!"

Much of our current understanding of game rules is characterized by the work of Johan Huizinga, who was quoted earlier. His anthropological theory of the *Homo ludens*—"man the player"—sees the game as a voluntary activity that unfolds within set boundaries of space and time. Rules not only confine games to specific spaces and times, they also determine the course and character of the game; to wit, *Tetris* takes place on a two-dimensional grid of about 10 spaces wide by 20 squares high, and the game is over when a tetromino breaches the top line of the game field. If we were to characterize the dramaturgy of *Tetris*'s action we might say that it is generally wave-shaped, with ebbs and flows reflecting the dynamic tension of eliminating rows of shapes that grow in number until a sufficient number have been eliminated, thereby completing the level, or until they over-whelm the player's screen ending the game (e.g., its dramatic climax or catharsis).

Rules constitute the official parameters by which one can win within the game's "possibility space."[6] Rules likewise limit the player's range of action; one can't con-veniently set the falling tetrominoes aside when they don't fit. The existential ne-cessity of rules is often in conflict with the playability and the player exercising his or her agency within the emergent and contingent field of choices. Rules, af-ter all, are guidelines for action; they are not actions proper, meaning that play-ers ultimately decide what they can do within a gamic space, sometimes rules be damned, including breaking, quitting, ignoring, and cheating (as Steven Conway and Kelly Bergstrom discuss elsewhere in this book). This brings us to a problem of defining rules using Huizinga's formulation. His distinction is based on a clear separation between the game as a "magic circle" of play and the non–game world. However, such a distinction is only conditionally maintained for the video game.

Philosopher John R. Searle strikes an important and useful distinction between *constitutive* and *regulative* rules.[7] Constitutive rules are those that enable actions. Without these types of rules, the game and its competition between players could not exist. Constitutive rules are negotiated, are based on agreement, and are ex-plicitly stated.

Searle's regulative rules, on the other hand, are the sometimes ambiguous and implicit standards that structure intersubjective societal cooperation. They are closely connected to a society's "common sense" and are, for the most part, invis-ible and naturalized. Regulative rules are taken for granted and are social conven-tions that are accepted without question.

The problem with assessing video games rules is that they only seem to be de-fined functionally on the basis of their constitutive rules, those predefined terms for action and computational algorithms that adjudicate player choice. But this limited viewpoint excludes an essential gameplay act: the rule violation. Breaking constitutive rules does not lead to the abolition of the "gaming agreement," but it is—in fact—part of the game experience (often part of the gaming fun). As Huiz-inga argues, each game oscillates between the compliance of rules (often judged by an arbitrator like a referee) and the breaking of constitutive rules to gain some competitive advantage.

If rules differ in type, so, too, do their perceived violations. The dive in foot-ball/soccer, the moving screen in basketball, holding in American football—these are all tactical acts committed with the goal of winning. Cheaters commit these fouls. Spoilsports, by contrast, are those who rupture the magic circle by break-ing the regulative rules and shared social contract that cast the holding spell of gameplay. The spoilsport is the nudist who streaks across the baseball diamond to disrupt the invisible social membrane between athletes and ourselves, and it is

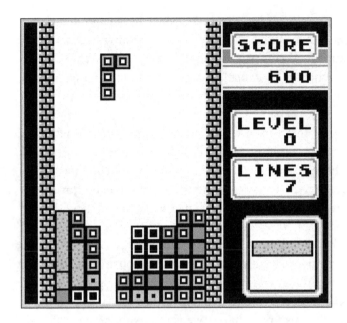

FIGURE 2.1
Tetris for the Nintendo
Game Boy.

the older sister who reminds her younger brother and his dice-wielding friends that they are not intrepid dungeon adventurers on the hunt for riches.

Rules are powerful things. Together, explicitly stated constitutive rules that are inscribed into the functional operation of the game as a technology, and all those implicit social regulations that help determine how a game is negotiated by players, have the combined effect of naturalizing and normalizing a game's metaphysics. Together, rules create the impression of a hermetically sealed autonomous world. In the nonnarrative universe of *Tetris*, certain questions go unanswered. Why do the tetrominoes always fall down? What exactly spawns the blocks? Where do they go after they've been aligned? Rules have a way of erasing that which lies beyond the field of play, just as it normalizes actions within the game space.

The rigid system of rules that delimit player agency would seemingly foreclose the possibility of locating liberating play in such games. Indeed, the presence of constitutive and regulative rules tamp down opportunities for open-ended play. If one evaluates games only by their sacrosanct rule sets or by the determinations of eagle-eyed referees, the medium would be an oppressive one. And this oppression would be enhanced by the obvious rigidity of the technical medium on which the game takes place: the computer.

But, of course, we know that there *is* cheating and free play in video games despite all the technical and social prohibitions to the contrary. Thus, a possible solution to this problem of where to find freedom in games, even in one as seemingly proscriptive as *Tetris*, is to conceptualize a space of rules outside and beyond the limits of the game itself. If we push beyond these conventional boundaries of technology and sociology, we may arrive at a new sense of gaming freedom.

Let's begin with "violations" of constitutive rules. On one hand, video games are perceived as regulated activities in algorithmically structured spaces: a square, two-by-two-shaped tetromino only fits in a two-unit-wide gap. On the other hand, the calculated tactical foul is part of the video game landscape. The internet abounds with sites cataloging hints, cheat codes, and walkthrough tutorials; they are an integral part of gaming communities. Using a cheat code to best *Tetris*'s unrelenting waterfall of shapes is not the overriding of a stated rule but an immanent possibility in the source code itself. Without leaving the fixed framework of the game, the player uses code in a more effective way: an unofficial hotkey slows the rate of falling cubes; an erase code deletes an inconvenient tetromino or allows a player to select a better shape.

The "violation" of the regulatory rules is similarly more open than it would initially appear. The unconventional ways gamers repurpose their gameplay (and that of others)—effectively deviating from mainstream views of how a game should be played—is most obvious in sandbox-style games with large worlds; *Tetris* makes for an admittedly bad example on this point. The degrees of spatial freedom and player choice in games such as *Grand Theft Auto V* (Rockstar North, 2013), *Fallout 4* (Bethesda Game Studios, 2015), and *Minecraft* (Mojong, 2011) encourage a wide range of regulative action. For example, members of "trick jumping" communities organize choreographed stunts. The machinima scene repurposes recorded gameplay to produce short films in a variety of genres (see Lowood's chapter in this volume on the history of this form). All these instances of play involve the breaking of constitutive and regulatory rules. These examples may be regarded as atypical player behavior, yet they are nevertheless expressive actions that deviate from the presumed norms regarding the way games are "supposed" to be played. Whereas rules are binary, play is a spectrum. This is just as true for nonnarrative, two-dimensional puzzle games as it is for narrative, three-dimensional sandbox titles.

The arcade classic *PONG* may better illustrate the extent to which Searle's rule binary explains the contextual dimensions of play in video games. The imperative—"Avoid missing ball for high score"—is only one of three regulating sentences appearing on the front of the original arcade machine. The three-part inscription reads: "Deposit Quarter. Ball will serve automatically. Avoid missing ball for high score."[8]

By unpacking these simple commands, one finds a series of more socially embedded values: video games are economic goods that activate only after a payment ("deposit quarter"), which then initiates an automated logic ("ball will serve automatically"), all of which aims to hide a computational artifice and history of design to arrive at a perception of great simplicity and effectiveness ("avoid missing ball for high score"). Game histories too often forget the first two rules of *PONG* even though they are essential for its operation. Thus, taking rules seriously means more than reciting them; it means excavating deeper levels of meaning that they attempt to normalize or elide.

To conclude, rules and regulations shape video games and gaming experiences. Some rules are quite visible to players; others are not. While playing *Tetris* we tend to recognize the obvious, constitutive rules: adjust every falling block to fill empty spaces below to clear the lines. The invisible rules of *Tetris*—"You have to do something otherwise you will lose," or convincing oneself "this exacting form of gameplay is, in fact, not work"—are operative but exist outside the formal contours of the gaming technology. It is only by critically examining the multiple layers of meaning that one can understand how *regimes of rules*—as expanded systems of internal and external regulations—play with gamers just as they play with games.

In addition to the gameplay rules, we must also attend to the more transparent discursive or design rules that dictate the kinds of games that get canonized as "classics" and those that are lost to history (i.e., those games labeled as classics because of their simple rules). Without opening a discussion about the canonization of games, it is worth asking ourselves if the normative evaluation of games is too often guided by the ensemble of visible rules? For certain kind of games (and players) the "less is more" paradigm seems to be a qualitative argument. Perhaps a step toward a nuanced game literacy would be to develop a sense for the presence of invisible rules. In doing so, we can recognize that even *Tetris*, for all its celebrated simplicity, may hide more rules than it reveals.

NOTES

1 For a detailed explanation of the (more than exciting) history of the development and release of *Tetris*, see Dan Ackerman, *The Tetris Effect: The Game that Hypnotized the World* (New York: Public Affairs, 2016).

2 Luke Hackett, "Tetris Gameboy Box Art," Super Luigi Brothers, www.superluigibros.com.

3 For an elaborated differentiation between different forms of play and game, see Roger Caillois, *Man, Play, and Games* (Chicago: University of Illinois Press, 1961).

4 Johan Huizinga, *Homo Ludens: A Study of the Play-Element in Culture* (Boston, MA: Beacon Press, 1955 [1938]), 10.

5 For the rich array of activities that surround gameplay, see James Newman, *Playing with Videogames* (London and New York: Routledge, 2008).

6 For a detailed discussion of the concepts of possibility, choice, rules, and narrations, see Katie Salen and Eric Zimmerman, *Rules of Play: Game Design Fundamentals* (Cambridge, MA: MIT Press, 2004): chap. 26.

7 John R. Searle, *Speech Acts: An Essay in the Philosophy of Language* (Cambridge: Cambridge University Press, 1969).

8 PONG Museum, http://pongmuseum.com.

FURTHER READING

Consalvo, Mia. *Cheating: Gaining Advantage in Videogames.* Cambridge, MA: MIT Press, 2007.

Juul, Jesper. *Half Real: Video Games Between Real Rules and Fictional Worlds.* Cambridge, MA: MIT Press, 2005.

Salen, Katie, and Eric Zimmerman. *Rules of Play: Game Design Fundamentals.* Cambridge, MA: MIT Press, 2004.

3

King's Quest
Narrative

ANASTASIA SALTER

Abstract: Games struggle with the apparent tension between interactivity and narrative as imposed story structures and goals restrict a player's agency in shaping their own experience through play. Anastasia Salter examines how the rebooted *King's Quest* series embraces the potential of games as a space for character-driven interactive narrative, where story becomes the motivation for exploration.

The *King's Quest* series (Sierra, 1984–1998) was one of the longest-running, best-selling franchises of its era and a landmark in the history of the adventure game genre. The series was designed by Roberta Williams, one of the most famous women in the history of computer games.[1] Adventure games (sometimes referred to as "point and click" because of their emphasis on exploring environments through mouse-based interaction) are characterized by a focus on narrative, with exploration, conversation, and puzzles driving the story forward.[2] The *King's Quest* series opened with *Quest for the Crown* (1984), which told the tale of Sir Graham and his search for three relics to save his kingdom. The game also established the mechanics of the genre, as Justin McElroy notes in his retrospective on the series: "*King's Quest* took players from staring at static screens . . . and shoved a representation of the player into the middle of the action. This shift from observer to direct participant was unprecedented, and it created a blueprint for the vast majority of adventure games that would follow."[3] Subsequent games in the series told increasingly complex tales, following Graham's ascension to king and the quests of his children (and, later, his wife) to escape captors, find love, journey to the underworld and back, and even save Graham's life.

However, the series ended badly with *King's Quest: Mask of Eternity* (Sierra On-Line, 1998), a three-dimensional (3D) debacle that represented a last-ditch attempt by Sierra to make the series fit a different genre by abandoning its roots in story and, particularly, the previous focus on the adventures of the royal family of Daventry. *Mask of Eternity* instead featured action-oriented gameplay that, at the time, was to be the future of gaming. Adventure games were declared dead, and many designers—including Roberta Williams herself—left the industry or moved on to other genres.[4] Sierra's adventure game development wing closed with the new ownership, effectively ending many game series at once.

It seemed that part of what had killed the genre was a fundamental tension between the competing demands of play and story—a tension that also played out in game studies.[5] Early on, game studies was presumed to be a divided turf, with narratologists (or narrativists), on one side, and ludologists (who advocated for the study of play and its mechanics), on the other side.[6] This dichotomy was an oversimplification, and over the years many game scholars have demonstrated the value that different disciplines and approaches bring to understanding games. Likewise, the appeal of a playable narrative hadn't died, and over the ensuing decades a number of designers took up the challenge of building a new future for adventure games while rethinking the possibilities for fusing story and interactivity.

On July 28, 2015, Activision published under the Sierra Entertainment brand name *King's Quest Chapter 1: A Knight to Remember* with a new design team, The Odd Gentlemen. *A Knight to Remember* fuses the generic traditions of the character-driven, quest-centered adventure game with newer approaches to modeling moral decision-making and agency. Adventure games center on narrative, or a sequence of events that may be experienced in a combination of orders but generally proceed through a dominant story arc. Because of this focus on narrative, adventure games limit player agency, which can be defined as the ability for the player to act in ways that change the game world or the direction of the narrative. Although it does include some fast-paced mechanics that resemble a more action-oriented genre, the fundamental experience of play is that of embodying a hero. *A Knight to Remember* is not a sequel to the old series, as it was intended to draw in a new generation of players. It is also not a remake. This new chapter reboots the series by reintroducing us to a much older Graham, telling stories of his past heroics to his granddaughter. Over the course of five chapters, players move through sequences drawn from the history of Daventry that both hearken back to and diverge from the original games.

The use of the elder Sir Graham's narration functions both to draw us into the character and add a framework of humor to the journey. It also serves an important role in signaling the potential (and limitations) of the experience as an interactive narrative. The reliance on the narrative framing device in *King's Quest: A Knight to Remember* is a textual acknowledgment that the story's destination is already set, but the details of his journey are not. Even though the fates of his family members are already known, Sir Graham's reminiscing leaves room for the player to control the details of his path from knight to king. Traditionally, this storytelling technique is used with narratives where the suspense is not in the outcome but in the process. Consider, for example, the film *Titanic* (James Cameron, 1997) wherein the elderly woman narrates her survivor story. We know how that story concludes, but we are nevertheless interested in her particular experience. The mechanics of *A Knight to Remember* allow for three distinct paths to victory, but that victory is guaranteed.

The variety of experiences possible is derived from the player's choice of values throughout. *A Knight to Remember* is built around three paths toward heroism: the Route of Bravery, the Route of Compassion, and the Route of Wisdom. These choices reflect an artificial binary that suggests a level of moralizing, recalling classic *King's Quest*, which favored nonviolence by awarding more points to decisions that didn't involve bloodshed. Later, the routes diverge, giving players a sense of consequence to their actions as well as providing nonlinear gameplay. This builds on the "string of pearls" approach to narrative design, which Roberta Williams perfected working on the original *King's Quest* games.[7] This design strategy linked scenes that the player can experience in any order while progressing toward the next big narrative moment or plot point. Essentially, this gives players the illusion of agency by allowing them to explore different parts of a story during sections of the game, even though ultimately the player will end up in the same place.

The game opens with a young Sir Graham putting on his adventurer's cap: the same blue cap with a red feather that he sported (albeit in a much more pixelated form) in the original game. The player is dropped into a 3D environment near a well without much explanation or context other than Graham's voice-over: "I had not been back there in years, but it was the last place left to look." As the player moves deeper into the cave, the landscapes grow lusher and menacing, leading the player to an encounter with a dragon. This event can be resolved in several ways: the player can choose direct confrontation, or *bravery*, and shoot the dragon in the eye to blind him. The player can notice that the dragon is a captive and choose to shoot a switch that frees it, demonstrating *compassion*. The player might also notice that there is a bell in the area and shoot it to trick the dragon into retreating, demonstrating *wisdom*.

Each choice plays out slightly differently. For example, after making the choice to shoot the bell and distract the dragon, the player guides Graham out of the dungeon and the final cutscene of the sequence takes over, with a much older Graham narrating the adventure to his granddaughter Gwendolyn (as in figure 3.1). When Gwendolyn asks how Graham knew how to overcome the dragon, he replies,

FIGURE 3.1
Graham-as-narrator
in *King's Quest*.

"Over the years I had realized the dragon was not the despicable, hideous beast Daventry had made him out to be. He was just a caged animal that was very hungry. I too would be violently angry if I could only eat when my neglectful owner rang the bell." After the story, Gwendolyn tricks her obnoxious cousin Gart in the same way, demonstrating the consequences of the player's choice of values through Graham's influence on the young.

The dialogue only differs slightly if the player sets the dragon free: "I set him free because, well, over the years I realized the dragon was not the despicable, hideous beast Daventry has made him out to be. He was just a caged beast that was never shown any kindness. On that day, I forgave the dragon for his atrocious past." The two statements demonstrate how any of the three decisions can be rationalized depending on the chosen value: the decision to free the dragon could be cast as heroic or foolhardy. Once again, the impact on Gwendolyn shows as she reacts to his attempt to scare her directly, opening the door and announcing, "You're free!" These small moments seem to foreshadow the larger significance of Graham's small choices—the choices the player controls, which, in turn, shape Graham's character.

After hearing that Gwendolyn plans to face off against him in the tournament, her cousin Gart makes the self-reflexive comment: "Well, perhaps this is the time to stop listening to stories and finally make some of your own." Immediately following this statement, the player regains control as Graham gives Gwendolyn advice for the duel, with the option of suggesting a deft maneuver, a quick-witted distraction, or an act of kindness even in victory. Whatever the player chooses, it transitions into a story about a tournament, where the player will have to demonstrate heroic virtues and will ultimately influence Gwendolyn's behavior based on the choices made throughout. In another self-reflexive observation, Graham notes, "There is so much more to my stories than dragons. I hope this old cap will be remembered for far more than the action tattered across its brim. Sewn into the seams are many hidden adventures." Coming as it does from a character whose games form the foundations of the adventure game genre, the statement could be read as a critique of more action-oriented game genres.

Following this framing conversation with Gwendolyn, the central part of Graham's first adventure begins with him retelling the story of his tournament for knighthood. The sequence is more open for exploration than the linear opening, as Graham tries to get to the tournament but finds himself barred by fallen bridges surrounding the city. The player then encounters a number of characters, many of whom display intertextual connections and references to other works, particularly the film *The Princess Bride* (Rob Reiner, 1987). But the player is asked to be continually conscious of virtue, which is at the center of every challenge. Even ordinary-seeming adventure game mechanics have a moral component. For instance, when Graham first arrives in town, he visits a blacksmith, a bakery, and a magic shop. The player needs to take supplies from each shop but can only leave one tip, which, in turn, will impact later interactions with the shopkeepers. Graham faces a series of trials to prove his worth and has a choice over which virtue to demonstrate. Although he will have to face all the trials, the choice of the first virtue has an impact on both the player's relationship with other characters and the path available to complete the challenge.

The most significant choice is how to collect the required eye of a hideous beast. Graham can earn the eye through kindness, by bringing food to a bridge troll, Olfie, who then helps Graham get the eye of a Snarlax. Or Graham can choose the path of bravery and pursue a younger version of the dragon from the previous encounter, taking his eye. An adventure game veteran is most likely to instead take the third path, wisdom, and find and dye a pumpkin lantern to resemble the required eye.

There are several approaches to adding a sense of agency in narrative games, even if that agency is often illusory. One of the best known is the Telltale Games formula, demonstrated in a range of adapted (and, more rarely, original) narratives from Telltale such as *The Walking Dead* (2012), *Game of Thrones* (2014), *The Wolf Among Us* (2013), and *Batman: The Telltale Series* (2016). These games use a core mechanic of decision making through timed choices in dialogue and action, although most major plot points are inevitable and the player is only truly in control of the details. All the Telltale games rely on a similar notion of memory: as the player makes decisions, particularly in choices of conversational gambits and attitude, a message will flash at the top of the screen reminding the player that the other character "will remember that." This idea of building a character's reputation within the story world is one way to provide a sense of narrative consistency, progression, and moral complexity—experiential features that are often lacking in adventure games (traditionally, a player could revisit a conversation over and over again without the character reacting or changing their responses). Conversations as a method of investigation are a standard mechanic of the adventure game—one perfected by Jane Jensen in her *Gabriel Knight* series.[8] The conversations in *A Knight to Remember* resemble a hybrid of these two approaches, with several dialogue options giving the player a chance to explore different values. The first chapter ends after Graham has successfully achieved knighthood. When the game switches back to the framing story, Graham reminds Gwendolyn of the value of whichever virtue the player preferred, even if the player had chosen a different virtue before starting the encounters. Graham notes, "Sometimes it's better to do as I do, not as I say."

The ending of the first chapter demonstrates both the big and small ways the player's actions have had an impact on the world; for instance, Graham's facial expression will change to reflect the player's emphasis on bravery, wisdom, or compassion. The dragon will appear eyeless if the player shot him, chained if the player rang the dinner bell, or chainless if the player freed him. The player's choice of eye from the competition—dragon, jack-o-lantern, or troll—will also be on display. This mechanic draws on a precedent from *King's Quest VI: Heir Today, Gone Tomorrow* (Sierra On-Line, 1992), co-designed by Roberta Williams and Jane Jensen: the game allowed for multiple endings, with various characters present only if the player had rescued them.[9]

Although these multiple endings do not create a significantly nonlinear story, they do play with the narrative structures of the adventure game genre. Game scholar Espen Aarseth observes that studying adventure games is particularly difficult because they are not "literary" in a way that can be easily recognized, despite their apparent connections to established genres of fiction.[10] In *On Interactive Storytelling*, famed game designer Chris Crawford suggests that these differences are part of what lets games get away with inconsistent narratives that don't "follow the protocols of storytelling."[11] Certainly, *A Knight to Remember*'s story-within-a-story conceit combines the instability of memory with the devices of oral storytelling to create narrative tension where the present is seemingly fixed while the character's past self is controlled by the player.

Adventure games began closer to what scholar Mark Meadows terms an impositional interactive narrative, which keeps the player on track with strict rules.[12] This contrasts with what Meadows terms expressive games, which use environments to tell a story while the player explores with relative freedom. *King's Quest Chapter 2: Rubble Without a Cause* (2015) ends with a summation that suggests the designer's focus on the journey, rather than the destination: "And that's my story. Some of the details might have changed over the years, and I certainly left out some parts I wasn't fond of, but I've found it's best to enjoy stories for what they are and not for what you hoped they would be." Today's interactive narratives similarly explore this space between imposed and expressive narrative, finding opportunities to create meaning from player's choices within the guiding framework of a world and its character.

NOTES

1 See Laine Nooney, "A Pedestal, a Table, a Love Letter: Archaeologies of Gender in Video-game History," *Game Studies* 13, no. 2 (2013), http://gamestudies.org/, for a discussion of Roberta Williams in the game industry.

2 See Anastasia Salter, *What Is Your Quest? From Adventure Games to Interactive Books* (Iowa City: University of Iowa Press, 2014), for an in-depth discussion of this genre definition.

3 Justin McElroy, "Royal with Cheese: A King's Quest Primer," *Polygon*, July 28, 2015.

4 See Old Man Murray, "Who Killed Adventure Games?," *Old Man Murray*, September 11, 2000, oldmanmurray.com, for an account of the different events preceding the supposed death of the genre.

5 See Janet H. Murray, "The Last Word on Ludology v Narratology in Game Studies," 2005 *Digital Games Research Association Conference Proceeding*, https://www.researchgate.net/, for an overview.

6 See Gonzalo Frasca, "Ludologists Love Stories, Too: Notes from a Debate that Never Took Place," 2003, www.ludology.org.

7 Marek Bronstring, "The Future of Adventure Games," *Adventure Gamers*, December 19, 2003, adventuregamers.com.

8 See Anastasia Salter, *Jane Jensen: Gabriel Knight, Adventure Games, Hidden Objects* (New York: Bloomsbury Academic, 2017) for a discussion of dialogue in Jensen's games.

9 Salter, *Jane Jensen*, chap. 1.

10 Espen J. Aarseth, *Cybertext: Perspectives on Ergodic Literature* (Baltimore, MD: Johns Hopkins Press, 1997), 109.

11 Chris Crawford, *Chris Crawford on Interactive Storytelling: Second Edition* (San Francisco: Peachpit, 2012), 14.

12 Mark Stephen Meadows, *Pause and Effect: The Art of Interactive Narrative* (Indianapolis, IN: New Riders, 2002), 62–63.

FURTHER READING

Ryan, Marie-Laure. *Narrative as Virtual Reality: Immersion and Interactivity in Literature and Electronic Media*. Baltimore, MD: Johns Hopkins University Press, 2001.

Wardrip-Fruin, Noah, and Pat Harrigan. *First Person: New Media as Story, Performance, and Game*. Cambridge, MA: MIT Press, 2006.

4

Grand Theft Auto V
Avatars

HARRISON GISH

Abstract: The term *avatar* is frequently deployed in both casual and scholarly discussions of video games, but its ubiquity belies the avatar's potential complexity. Focusing on *Grand Theft Auto V*, Harrison Gish examines the range of aesthetic and functional customizations possible in this controversial crime epic, arguing that avatars embody a self-determined, dynamic incorporation of the player within the game world, existing in tension with the game's narrative, spatiality, rules, and design limitations.

Avatars are interesting because it is with and through them that we engage in, interact with, and explore the larger virtual worlds of video games. Avatars—discernible, modifiable figures that players control—exist at the locus of many of the concerns that invigorate game studies; a figurative and figural nexus between issues of technology, genre, spatiality, narrative, interactivity, and identity. As such, avatars are diverse in their construction. The avatar of *Super Mario Bros. 3* (Nintendo R&D4, 1993), a classic platformer from the 8-bit era, and the multiple avatars of *Grand Theft Auto V* (Rockstar North, 2013), a sweeping, violent contemporary sandbox game, differ greatly in their relationship to the aforementioned concerns. Such differences are important, as the existence of varied, diverse avatars denotes that being an avatar is not a singular thing, not just one half of an "either/or" dichotomy. In other words, an onscreen figure through which you, the player, experience a game, exists on a spectrum of "avatariality," bearing certain qualities that denote them as specific projections of the individual player playing while eschewing others. Uniting these figures is their malleability; avatars, as virtual projections specific to each player, may encourage the modification of their aesthetics, altering how they appear onscreen, and their functionality, altering how the player explores and interacts with the game world. Similar to the larger gaming world in which they are embedded, avatars are rule-bound systems that allow for limited and dynamic forms of engagement. As such, players not only play *through* a variety of avatars when playing video games but play *with* them as well.

In contemporary literature and scholarship, the term avatar is deployed in a variety of ways that challenge a singular understanding of the concept. Originating from the Hindi, where an avatar was the earthly projection of a deity, the term entered the contemporary vernacular in the 1990s with the publication of Neal Stephenson's cyberpunk epic *Snow Crash* (1992), which proposed a vast virtual world in which users created projections that varied according to their skill levels and real-world resources.[1] In game scholarship, the term *avatar* has been used variously to denote any figure the player controls, on one hand,[2] and only the most deeply customizable proxy present in role-playing games, on the other.[3] Uniting these assorted definitions is an understanding of avatars as surrogates for players in the virtual world, which reflect the players back to themselves, creating a feedback loop that declares players' presence within and influence on the game. Avatars dynamically entwine players within their virtual worlds, connect them to items they collect, and make them partners in narrative progression, thereby engendering varying degrees of player engagement.

GTA V presents the player with three distinct avatars through which they must explore Los Santos, the game's self-referential, highly sardonic representation of greater Los Angeles. Whereas a first-person shooter game like *Borderlands 2* (2K Games, 2012) requires the player to control and modify only a single avatar throughout its narrative campaign and a third-person RPG like *Mass Effect* (BioWare, 2007) necessitates that the player modify the skills of an entire team of intergalactic warriors while only playing as Commander Sheppard, *GTA V* is unique in that the player must engage with and through three distinct avatars, each with their own navigational and interactive attributes and detailed back stories to successfully complete the game. In effect, *GTA V* offers three case studies in how the act of play itself, and the spatial exploration that is frequently essential to that activity, dynamically interrelates predetermined design, narrative affordances, and player proclivities through the avatar.

GTA V's three protagonists, notably all men, represent three wholly different strata of criminality and class distinction in the game's rollicking tale of government subterfuge, high-profile robbery, and retribution. Franklin, who lives in an approximation of South Central, is dissatisfied with his life of boosting cars for unscrupulous auto dealers and possesses a self-awareness that marks him as distinct from the criminals with whom he plies his trade. Michael, a middle-aged retired thief overwhelmed by ennui, lives in the Los Santos equivalent of Beverly

FIGURE 4.1 By collecting and combining a vast array of accoutrements—from hats, shirts, and glasses to haircuts, beards, and tattoos—players modify their avatars' appearances and signify their own agency within the game.

Hills. In a witness protection program, he passes his time drinking whiskey, arguing with his family, and yearning for days gone by. Trevor, the most degenerate and perhaps most eloquent of the group, is a methamphetamine dealer in the central coast pursuing a life of debauchery and ultraviolent revenge against motorcycle gangs and narcotics competitors. As the game unfolds, the characters' lives entwine unpredictably; Michael, who becomes Franklin's criminal mentor after a botched car repossession, unwittingly ushers Trevor, his former accomplice who believed Michael to be dead, back into his life. The unlikely trio attempt to hoodwink federal agents intent on using the group as a proxy for carrying out extrajudicial kidnappings, murders, and assorted nefarious operations.

The complexity of *Grand Theft Auto V*'s narrative is at least, in part, a function of the game's design. As a predominantly third-person "sandbox"-style game, *GTA V* enables the player to travel through a great deal of Los Santos almost immediately. The game is nonlinear and features two maps—one within the heads-up display that appears during play and another that exists as a distinct menu screen—that denote where the player must go to complete missions that advance the game's narrative. However, a predominant pleasure in *GTA* is the exploration of the game's space, the expansive virtual world that is Los Santos. Although it is most certainly possible to complete mission after mission without diverting from goal-oriented play, the game rewards players who deviate from the most obvious path through the world, as doing so increases the possibility that they will locate unique characters, situations, secrets, items, and even visual perspectives on Los Santos. Additionally, *GTA*'s narrative missions require players to travel to far-flung areas of the map, encouraging further exploration in the pursuit of completing campaign objectives. That players may do this with three distinct avatars guarantees a continual variability. For instance, if players explore the fringes of Sandy Shores with Trevor, they may locate and detain criminals on the lam, returning them to Marge, a bail bondswoman (a series of side missions players cannot complete with Michael or Franklin). Exploring Vinewood with Franklin lets players interact with local paparazzi and document celebrities in compromising situations, whereas Trevor may break into a celebrity's home. In *GTA V*, exploration is a dynamic function of both player and avatar; the places players choose to go and the surrogate they travel as result in significant variations of game experience.

While exploring Los Santos, each avatar has a special ability affecting how he moves through and interacts with the surrounding environment. Franklin is capable of driving automobiles at extremely high speeds while in slow motion; Michael can fend off attackers in "bullet time," allowing him to aim and fire quickly as opponents slow down; Trevor can enter a "rampage" mode that reduces the amount of damage he takes while increasing the amount of damage he inflicts. As such, choosing among the different avatars has a narrative effect—in that the game unfolds from different perspectives and in a different order depending whom players control—and a functional effect as well, changing how players interact with and understand their abilities in relation to their surrounding environs and enemies. Such differences between avatar mobility and interactivity are predetermined functions of design, but players may differentiate avatars further, modifying their appearance in ways that have little to no functional effect on play.

Indeed, aesthetic modification is a core part of avatar construction, and although many games require players to determine an avatar's appearance prior to the beginning of campaign play, *GTA V* grants players abundant opportunities to define and redefine how their avatars look throughout the game—a vivid reminder of player agency. Located within the larger game world are clothing stores, barbershops, and tattoo parlors, retailing items and services that adjust how Franklin, Michael, and Trevor appear onscreen. Adorning the trio with such alterations is the most obvious form in which players engage in an individualized customization of their avatars, marking the trio as distinct visual expressions of player intentionality (see figure 4.1). Players may dress their avatars in an expansive number of clothing combinations, choosing among a highly variable selection of shoes and boots, pants and shorts, shirts and T-shirts, glasses, and hats, as well as suits and other full-body regalia. These options include conservative dress designed to emphasize character, such as Franklin's basketball shorts and hooded

FIGURE 4.2 As players travel through Los Santos as Franklin, they simultaneously improve his unique skills and increase their own ability to modify and personalize the Franklin avatar.

sweatshirts displaying his gang affiliation, Michael's jeans and leather jackets, and Trevor's bloodied sweatpants and dirty tank tops. Yet players may also elect to go with utterly flamboyant options, adorning Michael with puffy pastel vests, Trevor with three-piece skinny plaid suits, and Franklin with conservative peacoats, that break radically with the designers' narrative, a choice that elevates player freedom above diegetic consistency and coherency.

With the ability to adjust certain aesthetic elements of *GTA*'s antiheroes, an important distinction between the concept of the *character* and that of the *avatar* exists; character is a function of an unfolding narrative, whereas an avatar is a virtual representation of the individual interacting with the game. Dressing the avatar Michael in flashy pastels challenges the stoic, traditional character of Michael that the game's narrative constructs. This is more than playing virtual dress-up; it reflects the player's ability to self-determine how they conceive of the character and to project their personal predilections and identity onto and into the game. Going "off-script" through an avatar, players pleasurably challenge and even violate the unwritten social rules the game's narrative proposes. In so doing, the avatar's modifiability encourages players to perform their own identity work instead of accepting solely what the game suggests.

Such personalized modification and experimentation are, of course, restricted by *GTA V*'s design. For all its proposed openness, *GTA* can be surprisingly rigid.

While the game promises endless exploration, nuanced and diverse encounters with non-player characters (NPCs), and limitless avatarial variability, systemic limitations rapidly become apparent. The game is, after all, a rule-bound system that places constraints on play, limiting the ways in which the player may engage with it. Narrative missions impose linearity on the seemingly open game world, side missions occur under inviolable time limits, and the ways in which players may interact with most NPCs are limited to physical assault. Such regimentation exists throughout: the foundational narrative remains steadfast, the game world abounds with barriers, and the combination of numerous avatar accoutrements is finite. It is through the choice of how to play within these constraints that the player's agency asserts itself.

Importantly, certain elements of *GTA*'s avatars may not be modified. For example, although the player can shave an array of patterns into Franklin's hair, have him grow a beard, and dress him in an assortment of clothing that ranges from leisurely to formal, the player may never adjust the color of Franklin's skin. Players may never give Trevor a haircut that conceals his bald spots or remove several of his tattoos, options governing minutiae that are available in many other games where aesthetic avatar adjustment is possible. *GTA*'s unfolding narrative depends on Franklin being an African American escaping from South Los Santos, and necessitates Trevor wearing the marks of a life of substantial drug abuse. In other third-person open-world games, such as the *Mass Effect* franchise, players may alter gender, race, skin tone, and even the placement of the eyes with a high degree of specificity. Avatar adjustment in *GTA* is deeply informed by predetermined characters, emphasizing the importance placed on narrative within the game and acting as an important limitation on avatar modification.[4]

Avatar accoutrements are not free in *Grand Theft Auto V*, and players must complete lucrative missions, play the Los Santos stock market effectively, or rob the pedestrians or armored trucks that dot the landscape to attain the necessary funds. The potential for avatar adjustment is a function of in-game progress, and players must spend a nontrivial amount of time playing and exploring if they desire an extensive wardrobe. Additionally, though players may go to the same stores in Los Santos, the goods available differ depending on the avatar the players control, and the location of the various retailers reflect how economic differences are mapped across its virtual world. For instance, discount stores on the south and east side of Los Santos retail cargo shorts, sneakers, and T-shirts emblazoned with corporate logos, while boutiques in the game's equivalent of the upscale Rodeo Drive area sell more expensive wares, such as pleated slacks, dress shoes, and button-down shirts. In addition to completing missions to secure the finances necessary to attain clothing, players must travel to specific locations to purchase the quality of clothing they desire. In Los Santos, the aesthetic adjustment of the avatar implicates and critiques the spatialized class differences present in Los Angeles itself. With *GTA V*'s avatars, who literally wear their economic status on their sleeves, aesthetic adjustment is more than simply a pleasurable player whim; such aesthetics exist in continual tension with the game's virtual economy and critique of contemporary urban capitalism.

Although players may choose what their avatars will wear, the avatar's functional abilities automatically improve during both goal-oriented play and undirected exploration (see figure 4.2). Where other games award skill points that players must assign to such functional qualities through an interface after completing missions, *GTA* invokes a degree of realism by requiring locomotion to enhance statistics related to physicality. As players guide the avatar through Los Santos on foot, stamina and endurance will increase, as will the ability to rapidly maneuver through the cityscape as they spend time in the game's numerous vehicles. Certain avatars already have an advantage in such functional attributes, again informed by the game's story world, such as how Franklin's driving skill is far greater than that of Michael's or Trevor's at the game's beginning. Throughout their exploration of the world, players may work to build these skills for each avatar, but that such enhancements occur automatically as players travel through Los Santos foregrounds the importance of spatial movement to functional advancement.

Additionally, activities that directly improve avatars' functional abilities populate Los Santos. Optional mini-games present throughout the world directly alter specific skills with an exactitude that cannot be achieved during random encounters with NPCs and leisurely explorations of game space. For example, players may take each of their avatars to shooting ranges to improve their aim, draw and reload speeds, engage in races that overtly increase driving ability, or participate in triathlons that improve stamina and strength with a far greater efficacy than is possible during undirected play. Players' commitment to completing mini-games outside of the main campaign improves their avatar's functionality throughout the game while enhancing their ability to complete the core narrative.

Both the aesthetic alterations and the functional changes occurring during play inscribe the avatar as a vessel that bears the marks of player experience and choice. This is true not only for *GTA V* but also for any game in which the experience of play allows or demands changes to the player's in-game surrogate. Avatars are fundamentally dynamic figures informed by and existing between player proclivities, designer mandates, narrative affordances, spatial mapping, and sociological critiques present within the game. Rule-bound and therefore inherently restricted, their complex modifiability nonetheless allows for and encourages exploratory creativity, signifying player achievement aesthetically and functionally while altering the player's relationship to the virtual worlds they play within.

NOTES

1 Neal Stephenson, *Snow Crash* (New York: Bantam Books, 1992). Players of video and computer games potentially encountered the term in the mid-1980s, as Richard Garriott titled the fourth game in his immensely popular and influential *Ultima* series *Ultima IV: Quest of the Avatar* (Origin Systems, 1985). In Garriott's game, players quested to become an "avatar" for the mythical land of Britannia, an example of spiritual and moral enlightenment for others to emulate.

2 For a discussion of avatars as any figure the player controls and the psychoanalytic implications of the connection between player and avatar, see Bob Rehak, "Playing at Being: Psychoanalysis and the Avatar," in *The Video Game Theory Reader*, ed. Mark J. P. Wolf and Bernard Perron (New York: Routledge, 2003), 103–128.

3 For a discussion of avatars as specific to deeply customizable role-playing games, and a detailed ethnography of players who play such games, see Zach Waggoner, *My Avatar, My Self: Identity in Video Role-Playing Games* (Jefferson, NC: McFarland, 2009).

4 Notably, such modifications are possible in the game's online version, where narrative affordances are comparatively minimal. Players may adjust skin color, facial construction, hairline, and more. However, in keeping with the *GTA*'s cynicism, they may also add cold sores, acne scars, and various kinds of weathered skin.

FURTHER READING

Bayliss, Peter. "Beings in the Game-world: Characters, Avatars, and Players." In *Proceedings of the 4th Australasian Conference on Interactive Entertainment*, Melbourne, Australia, 2007.

Calleja, Gordon. "Digital Game Involvement: A Conceptual Model." *Games and Culture* 2 no. 3 (2007): 236–260.

Coleman, B. *Hello Avatar: Rise of the Networked Generation*. Cambridge, MA: MIT Press, 2011.

Nitsche, Michael. *Video Game Spaces: Image, Play, and Structure in 3D Worlds*. Cambridge, MA: MIT Press, 2008.

5

Sid Meier's Civilization
Realism

PETER KRAPP

Abstract: In a simulation game like *Sid Meier's Civilization* that spans centuries of game time, Peter Krapp contends that the series' realism is not anchored in a sense of historical accuracy but, instead, offers a playful exploration through abstract representations of what leads to the rise and fall of empires.

When games are consumed as entertainment offering unprecedented flights of the imagination, when a widely used game engine is called Unreal, when big developers sell interactive software that indulges in all manner of fantasy and escapism, what role could there possibly be for realism in gaming? Should gamers expect a series such as *Sid Meier's Civilization* (1991–today) to be realistic, and if so, what exactly does that mean? How much does this change over time so that what may have been accepted as "realistic" years ago perhaps does not pass muster today? Games across genres have laid claim to certain kinds of realism: whether in offering action that reflects recent news headlines or in depicting the skills of star athletes, the handling of exotic cars, the ballistics of weapons, the gyrations of planes, the finer points of military tactics, or the machinations of global economics. The interactions afforded by sports games, driving games, or strategy games may be fanciful, but attention to detail, to *verisimilitude*, is often a prominent feature of a game. Yet that kind of recognizable detail is just one possible meaning of realism. If we have come to accept that games are an art form, a media discourse, a social platform, then it pays to consider the full spectrum of how we use the term *realism* before checking how a particular game or game franchise—such as the *Civilization* franchise—negotiates that spectrum.

Instead of seeking a definition of realism, which may tie us up in philosophical and psychological arguments, let's consider what it is not: antonyms of realism include fiction and fantasy, utopian and dystopian critique, surrealism and other rejections of realist aesthetics, and different strands of idealism and visionary imagination. To call something "realistic" implies that there is also some way to relate to the world without those representational strategies. Realism aims for a practical or pragmatic naturalism—an appearance of representing our ordinary realm of observation in a literal, naturalistic, authentic manner. This fidelity to real life, to convey an accurate representation without recourse to idealization, abstraction or stylistic condensation, may not be an achievable goal, but game designers continue to strive for verisimilitude by crafting ever-more lifelike visual worlds and, in the case of strategy games, creating simulations that model predictive systems.

Civilization is a turn-based strategy game franchise that has sold more than 33 million copies since its inception in 1991. As conceived by Sid Meier, it is not only one of the most successful series in game history, it also deeply influenced other games and game genres. Designed first for MS-DOS, then the Commodore Amiga 500/600 and Atari ST, Apple and Microsoft Windows systems, and finally Nintendo platforms, the game's simulation balances infrastructure, research, economic income, culture, and military might. The sequel *Sid Meier's Civilization II* was published in 1996 by Sid Meier's company Microprose for computers as well as the PlayStation console. Activision acquired the rights to publish a title called *Civilization: Call to Power* in 1999. In 2001, Meier's new company Firaxis published *Sid Meier's Civilization III* for Apple and Microsoft Windows systems. Between 2003 and 2005 the franchise rights went to Atari, and since then the rights to the title have been with 2K Games. *Sid Meier's Civilization IV* was released in 2005, and five years later the fifth installment appeared. In October 2014, *Sid Meier's Civilization: Beyond Earth* was published, followed by *Sid Meier's Civilization VI* in October 2016. Although the game visuals, multiplayer gameplay, and player communities evolved over time, the player's basic task remains the same: guide your chosen people from the early Stone Age through human history to the present day and into the future by colonizing new lands and new planets. Players start with one village in 4000 BC, pick a leader for their virtual nation, and aim to conquer the world. The chosen leader is not inserted into the game as the player's avatar. Instead, the game gifts players with a godlike perspective, providing an intradiegetic point of action. The isometric perspective of the main screen is a world map with menu systems of actions that invite players to build, engage in diplomacy, foster science and the arts, and take steps to make their area of influence bigger, stronger, and richer.

This map can depict a realistic version of Earth or a fictitious world; the option *not* to resemble Earth is available, but either way, the various rhomboid (later hexagonal, as of *Sid Meier's Civilization V*) plots of sea, forest, desert, hills, and so on always touch at the edges, making it possible to circumnavigate the game world as a cylindrical playscape. However, *Civilization* is not merely a battle map—it is a map-in-time, a spatiotemporal model, bringing narrative tools to mapmaking. On this map, the story unfolds as players make decisions (see figure 5.1). For a

FIGURE 5.1 Agriculture, industry, and military units populate the map in *Sid Meier's Civilization V*.

new village, for instance, the player picks whether to go with a settler, a scout, or a warrior, and each unit selected will have value, changing the balance between expansion and preservation, offense and defense. Cumulatively, these decisions add up to the success or failure of one's strategy.

Sid Meier has said that, to him, games are a series of interesting choices.[1] Consequently, the story of a game such as *Civilization* is not embedded; rather, simulation games lend themselves to emergent narratives as they draw on a complex system of interrelated variables. Events in the game are propagated by the complexity of the intersecting game systems and often not necessarily in ways that were anticipated by the game's developers.

After completing *Railroad Tycoon* in 1990, Meier and his team decided to tackle something more audacious. When Meier and Bruce Shelley appeared at the 2017 Game Developers Conference to reflect on their first *Civilization* game, they pointed out how the new title commingled elements from *SimCity* (Maxis, 1989), the British PC war game *Empire* (Walter Bright, 1977), and a board game named *Civilization*.[2] Drawing on children's books rather than history and strategy references, the developers foregrounded humor and a lighthearted portrayal of political leadership. It is hardly realistic to pit nations against each other whose leaders are not even from the same century—Genghis Khan and Caesar, Napoleon and Cleopatra—but in opting for a turn-based game, rather than the flow of a real-time simulator, Meier had a hit on his hands. Evidently, players care less about "real life" scenarios or locations and more so about the affordances of this type of strategy game. Indeed, what *Civilization* models is not so much historical accuracy but sociological and anthropological processes.[3] The franchise became highly successful once the second iteration allowed user-created modifications, or "mods" (see James Newman's chapter in this collection for more on user-generated content). From the second installment onward, *Civilization* also dropped reams of demographic data and other statistics provided in the initial version of the game.

Turn-based strategy and simulation games are less invested in photorealistic graphics and surround sound that are crucial for the immersive first-person perspective of racing and shooting games. This genre also depends less on a suite of customizable choices that role-playing games make a central pillar of the second-person perspective. Instead, simulation and strategy games deal in abstraction—in a detached third-person perspective. Just as Chaturanga, chess, or the Prussian and English board and floor games of the nineteenth century served as training tools for strategic thinking, the planning games of the first half of the twentieth century featured controls and feedback.[4] From wargaming to flight simulators, and from radar screens to immersive graphic interfaces, the history of game technology shows how cybernetic feedback lends itself to training models. Obviously, simulation can be a useful tool for closed mechanical systems; for complex open systems, simulation can be a pretty good tool for introducing beginners to dynamic system behavior and a way to explore options or test the validity of assumptions. This has made simulation games a powerful training tool for policy advisors, military officers, and aspiring rulers.

The introduction of computing black-boxed a lot of the military and business tradition of the strategy game, but the 1960s saw a resurgence of the elements that characterized simulation gaming before World War I. Here it is noteworthy that *Civilization* features strategy consultants. These advisers will speak to you, but their avatars are limited to a few syllables of gibberish—"vollum follum" and "roboro"—which pales in comparison to the effort that went into creating complex, realistic languages for the television series *Star Trek* or *Game of Thrones*. Yet scenario planning or management simulations necessarily limit their real-time data input to avoid losing definition; most simulators are particularly focused and do not scale while a global model using data mining and artificial intelligence to make large-scale, messy situations tractable risks black-boxing parameters.

By the same token, and despite ongoing efforts to make its systems more dynamic to reflect the historical vagaries of ruling civilizations, there remains room for interpreting *Civilization* games as dystopian critiques of our lived experience, as counterfactual history, as make-believe untethered from basic economic, technological, and cultural tenets, even as sheer willful abstraction. One may be tempted to pursue the historical verifiability of a strategy game portraying human history through reductive mechanics, with reference to the stipulation of a settled scientific consensus on how technology, economics, diplomacy, warfare, culture, and so on lead humans from the Stone Age to the space age. Or one may opt instead to see lost opportunities and unheralded advances in human history that are not captured in their subtlety and consequence by the necessary abstractions and simplifications of the game. Even if we treat a given game as a tool to remind ourselves of critical perspectives on how we got here, that does not prevent us from recognizing the game as caught up in ideological representations and distortions of all the basic mechanisms that make it playable. Although few would judge *Civilization* by the rule book of socialist realism (glorifying depictions of communist values), many critics identify its design as capitalist realism (glorifying neoliberal market domination). If we understand "socialist realism" as officially sanctioned art (above all in visual arts but also in music and literature) in the Soviet Union and other socialist states between the 1920s and 1960s, the motivation was to foster arts that affirm a direct effect on the human organism. This discursive formation rejects futurism and other socialist movements, emphasizing instead a life circumscribed by the communitarian ethos of planned states. In turn, if we understand "capitalist realism" as the predominant form of approved arts in the United States and other capitalist states since the 1950s, the motivation is to treat all forms of human expression as commodities. This discursive formation describes the ideological and aesthetic dominance of corporate culture in the West, a life dominated by private consumption as exhorted by advertising and competitive sales. What these two opposed ideological formations have in common is that they assert realism as a bulwark against critique—they assert the fundamental validity of ideology over dissent. Each lay claim to a faithful objective mirror of our collective human truth. In short, although realism was a period style, it remains a perennial motive in literature, art, film, and games. Arguably, in *Civilization* a pronounced US-centric view of the world and its politics is on display.[5]

To take a concrete example of the limits of this particular strategy game, consider an aspect of strategy that has become an ideological battleground: weather and climate. Military historians argue that Napoleon's incursion into Russia was defeated, in large part, by a harsh winter that affected supply lines more than anticipated; similar claims are made about the Russian defense in World War II. Strategically speaking, the absence of meteorological complexity weakens the realism of *Civilization* as a simulation. Weather models constitute a formidable challenge to computing even today—modeling the fluid dynamics and systemic interactions for three to five days has become relatively dependable, but longer-term forecasts remain problematic.[6] Nonetheless, a complex game like *Civilization* ought to be able to include weather, along with terrain and diplomacy and technology and finance, into its calculus. *Civilization* does not thematize the Anthropocene, does not invite gamers to contemplate environmental catastrophe in the race for technological supremacy, and does not account for what happens to the losing side; indeed, what "counts" is that a player can achieve a military–scientific–diplomatic victory, regardless of how that win condition is reached. The roots of the turn-based strategy game, however, lie in simulations that model far more realistic interactions.

One can see what constitutes realism in any such game by checking its blind spots or omissions—here, for instance, weather and climate. This is why Jesse Ausubel's role in redefining the planning game is so intriguing. An influential environmental scientist, Jesse Ausubel was an organizer of the first United Nations World Climate Conference, in 1979 in Geneva, which substantially heightened the profile of global warming issues on scientific and political agendas. In 1980, he built a board game and two computer games about carbon dioxide emissions and global warming. Ausubel's book *Cities and their Vital Systems* found its way to the young Will Wright, who made extensive use of it for his 1989 release of *SimCity*, for which Ausubel also served as a beta tester.[7] Although unfairly ignored in game studies, this distinguished science advisor can rightfully be seen as the progenitor of what is now often called "serious gaming."[8] *Ice Core Quest*, for instance, developed by Carleton University as a modification of *Neverwinter Nights* (BioWare, 2002), offers quests to explore Antarctica and global warming. A game called *20,000 Leagues Under the Sea: Captain Nemo* (Mzone Studio, 2009) uses National Oceanic and Atmospheric Administration data to illustrate Captain Nemo's last refuge in Antarctica. A strategy game called *Last Hope Antarctica* requires the player to build a new base and manage its resources. The games *Penguin Adventure* (Konami, 1986) and *Antarctic Adventure* (Konami, 1983) require players to navigate a penguin around the perimeter of the continent along crudely mapped paths. A game developed by a Canadian team working on a cyber-cartographic atlas of Antarctica allows players to playfully explore with joysticks or keyboard controls the life of penguins, the landscape of the continent, and the conceptual dimensions structuring the atlas itself. Is all of this just armchair tourism or a step toward planetary consciousness? None of these serious games is more realistic than *Civilization* in terms of visual and sonic fidelity, but they at least attempt to account for historical changes in weather and climate. Even a training simulation as abstract as Buckminster Fuller's *World Game* (or "OS Earth") had more real-time data and complexity than did the technically advanced *Civilization* games.[9]

In the theory of knowledge, realism is a general theory of scientifically established facts, assuming that the world is independent of our knowledge-gathering activities, which not only produce assumptions and predictions but get us closer to the real nature of things; realism, in short, harkens back to an ancient struggle between common sense and abstract thought. Clearly playing a simulation game will require some of both. However, as players quickly discover, while playing games such as *Civilization* may rely on a balanced mix of theory-crafting and commonsense approaches, the same does not hold for designing such games. The design of game mechanics, of competing strategies, and of win conditions illustrates that games always pivot on abstractions. This is why game players not only play as *Civilization* guides them to but soon also explore the limits of the game design. Designing the game so that a "cultural victory" is possible (which in *Civilization* means accumulating architectural, religious, and artistic achievements) likewise requires a theory of culture that allows for this to become a game mechanic, whereby some cultural achievements are somehow superior to others and thus provide more "civic inspiration" or attract more tourism. Designing the game so that scientific progress follows certain steps implies a linear theory of science. Designing the game so that trade routes are advantageous or disadvantageous discloses a tacit theory of markets and their function over historical periods. Needless to say, these aspects of *Civilization* do not strike every scholar of trade and economics, of science and culture, as valid or historically realistic.

Perhaps nobody approaches a game in the *Civilization* franchise with the expectation that it would render true descriptions of observable aspects of our world, yet players nonetheless notice and discuss problems with how *Civilization* models social, political, economic, and cultural interactions. That *Civilization* games pivot around an ideologically reductive model of technology and conflict seems not to have lessened the popularity of the franchise. If the game has remained enjoyable despite its realism limitations, it is at least partly because players are not naïve consumers. Players recognize that even so-called entertainment software is imbued with values and ideologies, but within the range of interactions afforded, players find pleasure in discovering a game's underlying assumptions. Perhaps those players seek ever more control over possible worlds, even to the point of simulating utopian and fantastic emergent interactions.

NOTES

1 As quoted in Andrew Rollings and Dave Morris, *Game Architecture and Design* (Scottsdale AZ: Coriolis, 2000), 38.

2 Meier and Shelley were able to strike a deal with venerable British board game company Avalon Hill for the use of the *Civilization* name and certain elements of their board game title.

3 William Uricchio, "Simulation, History, and Computer Games," in *Handbook of Computer Game Studies*, ed. Joost Raessens and Jeffrey Goldstein (Cambridge, MA: MIT 2005), 327–338.

4 Chaturanga is an ancient Indian strategy game developed around the sixth century CE. It was adopted in Persia a century later and eventually developed into the form of chess brought to late-medieval Europe.

5 Kacper Poblocki, "Becoming-State: The Bio-Cultural Imperialism of Sid Meier's Civilization," *Focal—European Journal of Anthropology* no. 39 (2002): 163–172.

6 Gabriele Gramelsberger, "Story Telling with Code—Archaeology of Climate Modeling," *TeamEthno Online* (February 2006): 77–84.

7 Jesse H. Ausubel and Robert Herman, eds., *Cities and their Vital Systems: Infrastructure Past, Present, and Future* (Washington DC: National Academies Press 1988).

8 Jennifer Robinson and Jesse H. Ausubel, "A Game Framework for Scenario Generation for the CO2 Issue," *Simulation and Games* 14, no. 3 (1983): 317–344

9 *World Game*, also known as *World Peace Game*, was an analog educational simulation created by Buckminster Fuller as a counterpoint to popular tabletop war games. Players work cooperatively to solve global problems in a manner that benefits the most people with the least ecological damage or loss of life. In 1993, a computer-based version of the game was released by the nonprofit World Game Institute, and in 2001 the game was acquired by OS Earth, Inc. and since has been published as OS Earth Global Simulation Workshop, www.worldgame.com.

FURTHER READING

Dorr, Simon. "Strategy." In *The Routledge Companion to Video Game Studies*, edited by Mark J. P. Wolf and Bernard Perron, 275–281. New York: Routledge, 2014.

Friedman, Ted. "*Civilization* and its Discontents: Simulation, Subjectivity, and Space." In *On a Silver Platter: CD-Roms and the Promises of a New Technology*, edited by Greg M. Smith, 132–150. New York: NYU Press, 1999.

Galloway, Alexander. "Social Realism in Gaming." *Game Studies—The International Journal of Computer Game Research* 4, no. 1 (November 2004), http://gamestudies.org.

Pias, Claus. *Computer Game Worlds*. Chicago: Diaphanes, 2017.

6

Planescape: Torment
Immersion

EVAN TORNER

Abstract: Although scholars and critics often cite aspects of audiovisual design and quick-twitch gameplay as the primary means by which players immerse themselves in a game's fiction, *Planescape: Torment*—a highly rated computer role-playing game with dated graphics and sound—proves a counterexample to this discourse. In this chapter, Evan Torner discusses the importance of literary framing, affect, and narrative reincorporation—elements derived largely from novels and table-top role-playing games—for the game's achievement of that oft-heralded but ever-elusive aesthetic ideal of immersion.

Immersion is a contested and messy concept in game studies. This is no less the case for role-playing games (RPGs)—be they digital or analog—for it concerns the core aesthetic experience of a game, as well as how that game is framed and marketed. In RPGs, we want to take on the role of another. Moreover, we want our actions within the story to matter, to have consequences. However, things get a bit conceptually hazy from here. After all, what does it mean to call a video game "immersive"? Am I "immersed" when I feel like my own consciousness is merging with the character I am playing? Am I "immersed" when I am given a series of routine activities in a game world that stimulate dopamine in my brain on their completion? Am I "immersed" when a game's multisensory stimulation causes my actual physiology to respond as if it were real? Am I "immersed" when a certain culture of play tells me I should be?

Maybe it's better if we think of immersion as a *meta-concept*, as well as being an aesthetic ideal. A meta-concept is an idea that organizes ways of thinking about that idea. Immersion is thus never singular in its meaning; rather, it is a placeholder that is both intimately subjective and highly contextual. For example,

Space Invaders (Taito, 1978) was considered so immersive in the early 1980s that UK member of Parliament George Foulkes sought (and failed) to ban it outright. Immersion, in this case, meant the game's incentive systems that kept players involved were perceived as addictive and then pathologized. Meanwhile, Frank Rose in *The Art of Immersion* frames immersion as resulting from the participatory agency of fans within transmedia universes such as *Lost* (2004–2010) or *Star Wars* (1977–).[1] Immersion, in this case, means a deeper investment in a story universe because of seeing the impact of fan input play out in its various narratives. In this instance, collective imagination and social reinforcement make immersion happen. A design ideal, a personal experience, marketing hype: immersion is a textual invitation to lose ourselves in the act of play. This chapter examines those textual features of a computer RPG that encourage players to take this leap of faith.

As an aesthetic ideal, immersion is also something designers aspire to create for the player through specific design choices. If the aim is visual-sensory immersion, one might double down on creating realistic water effects. If the aim is to keep a player focused on game action, one might design rules and mechanics that require constant attention. Immersion does not necessarily mean only participation in a story universe or having access to pixel-perfect graphics and sound. It does mean, however, feeling involved in an experience separate from one's everyday reality. It turns out, for example, that much of what we call gameplay "immersion" corresponds with propositions and functions of engaging literary fiction.

This chapter considers the idea of immersion in light of *Planescape: Torment* (Black Isle Studios, 1999)—a game that neither offers cutting-edge graphics (even for its time of production) nor highly-responsive control schemes. In fact, it is an unrelentingly prosaic and narratively dense text. And yet, it is often hailed as being amongst the most "immersive" computer role-playing games (CRPG) ever designed or, in the words of PC Gamer, "one of the most inventive, entertaining role-playing games ever created."[2] The core gameplay and storytelling are so compelling, in fact, that an enhanced edition of the game was released in 2017, updated for play on contemporary hardware. At first glance, however, the game appears unassuming. This CRPG is played from a top-down isometric point of view, and it sports relatively rudimentary graphics and animations even for its time of production. Composer Mark Morgan, best known for his work on *Zork Nemesis* (Zombie Studios, 1996) and *Fallout* (Black Isle Studios, 1997), crafted the game's moody, angst-ridden MIDI-instrumental soundtrack. Black Isle Studios created *Planescape: Torment* using BioWare's Infinity Engine, a game engine previously used for *Baldur's Gate* (BioWare, 1998), which was set in the *Advanced Dungeons & Dragons* (*AD&D*) "Forgotten Realms" story universe. And the game

FIGURE 6.1
The Nameless
One awakes in
the mortuary of
a world full of
complexity and
mystery.

came packaged in an orange box with cover dominated by a massive blue face; the contents included a manual, poster, and the game subdivided between four CD-ROM discs.

In *Planescape: Torment*, you play as the Nameless One, an immortal but amnesiac being who wakes up on a slab in a supernatural mortuary (see figure 6.1). Each time you die, another being also dies in your place to give you new life; this sacrifice then haunts you as a ghost. The goal of the game is to recover your memory and break this quasi-Buddhist cycle of eternal recurrence of dreary life after death, hence the titular "torment." However, it turns out that you are not the first Nameless One, and previous versions of yourself have left their own legacy for you to deal with. A motley cast of characters accompanies the player on their quest, including the wisecracking floating skull Morte, the deadly half-fiend Annah-of-the-Shadows, the Limbo-dwelling githzerai fighter-mage Dak'kon, and the brutal armored phantom Vhailor, to name a few. The humanity and complexity of these characters reinforce the protagonist's own inward search for justice and purpose. The journey takes the player through the baroque *AD&D* setting of *Planescape* (1994)—David "Zeb" Cook's tabletop role-playing creation with multiple portal-linked planes of existence teeming with bizarre undead, terrifying demons, and intriguing locations with unforgettable local customs. In the vein of pulp fantasy-fiction luminaries such as Jack Vance and Michael Moorcock, *Planescape*'s city of Sigil offers both danger and weirdness in equal measure, with every corner harboring some unique textual description to be uncovered or new non-player character (NPC) to confront.

Nevertheless, these other realms also harbor a surprising level of content to intrigue players, and the game actively cultivates emotions to match. Greg M. Smith writes that we approach media "with an enormous collection of microscripts . . . [that] encourage the viewer to anticipate what will happen next narratively, stylistically, and emotionally."[3] *Planescape: Torment* employs microscripts that "makes a unique emotive mix out of our various generic expectations."[4] As the Nameless One seeks to exit the mortuary, for example, Morgan's grim soundtrack establishes a foreboding mood with drums, water droplet noises, and a morose flute. At the same time, however, Morte advises (in text) that the protagonist ought not to kill any of the female undead, which, through dialogue options, leads into a necrophilia joke. The excessively grim atmosphere enables dark humor to flourish. In contrast, the Nameless One's comrades sacrifice their lives in the Fortress of Regret at the end so that he may confront the Transcendent One, his mortality made flesh. The isometric visuals offer an un-cinematic depiction of your friends' corpses, but the gravitas of the music coupled with the Transcendent One's arrogant justification for killing them has brought seasoned gamers to tears. The game's mutually reinforcing soundtrack, plotline, and dialogue elements are only some reasons why *Planescape: Torment* maintains player interest.

Hungarian psychologist Mihaly Csikszentmihalyi's (pronounced "me-hi chik-sent-me-hi") concept of "flow" has become a particularly useful benchmark for game designers working to create an immersive state: a person moving pleasurably from the completion of one goal to the next.[5] Human happiness, according to Csikszentmihalyi, corresponds to a specific blend of short-term, medium-term, and long-term goals being regularly completed. American game designer Jane McGonigal most notably took the concept up in her book *Reality is Broken* as part of a larger argument that games can help us improve our lives.[6] *Planescape: Torment* delivers that precise blend of goals that produces experiential "flow" that has since been emulated and expanded on by subsequent generations of CRPGs and massively multiplayer role-playing games.

Here is how *Planescape: Torment*'s structuring of its core gameplay loop helps a player achieve "flow." First, player characters enter a new environment. They explore this environment by clicking on various objects to reveal text, store items in their inventory, or open conversation options with NPCs. Objects and NPCs then point player characters toward the next minor or major quest. Managing an increasingly complex mixture of narrative-based tasks and quests captures players' attention, putting them in a flow state. The first half-hour of *Planescape: Torment* functions as a tutorial level that orients players to the game's series of quests and task resolutions—action that begins with waking on a cold mortuary slab in a strange, multiplanar city, followed by meeting a floating, talking skull, then finagling a key from zombie workers, all in an effort to locate a missing journal.

Although well executed, none of these design devices are revolutionary. Instead, *Planescape: Torment* distinguishes itself from similar-looking CRPGs through its literary ambitions. In many ways, the game seeks not only to engender the flow of a pleasing task structure, but it also re-creates the experience of reading a really good book. What keeps a player immersed is its long stream of engaging prose. *Planescape: Torment* is less a traditional CRPG than it is a masterpiece of interactive fiction with a thin layer of *AD&D* on top. Combat, a mainstay of most *Dungeons & Dragons*–based CRPGs, is de-emphasized in favor of dialogue. Indeed, there are few fights that a player could not talk their way out of. This encourages many players to build their characters around the stats of Wisdom, Intelligence, and Charisma, with the goal of maximizing their dialogue options. In other words, players are tempted by textual storylines to change their entire approach to gameplay.

Good storytelling, comments artist and critic John Berger, puts its listener "in an eternal present."[7] That, too, sounds like immersion. The game's narrative conceit— an exploration of the Nameless One's past lives and answering the timeless question posed by Ravel the Hag, "What can change the nature of a man?"—imbues the side quests with the same meaningfulness of the main campaign quests. The Nameless One is on an existential quest to find himself. The game's players are also on journeys of self-discovery where they make difficult decisions over many hours of gameplay. The script abounds with pregnant aphorisms, such as "All people love themselves too much to be changed by something as simple as love" and "There is only one truth in the multiverse. The multiverse shall be sharpened upon the blade of justice." The game even makes numerous literary and philosophical allusions. Nordom the four-armed mechanoid invokes René Descartes—"I think, therefore I am . . . I think"—whereas Morte echoes Shakespeare: "Alas Dak'kon, I knew him well." The text inscribed on the Nameless One's back mirrors that of Franz Kafka's "In the Penal Colony" (1919) or Christopher Nolan's *Memento* (2001). "No wonder my back hurts," the Nameless One comments. "There's a damn novel written on it." Indeed, this damn novel of a game serves as a bridge between nerd culture and the broader Western literary canon, playing with self-reflexivity, soul-searching, and emotional ambiguity in many of its scenarios. Such ambitious themes convince the discerning player that this CRPG aspires to high art status and is thus worthy of the reverence usually reserved for such cultural fare.

Planescape: Torment combines its literary referentiality with a series of tasks and dialogue options that lead players to agonize over their character's decisions because they are meaningful and feel consequential.[8] One of the reasons why the decision-making moments have such gravity is because the game utilizes a powerful technique common to tabletop RPG theory: *reincorporation*.[9] Narrative reincorporation is the simple act of bringing prior player character actions into conversation with a later scene. The Nameless One may undertake an action in one scene and, then 10 gameplay hours later, experience the ripple effects of that decision. There is no better illustration of this than with the Fortress of Regrets, which not only has its entrance near where you start the game but also contains Shadows of beings that you have killed along the way. Obstacles that you eliminate return to haunt you. Meeting previous versions of yourself cements the idea that your current incarnation of the Nameless One is but one of many. This is both a commentary on the replay and repetition at the heart of the video game medium and a means of blending the identification of the fictional character with the gamer playing that character. The Nameless One is a sufficiently blank slate, an avatar that functions as a projective surface. Reincorporation, coupled with sophisticated tracking of player decision trees, encourages the player to believe that their play has had an impact—that their choice *mattered*. Player agency coupled with narrative impact may be one of the most powerful formulas for producing a sense of immersion, in fact.

Planescape: Torment nurtures the belief that video games can aspire to high-art status, aiming for the same modernist literary heights such as Joyce and Kafka. Game scholar Diane Carr writes, "The game resists resolution or even comprehension. A rambling text like *Planescape: Torment* bounces when you try and nail it down, it resists totalization. It has its moments of 'rush' and of confrontation, but it wants to be savored, wandered through, in the company of armed companions."[10] Whereas we face monotony, interruptions, and oft-meaningless work in our real lives, gameplay immersion results from a combination of emotional attachment, task flow, and appreciating the results of previous decisions. Despite its origins in a remote *AD&D* universe and its lackluster visuals, *Planescape: Torment* is remembered as a deeply immersive and emotionally affecting title for conveying hundreds of thousands of words over the course of 30-plus hours of play. This is partly because of its mixing of narrative reincorporation and literary recursivity. The Nameless One becomes the ideal avatar for his state as a blank, projective surface, as well as being a critical vehicle for commentary *about* that very act of ego investment. A journal full of activities keeps players busy, and the ambiguous effects of gameplay choices keep them in suspense about how their decisions will play out.

Planescape: Torment gained a cult following for its philosophical and literary pretensions that are cloaked in the garish orange-and-blue box of a cheap piece of genre fiction set in an obscure tabletop story universe. Yet gamer cultures affirm *Planescape: Torment* as a "must-play" experience and one that players need neither spoilers nor cheats to complete. The expansive world-building and visual panache of later CRPGs such as *Mass Effect* (BioWare, 2007) or *The Elder Scrolls*

V: Skyrim (Bethesda Game Studios, 2011) seem less impressive in the face of old-fashioned storytelling, the written word as the primal site of revelation and belief. To quote one of the Nameless One's conversation options: "Belief can change the nature of a man." When we believe in them, games can change us too.

NOTES

1 Frank Rose, *The Art of Immersion: How the Digital Generation is Remaking Hollywood, Madison Avenue, and the Way We Tell Stories* (New York: W. W. Norton, 2011).

2 Michael Wolf, "*Planescape: Torment* Review," *PC Gamer*, August 3, 2014.

3 Greg Smith, *Film Structure and the Emotion System* (Cambridge: Cambridge University Press, 2003): 48.

4 Smith, *Film Structure*, 49.

5 Mihaly Csikszentmihalyi, *Flow: The Psychology of Optimal Experience* (New York: Harper & Row, 1991).

6 Jane McGonigal, *Reality Is Broken: Why Games Make Us Better and How They Can Change the World* (New York: Penguin, 2011).

7 Kate Kellaway, "John Berger: 'If I'm a Storyteller, It's Because I Listen,'" *Guardian*, October 30, 2016.

8 After all, you can *fail* conversations in *Planescape: Torment*, so dialogue options must be chosen with care.

9 "Games that actively support reincorporation" discussion board, *Story Games*, March 2008, http://story-games.com.

10 Diane Carr, "Play Dead: Genre and Affect in *Silent Hill* and *Planescape: Torment*," *Game Studies* 3, no. 1 (May 2003), http://www.gamestudies.org.

FURTHER READING

Adams, Ernest. "Postmodernism and the Three Types of Immersion." *Gamasutra*, July 9, 2004. www.gamasutra.com.

Ermi, Laura, and Frans Mäyrä. "Fundamental Components of the Gameplay Experience: Analyzing Immersion." In *Worlds in Play*, edited by Suzanne de Castell and Jennifer Jenson, 15–27. New York: Peter Lang, 2007

White, William J., Emily Care Boss, and J. Tuomas Harviainen. "Role-playing Communities, Cultures of Play, and the Discourse of Immersion." In *Immersive Gameplay*, edited by Evan Torner and William J. White, 71–86. Jefferson, NC: McFarland, 2012.

7

Don't Starve
Temporality

CHRISTOPHER HANSON

Abstract: Among the many pleasures of digital games are how they often allow play-ers to control time and experience temporality in new ways. By contrast, Christopher Hanson argues that *Don't Starve* inverts these pleasures to greatly restrict the player's control over temporality and foreground the function of time as an essential resource of its gameplay mechanics.

Many gaming pleasures are temporal: we play to "pass the time," we may lose track of time when immersed in gameplay, and a timed game's final few seconds can be thrilling for players and spectators alike. Games permit us a separation from work, other obligations, and our everyday lives by creating experiences in which we have power over time such as calling a "time-out" in a sports match or taking back a move in an analog board game. Digital games enhance these tem-poral pleasures, often allowing players to manipulate and traverse time through pausing and saving a game in the middle of a campaign or to employ time-based gameplay mechanics to achieve fantastic feats. However, as *Don't Starve* (Klei En-tertainment, 2013) illustrates, games may also impose time restrictions that mir-ror our everyday lives and invert games' pleasurable temporal control to instead make the lack of control part of their allure.

In *Don't Starve* players are tasked with the ostensibly simple and straightforward titular goal as they control Wilson, a "gentleman scientist" who, after an experi-ment, has awoken in a strange and unforgiving world. Initially, players may wan-der the procedurally generated landscape and try to get a sense of their bearings. A variety of flora and fauna populate the game world, some of which are benign while others are downright dangerous. However, the potentially hostile creatures and plants in *Don't Starve* only constitute a portion of the world's dangers. The player must also carefully monitor their avatar's physical and mental health while simultaneously developing short- and long-term strategies for survival. Klei Entertainment describes its title as an "uncompromising wilderness survival game" that intimates the countless ways in which the player's avatar may meet an untimely and utterly unexpected death.[1]

Time functions as an overt resource in a number of games and genres. For example, arcade games such as the racing game *Out Run* (Sega AM2, 1986) or the shooting game *Time Crisis* (Namco, 1995) limit game sessions to set periods. Play time may be extended upon successfully reaching checkpoints, allowing continued play until that new deadline expires or—as is often the case in arcade games—additional coins are deposited into the machine. A number of competitive analog sports games limit game time as well. A game clock tracks the time remaining in many sports, requiring teams to outscore one another before time expires. Time management extends to more granular components of gameplay. For example, a "shot clock" in basketball requires teams to shoot the ball within a set amount of time. This timer discourages teams from holding on to the ball to foster a more fluid flow wherein each team must continuously try to score. Competitive chess game clocks restrict the total amount of time players may use to execute their moves. The timer both helps expedite matches, and it balances games between differently skilled players by giving novices more time than more experienced players receive.

Don't Starve uses restricted time as a core play mechanic, giving the player only a set amount of time to accomplish essential tasks. The consequences of running out of time are dire. For instance, Wilson will die the very first night if the player does not find or craft a source of light. Survival requires adherence to these implicit timers, so food must be found before the avatar starves just as warm clothing or a fire pit must be made before the timed onset of winter.

Don't Starve's resource gathering and management are apparent upon starting a game. Virtually all of the game's objects can be examined, harvested or otherwise collected, and the player is prompted to build items essential for survival. This resource collection soon morphs into resource management as the player may only carry a set number of items at a given time. In the vein of *Minecraft* (Mojang, 2011), a player must find and combine resources to "craft" tools, weapons, and survival gear.

But what the game does not make immediately obvious is how time itself becomes one of its premier resources. Although it cannot be collected, time is decidedly finite in each game session. It is only through player actions and strategies that this resource can be extended. After all, it is simply a matter of time until the player's character will do exactly that which the game's title impels the player not to do.

Like *Minecraft*, every *Don't Starve* game session is its own, unique procedurally generated world. As a result of this randomization, *Don't Starve* is often described as having "roguelike" elements, named for the 1980 role-playing game *Rogue* (Michael Toy, Glen Wichman, and Ken Arnold). In this original game and the genre named for it, a variable game world is created for each game session according to a set of predefined rules and parameters.

In addition to this variability, roguelikes generally feature "permadeath," or permanent death, wherein the player character's death cannot be reversed and whatever progress made in that game session is lost. *Don't Starve* primarily uses permadeath, albeit with an occasional exception. One or two rare game elements in *Don't Starve* such as the discoverable "Touch Stones" allow the player to resurrect Wilson one time by reincarnating the player's character at a previously found Touch Stone, albeit with reduced health and dropping all carried items at the site of death. However, death is otherwise irreversible and permanent. This makes the gameplay all the more "uncompromising" and temporally constrained, as each hazard encountered may prove fatal and end the game in short order.

Digital games often allow methods of temporal manipulation and control in the form of pausing and saving. These features first emerged on computers and then on home game consoles in the 1970s. Pausing functionality can be found on the game console itself such as in the "Hold" button on the Fairchild Video Entertainment System/Channel F (1976). Subsequent consoles moved pausing to the controllers, allowing players to more readily pause games. Pausing has become such a standard feature that it now is more noteworthy when it is absent, such as in online-only games or more explicitly in games such as *There Is No Pause Button!* (Scott Cawthon, 2014). However familiar it may be, pausing constitutes a radical alteration of temporality that defies the continuity of our lived experience. This remarkable capacity to freeze and resume time's passage is actually a core pleasure of many games as the player is granted complete temporal control over the game world.

Saving and restoring further this temporal manipulation, and many digital games allow players to save their progress to continue later, thus allowing navigation of the game's temporality. In games that feature multiple save slots, one can save a game at different points in their progression, facilitating the movement backward and forward through game timelines at will. Some games feature "auto-saving" in which player progress is automatically saved at moments or areas designated by designers. Auto-saving ostensibly allows players to remain in what psychologist Mihaly Csikszentmihalyi calls a state of immersive "flow" by not forcing them to be continuously aware of the last time that they saved their progress. Auto-saving moves saving to the "background," letting players focus on gameplay.[2]

Like many roguelikes, *Don't Starve* restricts the ability to save. However, the game does allow the player to save when exiting the game, and it also auto-saves intermittently during gameplay. But these manual and auto-saved games are assigned to the same save slot for a given game session, meaning that any progress always overwrites the previously saved game of that session. Furthermore, when the avatar dies, this saved game is deleted. Actions in *Don't Starve* game sessions therefore have permanent consequences, as the player is unable to simply restore an earlier saved game to avoid an error.

In the spirit of the roguelike's permadeath, a *Don't Starve* player is unable to restore a saved game after the avatar's death. Instead, this character is lost forever, except for a listing on the game's "Morgue" page. Accessible from the main menu, this page lists the "Obituaries" of previous play sessions including information such as the number of days survived and the cause of death. The Morgue thus emphasizes temporal precariousness by explicitly drawing attention to the player's previous game sessions that resulted in permadeaths.

Death is central to playing *Don't Starve*. The first-time player must stumble about as they learn how the game world works to develop play strategies. An opening animation depicts Wilson creating an apparatus that transports him to the game world. Just before he awakens, a peculiar man appears and warns that Wilson "better find something to eat before it gets dark!" The figure disappears and the player then must try to determine what to do next. Unless referring to the game's numerous online wikis, strategy guides, and frequently asked questions, this introduction is all the information that the player is given. One instead must learn through a process that is largely composed of trial and error. For the player to be successful over the long term in *Don't Starve*, it is necessary to die a great deal.

Don't Starve requires its players to replay the game over and over to discover more successful strategies. This a familiar mechanism in digital games, which often necessitate repeatedly replaying sequences to master them. Rolf Nohr refers to the mode of repetition as the player's willing subordination to a procedure of "self-optimizing" practicing to complete levels in a video game (Nohr addresses the function of rules in *Tetris* [Alexey Pajitnov, 1984] in this anthology).[3] *Don't Starve* is clearly structured through this logic, which the game reinforces when the avatar dies. Upon death, the screen reads, "You are dead. You survived X days." A progress bar shows the player's total experience points, and the bar fills incrementally for surviving for longer periods and taking new actions in the game (see figure 7.1). These experience points accrue over multiple game sessions, eventually unlocking other avatars that have different traits and abilities. Such unlockable characters include the pyromaniac Willow, who starts game sessions with a lighter and is invulnerable to fire but who also intermittently starts fires of her

FIGURE 7.1
The death screen in
Don't Starve, depicting
player progress toward
unlocking the next
character, Willow.

own volition when her Sanity meter is low, and Wolfgang, who becomes stronger when his Hunger level is low but is afraid of monsters and the dark. The player must therefore play and fail and replay and fail again and again to not just learn general strategies but to also experiment with new characters and tactics.

Time's passage in *Don't Starve* is continuous, and it is communicated through both visual and aural elements. The player may decide to stand still upon starting the game, but the procedurally generated world will operate on its own, with creatures wandering about and fluttering past. The wind blows, distant birds squawk, and the trees and grasses sway in the breeze. More gradual changes occur, too, as saplings grow progressively into mature trees and harvested berry bushes eventually grow back their fruit. The game gives the distinct impression that this living and vibrant virtual world is one that persists without their input. *Don't Starve* thus emulates the constant change around us in the real world and challenges the popular notion that games require player input in order to function. Crucially, just as in their real-world non-game life, players cannot control time's continuous forward progress in *Don't Starve*, and the game thus undermines the usual gaming pleasures of manipulating and navigating time.

Don't Starve's day-and-night cycle further foregrounds the game's temporality. Several meters populate the top-right corner of the screen, dominated by a large circular dial that reads the current day number in its center (see figure 7.2). The dial is broken into 16 segments, each representing roughly 30 seconds of gameplay. These segments are broken into larger groupings to represent day (yellow), dusk (red), and night (blue). The dial's pointer gradually rotates clockwise, pointing to the game's time of day. Its prominence is a persistent reminder of the importance of time in *Don't Starve*.

The behavior of in-game elements changes at different times during the day, and as in many games, nighttime poses particular dangers to the player. When dusk starts, the visibility diminishes and the player is given an onscreen warning

FIGURE 7.2 *Don't Starve* gameplay, depicting the day-and-night dial in the top right, along with other meters tracking the player character's state of being.

that it will be getting dark soon. The fading light makes it more difficult to navigate the world as it becomes more challenging to decipher game world elements. Dusk's in-game reminder spurs the player to find a source of fire for warmth and light before night descends. By nighttime, visibility reduces to complete darkness, leaving only the game interface discernible. An unseen threat soon attacks the player unless a torch or other light source has been built and utilized. This invisible assailant (known as the "Night Monster" or "Charlie") will quickly kill the player's avatar in the absence of a light source. The player must therefore rapidly craft a light source before the first nightfall, or else the game will end shortly thereafter.

Three other meters are present beneath this day–night dial, all of which must be carefully monitored. A stomach represents the avatar's Hunger and a heart symbolizes Health, the latter of which is reduced by incurring injuries. The third meter, a brain, denotes the avatar's Sanity or mental health and is negatively affected by play mechanics such as being frightened or being alone. As is the case with the game's shifting time of day, attentive monitoring of each of these meters is essential to success and survival within a game session.

Like the day–night cycle, these three meters are all affected by time's passage. The player grows gradually hungrier over time, and when the Hunger meter reaches zero, the Health meter will decrement until food is consumed or the Health meter runs out—resulting in the titular starvation. When game mechanics or player actions substantially impact these meters, they flash or indicate with an arrow their change accompanied by a sound effect. Either through trial and error or research conducted outside of the game, the player learns successful strategies to maintain these meters, such as crafting a flower garland in order to preserve the Sanity meter. The game's incessant forward march of time is fundamentally bound to the resource collection and management, as players must gather items and prioritize their use in light of the current moment and plan for times to come.

Just as the avatar will die if a source of light is not secured before nightfall, the game's title broadcasts the importance of keeping the avatar fed. Unless food is consumed, the avatar will starve by the start of the third game day, impelling the player to prioritize searching for edible items. Different foods will positively impact the player's Hunger meter so that eating raw berries will increment the meter slightly while eating cooked berries or something more elaborate will increase the meter substantially more. The resources themselves are prone to decay, including certain perishable foods which can damage the player if they are not consumed quickly enough. In a game mechanic reminiscent of the "survival mode" in the aforementioned *Minecraft*, successful play thus shifts from finding necessary items for initially remaining alive while developing strategies for longer-term survival. As Kevin Purdy notes, *Don't Starve* is structured by the logic of Abraham Maslow's "hierarchy of needs" wherein the player must address both immediate and more abstract necessities.[4]

Surviving for any significant time in *Don't Starve* requires planning and preparing for inevitable seasonal change. After about 20 in-game days, winter arrives. The days then become shorter and the nights longer, requiring the player to plan accordingly and to secure sustainable sources of light and heat for keeping the avatar warm enough to prevent freezing to death. Some of the animals and insects hibernate while others change and new creatures appear, and the sudden scarcity of many sources of food that were abundant during the summer months requires the player to alter strategies. In the default settings, winter lasts for about 15 days before it turns to summer again, and the cycle continues for as long as players can sustain their avatar.

Games offer us self-contained worlds in which we can often control time and experience temporality in ways to which we would otherwise not have access. We may play games to escape the constraints of our lived experience, enjoying the pleasures of an empowered avatar or the agency over game elements, including time. But *Don't Starve* inverts this familiar pleasure by emulating the real world and structuring its challenges and play mechanics around the player's lack of temporal control. Perhaps most tellingly, there is no winning endgame in *Don't Starve*—no way to win other than to simply survive as long as possible.[5] *Don't Starve* powerfully reminds us that as players and as humans, our time is limited.

NOTES

1 The Jibe, "Don't Starve | Klei Entertainment," 2017, https://www.kleientertainment.com.
2 Mihaly Csikszentmihalyi, *Flow: The Psychology of Optimal Experience* (New York: Harper Perennial, 1990).
3 Rolf Nohr, "Restart after Death: 'Self-Optimizing,' 'Normalism' and 'Re-Entry' in Computer Games," in *The Game Culture Reader*, ed. Jason C. Thompson and Marc A. Ouellette (Cambridge Scholars Publishing, 2013), 67.
4 Kevin Purdy, "Dying as a Feature: Don't Starve and Impermanence (and Beefalo)," *Games on Delay*, August 21, 2014, www.gamesondelay.kinja.com.
5 Other than in the game's Adventure mode, which adds completable successive levels.

FURTHER READING

Hanson, Christopher. *Game Time: Understanding Temporality in Video Games.* Bloomington, IN: Indiana University Press, 2018.
Juul, Jesper. *Half-Real: Video Games between Real Rules and Fictional Worlds.* Cambridge, MA: MIT Press, 2005.
Nitsche, Michael. "Mapping Time in Video Games." In *Situated Play: Proceedings of the Third International Conference of the Digital Games Research Association DiGRA '07*, edited by Akira Baba, 145–152 Tokyo: University of Tokyo, 2007.
Zagal, José P., and Michael Mateas. "Time in Video Games: A Survey and Analysis." *Simulation & Gaming* (August 5, 2010): 1–25.

8

Braid
Indies

JESPER JUUL

Abstract: In this chapter, *Braid* is examined as a game that deliberately foregrounds its design as an independent (or "indie") game created in direct opposition to mainstream game titles. Jesper Juul argues that there is a close loop between independent game design strategies and new game reading strategies, strategies that borrow tropes from mainstream "highbrow" cultural criticism where the ability to correctly read such games offers ways for players to demonstrate both their cultural knowledge and their knowledge of video game history.

Video games continue to be dismissed as meaningless pastimes, marketed by a gigantic faceless industry, and lacking in innovation. Against this, there is broad agreement that *Braid* (Number None, 2008) is something else: that it is an independent, or indie, video game. Yet independence has three quite different meanings.

On the surface, independent means independent in a *financial* sense: independent of large game publishers or made without the external influence of investors. This contains a promise of democratizing game development by making it accessible to people with few financial means. Games can also be independent in an *aesthetic* sense when the design of independent games becomes distinct from mainstream games. Finally, games can be independent in a *cultural* sense, usually promoted as reactions to the perceived ills of the mainstream game industry. Independent games, it is said, are made by small teams, express personal visions, represent more diverse experiences, are (sometimes) made by diverse development teams, are wildly innovative, and challenge conventions. They are meaningful; they address what it means to be human. As we will see, this cultural sense of independence contains several contradicting ideas within it.

A 2012 profile of *Braid* developer Jonathan Blow outlines the cultural argument simply: "In a multibillion-dollar industry addicted to laser guns and carnivorous aliens, can true art finally flourish?"[1] This is a common David-and-Goliath understanding of independent games where the small budgets of independent games are contrasted to the "multibillion-dollar" industry, and the art of independent games is contrasted to the embarrassing and lowbrow gun battles of the mainstream industry.

The term *independent game* also conjures up ideas of independent cinema or independent music. However, because these three media have very different histories, we cannot simply assume that independent games are similar to these other independent forms. What we *can* say is that games are described, by developers, reviewers, and players, as independent to *signal* that they belong in a category with independent cinema or music.

At the same time, the comparison also shows that independent games in the cultural sense contain a contradiction: early independent music, especially punk music, is usually understood as a democratization of music-making, as a movement that allowed "everybody" to make music. Contrarily, independent cinema is associated with reaching a small audience or even targeting a small group of connoisseurs.[2]

The idea of an independent game in a cultural sense only gained traction around 2005. Prior to that, there had been many independent games in a financial sense, especially early home computer games of the 1980s that were often made by small development teams of one or two people and distributed through low-tech means, such as the manual duplication of cassette tapes or floppy disks. The influential Independent Games Festival started in 1999, but the first few years featured games that were not obviously distinguishable from mainstream video games. Only around 2005 did we see the appearance of a particular style of independent games, as well as the claims for independent games as a better type of game or a type of game that was meant to be understood as more than entertainment, as something meaningful and culturally valuable.

Comparing the independent games of today with the influential first-person shooter *DOOM* (id Software, 1993), developed by a small team, distributed for free as Shareware (where players had to pay for the full version), is instructive. *DOOM* is certainly independent in a financial sense, but there was no claim or attempt at creating an independent game in a cultural sense, no indication of providing a culturally valuable video game[3].

Since then, independent games have become *institutionalized* in that there are now independent game festivals, online media, YouTube channels, and even selected journalists in traditional print media who are interested in writing about independent games. A game developer can therefore develop a game on a small budget, declare it to be an independent game, and target it toward these venues.

Independent games are not any single game genre but are rather defined by their venues, by festivals, and by the promotion of independent games as personal, authentic, or artistic games.[4] For better or for worse, the 2012 documentary *Indie Game: The Movie* (James Swirsky and Lisanne Pajot, 2012) promoted the idea of independent games to a wide audience. Following three games—*Braid*, *FEZ* (Polytron Corporation, 2012), and *Super Meat Boy* (Team Meat, 2010)—the movie presented independent games by focusing on the one- or two-person team expressing themselves by making the game that only they could make, with ongoing commentary from the developers promoting the status of video games as an art form. It also emphasized the production process in a way that is absent in the coverage of most large-budget games: the movie presented independent game development as a long, personal struggle in the face of adversity and highlighted the fears and hopes of the developers. However, the lack of diversity among the developers represented in the film was rather striking, and many commentators pointed to the fact that *Indie Game: The Movie* presented, in Anna Anthropy's words, only one possible "narrative of game creation: one in which straight white guys who grew up playing Super Mario sacrifice every part of their lives to the creation of personal but nonetheless traditional video games . . . for sale in a commercial marketplace."[5]

The movie presented indie games not as anonymous products for purchase but, rather, aligned indie games with romantic notions of the work of art, as developed by struggling, and sometimes suffering, individuals who eventually became financially successful. The questions of diversity among developers and of whether independent games are or aren't tied to financial success have become points of discussion in the independent game community especially since the premiere of the movie.

So, to play an independent game is not simply to *play a game* but also to become involved in the way that game is promoted and discussed. When reviewers and jury members evaluate a game as independent in the cultural sense, they are often explicitly rejecting traditional review questions, such as whether a game is "fun," and, rather, are looking at the cultural or political merits of a game.

It is not that you can't play an independent game, such as *Braid*, without considering its cultural or artistic merit, but that the *promotion* of this specific game is tied closely to its status as an independent game. Moreover, various aspects of the game's design, discussed in the following, nudge us toward thinking about the "independent-ness" of the game. All video games are made by people and can be evaluated artistically or culturally. However, the category of "independent games" specifically presents itself as focusing on the developers of each game and asks us to consider it as culture and art rather than as just entertainment products.

Braid is a game in the platform genre, where players run and jump their way through a world that is seen from the side. Various obstacles, monsters, and

FIGURE 8.1
Braid presents a
new take on the
platform genre
with its unique
visual style and
time manipula-
tion gameplay
mechanic.

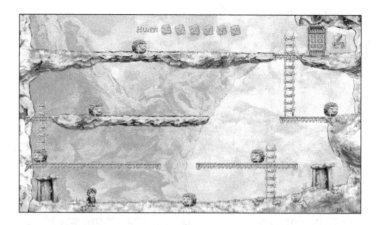

puzzles stand in the way of players. As can be seen from the screenshot of *Braid* (figure 8.1), the monsters and the layout of the screen directly reference the early platform games *Donkey Kong* (Nintendo R&D1, 1981) and *Super Mario Bros.* (Nintendo R&D4, 1985). Many popular independent games share a preference for the platform genre and for *Super Mario Bros.*, in particular.[6] However, independent games are not simply remakes of old genres: they tend rather to selectively reuse elements of early genres while adding modern touches. This allows a game to be playable and enjoyable by modern standards while also allowing for players to recognize and comment on references to video game history.

Braid asks us, stereotypically and like *Super Mario Bros.* before it, to save the princess. However, the core addition of *Braid* to the traditional platform formula is the ability to manipulate and rewind time. At first, this simply gives the player the ability to undo a mistimed jump. But as one progresses through the game, temporal manipulation becomes more complicated. After a while, we encounter objects that do not respond to time being rewound, allowing us to capture a key in a hard-to-escape place but then to rewind time with the key still in our possession. On one level, we can control time by moving left and right, and at one point a ring appears, which slows time for objects in its vicinity. The core challenge of the game is to use these new abilities to solve the game's puzzles in ways that are completely different from traditional platform games. This is characteristic for many independent games: the reuse of an old genre but with a twist.

The modern touches of independent games serve multiple functions. They signal that even though a game can seem a throwback to earlier times, this is more than nostalgia; it is, in fact, a conscious reimagining and reinterpretation of the older game (see Vanderhoef's chapter on "nostalgia" in this collection). The modern touches often revolve around adding contemporary graphical effects or a wider range of colors to what would otherwise be dated graphics. In terms of game design, we often see the inclusion of unlimited lives to genres that used to offer only limited lives to players. The fictions of independent games are often either irreverent or antiheroic or focused on more quotidian experiences than we see in mainstream games.

This is also manifest in *Braid*. Like traditional video games, *Braid* has levels ("worlds"), but here the levels are interspersed with text, outlining the story of protagonist Tim and his broken relationship with the princess. Each world then is a concrete manifestation of a question asked in the text. Before World Two, the text asks, "What if our world worked differently?" and the game then introduces the option to rewind time. (Much like chapters of Alan Lightman's novel *Einstein's Dreams* [1992], each world is a take on what it would be like if time worked differently.)

Finally, at the very end of *Braid*, there is a reversal. Time starts moving backward. The princess, who we always seem to be on the verge of rescuing, turns out to have been running away from us during the whole game. We are not the hero but the stalker, the villain of the game.

What are we supposed to do with *Braid*? To play *Braid* is to become enmeshed in more than the physical act of completing it. When the game breaks with video game tradition by suddenly casting the player as the villain at the end, it prompts us to interpret what the game means. As is often the case with interpretation, the reversal can be read in several ways. Most obviously, it may be a criticism of the stereotypical narrative structure of traditional video games. Do we *know* that the princess wants to be rescued by the player?

Or the reversal may relate to some of the text in the game. Toward the end, the game includes the sentences "On that moment hung eternity. Time stood still. Space contracted to a pinpoint. It was as though the earth had opened and the skies split." Although not credited in the game,[7] fans quickly discovered that this was a quote from a description of the Trinity test, the explosion of the first nuclear bomb in 1945. Of course, this opens for a range of possible interpretations, all explored by fans: Is the nuclear bomb a metaphor for relationships or for the relationship in this game? Is the whole game a metaphor for the nuclear bomb? Is the nuclear bomb a metaphor for the gaining of terrible knowledge that cannot be unlearned? and so on. The point is not that any one of these interpretations is the right one but that the game includes these unusual quotations, encouraging players to look up their sources and thereby quite directly asks players to attempt interpreting the game.

In the history of cinema, *auteur theory*[8] of the 1940s and 1950s claimed that the movie director is the central author behind a film—not the scriptwriter, not the cinematographer, not the actors. In effect, auteur theory reconceptualized film, usually made by large teams, as something that could express the artistic vision of a single person. We are, by now, accustomed to thinking of film in this way—as flowing from the creativity of the director. Video games share a similar conundrum to early film inasmuch as games are often considered to be purely technical creations made by large teams. Against this, *Indie Game: The Movie* presents Jonathan Blow as a sagelike genius creator, expounding his visions and the artistic value of his game. In this way, the appearance of *Braid* and its promotion were part of the gelling of a conception of independent games—that of the auteur-creator promoting a personal vision. As we can see, the small team behind an independent game makes it an easy fit for traditional ideas of creativity as coming from creative individuals, rather than from large groups, even without having to arbitrarily identify a single individual on a 1,000-person team as the sole creative person behind a video game.

Still, comparing *Braid* to other independent games also reveals that *Braid* is somewhat unusual in its visuals and sound. Most independent games, including *Braid*, use a style of a "representation of a representation," where modern technology is used to emulate older technological styles (pixelated graphics) or analog visual styles such as drawings.[9] Many other independent games emulate cheap or improvisational graphics such as crayons and torn paper to signal a kind of humility and deliberate choice of a low-budget expression.

But *Braid* emulates watercolor, more associated with fine art, and features violin-based music, an instrument associated with classical music. In this way, *Braid* openly signals a desire to be understood in relation to such established art forms. Similarly, the *Braid* credits thank literary authors Italo Calvino, Milorad Pavić, and Alan Lightman, asserting that this is the world to which *Braid* belongs. In this way, *Braid* is exactly a game that promises to be something *more* than other games, promises to be a game with higher cultural status.

As discussed in the beginning, the term *independent game* concerns both financial independence and a specific kind of cultural positioning. As we can also see, cultural independence has three different sides: first, *independence as highbrow*: *Braid* is an independent game that aligns itself with established forms of culture—literature, classical music, painting. The obvious comparison here is not to independent cinema but, rather, to art-house cinema, cinema that speaks to a small and often well-educated audience; second, *independence as a democratic game*: compare this to openly personal games, such as *Dys4ia* (Anna Anthropy, 2012), and to the *Rise of the Videogame Zinesters* manifesto by developer Anna Anthropy, where she argues for video games as an art form that we should all "take back" and use for expressing ourselves. This would be comparable to the promises of punk music, as a do-it-yourself type of music that is accessible to everyone. This is also chained to issues of diversity both onscreen and among developers; and third, *independence as craft and personality*: finally, several games made by small teams and promoted as independent games are neither claiming to be part of a democratic movement nor aiming to be elevated as a particularly refined type of video game. For example, *Super Meat Boy* takes its cue from the same platform game genre as *Braid*. Yet the stated aim is not to make art but to make a *good* video game, where the small size of the team is explained as a way to guarantee the craft of the game.

In short, *Braid* is a game that demonstrates most of the features now expected from independent video games, and its promotion helped cement the idea of independent games in popular imagination. To play an independent game is to become involved in these arguments about the meaning and future of video games, both what they've been and what they can become.

NOTES

1 Taylor Clark, "The Most Dangerous Gamer," *The Atlantic*, May 2012.

2 *Indie Game: The Movie* opens with Jonathan Blow arguing against making "polished" games that "serve as large an audience as possible" and claims that this is the opposite of making something personal.

3 If anything *DOOM* was more violent and clichéd than mainstream games at the time, so it could be said to have made the unusual cultural argument that being financially independent allowed developers to make games that exaggerated the trends of mainstream games, going where big publishers didn't dare tread at the time.

4 Juul, Jesper, "High-Tech Low-Tech Authenticity: The Creation of Independent Style at the Independent Games Festival," in *Proceedings of the 9th International Conference on the Foundations of Digital Games Conference* (Santa Cruz, CA: Society for the Advancement of the Science of Digital Games, 2014), www.jesperjuul.net.

5 "Indie Game: The Movie," *Auntie Pixelante* (blog), March 25, 2012, http://auntiepixelante .com.

6 Probably due to the fact the early video game consoles such as the Nintendo Entertainment System (NES) were much less common in Europe than in the United States, and European developers were therefore less exposed to games like *Super Mario Bros*, the Irish/UK independent game *VVVVVV* (Terry Cavanaugh, 2010) rather references the early European platform games *Manic Miner* (Matthew Smith, 1983) and *Jet Set Willy* (Software Projects, 1984).

7 Journalist William H. Laurence is thanked in the credits.

8 François Truffaut, "A Certain Tendency of the French Cinema," in *Auteurs and Authorship: A Film Reader*, ed. Barry Keith Grant (Malden, MA: Blackwell Publishing, 2008), 7–9.

9 Juul, "High-Tech Low-Tech Authenticity."

FURTHER READING

Anthropy, Anna. *Rise of the Videogame Zinesters: How Freaks, Normals, Amateurs, Artists, Dreamers, Dropouts, Queers, Housewives, and People like You Are Taking Back an Art Form.* New York: Seven Stories Press, 2012.

Juul, Jesper. "High-Tech Low-Tech Authenticity: The Creation of Independent Style at the Independent Games Festival." In *Proceedings of the 9th International Conference on the Foundations of Digital Games Conference*. Santa Cruz, CA: Society for the Advancement of the Science of Digital Games, 2014, www.jesperjuul.net.

Swirsky, James, and Lisanne Pajot, dirs. *Indie Game: The Movie*. Winnipeg, Manitoba: Blink-Works Media, 2012.

9

BioShock Infinite
World-building

MARK J. P. WOLF

Abstract: World-building and environmental storytelling are critically important design strategies for creating product differentiation in a gaming marketplace that is saturated with first-person shooters. In granting players the freedom to explore an immersive and richly textured America that never was, Mark J. P. Wolf argues that *BioShock Infinite* invites players to consider how this alternative, fictional world reveals certain truths about our own reality.

As the genre name suggests, first-person-shooter (FPS) games represent their universes from a first-person perspective while tasking the player with firing at an opponent or target. Since their emergence in the early 1990s, FPS games have grown to become one of the most popular genres for home console and PC markets, and FPS titles make up some of the most popular competitions in the esports scene.[1] FPSs, or "shooters" as they're commonly called, locate the spectator in a three-dimensional (3D) space through which the player moves, shooting at multiple assailants and targets in the game world. The depiction of the game world as a navigable, 3D space means that players negotiate it in much the same way as they would physical space in that, by using a controller, players' virtual movements in the game mimic how one physically moves through space by running, jumping, strafing, and so on. Because these 3D spaces play such a potentially important role in the player's gaming experience, world-building emerges as a critical creative opportunity for video game designers. This is no more the case than in the FPS genre where the titular game mechanic—shooting opponents and obstacles ad nauseam—often differs little from game to game. Thus, the diegetic or story world is one place where shooters can distinguish themselves from one another.

BioShock Infinite (Irrational Games, 2013), directed by *BioShock* series creator Ken Levine, presents a strong case study in how a carefully crafted game world grants producers with a flexible storytelling resource—one that holds considerable gameplay potential by fusing the construction of a virtual 3D space with action opportunities within that narrativized space. Furthermore, and in keeping with the political critiques of its predecessors, *BioShock Infinite*'s alternative history makes the familiar strange by twisting American ideals and recasting them in a distorted light.

BioShock Infinite takes place in an alternate version of America in 1912 and is set mainly in the flying city of Columbia.[2] As the story goes, Columbia's racist and elitist founders came to view the rest of America with contempt, and the city seceded from the Union by flying off on its own. The game's main playable character is former Pinkerton detective Booker DeWitt, who is sent to Columbia to rescue Elizabeth, a young woman who is being held captive. Along the way, Booker encounters the Founders, who rule Columbia and whose ugly political views determine much of Columbia's culture. Columbia's oppressive ruling class catalyzes the emergence of the underground rebel group, Vox Populi, who go to war with the Founders (and, we find, end up sharing their love of violence and other vices). Once Booker frees Elizabeth, the two work together to navigate the warring factions and attempt to leave Columbia, which—of course—becomes more difficult than expected. Throughout the game, the richly detailed graphics reveal an alternative American history that is visually inspired in equal measure by a nineteenth-century retro-futurism of steampunk-inspired technologies with the wonder of Jules Verne–style industrial design. This colorful and distinctive aesthetic infuses the design of the many objects that fill Columbia: the weapons, the robotlike Handymen, the airships, and the Sky-line system of elevated rails for moving goods and transport. Columbia is also imbued with turn-of-the-century Americana—flags, buntings, and fireworks decorate the regal buildings—while posters and billboards of political propaganda fuse late nineteenth-century and early twentieth-century decorative styles with fictional characters and events, a marked change from the submerged Art Deco–styled worlds of the previous two *Bioshock* games (see figure 9.1).

Unlike the open worlds found in games like *Grand Theft Auto V* (Rockstar North, 2013), the player moves through *BioShock Infinite*'s story world in a somewhat linear fashion; while each setting can be freely explored to some extent, it is limited to the area between the point where a player enters and the point where the player exits to the next section or chapter of the game. Each section of the game, once completed, leads either to additional narrative events or to a portal that transports the player to the next area. Occasionally, the player can backtrack to previously explored spaces. However, more often spatial freedom is limited

FIGURE 9.1
The flying city
of Columbia
in *BioShock
Infinite* offers
an alternate
version of 1912
America.

to support the game's overarching narrative demands. Furthermore, Columbia's spaces do not appear to fit together into a coherent geography. The transitions between gameplay spaces contain little geographic information about how the city's locations are physically linked, making it difficult, if not impossible, to piece together a complete map of Columbia. Instead, the game's smaller maps—like those of Soldier's Field and Downtown Emporia—reveal the relative positions of buildings to one another, but they do not offer any broader spatial context. Despite granting the player the ability to see parts of the city floating in the distance, thereby conveying a sense of a vast network of structures, Columbia does not appear to be designed with a single, consistent, geographical layout in mind.

Although this does not alter the gameplay proper, the lack of a single overall map uniting all the locations affects how *BioShock Infinite* is experienced (compare this, for example, to a game like *Grand Theft Auto V*, which connects all its spaces on a single map and allows players to move about freely between the map's locations). In *Bioshock Infinite*, on one hand, the story and travel through Columbia flow well enough that the player is usually unaware of any geographical inconsistencies, and the uncertainty of where locations are relative to each other only adds to the feeling of the city's vastness. On the other hand, it can also convey the feeling that the game was developed piecemeal, scene after scene, with little or no concern for the overall design of the city itself. There is, of course, also the possibility that the buildings of the city could be occasionally untethered and rearranged, changing the airborne geography as old buildings are destroyed or new ones are built; in fact, several of the game's locations are the decks of airships, some the size of buildings with multiple floors. There is both enough consistency and ambiguity present in the design of the geography to keep players speculating without ever being able to establish definitively how Columbia's

FIGURE 9.2
The museum's
timeline offers a
state-sponsored
version of his-
torical events.

buildings are arranged. This makes Columbia appear larger than it is (because no single map contains it all), and it suggests, too, that there may be areas the player has not seen. This creative choice to withhold information, ironically, makes the world seem more complete, even as it retains an air of mystery.

In addition to maps and geography, historical timelines are another way of structuring an imaginary world (see figure 9.2). Besides the narrative backstories discussed earlier, *BioShock Infinite* also includes alternate realities and alternate timelines, some of which include time travel. Elizabeth has the power to open "tears" into parallel universes. Other characters, such as the scientists Robert and Rosalind Lutece, are also able to work with the tears, using them to bring new technologies to Columbia. These tears are used to advance the storyline conveniently, as when Booker and Elizabeth have a stockpile of guns that they are supposed to distribute; instead of having scenes convey the logistics of such a transfer, Elizabeth can open a tear into an alternate reality where the guns have already been distributed. At other times, the tears are used for time traveling, as when an elderly Elizabeth introduces Booker and Elizabeth to a possible future of Columbia.

The world-building and world design of Columbia combine the familiar and the fantastic to make Columbia full of surprises yet generally recognizable to the player who has knowledge of American history. Much of Columbia's architecture, citizens' clothing, and the interior and graphic design is modeled after historical elements typical of early 1900s America. For instance, Scott Joplin piano rags, popular during this period, play during the game's loading screens. Together, these visual and sonic elements evoke simultaneously the mood and atmosphere of an earlier time and that of a place that never existed. Populating this bright and colorful cityscape are the airships, weapons, and other fantastic technologies, including the infrastructure that connects the city's floating structures. Functionally, the city's locations are common to the FPS and adventure genres: stores, banks, taverns, stations, government buildings, monuments, private homes, science labs, and so forth. The player character's needs are woven into these locations, as one finds food, ammunition, weapons, and money to spend at vending machines, strategically placed throughout the game's locations. Sometimes, however, these design conventions strain plausibility and undercut the world-building effort. When can you eat cotton candy found in a trash can and have it improve your health?

BioShock Infinite's Columbia is more than just an exotic backdrop for the game. Although the game's main story unfolds as Booker and Elizabeth make a series of discoveries during their adventures in the city, much of the information that they need to act on, including Columbia's backstory, is woven into the world design. Billboards, posters, and monuments relate past events and introduce characters and the relationships between them. The game's media devices, such as the 11 telescopes (usually aimed at monuments), 26 kinetoscope machines (with brief silent films about Columbia), and 85 voxophone recordings (in which characters discuss their history), serve similar narrative functions. These artifacts relate characters' backstories, previewing the world's broader history and its characters before a player encounters them in the game's unfolding narrative. The net result of this strategy is that players feel a part of the world.

Information is not all that the player can receive from these devices. Using all the telescopes and kinetoscopes earns the player the "Sightseer" achievement/trophy. Listening to all the voxophone records is rewarded with the "Eavesdropper" achievement/trophy. Such incentives encourage players to seek out these optional, environmental props. These tasks are not required for completing the game, but they enrich the exploration of the world, providing backstory and motivation for the game's characters. World details can enhance the story, even though they are not necessary for understanding or advancing it and demonstrate that storytelling can be direct (like a voice-over) or indirect, hidden among the details of the world (environmental storytelling). Both can be used together, strengthening the other; conversely, they can be used to purposefully contradict each other, prompting the player to question the dominant narrative of the game and the motivations and backstories of characters.

The game's locations function as narrative vehicles for Columbia's history. The curious player who stitches together the city's backstory from historical tidbits found at the city's cemetery, public halls, and museums collects environmental clues in a process of decentralized story-gathering interpretation. For example, Columbia's "Hall of Heroes" is devoted to honoring Zachary Hale Comstock, the self-proclaimed prophet and founder of Columbia, and his strange religious zealotry that valorizes America's Founding Fathers but promotes white suprema-cism and racial segregation. Arriving at the Hall of Heroes, Booker and Elizabeth find ticket booth employees and other people slain by the troops of Captain Cor-nelius Slate, an enemy of Comstock who has also defaced many of Comstock's monuments. The main hall features a timeline of Columbia history, complete with Motorized Patriots who repeat propaganda and refer to historical events, their speeches arranged in rhyming verses. In two side halls are elaborate walkthrough museum exhibits designed to elevate and promote Comstock's alleged military accomplishments, one about Wounded Knee and the other about the Boxer Re-bellion, and demonize Native Americans and Asians through vicious caricatures and stereotypes. It is also here, among these halls of displays, where Booker and Elizabeth battle Slate's men while attempting to find Slate himself. As the player explores Columbia's spaces, one senses a growing divergence between the "official" state-sponsored history of the museum displays and media and the experience of the common people—an overt critique of how national histories are crafted by the powerful to promote a point of view that supports their preferred ideology.

Even though the player spends relatively little time with the political figures battling over Columbia's future, the game's environmental details communicate a great deal about that political struggle. Seeing the devastation caused by the con-flict and how both sides demonize the other, the overall message appears to be that power corrupts and that stilted propaganda has replaced honest debate. The careful examination of world-building design choices allows the curious player to understand how a game's world is brought to life *and* to ascertain how cultural ideas might be embedded—consciously or not—into those virtual spaces.

BioShock Infinite demonstrates that video games not only tell engaging stories and can introduce us to immensely detailed imaginary worlds but also invite us to reflect on our own world. Even when the worlds depicted are overtly fantastic and unrealistic, they can nevertheless create desires in their audiences, cravings for new technologies such as flying cars or for alternative social configurations, as so many utopic worlds have depicted (and dystopias have critiqued). Imagi-nary worlds can be shared thought experiments about speculative, "what-if" pos-sibilities. For example, the geostationary communications satellite was invented by science-fiction author Arthur C. Clarke, and the world-building done for the movie *Minority Report* (Steven Spielberg, 2002) resulted in more than 100 real-world patents.[3] Imaginary worlds, therefore, can sometimes provide a glimpse into our own future.

Regardless of their feasibility, imaginary worlds exercise our collective imagi-nation, opening us to future possibilities and daring us to consider innumerable what-ifs that we may otherwise never imagine. Imaginary worlds can encourage us to reconsider common assumptions—a first step in any attempted paradigm shift, whether in technology, society, or culture. Inventions and discoveries continue to be made, but imaginary worlds offer wider insights about common visions and public dreams. The imaginary worlds of video games allow us to experiment with possible futures, level after level.

Given the possibility space that imaginary worlds create then, a critical analysis of these worlds and the gameplay made available in these spaces should ask, "What worlds and which world-builders are currently shaping the public imagination of today?" "Where are our imaginary worlds taking us?" "Conversely, what destinations might they be avoiding?" and "To what future imaginary worlds will they lead—and to what future for the real world in which we will live?"

NOTES

1 See, for example, Emma Witkowski's chapter on *Counter-Strike* and Henry Lowood's chapter on *Quake* in this collection.

2 The city derives its name from the "Columbian Exposition," the Chicago World's Fair of 1893, which celebrated the 400th anniversary of Christopher Columbus's arrival in the New World.

3 According to *Minority Report*'s production designer Alex McDowell in The Future of Storytelling (video), https://futureofstorytelling.org.

FURTHER READING

Carson, Don. "Environmental Storytelling: Creating Immersive 3D Worlds Using Lessons Learned from the Theme Park Industry." *Gamasutra*, March 1, 2000. www.gamasutra.com.

Morris, Dave, and Leo Hartas. *The Art of Game Worlds.* New York: Harper Collins, 2004.

Ryan, Marie-Laure, and Jan-Noel Thon, eds. *Storyworlds across Media: Toward a Media-Conscious Narratology.* Lincoln: University of Nebraska Press, 2014.

Wolf, Mark J. P. *Building Imaginary Worlds: The Theory and History of Subcreation.* New York and London: Routledge, 2012.

10

The Legend of Zelda: Ocarina of Time
Music

DAN GOLDING

Abstract: Video game music is a unique form that takes influence from longer musical traditions while also using the possibilities of digital technology to create new musical practices. Through an analysis of *The Legend of Zelda: Ocarina of Time*, Dan Golding argues that video games have birthed a form of music that can be thematically complex, action-led, interactive, and an important part of fan cultures.

I always thought of *The Legend of Zelda: Ocarina of Time* (Nintendo EAD, 1998) as a kind of musical. That might not make a lot of sense—there's no voice acting in the game, let alone the lyrical singing you would normally associate with a musical—but music is such a crucial part of *Ocarina of Time* that it needs to be accounted for. Playing *Ocarina* as a teenager, I discovered that most of the key moments of the game were musical ones: from riding my horse over a Hyrule hilltop and being greeted by the main Zelda fanfare to battling Ganon's evil creatures to suspenseful combat music to even performing melodies on the titular ocarina itself to bring the game world to life. Composer Koji Kondo was equally responsible for my experience with the game as, say, its legendary producer, Shigeru Miyamoto.[1] Today, when I recall my time with *Ocarina of Time*, my memories are defined by melodies, by sounds, and by rhythm.

Ocarina of Time may not, strictly speaking, be a musical, but it is, in many ways, an ideal case study to think about how video game music works—and, importantly, how video game music is different from music in other media forms. Video games often seem to work in similar ways to other media forms: like film, they have main themes and melodies associated with characters and places. But they're also dramatically different, with music that changes and responds to player action and input: music that, in some ways, is alive in our living rooms. Even to-day, two decades after *Ocarina of Time*'s release, and taking into account the Nintendo 64's limited sonic abilities on "withered technology,"[2] its music is a fine illustration of the possibilities of video game music. This is a musical form fixed among tradition, technology, and the promise of interactivity. Video game music borrows heavily from the sound practices of film, but the affordances of video game technology make possible an experience particular to the medium: that of musical interactivity.

Where would *The Legend of Zelda* be without its musical themes? Although Kondo initially considered using Ravel's famous *Bolero* as the theme for the first game in the series in 1986, the Zelda series is today almost unimaginable without Kondo's original main Zelda theme and lullaby compositions, both of which make strong appearances in *Ocarina of Time*. However, each game in the series has its own variants, its own musical tapestry for supporting characters, dungeons, and fantasy locations.

The idea of having musical melodies associated with particular characters or places has a long cultural history that flows through video games to television, cinema, radio dramas, theater, continuing all the way back to ballet and opera. This is a technique called leitmotif, and it is usually associated with Richard Wagner, a hugely influential German composer from the nineteenth century most famous for his epic Ring cycle series of four operas that contain an intricate pattern of dozens of characters and musical themes. Using leitmotif, a character, place, or narrative theme is given a musical idea that is returned to and usually developed across the course of a work. After Wagner's time, the logic of the leitmotif subsequently gained popularity with European composers such as Richard Strauss and Claude Debussy, and it was brought to popular film music when Viennese composers Max Steiner (*King Kong* [1933], *Gone With The Wind* [1939]) and Erich Wolfgang Korngold (*Captain Blood* [1935], *The Adventures of Robin Hood* [1938]) moved to America and began composing for Hollywood.

Leitmotif, especially in cinema, provides audiences with an easy way to connect music with image. Indiana Jones appears and his theme music (written by John Williams) plays, for example, indelibly associating each with the other. They become inseparable: when children play as Jones, they hum a bit of John Williams; when they take a turn at James Bond, Monty Norman's 007 theme usually comes out.

The musical language of cinema has been a huge influence on video game composers like Kondo, and so, leitmotif is one way of thinking about the way *Ocarina* works. We need only think of Zelda's lullaby, one of the most iconic melodies of the series and one that plays habitually when Princess Zelda—a character who often appears only in cutscenes—is present. Or we might think of music associated with particular locations within the game. Take the absurdly cheery shop music, for example. As a player, you can't be present in any of the regular Hyrule town stores without hearing this tango-style tune performed on an accordion. It defines the experience of the shops and sets the tone for what you can expect to find there: it is jaunty to the point of self-parody, aligning perfectly with the eccentric shopkeepers that inhabit Zelda's world. Most of *Ocarina*'s main locales have their own musical themes which play on repeat: Kakariko Village, the Lost Woods, Lon Lon Ranch, Gerudo Valley, Goron City, Zora's Domain, and all the temples have their own distinct music. Some of these melodies in *Ocarina* are developed from previous versions in older Zelda games; a great many would be further built on in future installments.

A distinction should be made between music that plays over player-led action and music that plays over noninteractive sequences. Think here of the kind of music that plays over the game's first cutscene, which moves from Link's nightmare dream portending a future encounter with Ganon to a mystical vision of Link's fairy, Navi, being called to him to finally Navi flying through the village and entering the sleeping Link's home. The music changes with each scene: dramatic and frightening for Ganon, mysterious for Navi's calling, playful for the flight through the village, and, finally, light and domestic in Link's home. The music responds to these sequences as they change. For example, Ganon's dramatic music only begins when he enters the screen.

This music has much in common with cinema and television. It is music that is locked into the image (to a significant degree at least as, in *Ocarina*, players still control the length of some sections through button presses to dismiss lines of dialogue). In a terrific and rarely seen BBC documentary from 1980 called *Star Wars: Music by John Williams*, we see the composer at a recording session for *The Empire Strikes Back* (Irvin Kershner, 1981). As Williams conducts, he faces the film as it is projected, allowing him (and us) to see not just the film's action but also an array of signals overlaid on the film to allow him to conduct correct time. "My first concern is a rhythmic one," Williams adds in a voice-over. "I sense a speed to a film, where every scene seems to have an underlying tempo, or series of tempi." A line moves across the image to indicate pace and tempo while a large dot flashes to mark the beginning of a new section. The music takes us from moment to moment, matching the film's emotion, cuts, and style.

This is one way that a lot of video game music works, and not just the early video games such as *Donkey Kong* (Nintendo R&D1, 1981), which took their cues from silent cinema.[3] Especially in contemporary video games that are more self-consciously "cinematic" (I'm thinking here of series such as *Mass Effect, Call of Duty*, and *Red Dead Redemption*), music is often locked to the image, aiming to evoke the right emotion at just the right beat of the scene. This approach is not without its critics, even in cinema: in 1947, at the height of a particularly slavish mode of Hollywood-style film music, Theodor Adorno and Hanns Eisler claimed that film music "points with unswerving agreement to everything that happens on the screen" and that "by the use of standardized configurations, it interprets the meaning of the action for the less intelligent members of the audience."[4]

Yet particularly with the leitmotif system, video game music, like film music before it, is music with an impenetrably close relationship to image and iconography. When Link turns up in a different game, such as *Super Smash Bros.* (HAL Laboratory, 1999) or *Mario Kart 8* (Nintendo EAD, 2014), we know what to expect. His music helps perform his identity in any context.

Of course, video game music is not always tied just to image alone. Famously, media theorist Alexander Galloway argued that video games are not just images: they are also complex circuits of action between a player and a computer program.[5] Players do things to games, and in turn, games do things back to players. Because the moment of gameplay is made up of innumerable such interactions, the relationship between music and game is often more active than that of music and film or music and theatre. As a result, video game music often falls across a spectrum of dynamism and reactivity: from static beds of music that repeat for entire sections (as we have already seen in the shop scenes in *Ocarina*) to music that reacts to changes in the game state. Such liveliness in video game music is not at all new—even the tempo of *Space Invaders'* music (Taito, 1978) increased as enemy numbers thinned while the SCUMM technology created by and used at Lucasfilm Games in the late 1980s and early 1990s allowed complex layering and dynamism in the music for games such as *The Secret of Monkey Island* (Lucasfilm Games, 1990).

What this means in practice is that my enjoyment of the Hyrule Field theme in *Ocarina* is completely disrupted the moment I run into one of the game's many enemies. The music immediately jettisons the romantic main melody and becomes static and nervy: a snare drum flutters its tense rhythm while low woodwinds add some minor-key menace. This is a very different proposition to how film music works, or really, music for any other medium. The player is jolted to attention as the game's soundtrack changes to account for the player's current actions.

The actual music itself is not being written on the fly by the game—it is the same version that everyone hears. But what is different is when and how the player hears it. This music is no less tied to its associated material as a film score, but it is connected to it in complicated ways. Digital music scholar Karen Collins suggests three ways of thinking about this kind of music: interactive audio, which reacts directly to the player's input; adaptive audio, which reacts to changes in the game; and dynamic audio, which includes both.[6] Although drawing on the same composed and coded material, players frequently experience the music of video games in unique and utterly unrepeatable ways.

Taken to one extreme in video games, music can start to sound a lot like sound design. When used to signal player success or failure, video game music reacts to the game world and gives us information about it. Think of the fanfare that plays when Link acquires a new item in *Ocarina*. This is still a musical composition from Kondo—it is part of the soundtrack—but in the game its primary function is not mood, character, or location but action. Well beyond the traditional functions of music in film and television, video game music can also tell us about our own success.

Of course, *Ocarina of Time* also provides us with an even more complex and illuminating example of video game music and action blending into one through the titular Ocarina itself. Once I receive this magical musical instrument, as Link, I must learn several short songs in order to complete the game. I play these songs by pressing different buttons on my controller, and I use these songs to solve puzzles, change the weather and the time of day, and call my horse. In some ways this is quite like playing an actual musical instrument as I control which notes are selected and the speed at which they are played—more evidence for *Ocarina* being a bit like a musical. But in this case, as Collins points out, we're not just *listening to* the music; we're *interacting*.[7]

What's especially interesting about this is how Kondo had to balance composing interesting and memorable melodies with the limited amount of buttons available on the Nintendo 64 controller. Kondo's solution was a clever one: on the Ocarina, the player effectively performs a series of short "trigger phrases" that, when played correctly, are answered by the game with longer and more complicated non-interactive phrases and orchestration. As Link, I can play "The Bolero of Fire" on my Ocarina using just four buttons (↓A↓A→↓→↓; see figure 10.1), which the game answers with a complex phrase that would be impossible for me to perform on the game's Ocarina. This illustrates the complex ways that video games can anticipate and produce music as well as simply have it accompany the action. Players learn, respond, and perform these pieces of music.[8]

The Ocarina also nicely preludes something that would become popular a few years after *Ocarina*: the music rhythm game. These games, epitomized by *Guitar Hero* (Harmonix, 2005), ask players to use custom controllers that mimic actual musical instrument designed to perform popular songs by following along with button-notation that scrolls onscreen. This enormously popular genre shows that video games and music share some interesting affinities for performance—affinities explored, in part, in *Ocarina*.

FIGURE 10.1
The player controls Link in learning to play the "Bolero of Fire" on the in-game Ocarina.

If all this music is so memorable, however, then surely people want to explore it beyond their play experience with the game itself? They certainly do—but not without some interesting problems. Although it has been easy for decades to listen to audio recordings of film scores or to attend concerts of suites or even entire film scores, unpicking music from the video game can be a much more challenging task. Video game melodies are often approached with a nostalgic sheen—when approaching Nintendo for the rights to use their game's music in his film *Scott Pilgrim vs The World* (Edgar Wright, 2010), director Edgar Wright described them as "the nursery rhymes of a generation."[9] Yet official video game soundtracks can be poorly assembled, either too lengthy or too short, and difficult to find. Take, for example, Mark Griskey's score for *Star Wars: Knights of the Old Republic II: The Sith Lords* (Obsidian Entertainment, 2004), which, although widely praised, was only available through the fan-led identification of 71 .wav files in the game's installed content directories, some of which last less than one minute and come with mundane titles such as "Battle Suspense 6."[10]

Yet video game music lives on in unpredictable ways through fans. A YouTube search for "Zelda theme cover," for example, yields more than 6 million results, with top videos including a guitar cover of *Ocarina*'s Gerudo Valley, an *a capella* version of the main theme featuring the same singer dubbed multiple times (a particularly popular YouTube musical genre), a duo performing on marimba, and *Ocarina*'s "Song of Healing" performed on wine glasses. The prominence of fan-driven performance as a site of video game music recalls philosopher Michel de Certeau's understanding of the way people appropriate culture within their own contexts and frameworks.[11] Through such performances, players can claim a little of *Ocarina* and its music for themselves. Such musical performances allow both the performer and the listener (or the viewer, in the case of YouTube) to revisit and rearticulate their relationship with the music of video games, just as it empowers it to form part of an ongoing vernacular of how music works outside the medium itself.

The need for action in the video game means that its music will always be a little more complicated when compared to more straightforward forms such as film and television. The video game is too lively and too dynamic to have the same overt rhythmic dependencies as cinema music: players listen, yes, but they can also play with the music and have it respond to both their actions and the changes in the game itself. *Ocarina of Time* is an excellent illustration of this point in this case as its music functions across many different registers, and this not only changes the way we need to think about the music, but it also changes the music itself.

Ocarina of Time might not really be a musical, but maybe it's even a step better: players listen to leitmotifs, the game reacts with active music, and players perform with their Ocarina. It's a negotiation, a call and response. In *Ocarina*—as in many video games—the player and the game make music together.

FURTHER READING

Austin, Michael, ed. *Music Video Games: Performance, Politics, and Play.* New York: Bloomsbury, 2016.

Donnelly, K. J., William Gibbons, and Neil Lerner, eds. *Music in Video Games: Studying Play.* London: Taylor and Francis, 2014.

Kamp, Michiel, Tim Summers, and Mark Sweeny, eds. *Ludomusicology: Approaches to Video Game Music.* Sheffield, UK: Equinox, 2016.

Whalen, Zach. "Play Along—An Approach to Videogame Music." *Game Studies* 4, no. 1 (November 2004). www.gamestudies.org.

NOTES

1 For more on Miyamoto, see Jennifer deWinter's chapter in this collection.

2 Roger Moseley and Aya Saiki, "Nintendo's Art of Musical Play," in *Music in Video Games: Studying Play*, ed. K. J. Donnelly, William Gibbons, and Neil Lerner (London: Taylor and Francis, 2014), 51.

3 Neil Lerner, "Mario's Dynamic Leaps: Musical Innovations (and the Specter of Early Cinema) in *Donkey Kong* and *Super Mario Bros*," in Donnely, Gibbons, and Lerner, eds., *Music in Video Games*, 2.

4 Theodor Adorno and Hanns Eisler, *Composing for the Films* (Oxford: Oxford University Press, 1947), 60.

5 Alexander Galloway, *Gaming: Essays on Algorithmic Culture* (Minneapolis: University of Minnesota Press, 2006), 3.

6 Karen Collins, *Game Sound: An Introduction to the History, Theory, and Practice of Video Game Music and Sound Design* (Cambridge, MA: MIT Press, 2008), 4.

7 Karen Collins, *Playing with Sound: A Theory of Interacting with Sound and Music in Video Games* (Cambridge, MA: MIT Press, 2013), 4.

8 Stephanie Lind describes this is as active and reactive listening and performance. Stephanie Lind, "Active Interfaces and Thematic Events in *The Legend of Zelda: Ocarina of Time*"

in *Music Video Games: Performance, Politics, and Play*, ed. Michael Austin (New York: Bloomsbury, 2016), 86.

9 Nancy Miller, "Director Edgar Wright, Actor Michael Cera Crack Wise about Scott Pilgrim," *Wired Magazine*, June 22, 2010, www.wired.com.

10 "Knights of the Old Republic II PC Soundtrack," Mixnmojo.com, accessed September 3, 2017, http://soundtracks.mixnmojo.com.

11 Michel de Certeau, *The Practice of Everyday Life* (Berkley: University of California Press, 1984), xiv.

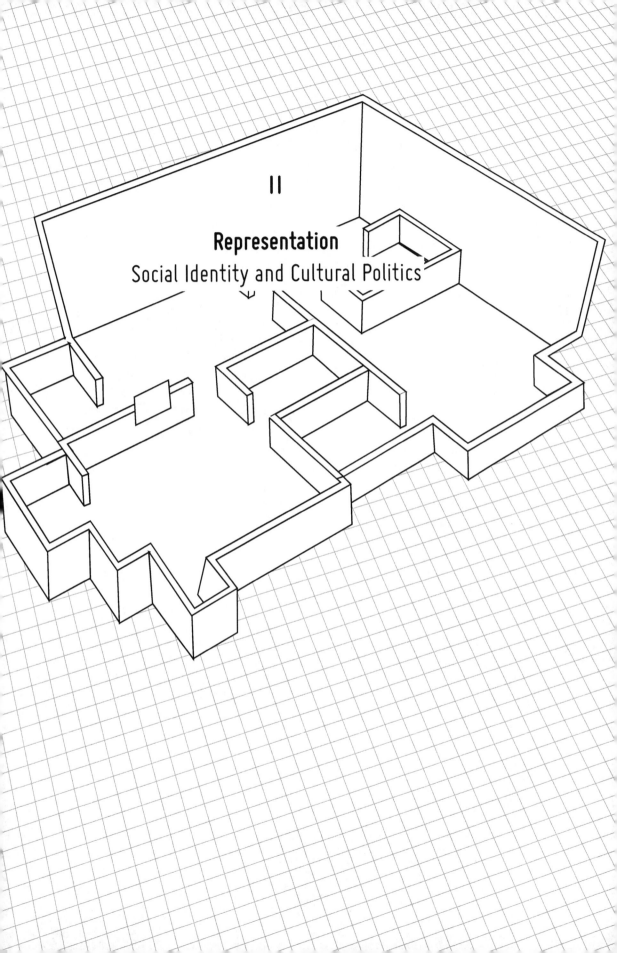

II

Representation
Social Identity and Cultural Politics

11

Kim Kardashian: Hollywood
Feminism

SHIRA CHESS

Abstract: Kim Kardashian has received much attention for her media empire, including her game, published by Glu Mobile. The game's premise plays a role in what Shira Chess characterizes as "Feminine Play Style," an emerging mode of video games that functions through assumptions about an idealized vision of the woman player and her relationship with leisure time.

Feminism is a messy topic for video games. Video games were long seen as a kind of "boys' club" wherein men and boys defined the industry. From the late 1980s through the 1990s, video games were primarily made by men for masculine audiences. In turn, early feminist critiques of video games have long focused on the problematic representations of female bodies, such as Lara Croft from the *Tomb Raider* series (1996–present) and other characters primarily made for a presumed male gaze.

By the late 1990s and early 2000s, however, audiences began to shift slightly. Research demonstrated that girls who played video games were more likely to be interested in science, technology, engineering, and medical careers, fostering an increased interest in player politics.[1] Video game companies began to market to girls, some as a feminist response to the industry and others commodifying a demographic. Eventually, by the mid-2000s, game marketing and design also began to target adult females. These games were often shorthanded as the "casual games market." Casual games (such as *Diner Dash* [Gamelab, 2004]), hidden object games, and cell phone puzzle games) are cheap or free, easy to learn, and minimalist in narrative. They also easily fit into busy schedules by being playable for either shorter or longer periods, depending on the needs of the player.

Technological changes made video games rapidly available to more diverse audiences. Around 2006, Nintendo was highly invested in marketing to women audiences via its portable Nintendo DS system and Wii gaming console. Equally important, the rise and popularity of smartphones made gaming more accessible and ubiquitous to a variety of people—many of them adult women. In this way, video games as a feminist topic have rapidly shifted from only conversations about "hard-core" games that are not necessarily intended for women to an equal amount of research on the steady influx of games that are intentionally made for feminine audiences. These games have a necessarily messy relationship to feminism: they are often essentializing yet liberating, condescending yet intoxicating.

It is within this context that we can consider the wonderful, terrible, fascinating, glorious, and troubling world of *Kim Kardashian: Hollywood* (Glu Mobile, 2014). Certainly, both scholars and media commentators have remarked on the game's namesake, who, in a variety of ways, has maintained a stronghold on popular culture for the last decade. *Kim Kardashian: Hollywood* (*KK:H*) appeared in a cascading wake of Kardashian-centric media and products. The Kardashian family has brought to market multiple television shows, makeup lines, perfumes, books, music, and clothing. Yet, in many ways, *KK:H* is unique. Created by Glu Mobile (as a re-skin of an older title, *Stardom: The A-List* [Blammo Games, 2011]), the game gives agency to the player, allowing her to sample, taste, and dabble in the unfathomable world of the rich and famous.

The sheer popularity of *KK:H* tells us the game is worth examination. The game brought in more than US$200 million in its first year, and the stock of Glu Mobile rapidly rose 42 percent in value.[2] As a game, *KK:H* was both commercially popular and widely discussed. But is the game feminist?

Asking if a video game is feminist can be a bit like asking if a television set is capitalist. The television set may be made by individuals that align (or do not align) themselves with capitalist ideals, it may be inhabited by programming that promotes (or does not promote) capitalism, and it may be read in a variety of polysemic ways that allow the viewer to reinforce (or not reinforce) their own beliefs vis-à-vis capitalism. The television set, however, is not itself for or against capitalism; it is a technology that can be imbued with a variety of beliefs. In other words, a variety of market conditions, institutional structures, and individual beliefs all simultaneously influence the outcome of a game. Thus, analyzing a video game in terms of its relationship to feminism is about reading underlying textual and industry cues to understand the game's different possible messages (both intentional and unintentional). At the same time, unpacking a game's relationship to feminism—particularly a game that is so readily marketed toward women audiences—is worth pursuing. By asking the question about the game's relationship to feminism, we can better understand the nuanced market conditions, social structures, and ideologies from which the game emerged.

Much of the trickiness of considering *KK:H* as feminist is in its relationship to "intersectionality." Intersectionality is a concept in feminist theory that acknowledges that gender oppression occurs neither in a vacuum nor equally across other modes of oppression. Intersectional feminism works to acknowledge that in addition to gender, other factors such as race, ethnicity, social class, disability, sexuality, and age create overlapping systems of oppression and discrimination. Intersectional feminism is meant to rethink the inherent whiteness of earlier feminist theories and find ways to talk about the range of experiences and modes of oppression that are experienced on global and local levels. Intersectionality, as it was originally proposed by Kimberlé Williams Crenshaw in the early 1990s, was a way to push back against the assumptions that all women's experiences are equal and follow similar trajectories.[3]

From an intersectionalist feminist perspective, *KK:H* is a mass of contradictions. On one hand, the game provides a great deal of agency in terms of player selections. On the other hand, those choices are limited to experiences of privilege. *KK:H* allows us to consider how a game object can simultaneously aspire to some feminist goals while simultaneously ignoring experiences of diversity and intersectionality.

When players first enter the game world of *KK:H* they have nothing but their plucky ambition. Before the narrative begins, players are permitted to decide on sex (limited to male or female and unchangeable once the game begins), a name, as well as a limited number of options of outward appearance, all later changeable. To start, the player is placed in a small clothing boutique in Los Angeles. Only minutes into the game, the player is approached by Kim Kardashian who is having a "fashion emergency" and desperately needs help. In helping Kim select a dress for an event, the player is subsequently invited by Kim to join her for a photo shoot—the first of many. This "in" allows the player to navigate the ins-and-outs of Hollywood, getting an agent and a publicist, meeting famous people (from other members of the Kardashian family to famous designers and stylists), and working one's way up from the "E-List" to the "A-List."

In addition to gigs for cash, the player is also given opportunities to date, as well as engage in personal and relationship "drama" in the game. Sexuality in *KK:H* is relatively fluid—while the player is asked early on to declare a sexual preference, the game world is ambivalent to these choices, and both men and women will flirt. Dating, however, creates drama, and a relationship that is not well nurtured ends in dramatic breakups or angry phone calls. Other in-game "drama" comes from non-player characters that wish to interfere in the player's climb toward stardom.

The gameplay is simultaneously simple and complex. The player moves up in ranking number (sets of numbers assigned to E-List through A-List). Experience points are gained via fictional followers on a fake Twitter feed. Followers determine the player's popularity, which, in turn, determines his or her position within the world of the game. Followers are gained through a variety of things: successful "gigs" (fashion shows, photo shoots, appearances), relationship work (nurturing a successful relationship from courtship through marriage through eventually adopting a child), and throwing parties. Additionally, followers can be gained through purchasing in-game items such as clothing, accessories, furniture, and pets. Mobility, however, is not only upward; the player can lose followers as well. Neglecting a relationship and being dumped, as well as doing poorly on a gig, can cause followers to drop. Players can also lose followers for not playing the game for a while. In other words, the more you play, the less likely you are to lose fictional fans.

Getting and keeping fans takes money. While gigs pay minimally (even for an A-lister), other things cost money: the player must pay to take paramours on dates, purchase homes for hosting parties, and purchase clothing or other in-game accessories to be declared a fashion icon. Despite the vast wealth of the empire that the game world is replicating, money is hard to come by. Other than completing gigs, there are really only two ways to acquire in-game cash: through hitting hidden "hot spots" (a few can be found in each game location) or through purchasing it with real-world money. Hidden hot spots supplying experience points, cash, and energy are typically understated, snuck under birds, inside of shrubs, under beer mugs, or at fire hydrants.

Despite the wealth of the game's namesake, the game replicates poverty far more than affluence. The constant struggle to get money to ultimately gain fans puts players in a situation where they are wandering around the streets, grabbing up every dollar bill they can find, and relishing the few hundred they gain from a modeling gig.[4] Players are in a constant struggle to find enough money to survive in the fast-paced Kardashian world. To "Keep up with the Kardashians" (so to speak) players must either play all the time or use their own money, thus ultimately contributing to the Kardashians' vast real-world media empire.

The relationship with consumerism and consumption puts *KK:H* in an awkward position vis-à-vis feminism, in general, and intersectional feminism, in particular. The game—both in terms of inner narrative and outward mechanics—constantly suggests the import of consumerism. To be successful, players must constantly spend in-game money, which ultimately translates to extra-game money. This is because it is almost impossible to win without supplanting in-game winnings with real-world money.

The game employs two congruent forms of currency: cash and K-stars. Cash, represented by dollar bills, is rarely the equivalent of actual monetary values.

For example, a T-shirt might cost several thousand dollars, but a flight to Dubai might only cost $90. Money and prices seem to be distorted as though reflected through a fun-house mirror, making them lose meaning and scope. Cash in the game is both simultaneously necessary and useless in how it maps back to real-world experiences. At the same time, K-stars are a harder-won kind of currency, not representative of any actual cash value but monetizing the charm of celebrity and the Kardashian family itself. K-stars are used for certain "special" items (nicer articles of clothing, pets, personal jets, etc.) or else used to "charm" individuals into doing your bidding. The two competing forms of currency help to establish that in the real world, there is money and then there is the money of wealthy people. The latter gives access to things that might be otherwise unattainable. The currency systems of *KK:H* are simultaneously unrealistic and spookily accurate.

There is an underlying conceit to *KK:H* that this kind of game—ultimately a shopping and beauty game—is what women and girls want out of their play. One does not have to look far online or in app stores to find shopping and beauty games marketed heavily to feminine demographics. This, of course, is unsurprising. There is a long history of marketing beauty, fashion, and consumerism to women and girl audiences, suggesting that members of this audience always want to "improve" their appearance and that the proper mode of this improvement is necessarily through acts of consumption. These presumptive links between women and consumption become normalized in such a way that we don't often think twice about the quandaries of expecting women to purchase their attractiveness and buy into a culture. *KK:H*, like other fashion and beauty games, does just this. Similarly, as researcher Alison Harvey points out, it reifies an inherent devaluation of feminine labor practices both in the game space and outside of it.[5]

From an intersectional perspective, the focus on consumption is equally troubling. The points of intersection between gender and class are often difficult to articulate. Social class is a topic that, while affecting both men and women on a global level, is often invisible or dismissed. In the United States the Horatio Algers "rags-to-riches" myth has become emblematic of the larger depiction of the "American Dream." Like a Cinderella story, there is an implicit suggestion that those who do not achieve wealth or success attached to the American Dream are lazy, immoral, or stupid. This, of course, is not only untrue but it is a dangerous point of view: blaming lower-income people for their lack of success only sets them up for systemic and institutional oppression.

KK:H is based on the core premises of this Horatio Alger story.[6] We play the role of the "main character" traversing the ladder of fame, fortune, and success. Although players might experience bumps and falls, they will thrive so long as they continue to play. In other words, the primary narrative of the game is one

FIGURE 11.1

The author's avatar in the game *Kim Kardashian: Hollywood*, a game with a complex relationship to feminism.

that values meritocracy, but that meritocracy occurs with an ease that suggests the experiences of already privileged lifestyles.

KK:H allows players to experiment with intersectionality in ways other than class privilege. As already noted, sexuality is fluid; the game lightly supports homosexuality and bisexuality. However, as open as sexualities are in *KK:H*, they do not necessarily imply a similar fluidity to gender assignment. Players are bound to the sex they select at the beginning of the game. Although hairstyles might give some sense of gender nuance, players' inability to change body type (curvy for women, flat and straight for men) implies that one can experiment with sexual preference; however, there are some things that should remain unchanged.[7]

Bodies are simultaneously fixed and fluid in *KK:H*. Certain features are infinitely mutable; players can change their hair, faces (noses, eyes, lips, facial structures), skin color, hair color, eye color, makeup, and clothing infinitely. These changes do not affect gameplay. This setup reflects a larger trend in video game design, often referred to in the video game industry as "invest/express." In invest/express games, players are given a minimal palette and the ability to earn currency to express personal taste into their gaming space. In a game like *FarmVille* (Zynga, 2009), this results in a personalized farm, styled to players' whims but having no effect on the outcome of play. Similarly, in *KK:H*, the gameplay and design attributes seem to occur in tandem—the player spends long periods working gigs and throwing parties to gain enough in-game cash to get cool things. In other words, consumerism—and the concurrent desire for class mobility—is at the heart of the invest/express style of *KK:H*.

Yet, the *limitations* on bodies in the game are equally telling. The one thing that the player cannot modify is body type. As noted, the player is only given two body type options: feminine curves or masculine flatness (see figure 11.1). Non-player characters (in particular, celebrity characters or those that are part of the Kardashian family) are permitted other shapes. For example, Kim's body is more voluptuous than any other character, whereas Kendall Kardashian's body is waifish and small. Height cannot be changed, either. The rhetoric seems to be that you can look like whatever you want so long as you have the correct body.

The inherent contradictions of bodily selection, yet denial of many important forms of selection supports the messiness in *KK:H*'s relationship to intersectional feminism. The feminist implications of selection seem far more poignant in *KK:H* as opposed to older-style, single-avatar games such as *Tomb Raider*'s Lara Croft. Yet, even with this fluidity—and even in a game that is clearly, deliberately intended for a feminine audience—we are still stuck with perfect bodies, ones with curves yet no cellulite and ones that cannot challenge cultural constructions of beauty.

To a similar extent, we can reassign our skin colors in *KK:H*, limited to five choices. The game is ambivalent to this, responding neither to your skin color nor to your other bodily features. Yet, given the inherent sexism, racism, ageism, ableism, and classism of Hollywood, it seems almost like an awkward omission that the upwardly mobile starlet is untouched by these things. The game seems to suggest that we live in a world that is blind to all the things that are so deeply rooted in modern entertainment culture.

KK:H is simultaneously both feminist and not feminist. The game's constraints, bodies, and the emphasis on consumptive practice illustrate a tenuous relationship with the lived experiences of players. However, aspects of the game, and the decision to design it for feminine audiences, suggest a push against more traditional (read: masculine) modes of gaming. Like other games developed for feminine audiences, the results are both essentializing and liberating. In this way, *KK:H*, as a feminist text, bears all of the possibilities and all of the problems inherent in mass-produced media.

NOTES

1 Justine Cassell and Henry Jenkins, *From Barbie to Mortal Kombat* (Cambridge, MA: MIT Press, 1998).

2 Caitlin McCabe, "Hit Kardashian Video Game Lifts Glu Mobile From E-List," *Bloomberg Tech*, July 10, 2014, https://www.bloomberg.com.

3 Kimberlé Williams Crenshaw, "Mapping the Margins: Intersectionality, Identity Politics, and Violence against Women of Color," *Stanford Law Review* 43 (1991): 1241–1299.

4 Players can also get cash from daily "bonuses," although the results of these contests are inconsistent and only occasionally is cash awarded.

5 Alison Harvey, "The Fame Game: Working Your Way Up the Celebrity Ladder in *Kim Kardashian: Hollywood*," *Games & Culture*, published ahead of print February 21, 2018, https://doi.org/10.1177/1555412018757872.

6 Shira Chess and Jessica Maddox, "Kim Kardashian is My New BFF: Video Games and the Looking Glass Celebrity," *Popular Communication* 16 (2018): 196–210.

7 This seems notable because soon after the game's release, Kardashian family member Bruce Jenner, after a sexual reassignment, went public as Caitlyn Jenner. Given the family awareness of transgender identity, it is noteworthy that characters must always remain cisgendered.

FURTHER READING

Chess, Shira. *Ready Player Two: Women Gamers and Designed Identity.* Minneapolis: University of Minnesota Press, 2017.

Harvey, Alison. *Gender, Age, and Digital Games in the Domestic Context.* New York: Routledge, 2015.

Kocurek, Carly A. *Coin-Operated Americans: Rebooting Boyhood at the Video Game Arcade.* Minneapolis: University of Minnesota Press, 2015.

Shaw, Adrienne. *Gaming at the Edge: Sexuality and Gender at the Margins of Gamer Culture.* Minneapolis: University of Minnesota Press, 2014.

12

The Last of Us
Masculinity

SORAYA MURRAY

Abstract: Mainstream video games often position players in the role of a hyper-masculine hero, with superhuman strength, mastery of combat skills, decisiveness, fearlessness, and an inclination toward domination. Through a close look at one iconic example, *The Last of Us*, Soraya Murray discusses the notable break from the invulnerable male protagonist, and how it signals larger Western cultural ambivalences and anxieties.

The Last of Us (Naughty Dog, 2013) is a third-person perspective survival-horror action game set in a post-apocalyptic United States full of disorder, desperation, and brutality. Highly praised at the time of its release, *The Last of Us* is an iconic example of its genre and one that is exceptionally well executed as a kind of parting magnum opus for the Sony PlayStation 3 in terms of its music, character development, voice acting, emotional resonance, and mature aesthetic sensibility.[1] Joel, the primary playable character, is a single father and a Texas construction worker. In an inciting incident set in the present day of the game's release, Joel has a sweet exchange with his pale blonde daughter, Sarah, late in the night after he returns from a hard day at work. It is his birthday, and she has waited up to give him his present. But this is also the fateful eve of an outbreak that will decimate the United States. Before we know it, the town has succumbed to violence and mayhem that, based on discoverable clues such as newspaper and television reports, has erupted nationally. There is panic, and despite his desperate efforts, Joel is unable to protect his daughter from it all. Before the title sequence has even begun, we see young Sarah whimpering and bleeding out in the dark night, cueing the player that this journey is bound to be harsh.

We meet Joel once again, 20 years into the pandemic, now grizzled, battle-worn, and emotionally damaged from the traumatic loss of his daughter. He physically embodies the "heartland" American man: white, able-bodied, presumed straight and of Christian stock, verbally reserved, solidly built, and pragmatic. Joel is resourceful, but he is also deeply jaded, plagued by survivor's guilt, and morally compromised by what he has done to stay alive. He is a smuggler and a killer, subsisting on rations and whatever opportunity he and his partner, Tess, can drum up. Joel lives in a militarized quarantine zone in Boston, which is besieged by warring factions, as well as the aggressive victims of an airborne fungal pandemic. As the fungus attacks their brains and grows, the infected become increasingly violent, deformed, and inhuman.

The scarcity of supplies is a problem, and scavenging is a primary game mechanic. It's a world that would be familiar to fans of the post-apocalyptic narrative in cinema like: *28 Days Later* (Danny Boyle, 2002), *Planet Terror* (Robert Rodriguez and Quentin Tarantino, 2007), *The Road* (John Hillcoat, 2009), *Zombieland* (Robin Fleischer, 2009), *The Book of Eli* (Albert Hughes and Allen Hughes, 2010), *Rise of the Planet of the Apes* (Rupert Wyatt, 2011) and *World War Z* (Marc Forster, 2013). Like these films and popular cinema-inspired survival-horror franchises such as *Resident Evil* and *Silent Hill*, they present visions of Western culture in ruins. Within these narratives, a compromised hero often contends with the crumbling of Western notions of progress, and the unsustainability of that way of life. This is demonstrated on two levels: in the individual narrative of survival hardship, and in the larger backdrop of civilization's breakdown due to an ecological crisis and the ensuing desperation.

A complication is introduced in the form of Ellie, a girl whom Joel is tasked with smuggling to another quarantine zone. Fourteen, imperiled, and of mysterious significance to the rebel "Fireflies" militia, Ellie is a painful reminder of Joel's lost daughter. She also rekindles his flickering sense of purpose. Between the infected and human threats, as well as the perils of this dystopic space, Joel is repeatedly forced to protect the innocent Ellie—which he does grudgingly at first. Over the course of the game, Joel's relationship to Ellie shifts from exasperated guardian to mentor, to protector, and finally surrogate father. Much of the gameplay involves stealth, combat, shooting, puzzle-solving, scavenging, and crafting. A poignant score by an Academy Award–winning composer combined with the strong storyline and unrelenting scenarios invoke pathos and concentrated emotional affect. The cinematic nature of the vision provides an immersive sense of place. *The Last of Us* presents, in the shape of a post-apocalyptic context, an extremely well executed opportunity to engage with some of America's deepest myths and fantasies of rugged individualism, man versus man, man versus nature, and in a way, the frontier narrative—all of which bear heavily on notions of masculinity.[2] As representations that are playable, games present constructions that users operate to catalyze actions that advance the game narrative.[3] Thus, playable representations are a key component through which players engage with the game and its unfolding story.

Visual studies–based scholarship of representation has long acknowledged the multiple and shifting notions of masculinity in culture, which are invented and shored up by various signifying practices and social mores, in keeping with the specific historical moment.[4] Overwhelmingly, most mainstream games with human characters still adhere to a traditional highly militarized masculine ideal of strength, resourcefulness, combat readiness, a competitive spirit, a penchant for violence, and dominance in the theater of war.[5] Stephen Kline, Nick Dyer-Witheford, and Greig de Peuter unpack the notion of "militarized masculinity" in relation to games, pointing to its relevance on multiple levels: "Militarized masculinity is a matter not only of designing cultural narratives of violence and gender but of computer technology's legacy of military applications and—of special importance—marketing practices aimed at commercially valuable hard-core male players."[6] As they observe, there is a connection among in-game representations that glorify a fantasy of militarized manhood, the military origins of the technology employed in video games, and the primary market audiences of games. Since these kinds of games have been wildly successful, the formula is repeated. But their success may also be due to having tapped into fears, anxieties, and hopes that operate on a deep cultural level and resonate with mainstream audiences. In his research on video games, masculinity, and culture, Derek Burrill notes these kinds of games are gateways for male players to access a kind of "boyhood, or the state of premature masculinity that is accessed by males seeking to re-engage their youth/virility/power/dominance over forces that appear to be encroaching on their former footholds . . ."[7] For him, "[v]ideogames in the 21st century serve as the prime mode of regression, a technonostalgia machine allowing escape, fantasy, extension, and utopia, a space away from feminism, class imperatives, familial duties, as well as a national and political responsibilities."[8] In other words, games become spaces to enact and negotiate one's relationship to lived-world pressures. This sense of losing a foothold, particularly on a national and a political level, will become important for an understanding of what is at work in *The Last of Us*.

Today, primary playable characters (if human) are still most likely to be male, and often adhere to a stock "type" (white, brown-haired, unshaven, brooding) that has prompted scrutiny for its ubiquity, exclusions, and lack of variation. The titular character of the *Max Payne* series (2001–2012), Nathan Drake of the *Uncharted* series (2007–), Niko Bellic of *Grand Theft Auto IV* (2008), John Marston of *Red Dead Redemption* (Rockstar San Diego, 2010), Booker DeWitt of *BioShock Infinite* (Irrational Games, 2013), Aiden Pearce of *Watch Dogs* (Ubisoft Montreal, 2014): these are just a few of the examples of a dominant "type" in games. The limiting nature of these representations often sidelines or excludes women, the non–gender conforming, and people of color. This systematic omission has raised repeated criticisms from women and minority players, journalists, and academics and has frequently surfaced in public discourse.

Because the game industry, game culture, and games themselves remain so male-dominated, studies in gender and video games have overwhelmingly focused on females and, particularly, girls.[9] Men and boys persist as the primary target audience of commercial games, their marketing, and their larger culture, despite statistical evidence that all genders play, and females play almost as much as males.[10] Despite this diversity, there remains a bent toward toxic forms of hypermasculinity in larger video game culture. However, some scholars, such as Ewan Kirkland, have noted that there is yet little understanding of the range of masculinities imaged and enacted in playable form, including those which may complicate and contradict the most regressive male roles associated with games.[11] As a part of this conversation, it is vital to interrogate the presumed norm not only in terms of masculinity but also whiteness, which has come under scrutiny in recent years yet persists as a "universal" onto which other kinds of players are often asked to map themselves.

Although Joel certainly does not conform to the conventional militarized masculinity of an iconic character like Snake in *Metal Gear Solid* (Konami, 1998), who is more immersed in "strongly gender coded scenarios of war, conquest, and combat," he does function as a cipher for an American rugged individualist.[12] And although Joel musters extraordinary strength at times, he does not possess the tactical combat skills of the militarized masculinity often presented in mainstream games. He is an antihero figure who is surly, deeply cynical, and self-serving. As the primary playable character and central representation of masculinity in the game, Joel is often presented as being vulnerable, imperiled, and victimized by a bleak existence. Much of the violence that takes place—while admittedly cinematic—is neither glamorized nor heroic. Most weapons are makeshift, and constant scavenging is necessary in order to find the most rudimentary tools and supplies to construct melee weapons and create distractions. One never feels the definitive domination of one's enemy, the rush of combat, or pleasure of highly technologized and fetishized weaponry. Whereas some military-oriented games can be almost balletic in their elegantly executed action, *The Last of Us* refuses to replicate this convention, instead presenting players with awkward, off-balance skirmishes. Indeed, at one point in the game, after Joel becomes seriously incapacitated, Ellie assumes the role of protector, hunting for their food and singlehandedly defending Joel against enemies.

White male victimization—a key pillar of the Men's Rights Movement and, more recently, the 2016 Donald Trump presidential campaign—is a clear political pushback against diversity in America.[13] The extreme survivalist scenario, when considered within a larger cultural moment in which there is a growing polarization between the West and a so-called axis of evil, suggests fears of being overrun, colonized, or perhaps becoming the losers of global competition and economic restructuring. It is hard not to read the representation of a beleaguered white normative American in light of such large anxieties of conflicted Western dominance across the world. Within the United States, for example, there is an increasing racially based anxiety around what it will mean for the nation when the demographic makeup renders whites the "minority"—which is projected in the near future.[14] In this regard, the American notion of whiteness, which operates simultaneously as a racial category, a term for power relations, and a term of normativity, weighs heavily on the representation of Joel, who is angry, disenfranchised, and subject to a radical otherness in the form of the infected, who have overrun his nation.

Despite the temporary shift to gameplay as Ellie, who eventually develops her autonomy and survival skills, several commentators discussed the game within a larger trend toward "dadification" in video games. That is, critics noted that several games have turned to a scenario of paternal relations between a primary male character and a younger female character who needs protection. Some have attributed this turn to game developers themselves becoming fathers and addressing this in their work or to the tendency of these same developers to speak to an aging game player constituency whom they believe to be much like themselves. Yet others suggest that this move provides the opportunity to reassert protective male dominant characters in a new way while sidestepping the exhausted rescue-the-princess model.[15] Joel and Ellie exemplify this relation, but there were many others, including Booker DeWitt and Elizabeth in *BioShock Infinite* and Lee Everett and Clementine in *The Walking Dead* (Telltale Games, 2012). In *The Last of Us*, Sarah, the daughter who dies in the game's inciting incident, becomes the engine for many of Joel's drives. One infers quickly that the origin of his deep bitterness stems from his inability, as a father, to have protected her. Despite his best efforts, this drive becomes mapped onto Ellie, another young girl, albeit one born "native" to the pandemic and therefore more socialized into surviving its harsh realities.

A distinctly paternalistic relation between Joel an Ellie evolves over the course of their engagement—one that is reinforced narratively and visually within the game itself. Joel is unwillingly placed in a protectorate role, although, at first, he is barely able to even look at Ellie—suggesting his persisting difficulty in dealing with his prior loss. As Joel and Ellie traverse the game space, the girl is often exposed to the ravaged beauty of the land and to the thrill of discovering new experiences. Ellie's childlike wonder in leaving the Boston quarantine zone for the first time not only allows players to experience similar feelings vicariously but also functions to place Joel increasingly in a parental position. While the two wander the sublime spaces of nature as it reabsorbs their once-great civilization, conversations between them can be triggered at will by the player. This functions to build interiority in each of the characters and relations between them. Players notice as a part of gameplay that Ellie, who is small, can scramble into small spaces, and Joel, who is brawnier, can boost her up easily to ledges neither could reach alone. A kind of symbiosis is reached between them, where each organically makes the most of their respective physical assets, to solve gamic problems and navigate the space through collaborative effort.

Joel's fatherly impulses also manifest themselves in the various shielding gestures made by his character throughout the game. While crouched together in a cover position, Ellie eventually nestles into the crook of Joel's arm if near to him. When standing in a cover position behind a wall, Joel places an arm across her body like a barrier against harm, in a typically parental gesture (see figure 12.1). Ellie is also very petite when beside Joel, girlish in her form, wide-eyed, and representative of a kind of unblemished spirit that he increasingly desires to protect. He calls her "kiddo." This paternal relation is also represented through Joel's reticence to Ellie's use of deadly weapons and his desire to shelter her from having to kill. In one instance, Joel finds a bow and Ellie wants to use it: "I'm a pretty good shot with that thing," she says. Joel responds, "How 'bout we just leave this kind of stuff to me." Ellie protests: "Well, we could both be armed. Cover each other." "I don't think so," Joel admonishes. Of course, Joel's desire to spare Ellie this burden is unrealistic, and across the game this dynamic shifts. Ellie's gradual acceptance of her new, brutal reality intensifies as the two head west, culminating in an extremely cruel scene of mortal struggle between Ellie and a cannibal. In this and other desperate moments of almost losing her, Joel addresses Ellie as "Baby Girl," an endearment once reserved for his own child. This fatherly role, in which Joel is presented a second chance to save the girl, offers another kind of masculinity, one that is protectorate but emotionally vulnerable. What the paternal offers on an affective level is a narrative access point to the emotional inner lives of men as fathers while keeping intact the player's perceived sense of Joel's masculinity.

The Last of Us breaks with typical gamic hypermasculinity in significant ways that are built into both the core gameplay and the representational elements. The masculinity presented in the form of Joel typifies the triple-A title white male game hero but departs in ways that signal an ambivalence toward the exhausted militarized masculine types that have dominated mainstream games. The sense of overall privation and the lack of all the tools and mastery necessary interrupt

FIGURE 12.1 Joel protects Ellie, in *The Last of Us*. Image provided by Sony Interactive Entertainment America LLC. © Sony Interactive Entertainment America LLC. Created and developed by Naughty Dog LLC.

the sense of combat dominance. Even though he is a masculine protagonist who largely adheres to the generic white male "type," Joel is nevertheless almost always configured as despondent, as someone who is constantly innovating out of necessity. Furthermore, he is placed in a paternal role in relation to his young ward, Ellie, which places him in emotional peril relative to his tragic past. Protracted episodes of scrounging and scavenging provide a sense of desperation and vulnerability rather than control and dominance. There are never enough places to hide, the body fails, plans fall through, everyone is at risk, alliances are fragile, and collaboration is necessary.

Still, the game does not entirely ditch conventional male representation. Rather, it taps into concerns related to a fraught moment—particularly connected to the larger social engineering of a victimized white American masculinity. What results is an affective quality of a deep ambivalence, which trades on highly ideological perceptions of the white male as both normative hero, and as threatened by larger historical circumstance. This is an image of masculinity that mobilizes a moral high ground of victimization and alienation within the nation. It is an ambivalent whiteness, disadvantaged in a new world of profound threatening otherness embodied in the form of the infected. It is in this brilliant flattening of hero and victim into a single masculine form, that *The Last of Us* shores up a construction of white masculinity that is embattled by threats, both real and imagined.

NOTES

1 The Sony PlayStation 4 (PS4) was released just four months after *The Last of Us* hit the shelves in June 2013. An enhanced version of the game, *The Last of Us Remastered*, was released for PS4 in July of 2014.

2 See, for example, Sara Humphreys, "Rejuvenating 'Eternal Inequality' on the Digital Frontiers of Red Dead Redemption," *Western American Literature* 47, no. 2 (Summer 2012): 200–215.

3 Alexander Galloway discusses this in Alexander R. Galloway, *Gaming: Essays on Algorithmic Culture*, Electronic Mediations 18 (Minneapolis: University of Minnesota Press, 2006).

4 Sean Nixon, "Exhibiting Masculinity," in *Representation: Cultural Representations and Signifying Practices, Culture, Media, and Identities*, ed. Stuart Hall and Open University (London and Thousand Oaks, CA: Sage in association with the Open University, 1997), 291–336.

5 The term *militarized masculinity*, which is connected to "mastery, domination, and conquest" as values in games, is explored to great effect in Stephen Kline, Nick Dyer-Witheford, and Greig de Peuter, *Digital Play: The Interaction of Technology, Culture, and Marketing* (Montréal; London: McGill-Queen's University Press, 2003), 238.

6 Kline, Dyer-Witheford, and de Peuter, *Digital Play*, 196.

7 Derek A. Burrill, *Die Tryin': Videogames, Masculinity, Culture, Popular Culture and Everyday Life, v. 18* (New York: Peter Lang, 2008), 137.

8 Burrill, *Die Tryin'*, 2.

9 Justine Cassell and Henry Jenkins, eds., *From Barbie to Mortal Kombat: Gender and Computer Games*, paperback ed. (Cambridge, MA: MIT Press, 2000).

10 Entertainment Software Association, "2017 Essential Facts About the Computer and Video Game Industry," *The Entertainment Software Association*, April 2017, http://www.theesa.com.

11 Ewan Kirkland, "Masculinity in Video Games: The Gendered Gameplay of *Silent Hill*," *Camera Obscura* 24, no. 71 (May 2009): 161–83.

12 Kline, Dyer-Witheford, and Peuter, *Digital Play*, 247.

13 Hanna Rosin, *The End of Men: And the Rise of Women*, reprint ed. (New York: Riverhead Books, 2013); M. A. Messner, "The Limits of 'The Male Sex Role': An Analysis of the Men's Liberation and Men's Rights Movements' Discourse," *Gender & Society* 12, no. 3 (June 1, 1998): 255–76, doi:10.1177/0891243298012003002; and Michael Kimmel, *Angry White Men: American Masculinity at the End of an Era*, 2nd ed. (New York: Nation Books, 2017).

14 Hua Hsu, "The End of White America?," *The Atlantic*, February 2009.

15 Mattie Brice, "The Dadification of Video Games Is Real," *Mattie Brice* (blog), August 15, 2013, www.mattiebrice.com; Maddy Myers, "Bad Dads Vs. Hyper Mode: The Father-Daughter Bond In Videogames," *pastemagazine.com*, July 30, 2013, www.pastemagazine.com; Jess Joho, "The Dadification of Videogames, Round Two," *Kill Screen*, February 11, 2014, http://killscreendaily.com; Richard Cobbett, "Daddy Un-Cool: How Fallout 4 Falls into the Parent Trap," *TechRadar*, December 2, 2015, www.techradar.com; and Sarah Stang, "Controlling Fathers and Devoted Daughters: Paternal Authority in BioShock 2 and The Witcher 3: Wild Hunt," *First Person Scholar*, December 7, 2016, www.firstpersonscholar.com.

FURTHER READING

Murray, Soraya. *On Video Games: The Visual Politics of Race, Gender and Space.* London: I. B. Tauris, 2018.

Stang, Sarah. "Big Daddies and Broken Men: Father-Daughter Relationships in Video Games." *Loading . . . The Journal of the Canadian Game Studies Association* 10, no. 16 (2017): 162–174.

Watts, Evan. "Ruin, Gender and Digital Games." *WSQ: Women's Studies Quarterly* 39, no. 3/4 (Fall/Winter 2011): 247–265.

13

Leisure Suit Larry
LGBTQ Representation

ADRIENNE SHAW

Abstract: Much of popular and critical attention to lesbian, gay, bisexual, transgender, and queer (LGBTQ) representation in video games has focused on either same-sex romance options or explicitly LGBTQ major game characters, but little has been written about more minor but equally important forms of representation. In this chapter, Adrienne Shaw analyzes a game series that is at its core about heterosexual masculinity, *Leisure Suit Larry*, to explore how LGBTQ representation permeates texts even when they are "not about that."

Compared to other media, little academic attention has been paid to the history of lesbian, gay, bisexual, transgender, and queer (LGBTQ) content in digital games. To correct for this, my collaborators and I have been building a digital archive documenting all known LGBTQ content in digital games created since the 1980s.[1] In addition to allowing us to look at LGBTQ representation in games over time, the archive demonstrates the myriad ways LGBTQ people and issues are integrated into this medium. In this chapter, I use the game series *Leisure Suit Larry* (Sierra On-Line/Vivendi, 1987–2009) as an example for analyzing LGBTQ representation in digital games. Although the series is about a heterosexual man attempting to perform a version of white hegemonic masculinity, the game is rife with LGBTQ characters, content, and gameplay sequences. Although many of these examples are used in a homophobic or transphobic manner, the game offers a useful example for thinking about how games can include LGBTQ content holistically and not simply via same-sex romance options.

Leisure Suit Larry (*LSL*) is a comedic, adult video game series first released in 1987 and created by Al Lowe for Sierra On-Line. The company invested little in the original game. It was wholly written and programmed by Lowe, and the art was done by a single artist, Mark Crowe. Lowe was also asked to forego any up-front payment in exchange for a generous cut of the royalties on each game sold.[2] Although some distributors refused to sell or advertise it, blogger Jimmy Maher writes that "by the summer of 1988, the game's one-year anniversary, *Leisure Suit Larry in the Land of the Lounge Lizards* had become the biggest game Sierra had ever released that wasn't a *King's Quest*."[3] It has enjoyed continued cult popularity ever since.

Prior to a 2004 reboot of the franchise, *LSL* was a point-and-click adventure game series where players guided Larry Laffer, a middle-aged virgin (in the first game), through a series of interactions with women he was trying to seduce. The rebooted series from publisher Vivendi, created without Lowe and criticized by him, features Larry's nephew Larry Lovage.[4] The newer games have three-dimensional (3D) graphics and more movement challenges than logic puzzles. *LSL: Magna Cum Laude* (High Voltage Software, 2004), for example, requires players to navigate a smiling sperm around obstacles in a scrolling bar across the bottom of the screen. Successful navigation makes Larry more or less successful in his endeavors to seduce women. Not counting remakes and spin-off games, there are eight games in the main *LSL* series.

LSL is impressive for many "firsts" in Sierra's game development process, including beta-testing and an ability to respond to an impressive array of player inputs.[5] But *LSL* was also part of a long trend of sex-focused games. According to Maher, following Sierra's 1981 *Softporn Adventure* there was a veritable explosion of sex-themed games.[6] Conservative backlash, computer companies' hesitancy to have their products associated with adult-themed software, and software distributors' refusal to sell such software later made companies hesitant to invest in pornographic games. Following the mid-1980s game industry bust, however, publishers turned to sex games again to appeal to a largely young male computer enthusiast market. *Leather Goddesses of Phobos* from Infocom in 1986 was the first of the new wave of sex games and helped set the stage for *LSL* in 1987. Following its success, game developer Ken Williams at Sierra tasked Al Lowe with updating *Softporn Adventure* and making it funny.[7]

There is little academic research on *LSL*, although it is used as a passing reference in many pieces about sex and sexuality in games, and none address its LGBTQ content.[8] LGBTQ characters' gender and sexuality in the series are often conveyed via stereotypical signifiers (e.g., men acting effeminately or women acting masculine). This should not be read as bad in and of itself because as film scholar Richard Dyer discusses, sexuality is difficult to represent outside of those performative codes.[9] What are often critiqued as negative stereotypes are performances of identity that are a part of some LGBTQ peoples' lives (i.e., there are gay men who perform effeminately; there are women who identify as butch).

FIGURE 13.1
Shablee in *Leisure Suit Larry 6* (1993).

Dismissing them as unrealistic or bad dismisses people who are often marginalized within LGBTQ communities. Dyer argues that when we critique representations of homosexuality, rather than focus on questions of accuracy, we should focus on the purpose of using those stereotypes in the text. Are stereotypes used to demean and make other, or are they used as performative clues to signal a character's sexuality? How does *LSL* use LGBTQ characters?

Across six of the eight total *LSL* games, there are nine main non-player characters (NPCs) and several background LGBTQ characters. In *LSL 3* (1989), for example, Larry's wife Kalalau has left him for Bobbi, "an Amazonian, Harley-riding, former-cannibal, lesbian, slot-machine repairwoman." The game ends with Larry and a woman named Patti being captured by a tribe of lesbian cannibals. *LSL 6* (1993) has Gary, the gay towel-stand attendant; Shablee, "a dark-skinned make-up artist" who Larry discovers later is a transgender woman (see figure 13.1); and Cavaricchi, an aerobics instructor that on some sites fans have described as either bisexual or lesbian.[10]

In the reboot of the series *Leisure Suit Larry: Magna Cum Laude* (High Voltage Software, 2004), Larry Lovage seduces a fellow college student named Ione, who is interested in feminist poetry. Later in the game, she has come out as a lesbian and is now dating her bisexual roommate, Luba. During one sequence of the game Larry runs into Ione at the gay bar Spartacus. Finally, *Leisure Suit Larry: Box Office Bust* (Team17, 2009) includes a reportedly bisexual pornographic movie star, Damone LaCoque. In most of these cases, these characters are part of the overarching humor for why Larry fails so dramatically in his search for sex and love. He either goes after women who are uninterested in him or is pursued by people he is uninterested in.

It is interesting that even as the games' representations of gender and sexuality are problematic, they do show a wide variety of types of LGBTQ people. Each character draws on a different trope of LGBTQ representation, and the early games even have queer people of color. Bobbi is a classic "dykes on bikes" type of lesbian character and, although she does not appear in the game, is described as a native of the same fictional approximation of a Pacific Island Larry's wife Kalalau is from. Although the couple might mimic a tradition of showing queer women in butch–femme relationships, the representation of two Pacific Islander women together is rare in any medium. Shablee is used as the butt of a transphobic joke, but she is, as far as we know, the first transgender woman of color to appear in a game. She falls into the trope of an overly flirtatious and sexualized transwoman of color, one who uses her sex appeal to influence Larry to get things for her. Yet, until the final moment of their date, she is represented as a desirable woman who knows what she wants. The post-2004 reboot games are actually more problematic in many ways, and all of the LGBTQ characters appear to be white, including all the patrons of Spartacus. Marking Damone as bisexual involves a problematic conflating of sex work with sexual identity. Ione is clearly meant as a parody of the "typical college feminist" who inevitably "becomes" a lesbian and cuts off all her hair, while Luba is represented as an open-to-anyone (when drunk) bisexual. Although the entire series is about sexual humor, nonheterosexual and noncisgender characters occupy a particularly marginalized space in that humor. The jokes being told or shown, imply a player who has a similar identity to Larry (i.e., a heterosexual, cisgendered male). Certainly, actual fans of the game run the gamut of sexual and gender identities, but LGBTQ characters in this game are used in a marginalizing fashion. Returning to Dyer, the stereotypes deployed in their representation are meant to reinforce their marginalization.[11] Moreover, in the earlier games these characters' sexual identities are usually something to be discovered rather than an outward marker of their difference to be made fun of by Larry. This allows for a bit more opportunity of LGBTQ players themselves to be in on, and not just part of, the joke.

LGBTQ content also includes passing references found in the background or ambiance of the games. For example, in the first *LSL* game (1987) there are comedians the player can watch perform. Several of the jokes told are homophobic or are at least derogatory against LGBTQ people and women generally. In *Leisure Suit Larry 5: Passionate Patti Does a Little Undercover Work* (Sierra On-Line, 1991) there is an advertisement in the New York airport that reads "Gay?

Lesbian? Divorced? Single? Widowed? Depressed? Sorry, but the Blecchnaven Center offers weekly seminars for happy straight couples only." It is a random passing reference, which is seemingly unnecessary and inconsequential, but that makes its inclusion all the more purposeful. Every choice made in game design is intentional, and so we must ask, "What was the purpose of including such an unnecessary slight to homosexuals via a background ad?" Clearly it was meant for humor, as were the passing references to lesbian cannibals in *LSL 3*, but the humor was clearly at the expense of, not for, LGBTQ people. Interestingly, however, when the original game was released and distributors were refusing to openly display it and, in some cases, carry the game, Maher reports that "Ken Williams himself got nervous enough that he ordered all of the jokes about 'gay life' to be removed from future versions."[12] What drove this decision is unclear, however. Perhaps it came from a concern that references to homosexuality were crossing a line in a game that was already offending mainstream sensibilities. Alternatively, perhaps in the late 1980s and the rise of queer activism following the AIDS crisis, the company didn't want to be known as the software firm that traded in homophobic jokes.

Turning to the ludic (or play) and narrative aspects of the game, this marginalization of LGBTQ content is reinforced. The goal of the game is helping Larry successfully perform his role as a heterosexual, white, cisgendered male by having sex with various women.[13] In a game where heterosexual masculinity is the goal, however, one logical way to impede that goal and help make sexuality and gender funny is through LGBTQ characters and themes. At the end of *LSL 2* (1988), for example, Larry marries Kalalau. To continue the series, at least without dramatically rethinking what the goal of each game would be, Larry had to become single again. Certainly his wife could have left him for another man, but given how regularly homosexuality is used for humor in the series, a lesbian relationship provided a narrative twist to transition into a third game.

The ludic–narrative intersections in later games are more negatively framed. In *LSL 6* for example, Gary flirts with Larry throughout the game, but if Larry flirts back the game ends with an image of Larry and Gary holding hands and walking off into the sunset and the following text: "What an ignominious end to a sterling career as the ultimate swinging single!" In a game where the player is tasked with helping Larry get the ladies, his finding love with another man is apparently shameful. The mild homophobia of this "gay game over," however, is nothing compared to the explicit transphobia of Larry's reaction to Shablee. Larry tries to seduce her by finding a dress she's been searching for. In thanks she invites him to the beach for a midnight swim. Once they start to have sex Larry discovers she has a penis and begins to retch and spit on his hands and knees near the ocean. The screen goes dark, but the audio implies Shablee rapes Larry. The next scene shows Larry in a bathroom gargling furiously with mouthwash. He then proceeds to go back to the beach, however, and happily picks up the champagne Shablee left on the beach, proclaiming with a smile: "I earned this!" indicating the sex was not as traumatic as one might expect. The transphobic narrative is oppressive enough, but this scene also subtly reinforces the assumption that men (at least "real men") cannot be raped. Rape is punchline because there is no trauma to deal with after the fact.

In *LSL: Magna Cum Laude*, there are a great many more actions Larry can engage in tied to LGBTQ themes. Intending to foreshadow her sexual identity reveal later in the game, when Ione and Larry finally have sex she asks him to use a strap-on dildo instead of his penis. Later in the game, after meeting them in Spartacus, a gay bar, Larry eventually proclaims that he is gay and walks Ione and Luba back to their room to watch them have sex. This interaction results in the player getting a double-ended purple dildo as a trophy. In Spartacus there are also several different mini-games for Larry to play. In one a man named Julius wants the player to take pictures of the scantily clad, muscular Helmut (more points for crotch shots), although Larry can also sell these pictures to other bar patrons. He can also, after telling Ione he is gay, try to impress the gay men at the club by dancing with them via a rhythm mini-game.

Interestingly, although graphically the games became richer as time progressed, the relative agency of the player in exploring actions and reactions was reduced. In the early games much of pleasure is derived from typing in various words and seeing how the game responds (including seeing which nonnormative responses the designer accounted for). In *LSL 3*, Larry accidentally ends up in a woman's burlesque costume after having sex with her between acts. The player can go through a variety of inputs before realizing that "dance" is the only one that allows Larry to successfully move on (i.e., embracing gender nonconformity is the answer to the puzzle). In later games, however, players are asked to navigate kinesthetic challenges rather than solve riddles. The playful exploration of a variety of sexual or gender expressions in the earlier games is reduced to generally one-liners or sight gags in the later games.

These games span three decades, and although some specific aspects of the types of LGBTQ representation changed, the core messages that male homosexuality is undesirable, female homosexuality is only important to the extent that it is titillating to men, gender nonconformity is a mark of deviance, and transgender people are a joke are consistent. This challenges easy assumptions about the inclusion of marginalized groups in media being a story of linear and evolutionary progress. The tongue-and-cheek edge of the series' humor certainly makes as much fun of Larry as it does the various NPCs I have described, but in the end the player is meant to be on Larry's side. Heterosexual masculinity is joked about in the games, but it is not The Joke.

The developers' politics are clearly written into these games. In one interview Lowe claims the games were feminist because the women always get the upper hand and were smarter than Larry.[14] This demonstrates a *profound* misunderstanding of feminist politics. As Maher describes, the game "is at heart an exercise in bullying, looking down on safe targets from a position of privilege and letting fly."[15] Even Lowe's claims for why the game is appealing support Maher's critique. Lowe asserts, "The guys like him because even they aren't as dorky as Larry. It's someone they can feel superior to, no matter how bad off they are. And I think the reason women like the game . . . because they've all dated a jerk like that. And I think the games were very feminist, pro-female."[16] The end of *LSL 2* belies Lowe's claim that the game is feminist, however. The final text screens of the game read, "As we leave our hero. . . . we ask ourselves the burning question. . . . Is women's lib really dead? Is there still a feminist movement? . . . or will Al Lowe have to write yet another of these Silly Sin-phonies?"

According to Lowe, the "Boss" against which *LSL* is fighting, on a meta-level, is feminism. Every joke about folks whose very existence challenges normative heterosexual white masculinity are always more than jokes; they are attacks. Although the series attempts to use humor to undercut its own oppressive messages, it can never really escape the politics of its design. The takeaway, however, need not simply be "Leisure Suit Larry" is oppressive. Throughout the series LG-BTQ content is actually integral to the narrative. Looking past its sophomoric humor, designers operating under a different framework and politics could gain some useful insights from *LSL* for making a lighthearted game that represents a diversity of LGBTQ people. The act of tracing LGBTQ representation in games, in any medium, is not to simply document what has been. Rather, it is a starting point in figuring out why things are the way they are and then imagining how we can make things differently.

NOTES

1 Adrienne Shaw, *LGBTQ Game Archive*, accessed August 18, 2016, www.lgbtqgamearchive.com.

2 Jimmy Maher, "Leisure Suit Larry in the Land of the Lounge Lizards," *The Digital Antiquarian*, August 15, 2015, accessed September 12, 2016, www.filfre.net.

3 Maher, "Leisure Suit Larry."

4 Brenda Brathwaite, *Sex in Video Games* (Middletown, DE: Brenda Brathwaite, 2013); and Chris Kohler, "20 Years, Still Middle-Age: Two Decades of Leisure Suit Larry," *1up.com*, August 8, 2007, accessed September 12, 2016, www.1up.com.

5 Maher, "Leisure Suit Larry"; and Matt Barton, "Matt Chat 50 Part 1: Leisure Suit Larry Featuring Al Lowe," YouTube video, 10:02, published February 21, 2010, accessed September 12, 2016, https://www.youtube.com/watch?v=9PGGEFQdZuw.

6 Jimmy Maher, "Leather Goddesses of Phobos (or, Sex Comes to the Micros- Again)," *The Digital Antiquarian*, March 5, 2015, accessed September 12, 2016, www.filfre.net; and Al Lowe, "What Is Softporn?" *Al Lowe's Humor Site*, n.d., accessed August 18, 2016, www.allowe.com.

7 Maher, "Leisure Suit Larry."

8 Sue Ellen-Case, "The Hot Rod Bodies of Cybersex," in *Feminist Theory and the Body*, ed. Janet Price and Margrit Shildrick (New York: Routledge, 1999), 141.

9 Richard Dyer, "Stereotyping," in *The Columbia Reader on Lesbians and Gay men in Media, Society, and Politics*, ed. Larry P. Gross and James D. Woods (New York: Columbia University Press, 1999), 297–301.

10 "Leisure Suit Larry 6: Shape Up or Slip Out!" *Wikipedia*, n.d., accessed September 12, 2016, https://en.wikipedia.org.

11 Dyer, "Stereotyping."

12 Maher, "Leisure Suit Larry."

13 In the interest of space I do not go into the long histories of how different groups of men of color are represented as overly sexual or desexualized but will mention in brief that it would be hard to imagine a US-produced game about a black man or Asian man in Larry's role with whom the player is meant to identify.

14 Barton, "Matt Chat 50 Part 1: Leisure Suit Larry."

15 Maher, "Leisure Suit Larry."

16 Barton, "Matt Chat 50 Part 1: Leisure Suit Larry."

FURTHER READING

Benshoff, Henry M., and Sean Griffin. *Queer Images: A History of Gay and Lesbian Film in America*. Lanham, MD: Rowman & Littlefield, 2006.

Consalvo, Mia. "Hot Dates and Fairy-Tale Romances: Studying Sexuality in Video Games." In *The Video Game Theory Reader*, edited by Mark J. P. Wolf and Bernard Perron, 171–194. New York: Routledge, 2003.

Greer, Stephen. "Playing Queer: Affordances for Sexuality in *Fable* and *Dragon Age*." *Journal of Gaming & Virtual Worlds* 5 (2013): 3–21.

Shaw, Adrienne. "Putting the Gay in Games: Cultural Production and GLBT Content in Video Games." *Games and Culture* 4 (2009): 228–253.

14

The Queerness and Games Conference
Community

BONNIE RUBERG

Abstract: Studying video games most often means analyzing games themselves, but understanding the cultures and communities that surround games is equally important for those who are interested in how games relate to identity, diversity, and activism. Through a discussion of the Queerness and Games Conference, an annual event that brings together scholars and designers to explore the intersection of lesbian, gay, bisexual, transgender, and queer issues and video games, Bonnie Ruberg demonstrates how community is constructed at the margins of game culture, with an emphasis on the power as well as the pitfalls of creating space for self-expression and difference.

Understanding video games is about more than analyzing games themselves. When talking about game studies, it is common to talk about critiquing games as media objects—that is, deconstructing and reimagining games through various theoretical lenses. However, to make sense of the relationship between video games and society, considering the cultures that surround games is equally crucial. Games do not exist in a vacuum. As Mary Flanagan and Helen Nissenbaum have argued, games reflect the values and beliefs of the people who make and play them.[1] Even "fun" games, which do not seem to have a political or social message, communicate values with real-world implications. The same can be said for the importance of thinking about the people behind video games. All games are the products of the developers who build them, whether or not they are part of the professional "games industry," and all games are played by a wide range of individuals, all of whom bring their own identity and unique set of experiences to the game. If we only talk about games and not about people, we miss a huge piece of the equation.

Video games have long been intertwined with what is broadly called "games culture." Games culture refers to the activities and conversations that take place around games. Historically, before playing video games became mostly something that people do at home, game arcades were important places for the formation of games culture. Today, games culture largely takes shape in online spaces like websites, forums, and segments of social media that focus on video games. Feminists, people of color, queer people, and others have condemned games culture as toxic and reactionary.[2] Indeed, starting in 2014, a wave of large-scale, internet-based harassment campaigns targeted at "social justice warriors" made it clear that games culture can be a truly dangerous place for those who do not fit the traditional picture of the straight, white, male, cisgender "gamer."[3] Yet, the truth is that there are many games cultures, not just one. When the members of these subcultures are connected in some way—perhaps through events they attend off-line or through playing and discussing games online—they can be called a community. Some communities are vast; others are small. Examples of game communities include the "speedrunning" community, a network of players who compete to see who can complete games the fastest, and the "modding" community, who crack open and modify the code of existing games.

Community is an especially important topic for thinking about video games and identity. Identity relates to video games in a number of different ways. Analyzing the representation of characters onscreen is one approach that game studies scholars take to understanding identity. Investigating how players do or not identify with game characters is another. However, equally meaningful for identity are the subcultures and communities in which players take part. Often these communities are founded around shared life experiences and interests. For example, the organization I Need Diverse Games, which began as the Twitter hashtag #ineeddiversegames, has formed a community of game makers and players who share a commitment to increasing visibility around issues such as those faced by people of color in video games. This example also illustrates how community is a key component of the connection between diversity and activism. Because nonwhite, nonmale, and queer folks, to name only a few groups, have been pushed to the sidelines for much of video games' history, community organizing represents a valuable opportunity for marginalized people to come together and make their voices heard.

In the fall of 2012, three collaborators and I set out to build a kind of community we had never seen in games culture: one specifically dedicated to the intersection of queerness and video games. *Queerness* is a slippery word, but it is also a powerful one, and rich with meaning. Originally a pejorative, today *queer* has been largely reclaimed as an umbrella term that encompasses all gender identities and sexual orientations that fall outside the bounds of "heteronormativity"—the dominant cultural expectations for what it means to "normal." Used in this sense, each of the identities in the LGBT+ acronym (which stands for lesbian, gay, bisexual, and transgender) could be called "queer," although not every LGBT+ person identifies with that word. Especially in the academic context, *queerness* also has a number of conceptual meanings. The field of "queer theory," which was established in the late 1980s and early 1990s by now-famous scholars such as Judith Butler, approaches queerness as a way of desiring, acting, or simply being differently.[4] In this second sense, queerness is still linked to the real-life experiences of LGBTQ people, but it is also a name for disrupting expectations around identity and power.

Any new community faces obstacles, but the creation of a queer games community posed a number of particular challenges. LGBTQ people have rarely had an easy time in games culture. Video games with LGBTQ protagonists are still few and far between and homophobia is an ongoing problem in competitive online games, to cite just a few of the many reasons why LGBTQ players often feel discriminated against (see Shaw's chapter in this collection for more on LGBTQ game representations). Although private LGBTQ guilds in games like *World of Warcraft* (Blizzard Entertainment, 2004) have existed since the early 2000s, few spaces explicitly designed for LGBTQ gaming were yet available when my collaborators, and I began thinking about the type of community we wanted to build. Because of all this, we knew that video games culture desperately needed a place where queer people who cared about games could share their ideas—but we also knew that the very people we hoped to bring together might worry about feeling unsafe. Forming a queer games community was also difficult because many non-LGBTQ people still operate under the misconception that video games have little to do with queer issues. The fact that few "triple-A" video games, the industry term for large-budget games, include LGBTQ characters incorrectly suggests that LGBTQ experiences are not relevant to video games.

We knew differently, however. My collaborators and I were LGBTQ players ourselves: a mixed group of professional game developers and game academics. What we had in common was a passion for video games and the conviction that queerness in games was a pressingly important area that we, as a wider games community, needed to be discussing in the open. We wanted a space to call our own, a community to call our own, and so we built it.

In 2013, we founded the Queerness and Games Conference (QGCon) (see figure 14.1). Held annually, QGCon is a two-day conference dedicated to LGBTQ issues and video games. It is usually attended by about 300 people, many of whom travel from across the country or even the world. For its first three years, QGCon took place at the University of California, Berkeley; for its fourth year, the conference was held at the University of Southern California in Los Angeles. Unlike most

FIGURE 14.1 The organizers of the 2017 Queerness and Games Conference, hosted at the University of Southern California in Los Angeles, take a moment mid-event to show their excitement. Organizers, from left to right, are Dietrich Squinkifer, Christopher Goetz, Teddy Diana Pozo, Terran Pierola, Bonnie Ruberg, Jasmine Aguilar, Chuck Roslof, and Chelsea Howe (below banner).

conferences at universities, however, QGCon is not purely an academic event. Sessions include not only talks and panels but also video game "postmortems" (a format in which game designers reflect on the process of developing a recent game) and an arcade of "indie" games from queer designers. Over the years, presenters have spoken on a wide range of topics—from transgender representation in games to the obstacles faced by queer of color folks in the games industry to how to design games with "queer" rules. The event is founded on an ethos of inclusion and financial accessibility. Among many other things, building a diverse community requires thinking about who can and cannot afford to attend. Although attendees are invited to donate to the event, tickets are always available for free.

Of all the forms that our new queer games community could take, we chose to create a conference because we believed that face-to-face interactions were a crucial part of building meaningful, dynamic connections between LGBTQ game makers, players, scholars, and allies. While most contemporary gaming takes place in virtual spaces, such as massively multiplayer online games, there is a thriving tradition in games culture of players coming together off-line. "Cons" (short for "conventions") are among the most common types of these events. At cons, video game fans gather to celebrate the games they love and connect with others who share their interests. Other forms of in-person community game events are also becoming increasingly popular. One example is the "game jam," where participants work together over a brief but exciting period to develop their own games. Although QGCon is not a "con" in a traditional sense—nor is it a game jam—the conference takes inspiration from events like these, which demonstrate the power of building community off-line as well as on the internet.

While no event is perfect and no community above critique, QGCon has been immensely successful in building a community around queerness and video games that brings together individuals from across North America and beyond. This community is made up not only of the people who attend the conference—some only once, some year after year—but also those who join in the larger dialogue the conference has sparked. For many attendees, and for each year's cohort of conference co-organizers, it is truly moving to spend one weekend each year with fellow LGBTQ folks and allies. In the decade-plus that I have been attending video game events, I have never seen such diversity of gender identity as I do at QGCon. Yet it would be misleading to say that there is only one QGCon community. As is true with any community, ours is also made up of a number of overlapping subcommunities.[5] One of the most vibrant has been the network of academics now working on "queer game studies"—a new scholarly paradigm that has galvanized around the conference.[6] Queer game studies is bringing research on LGBTQ issues and video games into universities across North America, Western Europe, and beyond. In 2014 and 2015 QGCon also expanded to include a three-month workshop to teach queer students with limited prior technical experience how to build their own video games.[7] This created yet another subcommunity: a community of students who have since entered the workforce and have become the next generation of game professionals.

One of our biggest goals for QGCon, and also our biggest challenges, was creating a community that bridged academia and the games industry. Before returning to graduate school for my doctorate in new media, I worked as a games and technology journalist. I knew from my experience interviewing professional game developers that there was a surprising amount of bad blood between those who make games and those who study them. Not uncommonly, developers see game studies scholars as elites who criticize games from their ivory towers. While I have encountered academics from outside game studies who do look down their noses at video games, in truth those of us who make game studies our life's work have the greatest respect for games. My collaborators and I believed strongly that industry and academia had an immense amount to learn from one another. Facilitating those barrier-breaking conversations was a top priority, so the conference was designed from the ground up to be welcoming to attendees from different backgrounds. Over the years, we have seen this approach foster connections, collaborations, and friendships that cross professional divides—or even begin to break them.

Just as video games do not exist in a cultural vacuum, neither does the Queerness and Games Conference. A number of other important factors have contributed to the formation of a queer games community. The same year that QGCon was founded also saw the birth of events like GaymerX, an LGBTQ gamer fan convention that regularly attracts thousands of attendees each year. Other alternative games conferences, like Different Games and Lost Levels, were starting up as well, helping promote dialogues around diversity in video games. QGCon also came into being side by side with the rise of what could be termed the "queer games avant-garde." This is a movement, loosely defined and still ongoing, of LGBTQ game makers using accessible development tools like Twine to design small-scale video games about their own queer experiences. The work of some of these designers has made national news, spreading their mainstream visibility and the impact they have on games culture.[8] Other queer game communities continue to arise from outside the conference and related events. Fan cultures, for example, are increasingly bringing queerness to video games by reimagining game narratives and characters as queer.

A strong community is not necessarily made up of people who always agree, and QGCon, too, has had its share of internal conflict. Often these moments of friction arise around differing ideas about what makes a constructive dialogue and who should or should not be given the floor to speak. One such disagreement arose during the second conference, in 2014, about a speaker who had helped develop a game with arguably homophobic content. Some members of the QGCon community felt strongly that this speaker should be removed from the program. Others believed that his talk would start an important discussion among conference attendees about how LGBTQ characters are portrayed. Ultimately, we organizers decided against cancelling the speaker's talk—but we also asked him to take part in a live question-and-answer with another game developer who was critical of his game in the hope of creating an opportunity for productive self-reflection. This example demonstrates how conflict within a community can be highly productive. Our community spoke, and together we made the conference better.

Logistically, creating community is easier said than done—especially when doing so requires breaking new ground. Each year at QGCon, we learn new things about the nitty-gritty details of making our event more inclusive. Even when these things seem small, they can have a big effect. In our first year, for example, we knew that we wanted to designate a bathroom as "gender neutral." However, we made the mistake of placing the gender-neutral bathroom in the basement, making it the hardest for attendees to reach and creating the impression that we valued binary gender identities (represented by "men's" and "women's" restrooms) over nonbinary ones. At the end of the event, we held a town hall where attendees provided feedback on the conference—a tradition we repeat each year. The attendees not only pointed out our mistake but also suggested ways to improve in the future. Moments like these are key for the creation of communities. Individuals become community members when they take an active role. By contributing their own knowledge and passion to the group, they make their place within it.

The Queerness and Games Conference will not go on forever, and the communities that have emerged around it are already changing. This is how it should be. QGCon has been a springboard for a wealth of new conversations and connections at the intersection of queerness and video games. Now our community members are going out in the world, forming their own communities and growing the commitment to LGBTQ issues in video games that we all share. Whatever the future of queerness and video games brings, community will have played a crucial part in getting us there. As new challenges surface, it will continue to be an invaluable tool for those at the margins of video games.

NOTES

1 Mary Flanagan and Helen Nissenbaum, *Values at Play in Digital Games* (Cambridge, MA: MIT Press, 2014), 1.

2 Leigh Alexander, "'Gamers' Don't Have to Be Your Audience. 'Gamers' Are Over," *Gamasutra*, August 28, 2014, accessed October 11, 2016, www.gamasutra.com.

3 Nick Wingfield, "Feminist Critics of Video Games Facing Threats in 'GamerGate' Campaign," *NYTimes.com*, October 15, 2014, accessed October 11, 2016, www.nytimes.com.

4 Judith Butler, *Gender Trouble: Feminism and the Subversion of Identity* (New York: Routledge, 1990).

5 Adrienne Shaw, "The Problem with Community," in *Queer Game Studies*, ed. Bonnie Ruberg and Adrienne Shaw (Minneapolis: University of Minnesota Press, 2017), 153–162.

6 An introduction to the work of queer game studies, as well as a list of current work in this area, is available in my online piece "Queer Game Studies 101: An Introduction to the Field (2016)," published June 20, 2016, accessed October 11, 2016, http://ourglasslake.com.

7 Christopher Goetz, "Building Queer Community: Report on the Queerness and Games Design Workshop," *First Person Scholar*, February 25, 2015, accessed October 11, 2016, www.firstpersonscholar.com.

8 Laura Hudson, "Twine, The Video-Game Technology for All," *New York Times*, November 19, 2014, accessed October 11, 2016, www.nytimes.com.

FURTHER READING

Anthropy, Anna. *Rise of the Videogame Zinesters: How Freaks, Normals, Amateurs, Artists, Dreamers, Drop-outs, Queers, Housewives, and People Like You Are Taking Back an Art Form.* New York: Seven Stories Press, 2012.

kopas, merritt. *Video Games for Humans: Twine Authors in Conversation.* New York: Instar Books, 2015.

Ruberg, Bonnie, and Adrienne Shaw. *Queer Game Studies.* Minneapolis: University of Minnesota Press, 2017.

Shaw, Adrienne. *Gaming at the Edge: Sexuality and Gender at the Margins of Gamer Culture.* Minneapolis: University of Minnesota Press, 2014.

15

NBA 2K16
Race

TREAANDREA M. RUSSWORM

Abstract: The story-driven career mode in 2K Sports' basketball series has evolved from a simple character creation system to become the most anticipated and popular component of the annually released game. In closely examining the use of face-scan technologies and the story of *NBA 2K16*'s MyCareer mode, which includes the Spike Lee directed film-within-a game, *Livin' da Dream*, TreaAndrea M. Russworm explores the ways in which race and a lack of empathy have become central to what it means for gamers to simulate NBA superstar greatness.

The video game industry has a racial representation problem. It is tempting to think of this problem quantitatively, as a problem defined by a lack of "diverse" and "inclusive" characters and avatars—as a problem that can be addressed by simply creating more games with more racially diverse characters. Yet the video game industry's problems with racial representation are much more complicated than this. The representation problem has less to do with the pitiably limited number of characters of color who appear as playable protagonists in games and more to do with the ideological work those characters facilitate, including how gamers *feel* about and express empathy for such characters when they do happen to appear in games across genres.

Take sports games, for example, a segment of the industry that both generates millions of dollars of revenue each year and has always featured the highest number of racially diverse character representations in all of gaming.[1] Not only are sports games the "crown jewel" of the industry in terms of revenue; sports games are also necessarily diverse or, as David J. Leonard has explained, "eight out of ten black male video game characters are sports competitors."[2] If approximately 75 percent of the National Basketball Association (NBA) is African American, then thinking quantitatively about racial representation in sports games makes the obvious only clearer. That is, of course, the best-selling *NBA 2K* (Visual Concepts, 1999–) series would be considered "diverse"—the games in the series necessarily include a comparable number of black "characters" in creating, and in most cases motion capturing, the digital reproductions of actual NBA stars such as LeBron James and Stephen Curry. Beyond the numbers, however, sports games also offer *narrative* experiences, just like more traditional story-based games that feature diverse character representations: *The Walking Dead* (Telltale Games, 2014–2018), *Mafia III* (Hangar 13, 2016), and *Watch Dogs 2* (Ubisoft Montreal, 2016), to name a few. This chapter proposes that *NBA 2K16*, which in recent years has become a narrative game, struggles not at the level of visually representing racial difference. Instead, *NBA 2K16*'s competing cinematic story and simulation game mechanics disrupt gamic attempts at creating a sense of empathy for its fictional African American characters. In this case, the use of face scanning technologies, which would ostensibly strengthen an emotional connection to game world characters, seemed to further preclude immersion and empathetic association for nonblack players.

So how did a basketball simulation become a narrative game? Acclaimed sports game developer Visual Concepts turned its industry-leading *NBA 2K* series into a narrative game by gradually tweaking its "MyCareer" experience, a mode in the game that has catered to fans wanting storytelling and role-playing along with basketball gameplay. Once face scanning technologies became widely available with the use of smartphones and built-in console cameras, Visual Concepts and publisher 2K Games began fully marketing "MyCareer" as a playable "feature film."[3] These technological innovations enabled the creation of realistic digital self-representations and intensified a need for professionally written and directed stories that could help gamers feel even more emotionally connected to their in-game doppelgangers.

In an effort to do more than represent racial diversity quantitatively, MyCareer's fictional backstories have also centralized racial representation and thematized African American social and cultural contexts. *NBA 2K16*'s culmination of these efforts is a 90-minute film-within-a-game, *Livin' da Dream*, directed by Spike Lee, the legendary African American independent filmmaker known for films such as *Do the Right Thing* (1989) and *Malcolm X* (1992). To stress the significance of his directorial debut in a video game, Lee appears on camera at the beginning of *Livin' da Dream* and announces,

> This year *NBA 2K16* will take a new approach to your MyCareer story. Expand your world to something bigger and better than ever before. There is a lot more to being a great baller than what you see on the court. High school, college, choosing

an agent, getting drafted, developing a personal brand, and family, the pressures of stardom are very real for you and everyone around you but the rewards can be equally as powerful—if you're willing to put in the work. So let me tell you a story.

Then as the live-action session transitions to the digital realm with a jump cut to a digital representation of Lee standing in front of digital versions of the actors who were rehearsing, the lead actor onscreen is replaced with a digital representation of the gamer's likeness. "Shazam," Lee says, "step into my world where you can be the story."

Livin' da Dream was created by alternating lengthy, noninteractive cutscenes with the interactive gameplay of just a few highlights in your player character's early career. In the story that materializes as a result of this alteration between cutscene and limited basketball gameplay, with a nickname of "Frequency Vibrations" (Freq) you are born in Harlem, New York, to two working-class black parents. You also have a black fraternal twin sister with whom you share a close relationship. When the story begins, you are a high school basketball phenom, the very best at your position. With your parents, twin sister, and best friend (Vic) by your side, you select a college, play basketball for a year, and decide to become eligible for the NBA draft. As you ascend through the ranks of NBA stardom, attract sponsorships, capitalize on your talent, and turn your image into a carefully mediated brand, the only real blemish on your career is your association with your best friend. Vic, your "boy" from back in the day, crashes wild parties, often gets arrested, publicizes his connection to you (proudly broadcasts his status as a "Friend of Freq"), remains completely unfiltered on social media, and generally offends your family, your agent, and your team's owner. Proximity to him places you in jeopardy of violating the NBA's "morality clause." After everyone continually warns you to sever ties with him, you and Vic get into a heated argument (see figure 15.1) about your undisclosed past: a time when he took the blame for an accidental homicide you committed.

At the end of your first year in the NBA, Vic commits suicide in your car by high-speed chase. After he dies, even though you are in mourning for your friend, you are left to focus on your auspicious career as a true baller. *Livin' da Dream* ends with Vic's on-camera delivery of a poignant suicide monologue. At the completion of this narrative experience, MyCareer continues as a more traditional basketball sim played interactively without the further use of cutscenes or other storytelling devices.

Throughout the game's opening introduction of a black family drama, the player character Freq maintains a complex emotional connection to Vic. For instance, in one cutscene, a documentary segment where Spike Lee can be heard off camera asking Freq interview questions about the negative media attention

FIGURE 15.1
Vic and my player
character Freq.

Vic has been creating, Freq resolutely and compassionately defends his friend: "Let me tell you about Vic. He has his bad rap. . . . I understand some of his judgments might shadow his actual character. He's not that at all. . . . We actually have love for each other. We're brothers. Blood couldn't make us closer at all." In this scene, Freq acknowledges Vic's "actual character" as different from the perception of his mediated image. As the story progresses, Freq argues that there is essentially a tragic misrecognition of Vic, especially by the media and by the team owner who bans Vic from attending NBA games as a part of Freq's entourage. This narrative emphasis on Vic's complexity is further accentuated by Spike Lee's directorial style, including the use of a dolly and revolving camera to emphasize character introspection and interiority. The commitment to depicting Vic's emotional complexity is further accentuated by the film-within-a-game's diversion of screen time from the NBA star to Vic, who speaks directly and unguarded at the end of the narrative. In the concluding monologue of the story Vic reflects on *his* dreams, *his* hopes, *his* childhood experiences of growing with parents who died from AIDS. He asks those who would judge him indiscriminately to "stop, listen and really get to know me, Victor Van Lier."

Despite the use of filmmaking techniques designed to complicate and humanize the character, in echoing the sentiments expressed by the other characters in the story ("don't be a hero, cut that zero"), many longtime fans of the My-Career mode despised Vic. Countless blog posts complain that Spike Lee's story "broke the game." There is a Reddit thread called "Vic Hate Train," a Gamefaqs poll titled "Does Anyone Actually Like Vic Van Lier?" (249 participants voted "no," 80 "yes"), and there are several Vic parody death machinima.[4] Why was there such contempt for the character in fan communities? How did this more robust approach to storytelling in a sports game combined with the use of face scan technologies that placed gamers in visual proximity to Vic fail to create an engaged and empathetic gaming experience?

Appropriated from the study of art and aesthetics to psychology, empathy originally referred to an individual's capacity to feel one's "way into an inanimate work of art."[5] In video game studies empathy is often discussed as a cherished design goal. As Katherine Isbister argues in *How Games Move Us: Emotion by Design*, it is a mistaken assumption that playing video games "numb players to other people."[6] On the contrary, Isbister—whose work appears in this collection—contends that games can "play a powerful role in creating empathy and other strong, positive emotional experiences."[7] The bedrock of such an analysis is that games can create powerful emotions such as empathy through the careful coordination of design elements, like meaningful choice, flow, and social play (including role-playing and coordinated action with non-player-controlled characters).[8] If empathy is believed to be fostered, in part, by creating narrative opportunities to develop strong feelings and compassion toward characters who appear in fictional worlds, then, as philosopher Nancy E. Snow reminds us, there is an important distinction between feeling something *for* a character and feeling *with* a character. As Snow explains, "empathy is more accurately characterized as feeling an emotion with someone, and because the other is feeling it, than to portray it as feeling an emotion for someone, though the two phenomena are closely related and are often parts of the same complex affective experience."[9] So, to return to *Livin' da Dream*, instead of feeling antipathy *for* Vic during his monologue, truly empathetic players might have felt sorrow *with* Vic as he delivered his painful revelation that he did not fit in with Freq's pursuit of the American Dream.

How to explain the vast difference in emotional orientation between gamers and their self-represented player character Freq? Two design elements stand out as contributing to the disconnection. First, the closed narrative structure of the game (game as cinema) clashes with the open-ended simulation mechanics (game as sports sim) for which the title has been known. Second, because being "in the story" in this case also means starring in a black family drama, the tension between game as cinema and game as sports sim is inseparable from the game's representation of race. Put another way, the competing design elements are connected to the ways in which character construction—the game's default blackness—undermines empathetic role-playing.

One of the most notable aspects of the game's design is that unlike other games that also allow the customization of the player character's visual representation of race and other physical attributes (like the *Fallout* series, for example), when gamers insert themselves into MyCareer mode's story, the race of the surrounding supporting cast who appear in the cutscenes does not change. This means that when Asian, Latinx, and white gamers use the face scan technology to become their version of Freq, Freq's racial representation and skin tone onscreen changes to match the gamer's, but the character's biological parents, his twin sister, and Vic will always appear in the game as African Americans.

This fixed and default blackness is further crystalized during the many moments when the game functions as cinema, with its 90 minutes of noninteractive cutscenes. Thus, when fans of the series complained about Vic, their discontent stemmed most obviously from their engagement with the intractable role cinematic blackness plays in the game. That basketball fans could not accurately "see" themselves in these cutscenes because they could not change the race of Vic or the other non-player-controlled characters to match their own race was decried as "racist," as evidence of a "broken," "nightmare" of a game.[10] One fan wrote, "Having to be twins with a black sister and being part of a black family as a white person will never make sense to me and will make me not enjoy this my player experience."[11] Another fan complained:

> MyPlayer this year forces you to be a player named Frequency Vibrations from the projects in Brooklyn, and have an African American family with a twin sister. And it's called "Livin' Da Dream." Not joking. I'm trying to figure out how to reconcile these things as I hear the story and look at the Spaniard I have created to resemble myself. I can't decide if it's a reverse blindside or if my character is just having Rachel Dolezal type delusions [*sic*]. Spike Lee has made MyPlayer mode feel like it's choosing to exclude me, and make me feel that by participating I am appropriating a culture that is not mine. These are not things that are currently enhancing my experience.[12]

Although it might be tempting to mistake the circumstantial placement of all player characters into a black family as forced "cultural appropriation," this gamic condition only literalizes what players of all sports video games have done for decades: pretend to be someone they are not by fantasizing a superior athletic proximity to blackness. The main difference in the reception of *NBA 2K16* is that non-empathizing gamers preferred to enjoy the grand fantasy of themselves as NBA legends-in-the-making but could not stretch their imaginations to also include a familial association to blackness.

As these types of responses to the story mode indicate, for nonblack gamers there was something particularly prohibitive about role-playing as themselves *and* developing empathy for the black characters around them.[13] In addition to what these fan resistances reveal about perceived racial difference as a complicating factor in any discussion about video games and their presumed ability to create empathy, the ideological significance of *NBA 2K16*'s construction of Vic as a young black male merits some further consideration. As Freq's troubled and criminalized black friend who appears in a game that is licensed and endorsed by the NBA, Vic's violent banishment from the culture of the NBA by suicide sends a clear message that coheres with the league's long-standing punitive stance toward black player conduct. The "morality clause" that the fictional team owner uses against Freq solely because of his relationship to Vic reflects some of the ways in which sports culture writ large functions as a "space of contested racial meaning" that reinforces white supremacist assumptions about "good" versus "bad" black masculinities.[14] Or, as David J. Leonard has argued, the vilification of some black men and elevation of others in sports culture play out as its own popular "morality tale," a contest between "heroes and the villains who [are] routinely condemned, vilified and policed inside and outside of sports."[15] Relatedly, although Freq seems to understand his friend empathetically, the fact that Vic dies negates any real opportunity for the characters to serve as critiques of the NBA's prioritization of capitalistic surveillance over humanistic understanding. In the end, of course, Vic must die so that there can be no ambiguity around Freq's moral fidelity to the NBA's politicized image of respectability and exceptionalism. Yet, the way the story operates as fixed and as noninteractive before yielding to the nonnarrative simulation eliminates all opportunities for gamers to participate in these symbolic contests over racialized meaning with direct and consequential gamic action.

NOTES

1 Racial representation in sports games can be productively compared to other genres of video games, most of which have historically been criticized for lacking diverse representations. See, for example, Williams, Dmitri, Nicole Martins, Mia Consalvo, and James D. Ivory, "The Virtual Census: Representations of Gender, Race and Age in Video Games," *New Media & Society* 11, no. 5 (August 2009): 815–34.

2 David J. Leonard, "Performing Blackness: Virtual Sports and Becoming the Other in an Era of White Supremacy," in *Re:skin*, ed. Mary Flanagan and Austin Booth (Cambridge, MA, and London: MIT Press, 2009), 321, 322.

3 The game began including elliptical storytelling since the mode's debut in 2005. It is now billed as a "cinematic" experience replete with an opening film created to introduce your player as the star of his own movie. The face-scan technologies have been available in the game for the most recent releases, *2K15, 2K16, 2K17,* and *2K18.*

4 Tyus Tisdale, "Victor Van Lier Tribute (ACTUAL CAR ACCIDENT FOOTAGE)," YouTube video, 4:08, published October 20, 2015, https://www.youtube.com/watch?v=AmuaOTgwa5Q; and JaelenGames, "HOW VIC DIES! NBA 2K!^ MyCAREER (Vic's untold Story)—RockStar Editor, YouTube video, 5:11, published December 24, 2015, https://www.youtube.com/watch?v=956Fb50fNv8.

5 Warren S. Poland, "The Limits of Empathy," *American Imago* 64, no. 1 (2007): 90.

6 Katherine Isbister, *How Games Move Us: Emotion by Design* (Cambridge, MA: MIT Press, 2016), xvii.

7 Isbister, *How Games Move Us*, xvii.

8 Isbister, *How Games Move Us*, xviii.

9 Nancy E. Snow, "Empathy," *American Philosophical Quarterly* 37, no. 1 (2000): 66.

10 See, for example, this extensive Reddit thread about the game: https://www.reddit .com/r/NBA2k/comments/3mkw9e/livin_da_dream_more_like_livin_da_nightmare /#bottom-comments.

11 Comments posted by user "Schoonie30," *Metacritic* review, www.metacritic.com/user /Schoonie30.

12 The commenter is referring to the film *The Blind Side* (2009) in which an African American football player is raised by a white family. Rachel Dolezal, a former civil rights activist, made headlines for living her personal and professional life as African American until it was revealed in 2015 that she is not African American. Comments posted by user "Greedoinaspeedo," *Metacritic* review, www.metacritic.com/user/greedoinaspeedo.

13 How does the reception of this African American story compare to the reception of other black characters in video games? Although a complete answer to such a question is beyond the scope of this chapter, we can note that generally, games that feature black protagonists in lead roles (such as *Mafia III* and *Watch Dogs 2*) are less well received and reviewed by fans when compared to games that do not feature black characters. This does not mean that there are not exceptions, such as *Grand Theft Auto: San Andreas* (Rockstar North, 2004) or *The Walking Dead*, that fans seem to enjoy. However, such games tend to promote social messages about blackness that placate, rather than disrupt, ideologies of supremacy and racial bias. With its insistence that gamers see themselves as biologically related to a black family, *Livin' da Dream* makes an argument that falls outside of normative, popular representations of race in the video game industry.

14 David J. Leonard, "Never Just a Game: The Language of Sport on and off the Court," *Journal of Multicultural Discourses* 7, no. 2 (July 2012): 140.

15 Leonard, "Never Just a Game," 138.

FURTHER READING

Consalvo, Mia, Konstantin Mitgutsch, and Abe Stein, eds. *Sports Videogames*. New York: Routledge, 2013.

Oates, Thomas P., and Robert Alan Brookey, eds. *Playing to Win: Sports, Video Games, and the Culture of Play*. Bloomington: Indiana University Press, 2015.

Russworm, TreaAndrea M. "Dystopian Blackness and the Limits of Racial Empathy in *The Walking Dead* and *The Last of Us*." In *Gaming Representation: Race, Gender, and Sexuality in Video Games*, edited by Jennifer Malkowski and TreaAndrea M. Russworm, 109–128. Bloomington: Indiana University Press, 2017.

16

PaRappa the Rapper
Emotion

KATHERINE ISBISTER

Abstract: Games can evoke certain feelings in players that other media such as film and novels struggle to conjure. Katherine Isbister uses the PlayStation rhythm game *PaRappa the Rapper* to showcase core design techniques that engender emotions such as pride and affection that result from goal-oriented persistence and real-time collaboration.

What makes games fun? This is an enduring question for game scholars and game designers alike. One important aspect of the player experience is that games take us on a compelling emotional ride—evoking feelings that are interesting and satisfying moment to moment. Some of those feelings are a lot like feelings that we experience with other media—such as suspense, thrills and chills, and happiness or sadness about how narrative events play out within a story world. But there are additional feelings that games are particularly good at evoking in players—feelings that hinge on players taking consequential actions within game worlds. In this chapter, I explore the classic PlayStation game *PaRappa the Rapper* (NanaOn-Sha, 1996), drawing on both my scholarly experience in game design research and my direct experience as a player of this game to illustrate how designers evoke feelings of pride and affection in players.

Originally released for the Sony PlayStation console in 1996, *PaRappa the Rapper* was the first influential commercial rhythm game. Rhythm games are those that challenge players to synchronize gameplay actions with a beat or musical score. Other popular games of the genre include *Guitar Hero* (Harmonix, 2005), *Rock Band* (Harmonix, 2007), *Rhythm Heaven* (Nintendo SPD, 2008), and *Beat Sneak Bandit* (Simogo, 2012), to name a few. In *PaRappa*, the player learns to be a rapper who is coached by a series of MCs with different musical styles. To "rap,"

FIGURE 16.1
Parappa learns
to drive with
Instructor
Mooselini.

the player hits buttons on the controller in the right order, copying the rhythm of the rapping mentor characters. As a mentor MC raps, the player sees symbols above that character's head that correspond to buttons on the PlayStation controller—triangle, square, circle, and so on. The player must press each button at just the right time as the music plays. The game evaluates the player on a scale of "awful," "bad," "good," and "cool," shown on the right side of the screen (see figure 16.1). To complete each level, the player must manage to stay in the "good" zone for most of the song. Too many off-beat or wrong taps will drop the score to bad, then to awful, and the game will stop. After the first successful playthrough of a level, the player can also try for a "cool" rating by doing rhythmic improvisations, pressing additional buttons beyond those that are indicated, when he or she plays that level again. If the game decides the player's rap is cool enough, the MC will praise the player, then step off stage to allow a solo performance for the rest of the song.

The player's character (also known as an "avatar"), Parappa, is a naïve, young dog (see figure 16.1). Parappa's backstory and motivations are conveyed through cutscenes—prerecorded animated sequences that the player watches, which are interspersed between active gameplay levels, which set and advance a narrative background to motivate play. In the first cutscene, the player learns that Parappa's main goal is to impress and protect Sunny Funny, a daisy-headed creature. Parappa must learn different skills—such as kung fu, driving, and baking a cake—from each of his mentors as part of his efforts to woo Sunny. Of course, it's actually the player who is gaining these skills for Parappa, by performing a rap in each level's song to advance Parappa's goals. And through the process of learning and performing these raps, the player has a unique emotional experience particular to the video game medium.

Famed game designer Will Wright, who is responsible for such best-selling games as *The Sims* (Maxis, 2000), *SimCity* (Maxis, 1989), and *Spore* (Maxis, 2008), once said, "People talk about how games don't have the emotional impact of movies. I think they do—they just have a different palette. I never felt pride, or guilt, watching a movie."[1] But where does this emotional palette come from? In my book *How Games Move Us*,[2] I argue that the main difference between games and functionally fixed media like movies or novels is that players take an active role in the gaming experience, making choices that affect what happens next. While a reader or viewer can imagine making a protagonist's choices, a gamer actually makes those decisions—lots of them in fact (within the confines of what is plausible for the character as constrained by the game designer, of course). And because each choice results in feedback from the game world, great designers present players with interesting options that have emotionally resonant outcomes, including feelings such as pride and affection.

But how exactly does a game designer offer players choices that are meaningful and emotionally resonant? A primary mechanism is the player character or avatar. Avatars are the characters in a game's narrative world that are piloted by the player directly. Not all games have avatars, but they are one of the medium's most common design elements. (For more on avatars, see Gish's chapter in this collection.) An avatar serves as the player's puppet in the game world, but the puppet also ends up affecting the puppeteer. Game designers make many choices about the avatar that shape how the player feels moment to moment as they take action. Parappa is a great example of a well-designed avatar for reasons described in the following.

PaRappa's art style invites the player to easily identify with and feel connected to the titular avatar. All the game's characters, created by accomplished graphic artist Rodney Greenblat, are visually represented in a simple, cartoonish style. They look like paper cutouts living in a three-dimensional world. As cartoonist and comics theorist Scott McCloud notes, simple, stylized drawings (instead of detailed and photorealistic ones) make it easier for a person to empathize with a character's experience instead of being distracted by how it might differ from the spectator.[3] Why is this? Let's use Parappa as an example: the player does not look at Parappa and imagine him to be a dog that exists somewhere in the real world, with its own life history and preferences. Imagine if Parappa were drawn as a photorealistic German shepherd—would you find it easier or harder adopt and play as this character? For most readers, probably harder. The simplistic art style invites players to project themselves into Parappa's situation. And because it's more dreamlike than real, it becomes easier to merge player and avatar identities and goals. This is not a new phenomenon: digital games have a long history of using simple and highly abstracted art styles when depicting their virtual worlds.[4]

This aesthetic choice was first borne out of technical necessity; early computers and consoles simply could not render photo-realistic graphics. However, as time passed and as technological sophistication increased, some game designers remained committed to representing their characters and worlds in a more abstract and cartoonish visual style *precisely* because that choice made it easier for players to imagine themselves as being a part of that universe.

Another visual art style choice that shapes the player's emotions is Parappa's depiction as a wide-eyed, innocent-looking dog. His appearance as a young dog subtly encourages the player to want to take care of Parappa—to look out for him. It likewise predisposes players toward liking him and even feeling affection for him. There is a widespread tendency for people to respond to people or characters with babylike features (big eyes, round face, high forehead, small nose) with greater liking and trust. Psychologists call this the "babyface effect."[5] In the case of *PaRappa*, the designers use this psychological tendency to create the desire to protect the rapping avatar and to help him achieve his goals.

Game designers also direct the player's emotions by setting up a strong narrative frame around the avatar. The first cutscene in *PaRappa* is a dramatic scenario in which the player learns that Parappa needs to protect Sunny from a bully. This leads into the first game level, where Parappa raps to master a martial art so he can defend himself and Sunny. Game designers often motivate players' actions with a backstory that includes taking care of someone because they know that players can relate to similar social situations. Additionally, it's more emotionally interesting to be meeting a challenge if it benefits someone beyond yourself. It is worth noting here that while the "damsel in distress" is a problematic trope in video games—one that exacerbates stereotypical notions of women as weak and in need of paternalistic protection—the designers take an overtly tongue-in-cheek approach to presenting Sunny's dilemma.[6]

At the end of each cutscene, before the player is controlling Parappa, he cheerfully shouts his mantra for every tough situation: "I gotta believe!" This affectingly orients players to approach each rapping situation with enthusiasm and faith in their personal ability to persist and succeed. Parappa's exaggerated enthusiasm gives players an emotional boost heading into the next level. This, too, has a psychological foundation. Specifically, "emotional contagion" is when one person's emotional state similarly affects others.[7] In this example, game designers are aiming to infect players' emotional state through overt displays of Parappa's enthusiasm for the task at hand.

Game designers also shape players' feelings by making real-time changes in the atmosphere of a game based on players' performance, giving feedback based on their choices. As players press buttons to the rhythm of the music to match the mentor's rap, they can tell how they are doing not just by looking at the "U

Rappin" score meter but also through changes in the game music. When players fail to match the onscreen prompts, the meter falls and the sound gets tinny and muted. Conversely, when players perform in rhythm, the sonic quality improves as the score rises. When players complete the level, they receive praise from the mentor along with the sound of off-screen applause. The Parappa avatar celebrates by jumping up and down and waving his arms enthusiastically after passing a level. All this positive feedback heightens players' happy and proud feelings about succeeding at finishing the level.

Players feel a sense of pride and accomplishment as the Parappa avatar because they have been given reasons to identify with and care for this lighthearted character through an evocative art style and narrative motivation and because they have received positive feedback during gameplay. These design choices work together for me as a player, at least, to deliver a satisfying sense of accomplishment and pride.

Game designers also use non-player characters (NPCs) to shape player emotions. Although the game designers frame the game goal as Parappa wanting to be closer to Sunny, the strongest feelings of affection during gameplay arise from engaging with the NPC mentors. Instructor Mooselini (see figure 16.1), who teaches Parappa to drive so he can get his license to chauffeur Sunny, offers a good illustration of this teacher–student relationship. Instructor Mooselini is domineering and skeptical at first, informing the player, "You wanna learn how to drive, hunh? It's harder than you think it is." She flares her nostrils as she says this. At one point during the rap she stops the car and asks players (in rap, of course) if they know why "we stopped the car," making players nervous that they are going to fail, but then she says it's because "I forgot to close the door," slams it, and then player and mentor are off again. If players can muster some more quality rap-driving, at the end, Mooselini asks again if they know why the car was stopped before revealing that it is because players have earned their license. Parappa punctuates this achievement with enthusiastic whooping.

As this example illustrates, an NPC mentor such as Mooselini has real in-game authority over the player's ability to succeed or fail and, as such, can offer encouragement or criticism that matters emotionally. The emotionally invested player thus gets genuinely worried if the mentor is displeased and seeks praise at the end of a well-played level. The mentor NPC role is one that players can readily relate to—a teacher, a coach, a parent, or a caregiver. Players feel a sense of respect for and dependence on each in-game mentor in *PaRappa*—hoping they don't find fault and struggling to master each song. Each mentor is a bit stern at the start but also makes enthusiastic and encouraging comments in the end, if the player performs well. It might sound silly, but it can feel good to be praised by these cartoon mentors, in large part, because their validation is based on the player's actual, in-game performance.

Another aspect of *PaRappa*'s clever NPC design is connected to this unique genre. As a rhythm game, *PaRappa* makes use of the deep-seated tendency we have as humans to form affectionate ties with people with whom we are in close physical synchrony.[8] To succeed, players must closely copy the NPC mentor, contributing to a feeling of affection for them. If, like most people, players don't get the level right the first time, they end up spending quite a bit of time with each mentor, closely attending to their rap and trying hard to improve. By the time they've mastered the challenge, they may feel like they've really been through something with that character. And they've also likely bonded by sharing the same rhythm and words. Think of your own experience playing a sport or dancing or doing chores with someone—doing collective action together tends to help forge emotional connections over time.

The end of the game masterfully blends both avatar and NPC techniques to evoke player emotions. In the final stage, Parappa travels with Sunny to an exclusive event. They enter the club to find all his former mentors together with another MC. The final rapping test is done with everyone who has taught Parappa standing behind him on the stage. The whole group sings, "You gotta do WHAT?," as Parappa responds, "I gotta BELIEVE!" Parappa sees Sunny in the audience smiling. The very last round of play is Parappa engaging the crowd in a call and response (instead of being the one responding to a mentor MC), cementing his place as a master rapper. At the end of the game, Parappa thanks everyone and takes his bows with the others.

The game designers reward players at this level by changing the status of Parappa from student to master. They underscore and continue to build the affection players already feel for the MC mentors who have helped along the way by bringing them up on stage to rap with him, to be his backup. The player sees the cast of characters like Sunny and the other nonmentor NPCs, all cheering from the crowd. These numerous design choices coalesce to make the player feel great about investing the time to master the game's mechanics and to cause a warm sense of accomplishment, inclusion, and affection.

PaRappa offers a window into how game designers evoke emotion in their players, taking advantage of the active choice making that is at the heart of gameplay. The player is encouraged to feel pride and affection for Parappa as a result of the game's artful visual design, including the look of its leading, charismatic hero. Moreover, Parappa's narrative backstory emotionally motivates the player, as does seeing one's musical skill improve over time. The game's designers mold the player's response by building active relationships between the player's character and the NPCs in the game, setting up familiar relationships such as mentor/mentee. The core mechanic, copying the rhythm of the mentor, is something that is known to build rapport and connection in everyday human interaction. As the reader can see, some of these techniques are similar to those used in other media—for example, choosing art style carefully or telling a strong framing backstory. But others are unique to gameplay—such as creating a game mechanic of call-and-response rhythmic action. These design decisions evoke a different emotional palette than other media, contributing to feelings like pride of accomplishment and abiding affection for characters with whom the player has spent time and a shared set of activities.

NOTES

1 Alan Burdick, "Discover Interview: Will Wright," *Discover*, August 1, 2006, accessed August 24, 2015, http://discovermagazine.com.

2 Katherine Isbister, *How Games Move Us: Emotion by Design* (Cambridge, MA: MIT Press, 2016).

3 Scott McCloud, *Understanding Comics: The Invisible Art* (New York: Harper Collins, 1993).

4 Mark J. P. Wolf, "Abstraction in the Video Game," in *The Video Game Theory Reader*, ed. Mark J. P. Wolf and Bernard Perron (New York: Routledge, 2003), 47–66.

5 Katherine Isbister, *Better Game Characters by Design: A Psychological Approach* (Burlington, MA: Morgan Kaufmann, 2006).

6 Anita Sarkeesian, "Damsel in Distress," *Feminist Frequency*, https://feministfrequency.com.

7 Isbister, *Better Game Characters by Design*, 79.

8 Isbister, *Better Game Characters by Design*.

FURTHER READING

Fullerton, Tracy. *Game Design Workshop: A Playcentric Approach to Creating Innovative Games*, 3rd ed. Boca Raton, FL: A K Peters/CRC Press, 2014.

Karpouzis, Kostas, and Georgios N. Yannakakis, eds. *Emotion in Games: Theory and Praxis*. Cham, Switzerland: Springer Press, 2016.

Swink, Steve. *Game Feel: A Game Designer's Guide to Virtual Sensation*. Burlington, MA: Morgan Kaufmann, 2008.

Tettegah, Sharon, and Wenhao David Huang, eds. *Emotions, Technology, and Digital Games*. London: Academic Press, 2015.

17

Sniper Elite III
Death

AMANDA PHILLIPS

Abstract: This chapter seeks to understand the various mechanics surrounding death in video games, from the thrill of the hunt to the flopping of ragdoll bodies, using Rebellion Developments' *Sniper Elite III*. Amanda Phillips argues that understanding how a game treats death can reveal insights into how death operates in a wider cultural milieu: as a mechanism of power, as trauma, or even as a shared experience.

When we think about death in video games, we often think of ourselves. As Mario plunges into the abyss, we do not lament his passing; we're too busy shouting about how we just died—again. Death serves many purposes for gaming. In the arcade, it provides motivation to keep dropping quarters. On home consoles, it regulates difficulty and promotes competition. On YouTube, it is both a spectacle and a mark of virtuosity. In these modes, death is a mechanism of "self-optimization," a normalizing process by which gamers conform to the demands of the ludic and technological systems of a video game.[1] We can see discipline-by-death everywhere from the rise of "permadeath" games that end when the player dies to the call by queer game scholars to embrace failure, and, by extension, death, as a distinctly queer mode of play.[2]

But let's be real: video games encourage killing at least as much as they discourage dying. Our historical defensiveness about the effects of violence in video games has led many fans and academics to politely gloss over this fact and point to the games that prove otherwise. However, to say that death does not saturate gaming in one way or another is disingenuous. This chapter investigates what it means to be a perpetrator of death through an analysis of *Sniper Elite III* (Rebellion Developments, 2014), a third-person military shooter with a wide array of significant death mechanics.

Although not all games strive for visual fidelity or extreme violence, we can ask many of the same questions about death from any game: How does a game encourage or discourage death? How does it treat death as a sensory and procedural event? Whom does it encourage or discourage you from killing? Understanding how a game treats death can reveal insights into how death operates in a wider cultural milieu: as a mechanism of power, as trauma, or even as a shared experience.

From my hidden perch, I take note of multiple targets pacing in predictable patterns below me. I choose one and follow him through the crosshairs of my reticle, waiting patiently for a sputtering generator to begin the next series of coughs that will mask the sound of my shot. As the racket builds up, I hold my breath, refine my aim, and pull the trigger.[3]

In *Sniper Elite III*, the gamer plays as Karl Fairburne, an American sniper tapped by the British for their African campaign in World War II. Fairburne travels across Egypt, Libya, and Tunisia, taking out entire companies of soldiers, eliminating artillery positions with a single bullet, and battling one-on-one with tanks in an alternate-history game that culminates in blowing up a Nazi general's secret pet project: a giant building-sized tank called the Ratte. The plot is absurd and nonsensical, but as with many games, the narrative here is merely a vessel for compelling gameplay.

In the case of *Sniper Elite III*, the most compelling gameplay is the act of shooting a rifle. The game's stealth mechanics and high-energy shootouts are quite limited when compared to its exhaustive simulation of long-distance bullet ballistics. Wind, gravity, rifle model, muzzle velocity, recoil, and enemy trajectory all factor into the shot, and repetitive ambient sounds encourage the gamer to synch up with the rhythm of the environment before pulling the trigger. Most military shooter games prioritize fast-paced action over thoughtful movement and selective violence. The bullet ballistics of *Sniper Elite III* interrupt this impulse. Rather than the twitch reflexes of other titles, this game requires patience, thoughtfulness, and timing with each shot.

This isn't to say that the gameplay is any more realistic than run-and-gun shooters, such as the *Call of Duty* or *Medal of Honor* series. Appeals to realism ground so many contemporary games that it is often difficult to parse out what makes any one aspect of our virtual fantasies more realistic than others (for further discussion of realism in video games, see Peter Krapp's chapter in this collection). Frequently, it is synonymous with "painstakingly simulated details," from skin pores to historically accurate weapons arsenals. Detailed bullet ballistics fall into this category, but *Sniper Elite III*'s hunt gives the lie to its detailed rifle calculations. In real life, military snipers deploy in pairs at the very least, and frequently they are a part of even larger groups of soldiers, performing reconnaissance and support from afar. Their opponents would not easily give up the search for a killer who took out their friend and return to an isolated post as if everything were normal. Snipers do not hunt down tanks.

The contrast between painstakingly simulated rifle shooting and improbable hunting conditions encourages the gamer to cling to the detailed gunfire simulations. When exhaustive bullet ballistics deem it reasonable that an unmodified sniper rifle shooting standard ammo would penetrate the hull of a tank, the effect passes muster because the game offers a painstakingly simulated view of the interior of said tank, creating a visual argument that the expertly aimed bullet happened to slip between armored plates to rupture the highly explosive gas tank within. These visual arguments occur throughout the game in the form of the infamous "Kill Cam" (short for kill camera), a tool that repeatedly confirms that the developers put a lot of effort into simulating those bullets.

Time slows down as the bullet leaves my rifle. The camera follows as it spins toward destiny, its shockwave visible as ripples in the air. On approach, my target's skin peels back, then his muscles, as if an x-ray spotlight has settled on his body. I watch as bones shatter, eyeballs explode, and blood gushes from the wound before my view snaps back to the reticle. An XP report scrolls, logging extra points for stealthy flourishes and damage location. Head shot. Heart Shot. Lung Shot. Testicles. The vital organs of man.

The Kill Cam was introduced to the series in *Sniper Elite V2* (Rebellion Developments, 2012) and has become a fan favorite that continues in the series' most recent installment. Each iteration improves on the last: *Sniper Elite III* exaggerated the time dilation, added muscle layers, improved blood spatter, and simulated the guts of vehicles whereas *Sniper Elite 4* (Rebellion Developments, 2017) adds shrapnel damage and melee attacks to the Kill Cam repertoire. It is a variation on the "bullet time" special effect popularized by the 1999 film *The Matrix*, incorporating an internal-view mechanic that peels back the layers of the digital body: a fantastic medicalized vision that evokes the x-ray.

In a stealth game like *Sniper Elite III*, line-of-sight mechanics are an integral part of gameplay. Gamers must understand both how to see their enemies as well as how their enemies see. Reverse-engineering computer vision in such games is a key to gameplay success, and the inclusion of alternative modes of vision draws attention to the ways that procedural visual mechanics structure gameplay. The Kill Cam lies outside the moments of play, but it relies on the very principles of simulation that drive *Sniper Elite* in the first place: the bullet's specific speed, trajectory, and entry point drive the animation after the gamer takes environmental factors into consideration when aiming the rifle. Ultimately, the gamer determines the outcome of the animation (see figure 17.1).

The use of x-ray vision to portray damage to the body is a surprisingly old development in gaming, although it has risen to prominence only in recent years.

FIGURE 17.1
Promotional image from
Rebellion Developments detailing a Kill Cam animation
in *Sniper Elite III.*

In an interview, producer Steve Hart attributes the Kill Cam's inspiration to the
1999 Iraq war film *Three Kings*, which features a scene illustrating how bile can
seep into an abdominal gunshot wound.[4] This effect was later popularized by *CSI:
Crime Scene Investigation* in 2000. In 1997, *Samurai Shodown 64* (SNK) had offered a simple animated x-ray of breaking bones that popped up over the combatants as the player executed certain attacks. NetherRealm Studio's *Mortal Kombat* reboot deployed elaborately detailed injury scenes called "X-Ray Attacks" to
wide critical acclaim in 2011, a year before *Sniper Elite V2.*

Richard Swiderski calls x-ray vision an "image-idea" that exceeds the technology itself, giving viewers access not to the reality of an internal body but, rather,
to a "culturally meaningful set of insides" that combine the penetrative visual fantasy of the x-ray with other anatomical knowledge that circulates within culture.[5]
The type of vision enabled by these x-ray attacks is not possible in real life, even
though they suggest that we are seeing how physical bodies respond to extreme
violence. A real body is messier and quieter, its organs less easily distinguishable,
and each one deviates from the anatomical ideal projected by the animations. According to Deborah Jermyn, the so-called *CSI*-shot has the paradoxical effect of
increasing the audience's perception of realism through its appeal to the neutral
facticity of the body while simultaneously undercutting aesthetic realism by in-
voking the spectacular effects of science fiction and fantasy genres.[6] The same is
true for x-ray damage indicators in video games.

Unsurprisingly, the ability to shoot out an enemy's testicles is one of the most popular features of the game. The inclusion of the Testicle Shot in the Kill Cam's repertoire amplifies the anxious masculinity that underscores so many games but particularly one that trades in the nostalgic heroism and moral purity of World War II. Here, Swiderski's note about the cultural legibility of bodily interiors becomes particularly clear: the testicles are simulated in the Kill Cam alongside organs that we might otherwise recognize as necessary for life, such as the heart, lungs, kidneys, and liver. And although medical research indicates that gunshot wounds to the testicles, even by military-grade weapons, are survivable and frequently minor,[7] they are always instantly fatal in *Sniper Elite*, with bonus XP added to the kill. Whereas *Mortal Kombat*'s eviscerations and dismemberments preserve the game's veneer of fantasy, the gruesome thrill of vicarious castration in *Sniper Elite* confirms a deep fear that a man cannot (or, perhaps, should not) live without his testes.

As my targets die, their bodies crumple in unusual ways. They slide slowly down hills, twitch improbably as the game performs its animation calculations, and then settle, immovable, on the ground. They pile up against one another, and more than a few end up falling over with their faces on the ground, buttocks in the air. Sometimes they float just above the ground, an eerie reminder of the imperfect nature of algorithmic animation.

As with many games, killed enemies in *Sniper Elite* become ragdolls that flop to their deaths. Ragdolling is one perfect example of ludic objectification, the precise moment when the virtual subject leaves its body behind, creating a corpse rather than a character. Ragdoll physics are procedural, enabling the game to produce a theoretically limitless number of death animations. They are infamous in gaming for their glitchy behaviors, leading to gamer innovations such as teabagging and physics-based games such as *Stair Dismount* (Jethro Lauha, 2002). *Sniper Elite*'s ragdolls attract less attention than its exploding testicles, but they do manage to break the seriousness of the game at unexpected moments—whether by alerting the gamer to the limitations of its physics simulations or by inserting homoerotic tensions into the hypermasculine space of battle.

Ragdolls, with their improbable flexibility and compliant mobility, are always already erotic. It is no accident that activities like teabagging are virtual enactments of sexual violence. In his interview with *PC Gamer*, Steve Hart comments that "sniping is such an intimate thing, and it's got and [*sic*] almost voyeuristic touch to it—you're studying that person before you take that shot. You must know something about them."[8] This, of course, is not a new fantasy, but it plays out particularly well in *Sniper Elite*: the intimacy of the hunt, propelled forward by the sniper's intrusive gaze and massive gun, ending with the slow-motion penetration of the bullet and, ultimately, the frisking and handling of the body after death.

My personal playthroughs often resulted in inadvertently creating erotically posed corpses. Some enemies fell ass-up. One froze hip-thrusting the air. Others settled into each other's arms for their final repose. A YouTuber even documented a ragdoll in his game that appeared to be standing, bent backward, with a look of ecstasy on his face.[9] These floppy bodies are unruly, and they can fall in any number of configurations if not explicitly programmed not to do so. We might say that the ragdoll is the queerest death mechanic, a tool that defies corporeal expectations and whose sexuality is always threatening to erupt and impose itself on an innocent bystander.

As I progress through the campaign, anxious guards begin calling me "Wüstengeist"—the Desert Ghost. "You think you're safe and then . . . BAM! Your head's gone. Just like that!" I listen to the rumors from a concealed spot on a ridge. I have stalked and killed dozens of soldiers so expertly that the game propels me into Ghost Mode, granting an XP bonus for every undetected kill I rack up.

Although the "ghost" is a common designation in sniper culture, it is more accurate to note that Karl is as much a ghost-maker as a ghost himself. For a game about stealth and covert operations, *Sniper Elite III* encourages a lot of conspicuous violence, betraying the more sensible tactics of a true stealth master. Its achievements, like many games, are tied to body counts and creative methods of killing opponents, and its many collectibles are found deep in enemy territory, often requiring the gamer to clear the battlefield to complete minor optional objectives. No sniper would deploy so deeply into the field while killing everyone in sight, making Karl Fairburne less of a covert sniper and more of a one-man army.

Video game kill cams originally showed the player their own deaths on a multiplayer field in order to provide a bit of information about their attacker. *Sniper Elite III*'s Kill Cam, however, never shows Karl's death. When he succumbs to his injuries, there is no x-ray theater and no floppy ragdoll. He begins to fall, and the screen cuts to "Game Over." In one sense, this represents the gamer's endless cycle of death and rebirth, the goal to master the game or keep dying forever.

We might also read Karl's censored deaths in the context of the United States' contested history on photographing war dead. In 2009, under the direction of President Barack Obama, Defense Secretary Robert Gates lifted the 18-year-old ban on photographing military coffins arriving at Dover Air Force Base, opting instead to allow families to decide whether to allow images to be taken of their dead. Mobley notes that while much conversation around the so-called Dover Ban focused on how depicting war casualties affects public support for military action abroad, it is also important to understand how controlling images of the dead also helps governments reinforce their own necropolitical power.[10]

Similarly, the game claims sovereignty for itself by refusing to grant the gamer access to the gruesome death scenes of the player character, reinforcing Karl's position as the sole arbiter of death within the narrative. He is an untouchable, lethal hero fighting in what is remembered as the modern era's morally righteous war. However, the generic desert landscapes crafted to represent the game's narrative backdrop of North Africa during World War II simultaneously place Karl, out of time, in the theater of contemporary US military conflict. Suddenly, his strange position as an American soldier killing for the British makes more sense. *Sniper Elite III* ultimately evokes conflict in the Middle East. This blends not only time but morality as well, with Axis troops across the desert standing in for the West's ideological nemesis in the ongoing global war on terror.

NOTES

1 Rolf F. Nohr, "Restart after Death: 'Self-Optimizing,' 'Normalism,' and 'Re-entry' in Computer Games," in *The Game Culture Reader*, ed. Jason C. Thompson and Marc Ouellette (Newcastle Upon Tyne, UK: Cambridge Scholars Publishing, 2013), 66–83.

2 Bonnie Ruberg, "No Fun: The Queer Potential of Video Games that Annoy, Anger, Disappoint, Sadden, and Hurt," *QED: A Journal in LGBTQ Worldmaking* 2, no. 2 (2015): 108–124. See also the "Queer Failures in Games" section of Ruberg and Adrienne Shaw, eds, *Queer Game Studies* (Minneapolis: Minnesota University Press, 2017).

3 These vignettes are the author's narrativization of gameplay.

4 Henry Winchester, "*Sniper Elite V2*'s Testicular Animation Detailed by Dev: 'Sniping Is such an Intimate Thing,'" *PC Gamer*, December 2011, www.pcgamer.com.

5 Richard Swiderski, *X-Ray Vision: A Way of Looking* (Boca Raton, FL: Universal-Publishers, 2012), 191.

6 Deborah Jermyn, "Body Matters: Realism, Spectacle and the Corpse in *CSI*," in *Reading 'CSI': Crime TV Under the Microscope*, ed. Michael Allen (London and New York: I.B. Taurus, 2007), 80–81.

7 Abdulelah M. Ghilan, Mohammed A. Ghafour, Waleed A. Al-Asbahi, Omar M. Al-Khanbashi, Mohammed A. Alwan, and Tawfik H. Al-Ba'dani, "Gunshot Wound Injuries to the External Male Genitalia," *Saudi Medical Journal* 31, no. 9 (2010): 1005–10.

8 Quoted in Winchester, "*Sniper Elite V2*."

9 GoldLion20, "Sniper Elite 3 Ragdoll What," YouTube video, 1:01, published August 4, 2014, https://www.youtube.com/watch?v=O5Dk6idceGA.

10 Kayce Mobley, "Hiding Death: Contextualizing the Dover Ban," *Journal of Military Ethics* 15, no. 2 (2016): 130.

FURTHER READING

Christiansen, Peter. "Thanatogaming: Death, Videogames, and the Biopolitical State." In *Proceedings of 2014 DiGRA International Conference*, August 2014. http://www.digra.org.

Kocurek, Carly. "Who Hearkens to the Monster's Scream? Death, Violence, and the Veil of the Monstrous in Video Games." *Visual Studies* 30, no. 1 (2015): 79–89.

Smethurst, Tobi. "Playing Dead in Videogames: Trauma in *Limbo*." *Journal of Popular Culture* 48, no. 5 (2015): 817–35.

Wenz, Karin. "Death." In *The Routledge Companion to Video Game Studies*, edited by Mark J. P. Wolf and Bernard Perron, 310–316. New York: Routledge, 2016.

18

Papers, Please
Ethics

MIGUEL SICART

Abstract: Can a video game make a moral argument? In this chapter, Miguel Sicart examines how *Papers, Please* illustrates the expressive capacities of video games to explore complex moral topics, playfully engaging players not just as consumers but also, and more critically, as reflective ethical beings.

Ever since *Ultima IV* (Origin Systems, 1985) proposed a morality system to evaluate players' actions, game critics have examined the relationship between gameplay and morals, and designers have utilized game structures and mechanics to explore ethical topics. From *Fable* (Lionhead Studios, 2004) to *Fallout 4* (Bethesda Game Studios, 2015), numerous titles offer players moral choices. But what do we mean by moral choices? Do these choices engage players in ethical thinking? And how might games be designed to encourage thoughtful reflection? I engage these concerns by examining the independent game *Papers, Please* (3909 LLC, 2013) in light of the following three key questions: First, what do we mean by ethics and morality? Second, how do video games engage ethical thinking? And, finally, what role do games play in our moral life?

It may be a commonsense notion to dismiss morality when we play video games—the "it's just a game" argument. Classic theories of play, such as Johan Huizinga's "magic circle" (see the chapter by Steven Conway in this collection), present play as spatially and temporality demarcated from regular life during which society's rules are briefly suspended. As such, it is thought, we need not apply the ethical rules by which we live to our actions undertaken during play. Yet we make many difficult choices when we play games—quickly evaluating situations, calculating potential gains and consequences. Narrative game worlds frequently present us with ethical dilemmas that we don't encounter in our everyday

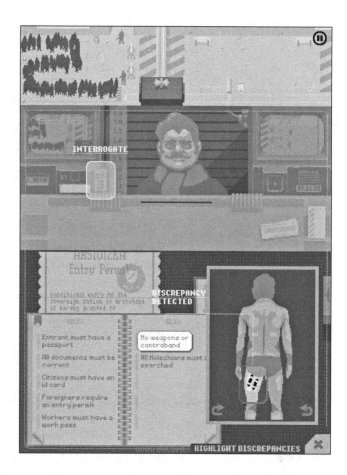

FIGURE 18.1
The user interface of
Papers, Please.

lives: to kill or not kill an enemy, to horde personal resources, or to share them with someone. However, although our gameplay choices may not have immediate or direct consequences on our nongaming lives (although this point is debatable), video games nevertheless inform our morality *while we are playing* and potentially affect our moral fiber once we're done. *Papers, Please* offers a great example of how video games can have those ethical effects.

Lucas Pope's *Papers, Please* turns players into border bureaucrats in the fictional Eastern-bloc country of Astorzska, which has just established a fragile truce after many years of warring with neighboring countries. Players are tasked with controlling the flow of people into the country, meeting quotas that influence the amount of money they earn (see figure 18.1). Players decide whether migrants are permitted entry into the country based on a migrant's documentation and other information via computer news. *Papers, Please* is a bleak simulation of border control protocols, the rhetoric of isolationism, and the fear of terrorism.

Before evaluating *Papers, Please*, we need to define a few basic terms. Ethics is the analytical examination of the principles from which we derive and evaluate moral rules. For example, ethics can propose a system that states that to make decisions, we should look at the consequences of our actions. If the consequences of our actions harm somebody, then that action is immoral. We call that system consequentialism. A similar system looks at who would benefit from a particular decision and the utility of that decision. If our choices have a positive effect on many, these choices are deemed to be morally good. We call that system utilitarianism.

Morality is a system of rules for guiding and evaluating individual and collective conduct. In simpler terms, morality is ethics *in practice*. Any time we make a decision or ponder a difficult situation, we are performing moral work; we are assessing how best to solve a moral conflict. Furthermore, moral systems have two main purposes: they exist to prevent harm and they exist to encourage the ethical development of individuals and collectives. Moral systems have four defining characteristics: they are public, rational, impartial, and informal. We can understand these elements in the world of games as follows. First, to play a game, everybody needs to know the rules of the game. For example, to play a pickup game of basketball you need to know the rules of basketball, plus the social rules of the neighborhood court where the game takes place. Everybody should know those rules, and everybody should agree on what constitutes breaking the rules. These shared rules governing this activity makes it a public system. Morality systems are *public* so that cultures can share agreed-upon notions of what is right and wrong— actions that both prevent harm and those that encourage human flourishing. A public system is any system in which everybody that is affected by the workings of the system has an understanding of the basic guidelines behind that system. Law, for example, should be a public system to ensure that everybody knows what is legal and illegal in a particular society.

One of the great design insights of *Papers, Please* is that it makes players feel as if they are living in an unjust society by keeping the operating morality system hidden from view. Players never know whether an action is "good" or "evil" or what long-term consequences their choices might have. A player might commiserate with an innocent-looking man who begs to enter the country to visit a dying mother, only to learn afterward that the man was a murderer. Or worse, sometimes players will let through a person they have suspicions about but will never learn whether their decision was right or wrong. It is through these choices that *Papers, Please* is an exploration of totalitarian bureaucratic systems and the banality of evil. Totalitarian bureaucracies can be designed to alienate decision makers from the consequences of their choices and, in doing so, allow participants to feel ethically detached from their decisions. The dull routine of these choices, such as the daily work of a border control guard, is bound up in rules and procedures, which can further remove the participant from feeling culpable. The emotional impact of *Papers, Please* is largely a result of this design.

In addition to being public, moral systems are *rational*—in that their principles can be argued using reason rather than emotion or faith—and they are *impartial*—seeking to treat people evenhandedly. (There are moral systems derived from faith, but these are developed under the domain of religious belief and structures and are outside of the scope of this chapter.) If we create a moral system in which some parts of the population are evaluated more harshly than others, then we are creating a biased system that will engender an inequitable and irrational society. For a moral system to work, everybody should be treated both fairly and consistently.

Returning to our analog and video game examples, ideally all players on both teams are treated equally by the rules and by the referees so as to create equity among players. We celebrate sporting competitions, in part, because we appreciate how athletes overcome the challenges of the game and their opponents on an even playing field. When a basketball referee applies game rules unevenly, favoring foul calls against one team more than the other, players, coaches, and fans may decry the game as unfair and protest the outcome. In contrast, *Papers, Please* explores what it feels like to live and work in a biased morality system. Some of the choices players need to take are clearly biased, harming people just because of their origin or because of biased suspicion. *Papers, Please* is also an exploration of what it takes to be a moral citizen in a morally failing state. In the game, players are told what to do, but the reasons behind the laws, the border rules they have to apply to let people in or out, are left in the dark. There are rules and laws in the state, but those are of obscure origins, brutally enforced, and subject to random changes. This is how authoritarian power operates.

Finally, moral systems are *informal*. This means that actions are open to interpretation and adaptation as the situational context demands. By having informal systems, we can negotiate the ways rules are evaluated on a case-by-case basis. Consider the informal aspects of pickup basketball games: there are rules to govern action, but there are typically no referees in attendance. Thus, players must police themselves and engage in ongoing negotiations to ensure everybody is playing under the same rules.

This is another aspect that *Papers, Please* engages creatively: players are not permitted to negotiate the moral impact of their actions. The game system rewards morally wrong choices and players cannot refuse to make a decision. The ethical system in *Papers, Please* is *private*, *partial*, and *rigid*, presenting a simulation of moral life under a totalitarian regime (see figure 18.2).

As the examples from basketball and *Papers, Please* demonstrate, games and ethics share some common traits. Games are informal public systems with rules

FIGURE 18.2
Choices and conse-
quences in *Papers,
Please.*

that indicate how to behave. In games, those rules of play tell us what to do in order to succeed. Similarly, morality uses rules as heuristics for leading a good life,
avoiding harm, and developing our potential as human beings. There are games
where the rules of play and its morality system are profoundly intertwined—
games such as *Undertale* (Toby Fox, 2015), *The Walking Dead* (Telltale Games,
2012–2018), or the *Mass Effect* series (BioWare, 2007–2017). However, *Papers,
Please* offers a different take on how video games can design ethical experiences.

Let's look more closely at *Papers, Please* to assess its novelty. This game engages
players in a number of ethical dilemmas in the face of imperfect and incomplete
information. How does one balance the risk of barring innocent migrants against
the threat of terrorism? Do players place their personal, financial well-being
above that of their fellow citizens, their state, or those seeking asylum? Most of
the time, players are given insufficient information, contradictory goals, and little
power beyond fulfilling their bureaucratic role as a border agent. Unlike other

choice-based games, *Papers, Please* does not quantify the player's actions according to predetermined values; rather, it is the task of the player to assign values to the exploration of the choices that are presented. In other words, the only moral guide one has in *Papers, Please* is the player's personal code. For example, players could evaluate the game's challenges by looking at the potential outcome of their decisions, therefore embracing a consequentialist ethics. Meanwhile, a utilitarian would weigh the pros and cons of a particular decision looking at both individual and collective outcomes, deciding whether to sacrifice one's self for the sake of the fictional country or to act selfishly to protect only those they care about.

The game does have up to 20 endings that conclude the scripted narrative arc. However, this large number of endings makes it very difficult for (casual) players to "play for the plot," that is, to try to achieve results by deliberately making choices based on their intention to complete a narrative. Most casual *Papers, Please* players will not know about the multiple endings or how to reach them, and thus, they are encouraged to make choices by following their moral compass. Dedicated players who want to see the different endings are playing "for the plot," but given how they must carefully make choices to reach a different end for each playthrough, it is likely that they have reflected about the meaning of those choices, resulting in a process of moral reflection.

Papers, Please is a brilliant example of ethical gameplay design because it allows for the application of different ethical theories to how it is played. This is *precisely* what computer and video games can do: create safe spaces for the exploration of different ethical choices and their resulting consequences. In fact, player agency is a key characteristic that makes games useful for posing ethical questions and for testing possible outcomes. In their influential *Rules of Play*,[1] Katie Salen and Eric Zimmerman describe games as systems that create a possibility space for players to explore. In games, this space of possibility determines the choices available to players who, in turn, develop strategies and tactics for negotiating and traversing that space.

The idea of gaming offering a "possibility space" is what allows us to think about them as potential vehicles for moral experiences that allow for the exploration of different ethical theories. In many cases, gamers traverse these game spaces simply by trying to optimize their chances of winning. However, games such as *Papers, Please* illustrate how games can model a ludic possibility space as an invitation for exploring personal and social values. In this way, gameplay is not necessarily about fulfilling a win condition, but the actions are directed back at players as a form of moral reflection. *Papers, Please* encourages players to interrogate the values and the logic behind their choices, as well as the philosophical systems that support those rules and behaviors.

Papers, Please demonstrates how ethical dilemmas in games should complicate players' choices, encouraging them to use their own inner moral compass as an instrument for decision making. In particular, the game deploys incomplete information and insufficient time as complementary gameplay mechanics. In contrast, many games present complete worlds where everything is clear to users, giving them enough information to act with confidence. But if the goal is to have players explore their unquestioned or underexamined values, there must be gaps in information and time constraints that generate difficult decisions, like the timed decision-making sequences in Telltale Games' *The Walking Dead*, that force players to take grave choices without having time to ponder about the nature and consequences of their actions. In that way, gameplay becomes an ethical practice as the possibility space becomes one of moral possibility. Ethical gameplay is not the act of choosing between options but of traversing the possibility space of a game with moral thinking.

Playing games is an act of leisure, a pleasurable activity pursued for escaping daily routines. Is it fair, then, to expect games to have ethical content? Should they encourage us to engage ethical thinking? Are these fair questions? Escapism from the burden of being a moral creature is a perfectly valid design and cultural goal for games. The moral role games play in society might be that of letting us be more relaxed moral animals. Games therefore needn't be under any imperative to morally engage us with ethically provocative content.

However, if *Papers, Please* teaches us anything, it is that the rhetoric of games and game design can create engaging moral experiences. Why not, then, use this medium to explore different ethical theories: different ways of acting, different ways of understanding why something might be a moral dilemma, and what makes a decision a moral or an immoral one? Also, we should forge beyond single-player narrative games to consider how ethical multiplayer games might be designed. What would the moral possibility space of an abstract or experimental game look like?[2] Such games might be difficult or impossible to bring to fruition. Yet that very impossibility would tell us something about games as a medium—about their limits and their affordances.

Games are exercises in ethical thinking, play instruments to train and sharpen our moral instincts. Like literature and the movies, games can help us formulate, explore, understand or reject ethical rules. The uniqueness of games is that this process takes place in a computational space of possibility that each player traverses in a particular way—players get to *practice* ethical theories and see their effects, both in the game and in their reflection on their gaming experiences.

Aristotle understood ethics as a practical science. Discussing the rules of morality was interesting if and only if we also lived morally and engaged practically with the complications of making choices. Games offer us the possibility of engaging directly with that practical science. This is not to say that because we have *Papers, Please*, the medium of the video game is mature. Rather, it is to say that playing can be a moral act, one that can help us better understand what we value personally, as well as what we value for the societies in which we live. If ethics is a practical science, then video games can be an ideal laboratory for moral research.

NOTES

1 Katie Salen and Eric Zimmerman, *Rules of Play. Game Design Fundamentals* (Cambridge, MA: MIT Press, 2004).

2 See, for example, Joseph DeLappe and Biome Collective, *Killbox*, https://www.killbox.info.

FURTHER READING

Flanagan, Mary. *Critical Play: Radical Game Design.* Cambridge, MA: MIT Press, 2009.

Flanagan, Mary, and Helen Nissenbaum. *Values at Play in Digital Games.* Cambridge, MA: MIT Press, 2014.

Sicart, Miguel. *The Ethics of Computer Games.* Cambridge, MA: MIT Press, 2009.

Zagal, Jose. *The Videogame Ethics Reader.* San Diego, CA: Cognella, 2012.

19

Age of Empires
Postcolonialism

SOUVIK MUKHERJEE

Abstract: Despite early depictions of colonization in video games, such as *Sid Meier's Colonization* or Microsoft's *Age of Empires*, there has been little game studies scholarship on postcolonial perspectives. Viewing the presentation of history and the narratives of the colonized Other, as well as the processes of control and expansion of empire through an analysis of *Age of Empires,* Souvik Mukherjee offers a much-needed postcolonial intervention in the ways in which imperialism and colonialism are presented in video games.

From early real-time strategy games, such as *Sid Meier's Colonization* (Micro-Prose, 1994) and Ensemble Studio's *Age of Empires* (1997), to their present-day sequels, gamers the world over have controlled empires, conquered lands, colonized peoples, and even changed history. Often, the countries they conquered and the people they colonized are their own, and there can be an underlying unease in such tacit participation of power, even in the virtual world. Recent discussions on diversity in video games have opened up ways to reassess the portrayals and politics of colonialism and the stereotypes of the colonized Other. This chapter analyses the roots of such portrayals taking the example of the early PC game, *Age of Empires* and following the trajectory of empire-building real-time strategy (RTS) games into the present moment. In doing so, this chapter engages with key ideas in postcolonialism that problematize such portrayals, and it prompts a re-thinking of how digital media responds to questions of colonialism.

Age of Empires (*AoE*), developed by the three-member Dallas-based company Ensemble Studios and published by Microsoft, was a major success when it was released in 1997—one that has spawned many sequels. The developers aimed at improving the RTS genre by combining "the historic and strategic elements of

FIGURE 19.1 Building the Hittite empire in *Age of Empires.*

Civilization with the real-time decision making and animations of *Warcraft* and *Command & Conquer*."[1] As a reviewer comments, despite the criticisms of the game's artificial intelligence, one major point where the game scored well was its representation of history: "the single most compelling aspect of this game is its feel, its atmosphere . . . instead of science fiction, or fantasy, the game draws on ancient history for its inspiration."[2] It is this lauded historical representation, however, that needs reexamining.

The game's title quite clearly identifies empire as its key interest. The closest parallel to the title in history books is Eric Hobsbawm's *Age of Empire: 1875 to 1914*, where the eminent Marxist historian traces the development of capital in what he calls the "long nineteenth century."[3] The last book in a trilogy, *Age of Empire* depicts a comparatively stable period albeit with internal contradictions and conflicts, and—of course—contact with multiple non-Western cultures under Western colonial rule. Unlike Hobsbawm's Marxist notion of the progression of capitalism, the *Age of Empires* video games, however, see almost all of human history as the history of imperialism. Beginning with the Hittites and the Babylonians in the ancient past and ending with the British and other Western empires in the nineteenth century, these games make imperial rule the norm and glorify the logic of empire (see figure 19.1). History, in its entirety, is written (and played) from the perspective of the imperial conquerors. Even when one gets to play (in multiplayer games or user mods) as the colonized and conquered peoples, the games still privilege the imperialist logic of conquest, control, and expansion. In this case, the sides may have been switched, but the logic of imperialism prevails.

This underlying logic of imperialism embeds a grim reality of race, class, and economic disadvantage for the colonized. As the postcolonial thinker Franz Fanon outlines,

> [t]his world divided into compartments, this world cut in two is inhabited by two different species. The originality of the colonial context is that economic reality, inequality and the immense difference of ways of life never come to mask the human realities. When you examine at close quarters the colonial context, it is evident that what parcels out the world is to begin with the fact of belonging to or not belonging to a given race, a given species. In the colonies the economic substructure is also a superstructure. The cause is the consequence; you are rich because you are white, you are white because you are rich.[4]

In reassessing *Age of Empires* two decades after its initial release, one wonders why the developers chose to avoid critiques of imperialism in their design. Such critiques have been voiced for decades, during the freedom struggles of many Asian and African countries fighting for independence from their colonizers and in the years afterward as newly independent countries. Postcolonialism is "resonant with all the ambiguity and complexity of the many different cultural experiences it implicates [and] it addresses all aspects of the colonial process from the beginning of colonial contact."[5] *Post* does not simply mean "after" colonialism but comprises a range of issues connected to the master discourses of the imperial West and the responses to them by Others. Some of the key problems it addresses besides the exploitation of resources in the colonies are the questions of how spatiality, identity, and even cultural history are affected by colonialism.

Before proceeding, a quick caveat is in order. As postcolonial literature scholar Ania Loomba rightly points out, European colonialism from the fifteenth century onward was a very different phenomenon from earlier imperial expansion (such as the empires of Rome or Egypt). Loomba notes that "[m]odern colonialism did more than extract tribute, goods, and wealth from the countries that it conquered—it restructured the economies of the latter, drawing them into a complex relationship with their own, so that there was a flow of human and natural resources between colonized and colonial countries."[6] The *Age of Empires* series, it is important to note, does *not* make such a distinction. Although the gameplay changes somewhat in *Age of Empires III* (Ensemble Studios, 2005), which includes bonuses based on the player's experience and removes the original game's ability to convert opponent units, the games follow a similar pattern and even have the same victory conditions (usually military conquest, regicide, capturing relics or ruins, and building a "wonder" or culture-specific significant building). These games, arguably, represent a notion of empire that envisages the total displacement of the opponent (or "the Other" in postcolonial terms). Any trade that happens between the player and other nations is usually to the advantage of the player (unless the other nations are allies). These and other features of the game design express an intriguing notion of colonialism that is examined in the following.

The "settlement of territory, the exploitation or development of resources and the attempt to govern the indigenous inhabitants of the occupied lands"[7] are the basic characteristics of colonialism, which is a specific form of imperialism. The *AoE* games usually conform to all of these—the logic of imperialism that they are based on, mirrors the workings of colonialism. In the case of *AoE*, the "empires" it represents from ancient history—such as Babylon, Greece, and ancient Japan— are each very different from the colonial systems of nineteenth-century Europe. The game, however, makes all of them work by the same colonialist logic. Indeed, the units for all the civilizations also look very similar on the whole. Some of the most notable differences are reserved for the how the game marks key socioeconomic characteristic of each ancient civilization. For example, unlike the Egyptian faction, the Greeks do not possess chariots, and their priests cannot convert buildings. Players select civilizations based on their specific tactical benefits. Victory is usually achieved in the *AoE* games with the overthrow of the opponent governments and/or the destruction of their entire populace. The adversaries in these games are the "Other" of postcolonialism. Edward Said, theorizing his notion of Orientalism, argues that the Orient is a construction of European nations, and as such, the Other is needed to imagine their own selves.

In *AoE*, these questions come to light when the player is presented with what appears to be a simulation of the colonial system. Addressing this issue in *Age of Empires II* (Ensemble Studios, 1999), which is set in the medieval period, Angela Cox comments that the game is involved in the "othering of time."[8] The game creates an ideal imagined medieval period just as it creates similarly idealized constructions of cultures. On its face, these imaginings comprise token elements from the various civilizations and cultures that the game represents. However, a closer look reveals something different. Cox rightly observes that "the Japanese, Chinese, and Korean buildings use the same sequence of visual development, erasing distinctions between these East Asian cultures, as do the buildings for the Britons and the Celts—both of which take a strikingly English appearance."[9] This is also true in the first *AoE* game, where the Greeks and the Babylonians share the same military units: the axmen look almost Neolithic, and the horsemen are richly armored, irrespective of their diverse history of martial cultures. The construction of diverse cultures and ethnicities using set stereotypes is problematic for the way this practice erases and elides cultural difference. In a way, the game reproduces through play the relation between the player and the opponents as that between the empire and its Other. When they are viewed together as the Oriental Other, the distinctions between the East Asian cultures are easy to erase. This is also evident in the later games, where Brian Reynolds, who heads Big Huge Games, comments about *AoE III* that "one other fun detail . . . you may be aware that for religious reasons Indians do not consume cows and so forth, and so indeed they do not in the game."[10] In this comment, he seems unaware that although the Hindus do not eat beef, there are many other religious communities in India that do (the Mughal rulers who were Muslim would be one such example), and there is already an oversimplification going on here. Even with the best intentions of accurate cultural portrayal, these games end up mired in Western stereotypes about the Orient. No wonder then that when commenting on the depiction of the Middle East in *AoE II*, game studies scholar Vit Šisler compares it to "orientalist discourses of European novels and nineteenth century paintings."[11]

One key element of the colonial enterprise is that the Other needs to be known: knowledge enables control. The game map is, therefore, extremely important in *AoE* as is the "fog of war," the dark space that signifies the unexplored area and that only becomes visible once the player's units pass through it. The sooner the player explores the dark areas of the map to reveal what is hidden, the better are the chances of finding resources such as gold, stone, wood, and food. Sending scouts is the usual method of exploring uncharted territory. Exploring through the fog of war also makes the players aware of the buildings of enemy civilizations and finding the Other is both literally and metaphorically a journey where darkness is brought under control. This is very similar to the colonial stress on mapping and surveying, which gave the world some of the most rigorous cartographic surveys such as the Great Trigonometric Survey that calculated the height of Mount Everest. In the colonial system, mapping allows the colonizer to surveil territory, with visibility implying control. In the *AoE* games one can increase visibility as well as control access to areas by building watchtowers. Watchtowers can be upgraded to increase their defensive capabilities and their line of sight. The player's ability to view uncharted sections of the map implies the power to control: *how* something is seen is crucial in knowledge creation and the consequent empowerment of those who create and possess such knowledge.

The upgrades in technology are an important part of *AoE*, as well as with the civilizations advancing from the Tool Age, to the Bronze Age, and then to the Iron Age. Different units can be upgraded for a price of wood, stone, food, and gold—the aforementioned resources. The technology trees available with the game (often as a glossy folding brochure) seem to privilege the notion of technological determinism—better technology—ensures a more successful nation. The cultural aspects of a civilization are not even acknowledged. The closest that the designers come to culture is the building of the national "wonder." The wonder is not so much a cultural artifact as it is a pathway to a victory condition: "if it is constructed and stands for two thousand years, the player will automatically win the game."[12] In the game, most technological research is aimed at obtaining military upgrades—reinforcing the notion that success is achieved by colonizing other nations and occupying more territory, often by military means.

As the player meets resistance during the attempt to capture and colonize land, there is another game mechanic that can be used against the adversary: conversion. The priests in the player's civilization can convert soldiers and, sometimes, even buildings. Conversion makes it possible for the empire to assimilate people outside its own group. The foreign and the resistant populations can be controlled by turning them into soldiers of the empire. This has resonances, on many levels, with how the Other is conceived as a problem in colonial regimes and then subjected to a "conversion" of sorts. At the same time, attempts are made to control the Other by making it more like the colonizer. In 1835, British historian Lord Thomas Babington Macaulay published a "Minute Upon Indian Education" that decreed that the Indian population needed to be educated following a Western model based on the premise "a single shelf of a good European library was worth the whole native literature of India and Arabia."[13] The Minute influenced the English Education Act passed by the British-controlled Council of India in 1835, which reallocated funds away from education in Indian languages and toward Western curriculum and English-language instruction. The conversion of the Other to the more acceptable European-educated subject was about to begin. In the stereotypical schema of *AoE*, such a conversion is depicted as immediate and totalizing. Of course, the act of the priest waving his arms and the opponent unit changing its color to that of the player's is akin to a total brainwashing, in the way it is often depicted in dystopian science fiction. The conversion could also be a metaphor for slavery—a key component of the colonial process that is often elided in empire-building games.

The easy acceptance of assumptions that make empire look inevitable is quite characteristic of *AoE*. Bruce Shelley, designer of the *AoE* games, states that "one of the key element in any *Age of Empires* game is verisimilitude—the idea that while a game doesn't have to be completely historically accurate, it should contain enough accurate elements that one gets the flavor of the period."[14] Esther MacCallum-Stewart and Justin Parsler contend that "history games cannot exist in a bubble, and need to be accountable for the version of history they present, as well as changing attitudes to historical theory and representation in the outside world."[15] Shelley's argument that *AoE* aims to provide a "flavor" of history raises questions as to what exactly that flavor is. As is obvious from the title, *AoE* posits the empire as the key system of governance and engine for social transformation, one that privileges colonial stereotypes in its construction of strategic gameplay. Of course, it is possible to tell the story in another way; games have multiple endings, after all. As a counterfactual historical exploration, it is possible to see historical events reversed and a different victor emerge as conqueror in this rendering of our world. This alternative history, however, would be the product of the same underlying logic of empire. As MacCallum-Stewart and Parsler note, one should exercise caution when using these games as teaching tools.[16] Beyond this, it is also necessary that players view the limitations of such games in relation to larger discussions in world history. Whether it professes to recount history or even just a "flavor" of it, *AoE* views history as stories of imperial greatness, something that current trends in historiography call into question. The game is unaware of debates in postcolonialism that have been popular in humanities discourses for more than half a century. Twenty years after its release, *AoE* continues to be popular among the historical RTS games; nevertheless, rereading (and replaying) it through a postcolonial lens provides a fresh perspective on both how the game represents history and how empire itself is constructed as a game to be played and won.

NOTES

1 Jeff Sengstack, "Microsoft Takes a Stab at the Golden Age of Wargaming," *GameSpot*, March 1, 2004, www.gamespot.com.

2 Old PC Gaming, "Age of Empires (1997)—PC Review," *Old PC Gaming*, July 31, 1994, www.oldpcgaming.net.

3 Eric Hobsbawm, *The Age of Empire: 1875–1914*, repr. ed. (New York: Vintage, 1989).

4 Franz Fanon, *The Wretched of the Earth*, trans. Homi Bhabha (New York: Grove Press, 2004 [1963]), 155.

5 Bill Ashcroft, Gareth Griffiths, and Helen Tiffin, *The Post-Colonial Studies Reader* (Abingdon and Oxford, UK: Taylor & Francis, 2006), 1.

6 Ania Loomba, *Colonialism/Postcolonialism*, 2nd ed. (London; New York: Routledge, 2005), 21.

7 Elleke Boehmer, *Colonial and Postcolonial Literature: Migrant Metaphors* (Oxford, UK: Oxford University Press, 2005), 2.

8 Angela Cox, "The Othering of Time in Age of Empires II | Play the Past," *Play the Past*, August 1, 2013, www.playthepast.org.

9 Cox, "The Othering of Time."

10 Steve Butts, "Age of Empires III: The Asian Dynasties," *IGN*, June 25, 2007, www.ign.com.

11 Vít Šisler, "Digital Arabs Representation in Video Games," *European Journal of Cultural Studies* 11, no. 2 (May 1, 2008): 203–220.

12 "Wonder (Age of Empires)," *Age of Empires Series Wiki*, 2016, accessed October 23, 2016, http://ageofempires.wikia.com.

13 Thomas Babington Macaulay, "Minute on Education (1835) by Thomas Babington Macaulay," *Project South Asia*, accessed October 23, 2016, www.columbia.edu.

14 Esther MacCallum-Stewart and Justin Parsler, "Controversies: Historicising the Computer Game," in *Situated Play, Proceedings of DiGRA 2007 Conference* (Tokyo: The University of Tokyo, 2007) , 203–210.

15 MacCallum-Stewart and Parsler, "Controversies," 206.

16 MacCallum-Stewart and Parsler, "Controversies."

FURTHER READING

Fanon, Franz. *Black Skins, White Masks*, trans. Richard Philcox. New York: Perseus Books, 2007 (1967).

Loomba, Ania. *Colonialism/Postcolonialism*, 2nd ed. London: Routledge, 2005.

Mukherjee, Souvik. "Playing Subaltern: Videogames and Postcolonialism." *Games and Culture* 13 (2016): 504–520.

Said, Edward. *Orientalism*. New York: Vintage Books, 1979.

20

Borderlands
Capitalism

MATTHEW THOMAS PAYNE AND MICHAEL FLEISCH

Abstract: Matthew Thomas Payne and Michael Fleisch argue that the inventory management at the heart of the *Borderlands* series reflects capitalism's ritual logic by celebrating the pleasures of maximizing wealth and commodity accumulation. Furthermore, the ways in which players both follow and break the games' rules of exchange reveal that capitalism is itself an uneven and exploitative gamified system.

It has been said that it is easier to imagine the end of civilization than it is to imagine the end of capitalism. As with much received wisdom, the origin of this aphorism is up for debate; some point to Marxist cultural theorist Fredric Jameson, others ascribe it to the philosopher-provocateur Slavoj Žižek, and still others credit cultural historian H. Bruce Franklin. Yet, importantly, the claim itself is hardly contested. The idea that capitalism can survive calamities ranging from giant asteroids to nuclear fallout resonates because it conforms to our shared imaginary popularized by post-apocalyptic fiction. Indeed, numerous fictional worlds have been decimated by natural disasters, leveled by bombs, or invaded by hostile aliens. Consider television's *Jericho, Falling Skies, Battlestar Galactica;* cinema's *Mad Max, Waterworld, Children of Men;* or the video game universes of *Fallout, Rage,* or *The Last of Us.* Despite the cataclysmic events that have befallen these realms, and for all the social and environmental upheaval that make them distorted versions of our own world, what endures in some distilled form is capitalism, an economic system of private ownership predicated on the accumulation of goods and mediated by a marketplace of exchange, all of which is propelled by conditions of scarcity, a desire for profit, and inescapable competition.

This, too, is the case for the *Borderlands* series of video games. In *Borderlands* (Gearbox Software, 2009) and *Borderlands 2* (Gearbox Software, 2012), the player is an adventurer seeking riches on the ravaged and dangerous planet of Pandora. In the years preceding the player's arrival, Pandora's mineral resources attracted waves of fortune seekers and corporations. After extracting what they could, these groups abandoned their facilities and released the criminals who were used as forced laborers. Pandora's remaining settlers were left to fend for themselves, competing for survival against the planet's indigenous monsters and the now-liberated criminal population.

The player is thrust into these harsh and unforgiving conditions with the primary goal of finding "The Vault," a legendary treasure trove of money, guns, armor, and assorted technologies. Along the way, players earn money and level up their characters and weapons until they are finally equipped to face the game's nastiest enemies. The sequel introduces more characters and settings, but the endgame remains the same: dispatch innumerable enemies en route to discovering and accumulating hidden treasures. The series showcases capitalism's excesses and its underlying logic in multiple ways. Narratively, Pandora's history is one of unchecked exploitation on a planetary level, a point consistently raised by the world's rusted ruins and its corporations' aggressive branding and advertising. Procedurally, the games require players to engage in endless cycles of item accumulation and marketplace exchanges. The drive to efficiently maximize in-game economic advantage finds its most fulsome expression in some players' pursuits of advantageous programming glitches and exploits. These unauthorized "solutions," and the backlash against using them, reveal that capitalism, as rendered and performed in the *Borderlands* community, is itself an uneven gamified system founded on exploitation and power imbalance.

The series has been a hit with gamers and critics alike, spawning the spinoff *Borderlands: The Pre-Sequel* (2K Australia, 2014); a graphic adventure game, *Tales from the Borderlands* (Telltale Games, 2014); a feature film that is in development as of 2018; and a commitment from Gearbox to create another installment. The franchise has been widely praised for its cooperative-preferred gameplay and for the darkly sardonic humor of its narrative campaigns. Conceived as a "*Halo-Diablo*" mash-up, these games combine the perspective and frenetic action of a first-person shooter (FPS) with the leveling-up and item-collection systems of a role-playing game (RPG). The gratuitous gun violence is tempered by cartoonish, cell-shaded graphics that—according to the developer's visual design team—give the games an "ill-mannered whimsy."[1] Furthermore, the games' procedural content generation systems add gameplay variation and tiered incentives to the otherwise repetitive quests and combat activities.[2] These content algorithms spawn an assortment of shields, guns, and items, virtually ensuring that no two treasure chests or loot boxes contain the same goodies. *Borderlands 2*'s promotional campaign boasts of "87 bazillion guns," a clearly tongue-in-cheek gesture toward the practically infinite combinations of gear and loot to be discovered.[3]

Yet this marketing hyperbole gestures at a substantial design challenge: how to guard against creating repetitive and rote tasks that lead to a sense of "grinding." Although the games' mechanics keep enemies at appropriate levels of difficulty to promote a balanced sense of experiential "flow"[4]—the enemy is rarely too easy (leading to boredom) or too difficult (leading to anxiety and frustration)—there is a great deal of noncombat content begging to be played. That is, although primarily pitched as a "role-playing shooter"—a term coined to describe the first *Borderlands'* unique mix of gameplay styles—much fun comes from contemplative, nonfrenetic moments of gathering, buying, selling, and trading items.

Hidden behind the comic-book veneer and cartoonish gunplay one finds an ostensible action franchise built on gamified file management. *Borderlands* is a game of data defragmentation supported by an ideological commitment to economic liberalism and private property. As a file-management FPS, *Borderlands* cycles fragging (slaying enemies to reap rewards) and defragging (economizing one's inventory), with each activity driving and reinforcing the other. The successful player painstakingly optimizes the endless inundation of guns, armor, and class-specific skills to unlock a variety of combat effects and benefits. Weaker items are traded or sold away to allow for the acquisition of marginally better goods. Indeed, in these protracted moments, this FPS franchise is better conceived of as a first-person spreadsheet.

To understand *Borderlands* simply as an action-oriented role-playing shooter is to elide some of its most basic, capitalistic pleasures—both sanctioned and unsanctioned. The games' rendering of laissez-faire capitalism engenders pleasures of accumulation by maximizing one's return-on-(playtime-)investment through the strategic management of in-game assets. This is the "right" way to play the game. There are likewise unsanctioned pleasures to be had by circumventing those systems with exploits and glitches. Thus, these games present a case study in a designed system of capital and how its users engage in *and* work around that system.

To illustrate how the *Borderlands* games reflect, internalize, and articulate reigning beliefs about free market capitalism, we discuss the repetitive cycling between the fragging that begets item accumulation and the decision-making that defrags one's limited inventory space. Next, we explore how the accumulation of property implicitly invites players to discover shortcuts to transform otherwise banal file management into the efficiently sublime. By attending to the designed trading systems, as well as gamers' pursuits of shortcuts, we demonstrate that Pandora is a post-apocalyptic wasteland that has been ravaged and exhausted by capitalism in appearance only. Instead, it should be seen for what it truly is: an idealized and thriving playground of late capitalism, a place where maximizing wealth accumulation remains the game's primary focus and where subverting the game's

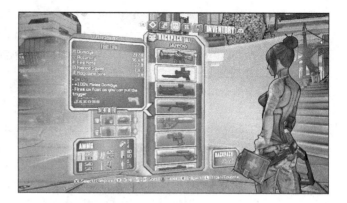

FIGURE 20.1
A player carefully
optimizes the inventory
options.

established economic system violates the letter but adheres to the spirit of capitalism's law.

Gun-based combat and the micro-management of one's inventory and skill
tree dominate the gameplay of *Borderlands*. As limited inventory space is filled by
loot collected from bested enemies and completed quests, gamers make repeated
trips to the vending machines that dot Pandora's landscape. These colorful machines are used to buy and sell guns, armor, grenades, and various class-specific
upgrades.[5] Not only are they critical to the game's leveling and asset management
processes, but because vending machines are insulated from enemies by a safe
remove, these sites also function as social hubs for players trading gear and tips.
Checking for daily specials, re-upping on ammo, selling less effective items, and
so on constitute a necessary pre- and postfight routine; one needs to gear up before a big battle and unload postconflict spoils. These vending machines serve as
veritable water coolers for collective strategizing on optimizing character builds
and synchronizing complementary skill sets. Over time, the repetitive vending
machine meet-ups transform into social rituals (see figure 20.1).

Gameplay repetition should not be confused with ritual. Through an iterative,
trial-and-error process players make sense of a game's rules and play mechanics.
Repetition is key for establishing the pattern recognition that is the foundation for
successful gameplay: green mushrooms give Mario extra lives; power pellets turn
Pac-Man's ghosts into vulnerable blue targets; completing a horizontal row of blocks
clears a line in *Tetris*. But pattern recognition does not necessarily give rise to meaningful and ritualized play. All game rituals involve repetition, but not all gameplay
repetitions carry ritualistic meanings. As Alison Gazzard and Alan Peacock note,
"[w]hile repetition is necessary within the game world, repetition that steps beyond
function and is understood as ritual provides the player with a significant moment
in the logic of the game."[6] A game's ritual logic is a culmination of repetitive actions

that bring about some essential transformation. Gameplay repetition offers information about what is possible, whereas gameplay ritual offers insight into the deep play structure representing broader cultural beliefs and social values.

Conceived along a spectrum, some repetitive activities are more functional or "automatic" in nature (i.e., necessary to make the game work) while others involve "conscious awareness" that imbue them with special meaning not found with the rote activities.[7] Counterintuitively, the automatic acts in *Borderlands* are the battles, whereas the plotting data management tasks are more ritualistic. Fighting and optimizing inventory are both repetitive and complementary actions. The better the gamer is at selecting the right items at the vending machines, the better equipped they are to fight enemies. And because Pandora is a perilous world full of numbers and multipliers that parade as colorful enemies and loot boxes, *Borderlands* grants gamers the visceral pleasure of immediately seeing the effects of their optimization efforts through quantified, aestheticized feedback: cascading rainbow numerals of drained hit points. Capitalism kills, beautifully.

What then is the ritual logic of *Borderlands*? What are those repetitive actions that, taken together, constitute a normative framework for understanding how Pandora functions as a fictional world while also revealing something about our own? Frequenting the vending machines in *Borderlands* is necessary for leveling up. As players review their inventories, a wealth of gaming information is shared between them: "Who needs a high-damage shottie?" "Is your assassin focusing on the rogue or gunslinger skill tree?" "How in the hell do you kill Skagzilla?" Information may be shared at any point, but the fact that it commonly happens in the safe spaces around vending machines transforms these sites into marketplaces for the exchange of items and gaming capital (see Mia Consalvo's chapter in this collection). The vending machine–based rituals of *Borderlands* present capitalism as a rules-based system that rewards incremental grinding and equitable economic exchange. When played "properly," *Borderlands* is a virtual lesson in the meritocratic virtues of capitalism and the Protestant work ethic, a post-apocalyptic American dream modeled through an interactive ritual logic. But this is not the only way to play the game. Indeed, how does one win at the game of capitalism? An obvious solution: one cheats.

If *Borderlands*'s ritual logic issues from the metered transmission of authorized, rules-based data, then it is a system begging to be hacked. As gamers repeatedly tear through *Borderlands*'s story campaigns in increasingly difficult playthroughs, they begin looking for alternative incentives beyond the narrative developments they have already experienced. Superlative item hunting becomes, for many, the enduring motivation for play; the pursuit of the most elusive, highest-level items evolves into a new, emergent endgame.

The *Borderlands* player community evidences passionate differences of opinion regarding their interpretations of what constitutes exploits and if and how these shortcuts should be utilized. Elite gamers up to speed on the latest discoveries thanks to YouTube and social media typically believe that these hacks fall into one of several categories: results of developer-intended design, unintended effects that nevertheless adhere to the game's parameters, clear software malfunctions, and cheat scripts uploaded by users. Moreover, the online discourse concerning these exploits tends toward moral positioning, the preceding list ordered by decreasing community acceptance, which maps precisely to perceived alignment with the developers' intent. This promotes a model of the producer–consumer dynamic along a spectrum of socio-moral norms, where the gamer community self-polices according to the rules they believe the developers want them to follow. Thus, any "cheating" becomes less about one's *own* gaming experiences and more about whether players who have "worked hard" to earn the top items truly have the most power versus those with whom they are not in contact—those who have "gamed the system." This oppositional framing mirrors the labor-versus-capital power struggle at the heart of many critiques of capitalism; is there greater potential for growth by grinding out a slowly improving bare survival (labor) or by leaping to access exceptional items (capital)? Who would you rather be: the dutiful gamer who maintains the sanctity of capitalism's magic circle of meritocracy or the "cheater" who games the system for personal reward, including showcasing the cracks in the system?

The best-known *Borderlands 2* exploit involved a marriage of legendary items: "The Bee" amp-damage shield (which added a large amount of damage to every fired projectile) and the "Conference Call" shotgun (which randomly fires between 5 and 77 pellets). Gamers quickly discovered that a single player could defeat nearly invincible super-bosses in just a few seconds. Within two weeks of release, the exploit had grabbed the attention of Gearbox CEO Randy Pitchford, who tweeted, ". . . Bee shield is so getting nerfed."[8] One month later, a patch required for online play dramatically weakened The Bee and similar amp-damage shields. Addressing the inevitable backlash, Pitchford again took to Twitter: "Bee was broken. Not nerfed enough, [in my opinion]. Some of you like broken games—I get it."[9] Gearbox has frequently rebalanced other aspects of gameplay with similar patches, usually igniting similarly passionate responses. "Hacking" bugs in programming code to produce a better outcome for one's character or team presents capitalism as a "meta" game, one where—instead of fighting more monsters for marginally better loot—players engage in complex but illicit innovating of the game itself. Meanwhile, Gearbox "corrects" its titles with patches while fans loyal to authorial intent take to discussion boards to shun and shame peers who manipulate its systems.

The core generic challenge in post-apocalyptic games is surviving with very little. The dramatic tension and, indeed, the fun of these titles come from managing a scarcity of resources. The ritual logic of *Borderlands* asks players to balance the pros and cons of a given character build and equip gear against the demands of a quest and the makeup of their party; *Borderlands* is a first-person spreadsheet in need of constant adjusting and balancing. Yet the state of artificial scarcity created and perpetuated by the franchise—a hostile environment defined by scant goods (despite the digital capacity to remedy any such shortage)—incents players to seek out exploits and glitches that offer elegant gameplay shortcuts.

Borderlands' content generation algorithms are calibrated (and recalibrated via patches and updates) to give players *just enough* of an edge to incentivize additional play while enterprising gamers find ways to beat the system. And although nearly all games, by necessity, keep overpowered objects from players to engender balance and a sense of challenge, few titles are so thoroughly imbued with a kind of neoliberal play economy where the design logic expresses an underlying market ideology.

Culturally and economically speaking, *Borderlands* is an exceedingly American game series. Pandora is a frontier-style, free-market universe populated by adventurers who dutifully grind hour after hour in pursuit of the next level. Once dedicated gamers complete the story missions and reach their level cap, they can continue the fight to collect and then display rare items to showcase their gaming acumen. But the circulation of tips that produce such digital goodies carries with it a radical gesture that belies its subversive counterplay; there is more than just "cheating" afoot.

Capitalism's ideological power is partly owed to its ability to appear neutral and natural and not as it is—a set of contingent and exploitative social conditions that mediate our relationships to one another and to our world. Similarly, the gameplay rules of *Borderlands* model capitalism as a cyclical fantasy of commodity accumulation in a never-ending pursuit of satisfying a perceived lack. But the calming balm of the next-best gun offers only temporary relief. The game's progression mechanic is a "bait and switch" trick that models capitalism's relentless spirit of perpetual accumulation. Gameplay satisfaction is fleeting in *Borderlands*. One can never have enough stuff, and there is always more stuff to be had.

The ritual logic of *Borderlands'* gameplay effectively conditions and supports character customization and optimization, a drive that is simultaneously perpetuated and satisfied by the franchise's vibrant fan community. But the pervasive discussion board theme of "proper" gameplay-turned-morality arguments, in tandem with Gearbox's frequent updates, sanction and forbid certain gameplay practices in service of maintaining a perfect relationship between utility and rarity on Pandora. This is the mythic and idealized state of meritocratic capitalism. With every newly discovered exploit, scarcity is revealed as but one possible universal precondition, and the existence of alternatives is incrementally reconfirmed, at least until the next patch; ironically, the game inadvertently reveals the truth that there is not a singular, natural capitalism but multiple, socially engineered capitalisms and that exploitations are not outside the system but are inherent to its nature.

In closing, it is worth asking, "What does it mean—culturally, ethically—that even in a cartoonish role-playing fantasy game, light-years removed from our own reality, that capitalism persists? Are *Borderlands* players who condemn others for gaming the system protecting Gearbox's rules of play, or those that govern free market capitalism? What will it take to reimagine the rules and rituals of the digital sandbox?" Perhaps the next *Borderlands* installment will feature a Pandora that privileges user creativity over the algorithm, user freedom over developer control, creative abundance over capitalistic scarcity. But, alas, as someone once said, that's a pretty hard world to imagine.

NOTES

1 Aaron Thibault, "Postmortem—Gearbox's Borderlands," *Game Developer* 17, no. 2 (February 2010): 27.

2 Julian Togelius, Emil Kastbjerg, David Schedl, and Georgios N. Yannakakis, "What Is Procedural Content Generation?: Mario on the Borderline," in *Proceedings of the 2nd International Workshop on Procedural Content Generation in Games*, June 28, 2011 (Bordeaux France: ACM, 2011), 3.

3 The developer has not shared the exact number of guns in *Borderlands 2*. However, the first *Borderlands* title holds the Guinness World Record for most weapons at a staggering 17.75 million. See Wesley Yin-Poole, "How Many Weapons Are in Borderlands 2?," *Eurogamer*, July 16, 2012, www.eurogamer.net.

4 Jeanne Nakamura and Mihaly Csikszentmihalyi, "The Concept of Flow," in *Handbook of Positive Psychology*, ed. Charles R. Snyder and Shane J. Lopez (New York: Oxford University Press, 2002), 89–105.

5 Jacob Brogan, "Why Did this Guy Collect 500 Screenshots of Soda Machines in Video Games? Because He Is a Genius," *Slate*, October 21, 2016, www.slate.com.

6 Alison Gazzard and Alan Peacock, "Repetition and Ritual Logic in Video Games," *Games and Culture* 6, no. 6 (2011): 505.

7 Gazzard and Peacock, "Repetition and Ritual Logic," 505–506.

8 Randy Pitchford (@DuvalMagic), "@AddyJohn_V Bee shield is so getting nerfed," Twitter, October 6, 2012, 12:38 PM, https://twitter.com/duvalmagic/status/254666987479904256.

9 Randy Pitchford (@DuvalMagic), "Bee was broken. Not nerfed enough, IMO. Some of you like broken games - I get it," Twitter, November 14, 2012, 7:38 AM, https://twitter.com/DuvalMagic/status/268709452096610304.

FURTHER READING

Consalvo, Mia. *Cheating: Gaining Advantage in Videogames*. Cambridge, MA: MIT Press, 2007.

Kline, Stephen, Nick Dyer-Witherford, and Greig de Peuter. *Digital Play: The Interaction of Technology, Culture, and Marketing*. Montreal: McGill-Queen's University Press, 2003.

Mandel, Ernest. *An Introduction to Marxist Economic Theory*. New York: Pathfinder, 2005.

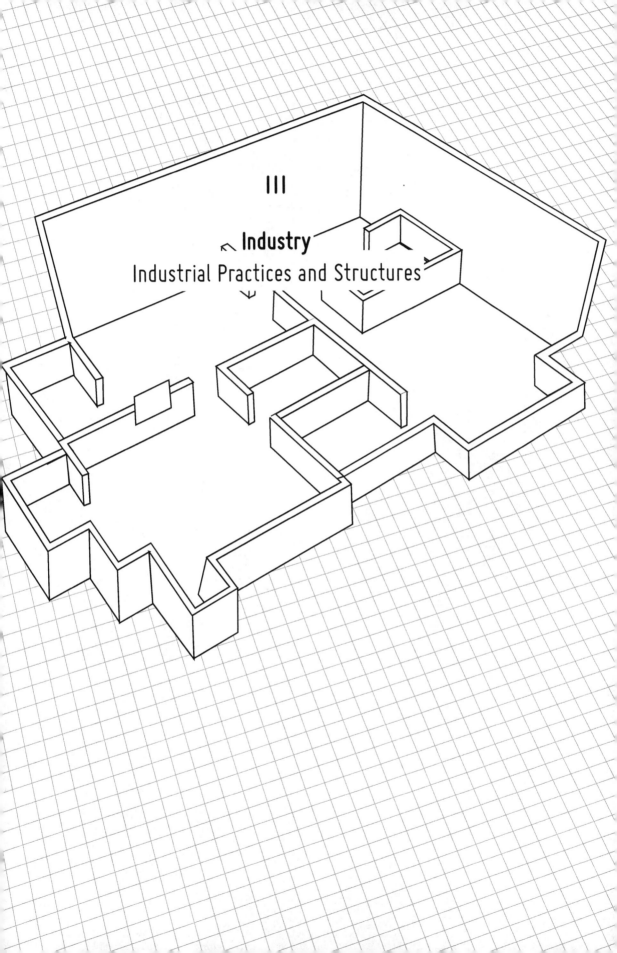

III

Industry
Industrial Practices and Structures

21

Miyamoto/Kojima
Authorship

JENNIFER DEWINTER

Abstract: Games are often celebrated for the fact that players are co-authors of their interactive experiences, yet turning attention to the designer shifts the conversation to the formation of the game as a designed, vision-driven experience. Jennifer deWinter uses Shigeru Miyamoto and Hideo Kojima—two Japanese game designers with very different backgrounds and visions—to explore how game designers author video games in significant and observable ways, which are embedded in personal, historical, and cultural contexts.

Game designers are charged with translating experiences into systems, such as intense confrontation, the closeness of teamwork, the betrayal of colleagues, or even love or despair. Game designers have to know how those systems will mediate experiences, from the game engine to the interface and controller. Players pick up the controller, start the game, and play with the rules and affordances crafted by designers. Ostensibly, "good" games are those where the designer's vision is the same as what the player experiences.

The challenge with analyzing a game as the product of a particular designer is that games are most often team projects with multiple points for creative input and technical decision making: game and physics engines, artificial intelligence, level design, story and character writing, concept art and art assets, and so on. Furthermore, the act of play feels so much like a process of co-creation between game and player that one can argue that the player is also part author for the game; player choice allows games to unfold in different and sometimes surprising ways. Auteur theory, then, might be more useful in accounting for the role of the designer. Auteur theory posits that film directors instantiate their vision through a host of cinematic elements: narrative design, visual style, editing, and so forth.[1]

Likewise, in the game industry, there are game designers who have strong visions of what their games should be and can mobilize their collaborators to create a single, unified text.[2] Unlike film directors, novelists, or television showrunners, people often struggle to name more than a handful of game designers. Yet these designers matter; they create the affordances of the game. As Gonzalo Frasca succinctly argues, "the simauthor [his word for the designer] always has the final word and remains in charge because total player freedom is impossible since it would imply that no rules are unchangeable and therefore the game could literally become anything."[3] The challenge is to account for games as created objects.

Game designers are at heart experience designers; therefore, an auteur approach to game designers needs to attend to how game designers are trained to think about experiences, how their cultural context shapes their worldview, and how their working conditions allow them to realize their visions. Comparing contemporary game designers will reveal how these factors shaped differing design philosophies of two Japanese game auteurs: Shigeru Miyamoto and Hideo Kojima.

Shigeru Miyamoto is synonymous with Nintendo. After completing a degree in industrial design and art, Miyamoto joined Nintendo in 1977. For a while, he did non-game-related design and painted arcade cabinets. His first game design opportunity came when he had a chance to redesign *Radar Scope* (Nintendo R&D1, 1979), a failed arcade game that left 2,000 unsold arcade cabinets in a warehouse. Under the mentorship of Gunpei Yokoi, an electrical engineer and toy designer, Miyamoto drew from his background as an amateur manga artist to create *Donkey Kong* (Nintendo R&D1, 1981). The game is notable because of its mangalike characters and continuous vertical space; the player's character Jumpman climbs the building to rescue Lady from a large gorilla. From these early experiences, Miyamoto-the-designer begins to emerge.

Miyamoto's design philosophy is heavily influenced by the fact that he is both a hardware and a software developer. He is also a product of his cultural context, with a tendency toward perfectionism and polish. Miyamoto's university training and his apprenticeship under the watchful eye of Gunpei Yokoi engendered a design sensitivity that sought to support community play for low economic investment. Yokoi's philosophy of *kareta gijutsu no shuhei shikou* (lateral thinking with withered technology) infuses Miyamoto's and Nintendo's approach to hardware design and reuse. Hardware doesn't need to be new and cutting edge to drive market demand; it just needs to allow for new applications and novel experiences at a low price point (such as repurposing the *Radar Scope* cabinet). This early training in hardware affordances, in fact, was foundational throughout Miyamoto's career. He was actively involved in hardware and controller development, understanding that controllers and platforms affect gameplay experiences just as much as his created levels. And finally, Miyamoto is dedicated to translating his life experiences

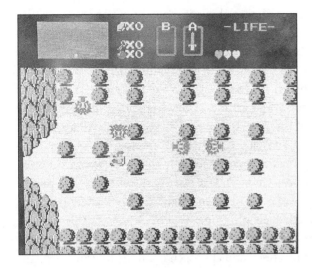

FIGURE 21.1
Link explores forests and
caves in this early level of
The Legend of Zelda.

into games, such as the joy he has for his hobbies, which is the heart of his experience design. This begins to solidify with his NES/Super Famicom undertakings (started simultaneously): *Super Mario Bros.* (Nintendo R&D4, 1985) and *The Legend of Zelda* (Nintendo R&D4, 1986).

For both *Super Mario Bros.* and *The Legend of Zelda*, Miyamoto was interested in translating his childhood experiences into gameplay. Miyamoto often speaks about exploring caves in Sonobe, Japan, as a child; thus, exploration became his signature core game mechanic. Perhaps more easily seen in *Zelda* (see figure 21.1), exploration is also a central part of what makes *Super Mario Bros.* such a successful game. Players discover pipes that they can go down, invisible blocks that they can climb to cloud kingdoms, and dungeons that they must traverse. Based on his love of playgrounds, *Super Mario Bros.* incorporates the joy of exploration with other playground staples—sliding, running, and jumping—all within a brightly colored landscape, which forever influenced subsequent platforming games around the world.

The Legend of Zelda, originally named *Mario Adventure* in early design documents, offered a different metaphor for spatial exploration in the form of a map. Players control the protagonist Link to find and explore hidden caves. Obviously, battle and puzzle-solving infuse this game as well, but the core experience of exploration and discovery is evident in this top-down action role-playing game. These two games, then, offer different instantiations of a single design vision, showcasing Miyamoto's ability to use the affordances of available technologies to realize different pathways and nuances to the same core experience.

In some ways, both games seem to diverge from the arcade design days preceding them. However, this is not actually the case. Miyomoto's early training with arcade game design strongly influences his approach to home console game design. The same characters from *Donkey Kong* now provide the starting point for his game design process—Jumpman is now Mario, and Lady is now Princess Peach. The call to action in all these games is essentially the same: the player must rescue the kidnapped lady/princess. What is less obvious but more important is the fact that Miyamoto understood that arcade games were about designing play experiences that would gratify those playing the game and attract and amuse on-lookers as well. He wanted people to laugh together, emphasizing video gaming as a communal experience. This makes sense in something like *Super Mario Bros.*, which is designed as a two-person game and is fast-paced enough that people can sit on the couch and enjoy watching a run-through. Yet even a solitary game like *The Legend of Zelda* compelled people to get together at school or at work and talk about the game, sharing secrets and strategies.

These seeds of game design philosophy and approach continue to grow through-out his career at Nintendo, and Miyamoto's core experiences shift to reflect chang-ing interests. For example, when Miyamoto took up gardening, he translated his joy of planting, tending for, and raising plants into the game *Pikmin* (Nintendo EAD, 2001). Likewise, when he became a dog owner, he enjoyed raising his dog so much that he created *Nintendogs* (Nintendo EAD, 2005). Importantly, these games are not simulations of what it is like to garden or the obligations of dog owner-ship, but they are about "the joy of" that experience, capturing the feeling of what brings people together. As a result, players can use Wi-Fi Connection on their Nintendo DS handheld consoles to let their dogs visit one another. Conversely, if players ignore their dogs (forget to clean up messes or take them on walks), nothing bad happens; dogs don't die in the game. There are no high-stakes conse-quences for the more laborious parts of dog ownership.

Although the mythology of Miyamoto has always emphasized his being a free spirit with long hair who likes to play banjo and draw manga, the fact is that his training in industrial design emphasizes the human operating within a defined system. Furthermore, as a product of Nintendo, he always worked at the inter-section of hardware and software to bring gaming experiences to the market as cheaply as possible for the greatest profit. A properly theorized understanding of authorship should account for the full complexity of the designer and his or her relationship with their corporate structures and teams. With Miyamoto, for ex-ample, people have uncritically embraced the compelling yet historically incom-plete view of Miyamoto as a beatnik designer who is disinterested in the business of the trade. This could not be further from the case. Another danger of employ-ing auteur theory is analyzing one designer and extrapolating those findings to any game designer in similar contexts. This is simply not so, as the story of Hideo Kojima demonstrates.

Kojima entered the game industry in 1986, almost 10 years after Miyamoto. Like Miyamoto, he thought that he wanted to be an artist and, like Miyamoto, his family and friends dissuaded him from pursuing this dream in lieu of a more stable and predictable career path. Interestingly, Kojima cites Miyamoto's *Super Mario Bros.* as one of the games that would inspire him to enter the game industry. However, this is where the similarities between the designers end. Kojima majored in economics with the goal of becoming a film director. This draws specifically from his childhood when he was left alone most of the time as a latchkey kid and ended up watching a lot of television and movies. This early emphasis on film finds its way into Kojima's design, appearing in his narrative structure and in the cinematic visuals of cutscenes and gameplay. Kojima joined Konami in 1986, surprising his friends that he was joining the ranks of video game development rather than working in film or television.

Konami is a Japanese media firm that produces and publishes a range of entertainment goods: video games, arcade cabinets and slot machines, anime and films, and trading cards. Unlike Nintendo, Konami was not in the business of manufacturing home consoles. Thus, when Kojima had the opportunity to create *Metal Gear* (1987), he had to do so within the affordances of the Microsoft MSX2 console (popular in Japan at the time), which limited Kojima's color palate (annoying enough for someone interested in cinematics) and combat mechanics. Despite these considerable limitations, what emerged was a stealth game in which players experience a camera angle that cinematically informs the viewer of constant threat and tension, a technique that he would cultivate over the following iterations of the *Metal Gear* franchise. Kojima's cinematic influence can be seen in the wide shots, narrative and character development, filmic scoring techniques, and changes in pacing to build suspense into his games.

Like Miyamoto, Kojima is Japanese; however, Kojima's generational cultural landscape was notably different from Miyamoto's. Whereas Miyamoto grew up watching (and therefore adapted stories from) *Popeye* and the Japanese children's show *Hyokkorihyoutanjima*, Kojima came of age 10 years later, consuming mecha and cyberpunk texts such as *Gundam, Macross, Area 88, Bubblegum Crisis,* and *Akira.* The broad themes and tropes that underpin these narratives find their way into Kojima games, such as the seemingly ubiquitous mecha units, theme naming of characters,[4] narrative betrayals by father figures, and a strong protagonist with significant emotional setbacks. All this is done within a coherent cinematic setting rather than in levels that discretely organize play experiences.

By the time Kojima is contracted to design *Metal Gear Solid* (Konami, 1998) for the PlayStation, the technologies of game production could finally support his demanding cinematic vision. The third-person game camera still places the main character in the foreground with the threat of enemies always revealed to the

FIGURE 21.2
Metal Gear Solid
emphasizes
cinematic features
including char-
acter placement,
camera angles,
and depth of field.

player (see figure 21.2), and the narrative remains built around masculine melo-
drama. Yet Kojima was interested in using the video game medium to integrate
the player into the cinematic diegesis. For example, he was interested in creating
responsive sound and music tracks for this game (something that he did not realize until later games). In an interview, Kojima explained, "Music is so important
in both film and games. It's not only melodious background music that defines a
soundtrack. Music can convey a character's inner emotions or foreshadow future
events. Sound effects can also assist the direction."[5] However, he was unable to
realize responsive sound for his 1998 game, but that didn't stop his commitment
to cinematic quality in games. He worked with the Konami Computer Entertainment Sound Team Japan to create a cinematic-quality score and soundtrack
for the game, which was subsequently released that same year. Additionally, the
narrative framework and pacing of the game continue to draw strongly from the
movies and anime that Kojima cites as lifelong influences.

All this speaks to Kojima's interest and training as an aspiring filmmaker
turned game designer. What is especially revealing is how Kojima exploits the
game system to translate his cinematic influences into gameplay. For example,
he often talks about Hitchcock films as an influence and the ways that Hitchcock used the medium specificities of cinema to create tension and fear. Because
players are free to make their own choices, decisions that may break deep emotional engagement and connection, Kojima has created alternative means of playing with the storytelling potential of games. For instance, to narratively engage
players during *Metal Gear Solid*'s Psycho Mantis battle, Kojima manipulated players' assumptions. Suddenly, the television was acting like it lost input from the
console device, and the antagonist could read all the moves of the player and

was thus unbeatable—unbeatable, that is, unless the player moved the controller plug from the player 1 port to the player 2 port. With this, the whole game system, television, console, and player were part of the puzzle of the video game, extending the magic circle out of the confines of the screen to more explicitly include the player's body and material reality into this digitally mediated play.[6] And this evolution—building on core storytelling strengths of the past and expanding those to fully exploit the possibilities of the medium—has many naming Kojima the first video game auteur.

The challenge with analyzing game auteurs is that not all games have a distinct vision attributed to a singular figure, which asks us to consider *why* some games seem to have a distinct vision while others do not. What catapults a person or group of people into auteur status when so many games seem to be made by nameless designers? Regardless, the work of designers (named auteurs, credited designers, or invisible creators) is equally important to game culture writ large. Games that are derivative are no less products of their creators and cultures. Furthermore, by focusing on the auteur, games criticism runs the risk of effacing the input and labor of others who may have also strongly shaped the gameplay experience. Miyamoto, for example, doesn't care about narrative, but he has narrative writers who do. As a result, he is praised for games like *The Legend of Zelda: Twilight Princess* (Nintendo EAD, 2006) because of the narrative complexity, yet the praise is rightly owed to his team. In other words, an auteur's cultural and business context, training, and personal design goals all matter, but so too do the teams they work with. One challenge of critical game studies is not to simply conduct close readings of games; it is also to articulate the design vision, the experience goals of the game designer, the relationship that the designer has with his or her team, and how that vision finds in-game expression. The other, and arguably more important, goal is to look broadly at game designers and to create an inclusive list of creative laborers, not simply those who earn the title of auteur or those with their names on game boxes. A broader approach to authorship makes a place for holistically interrogating a designer's (and a design team's) personal, historical, and cultural contexts to better understand what influences the games we play.

NOTES

1 In the early development of this theory, Alexandre Astruc proposed the idea of a "camera-stylo," or camera pen to create the analogy between what he does as a director and what a novelist does. Alexandre Astruc "The Birth of the New Avant-Garde: La Camera-Stylo / Du Stylo à la caméra et de la caméra au stylo," *L'Écran Française*, March 1948.

2 Yet even in adopting this approach, researchers must take care. Auteur theory can mask or efface the contributions of others, it can perpetuate an intentionalist fallacy that seems to claim all design choices come from careful and purposeful consideration and

overemphasize the designer's role in meaning-making while ignoring how players create meaning or even distributors and marketers shape meaning and messaging.

3 Gonzalo Frasca, "Simulation versus Narrative: Introduction to Ludology," in *The Video Game Theory Reader*, ed. Mark J. P. Wolf and Bernard Perron (New York: Routledge, 2003), 233.

4 Theme naming is a trope wherein characters or places are given a category of names. In MGS, FOXHOUND group members are all named after animals.

5 Hideo Kojima, "Hideo Kojima at the Movies: Hitchcock Films," *Official PlayStation 2 Magazine*, August 2003, archived on www.metalgearsolid.net.

6 For more discussion on the magic circle, see Steven Conway's chapter in this collection.

FURTHER READING

deWinter, Jennifer. *Shigeru Miyamoto: Donkey Kong, Super Mario Bros., The Legend of Zelda.* New York: Bloomsbury, 2015.

Kirkpatrick, Graeme, Ewa Mazierska, and Lars Kristensen. "Marxism and the Computer Game." *Journal of Gaming & Virtual Worlds* 8, no. 2 (2016): 117–130.

Kocurek, Carly A. *Brenda Laurel: Pioneering Games for Girls.* New York: Bloomsbury, 2017.

Salter, Anastasia. *Jane Jensen: Gabriel Knight, Adventure Games, Hidden Objects.* New York: Bloomsbury, 2017.

22

Clash Royale
Gaming Capital

MIA CONSALVO

Abstract: This chapter explores how gaming capital—the deep knowledge about how a game works—operates in Supercell's free-to-play, player-versus-player tower defense game *Clash Royale*. By examining high-profile YouTube content creators, Mia Consalvo explores how the video game strategy guide maker not only has garnered more attention from game fans and the industry but also now requires a greater commitment to producing content to stay relevant with constantly updated game releases.

The advent of home game consoles and increasingly sophisticated video games in the 1990s and early 2000s opened up new markets not just for games but also for various products that supported play. These products could be considered paratexts—texts that framed how to understand games or that helped players figure out how to play a video game—including game reviews, game magazines, books of cheat codes, and strategy guides.[1] For many of the most complex games, particularly those that drew on well-established brands from triple-A developers such as Capcom, Electronic Arts and Activision, a strategy guide was a must-have: it could help players through difficult (or perhaps even buggy) parts of a game, getting them back on track or helping them find well-hidden items or bonuses.

Within that ecosystem, at least for a time, two of the most well-known publishers of strategy guides were BradyGames and Prima. They often competed to create licensed official guides for blockbuster games from high-profile developers such as Square, Nintendo, and Konami. The publishers then employed staff writers or hired freelancers who were given weeks or months to create a guide, sometimes with notes from the game developer to work from and sometimes just from playing the game on their own. The work was precarious—guide writers were not often credited as authors—and many writers worked from contract to contract. With the rise of the internet and free guides appearing in a multitude of places, the guide business has, over time, contracted almost completely with BradyGames and Prima merging in 2015.[2]

Yet players still need help playing games, and into that void have come player-created online guides made by individuals and offered on sites like GameFAQs. But now we see more content creators turning to the production of video guides, walkthroughs, and tips posted on YouTube. This is only part of a larger output of user-generated content (see also James Newman's contribution on that topic in this collection) that includes gameplay videos (Let's Plays), game reviews, and commentary about games and the game industry. All these paratexts are one of the latest forms of gaming capital that circulates around games—information that players need not just to play well but also to appear informed and knowledgeable about a particular game, a genre, or game culture as a whole.[3]

One subset of those who post such videos on YouTube have replaced those original guide authors, becoming (or continuing on as) freelance professionals, generating thousands of views—and unknown amounts of revenue—for their labor. And their efforts are not just recognized by players. We increasingly see game developers and publishers working with the more successful "YouTubers," giving them early and exclusive access to new games and game updates, inviting them to company headquarters to consult about games, and offering them incentives to keep creating content that is game specific.

To better understand this process, looking at specific examples is helpful. In the following, I focus on gaming capital that surrounds the free-to-play (f2p) game *Clash Royale*, which was developed by the Finnish company Supercell in 2016. Supercell's success with *Clash Royale* relies in part on the gaming capital produced by high-profile YouTube content creators with whom they have formal and informal ties. That gaming capital is then consumed by *Clash Royale* players, benefiting the players, the YouTubers, and, of course, Supercell, all to varying degrees. Such content creators likely receive greater acknowledgments from both the industry and players compared to the original writers for strategy guide companies. But in other ways their work continues to be precarious, particularly in an industry where games are now delivered as services with constant updates and refinements. As a result, the capital produced via a strategy video by an independent YouTuber has a very short shelf life, particularly compared to those older printed guides.

Clash Royale is a collectible card style, multiplayer tower-defense strategy game built off characters from Supercell's previous hit *Clash of Clans* (2012) and is playable on mobile and tablet devices. In the game, players must collect and level up different cards that feature ground and air units, assemble them into a "deck"

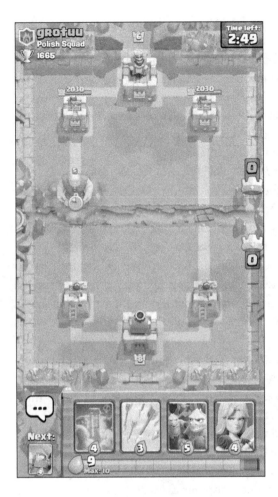

FIGURE 22.1
Clash Royale arena battle.

with which to do battle against other players, and work their way up through 8 levels to reach the Legendary Arena and compete against the best players in the world (see figure 22.1). The game is designed such that players are not required to spend any money to acquire cards or advance in the game, but of course, success is faster if one spends real money to acquire very rare cards and to level up existing cards. Supercell has been careful to ensure that paying is not the only way to succeed—there are viable f2p strategies for success—but many players admit to spending money if only to ease their journey or move more quickly to more advanced levels. In either case—paying or f2p—skill is essential for victory as players must learn how to balance their decks with cards that will counter likely opposition, and they must also determine the most advantageous strategies to use during battle, when and which cards to level, and how to manage the various currencies they choose to use.

In anticipation of writing this chapter, I returned to playing *Clash Royale*, which I had put aside several months ago after hitting a wall and experiencing almost nothing but a string of losses. I also returned to hunting for advice about the game, particularly as I advanced into new arenas and began facing cards that I had never encountered and did not own. Thus, my search for the acquisition of gaming capital became not just a scholarly interest but a necessity. What I learned is that the game has become so complex that devoting oneself to disseminating such knowledge easily requires hours upon hours of labor.

Creating gaming capital for *Clash Royale* players can be a full-time job, one that pays off for certain individuals in the form of content views for YouTube videos and page views for constantly updated websites. There is no permanent "meta" for players to learn that will ensure they are victorious in their battles—the strategies that are the agreed-on optimal ways to play. Instead, there are continual updates, additions, and balance changes made by the game developers to ensure that no one card, deck, or strategy dominates a game. This keeps play fresh, it prevents any one player or set of players from guaranteed victory, and it keeps YouTubers busy examining and explaining how the game should be optimally played—this week, this month, this year.

One of the most popular YouTube sites for learning about *Clash Royale* is Orange Juice Gaming (OJG), with 333,245 YouTube subscribers. A collective of three individuals, OJG posts short videos every few days that range from 2 to 12 minutes, focusing on game news and strategy for *Clash Royale*. Viewer counts for videos range from 91,000 views for a clip about a player tournament to highs of over a million views for information about four new "Mega Minion" cards. OJG's most popular efforts are about two things: detailing new cards that are being released and explaining how to use as well as counter popular cards and card combinations.

Another site for learning strategic and competitive play in *Clash Royale* is Ash's YouTube channel (with 324,550 subscribers). Ash's videos are slightly longer, ranging from 6 to 16 minutes, with some longer videos that feature recorded challenge events. Viewership also varies, from just over 40,000 views for a "sneak peek" at new loot chests to highs of more than 933,000 views for a guide on "How to counter & how to use inferno dragon."[4]

Both channels use advertising to gain revenue and offer players highly produced guided segments that provide strategy, detail game updates, show events such as challenges, and act as general boosters for *Clash Royale*. It's also unclear what if any revenue they receive from Supercell, but they do receive news and updates about the game before the public to keep enthusiasm high and give attentive viewers an edge when those changes do happen. Examining the two sites' videos more closely provides a useful way to see what elements are important enough to be mentioned and how content creators differentiate themselves and gain credibility in a sea of YouTube videos.

Looking at each site's video to introduce a new card—the Ice Golem—is instructive in seeing what they consider valuable gaming capital. Importantly, each is brief (less than 7 minutes in length) but packed with information and distinctive branding.[5] Yarn/OJG's video is only 5 minutes 10 seconds long, whereas Ash's is 6 minutes 43 seconds, but each includes background music, a professional voice-over, graphic overlays, split screens, and statistics that explain the new card, as well as its performance relative to most other game cards. Likewise, each video is not simply a match or two of the game showing how the Ice Golem performs (most *Clash Royale* matches last 3 to 4 minutes in length). Instead, they are heavily edited compilations of multiple matches or test events, demonstrating the range of possibilities that the Ice Golem offers to players and how they should either best use it or defend against its use by opponents.

Yarn begins his video by offering an overview of the Ice Golem in terms of its health and movement speed, showing a split screen comparing the Ice Golem walking up a lane with a Miner to show the relative speed and damage of each. The video is filled with similar shots, demonstrating how the Ice Golem compares in speed with the Knight ("it is slower than the Knight"), how its "Slow" spell works compared to other units that likewise can cast Slow, how it can be made to move faster by placing a quicker unit behind it to "push" it forward, and how the Ice Golem can act as a lightning rod, drawing the charge from a Lightning spell used by an opponent away from weaker units that surround it. Ash's video does similar work, echoing many of the points that Yarn makes about the Ice Golem. Ash further explains that he likes this particular card because "my favorite cards in the game are cheap cards that offer a lot of utility." Here Ash goes beyond merely pointing to the relative strengths and weaknesses of the Ice Golem to his "deck building" strategies more generally, explaining that he prefers cards that cost less elixir to cast—such as the Ice Golem which costs players only two elixir to use (cards range in elixir costs from 1 to 10 elixir; a player is constantly accumulating elixir in the game but can only hold 10 elixir maximum).

Through such statements, Ash refers back to the "meta" of the game—the larger strategies about the best ways to play and be successful. Yarn draws on similar terminology, explaining at one point that in using the Ice Golem to draw away a higher elixir card like the Mini-PEKKA, the player is engaging in "positive elixir trade." By deploying such terminology, Yarn is doing a couple of things. First, he's teaching viewers a strategy that would be considered savvy by the rest of the community—eliminating a threat by using the appropriate unit is, of course, smart—but in using a unit that also costs less elixir to play results in more elixir/

power remaining available for the player to engage in other actions. Second, it is another way for Yarn to show *he* is an expert in this matter. Use of the Ice Golem is strategic not only because the unit is powerful in a particular way—but it's also *cheap to use.* By using the lingo that the community has accepted as the "proper" way to discuss these matters—positive elixir trade—Yarn becomes trusted as an expert, and his critique is lent more weight.

Yarn and Ash also work diligently in their videos to constantly build brands for themselves and their individual channels and enterprises. These are clearly not Prima guides, where the writer's name is often hidden inside the book, rather than clearly visible on the cover. Partway through Yarn's video, the right third of the screen wipes to reveal the title "*Clash Royale* with Yarn from Orange Juice," with a ball of yarn pictured to remind viewers who they are watching. Yarn also ends the video by thanking viewers for watching and asking them to subscribe if they enjoyed it. As Hector Postigo explains, subscriptions bring revenue for You-Tubers and can help signal to other viewers the importance or influence of a particular channel—one with hundreds of thousands of subscribers and/or viewers is (by definition) more influential than a channel with only hundreds of views.[6] Ash takes self-branding even further, positioning his video as "everything you need to know" about the Ice Golem, and his channel as a site not just to learn more about the game but also a place to get "FREE Gems and Cards," an opportunity to join his Clan the "Altar of Elites" where "we're looking for the best players in the game with a minimum trophy count of 4000," and a thumbs-up for the video and for viewers to subscribe if they haven't done so already.

Despite their short length, such videos require massive amounts of time to assemble and produce. YouTubers like Yarn and Ash must be constantly playing the game, experimenting with new cards, analyzing newly balanced cards, and checking for emerging decks, as well as new styles of play, to counter or adopt. They must play multiple games or practice matches to assemble videos, script them, create voice-overs, apply graphical overlays, and make them consistent with their own branded style. And they have to do that several times a week, every week that the game is being played. Supercell is constantly adjusting how cards work. They regularly update the game and change card values, for example, by lowering the damage output on the Giant by 10 percent or increasing the durability of Minions by giving them another 100 hit points. Such changes have effects not simply on the cards affected but also on cards that counter them or on card combinations that rely on them.

Sites such as Orange Juice Gaming and Ash do valuable work not just for the players who want to play (and win) *Clash Royale*—they are also performing a vital role for Supercell. The most obvious way this happens is when they act as boosters, offering videos that simply preview upcoming cards or events, driving hype and interest in the game, and encouraging players to continue playing and perhaps continue (or start) spending money. But their guides that deconstruct troop abilities, as well as manage increasingly complex decks, are the real bread and butter of what they do. It's also what Supercell and players rely on most—offering more "serious" players seemingly evidence-based analyses of what works and what doesn't in competitive play.

Yet they are also on an endless treadmill. Supercell is continuously adjusting the values of different troops, which not only changes how a player might use a particular troop to attack or defend but also potentially upsets the balance of a certain deck. In that way, gaming capital is constantly draining away, much like the elixir that players consume. To ignore an update for even one unit risks one's guides and strategies falling into irrelevance, disuse, and the YouTuber lacking credibility with the larger player community. The loss of credibility can lead to the loss of revenue.

Players who create videos, guides, and forum posts that attempt to strategize the best ways to play *Clash Royale* must attend to all of these elements. Supercell is constantly working against the adoption of any persistent metagame strategy that players or YouTubers might create. Instead, YouTubers must continually labor to provide strategies that work for individual arenas, strategies for those who play but never pay for cards, strategies that account for constant updates, and so on. In the process YouTubers gain more prominence for their efforts than print strategy guide writers ever did, but with the fame comes the production treadmill. Gaming capital in this game is never something stable or unchanging. To be able to disseminate gaming capital successfully as Yarn and Ash currently do is to be seen as an expert, but it also means unwavering dedication and labor directed toward one game and its endless updates and changes.

NOTES

1 Mia Consalvo, *Cheating: Gaining Advantage in Videogames* (Cambridge, MA: MIT Press, 2007).

2 Jeff Grubb, "Prima Publisher Buys BradyGames and Merges the Strategy-Guide Giants," *VentureBeat*, June 1, 2015, accessed February 13, 2017, http://venturebeat.com.

3 Consalvo, *Cheating*.

4 Ash, "Clash Royale—How to use Ice Golem! (Strategy Guide)," YouTube video, published October 13, 2016, 6:44, accessed February 13, 2017, https://www.youtube.com/watch?v=INmS5OrsiWE.

5 Ash, "Clash Royale"; Orange Juice Gaming, "Clash Royale | Intro to Ice Golem | New Sponge!," YouTube video, 5:10, published October 13, 2016, accessed February 13, 2017, https://www.youtube.com/watch?v=XGCrH__nPp8.

6 Hector Postigo, "The Socio-Technical Architecture of Digital Labor: Converting Play into YouTube Money," *New Media & Society* 18 (2014): 332–349.

FURTHER READING

Banks, John. *Co-creating Videogames.* New York: Bloomsbury Academic, 2013.

Nieborg, David. "Crushing Candy: The Free-to-Play Game in its Connective Commodity Form." *Social Media + Society* 1, no. 2 (July 2015): 1–12. https://doi.org/10.1177/2056305115621932.

Postigo, Hector. "The Socio-Technical Architecture of Digital Labor: Converting Play into YouTube Money." *New Media & Society* 18 (2014): 332–349.

23

Game Dev Tycoon
Labor

CASEY O'DONNELL

Abstract: *Game Dev Tycoon* is a resource management game about running a video game design studio. In this chapter, Casey O'Donnell examines what a game about making games teaches us about this form of creative labor and what it fails to convey about the trials and tribulations of game development.

If there are games that simulate the building and maintaining of roller coasters (*Roller Coaster Tycoon* [Chris Sawyer Productions, 1999]), managing corporate agro-farms (*Farming Simulator 2016* [Giants Software, 2016]), operating a big trucking rig (*American Truck Simulator* [SCS Software, 2016]), or even being a "glitch" goat (*Goat Simulator* [Coffee Stain Studios, 2014]), then why wouldn't there be a game about running a game development studio? It seems the resource management genre (of which *Goat Simulator* is not, but the others are) is ripe for turning everyday jobs into simulation-style games. *Game Dev Tycoon* (Greenheart Games, 2012) is no exception. In this chapter, I examine what *Game Dev Tycoon* might teach us about video games, gameplay, and professional labor in the context of the video game industry.

It is important to begin by recognizing that *Game Dev Tycoon* was deeply inspired by another game development studio simulator, *Game Dev Story* (Kairsoft, 1997).[1] I first wrote about *Game Dev Story* as a footnote in my first book, a project that examined the everyday work and culture of video game developers. In that footnote, I observed,

> Oddly, a game industry game already exists. *Game Dev Story* was released for Apple's iOS platform in October of 2010. This resource management and strategy game challenges players to manage a game development studio. The game takes small

jabs at numerous aspects of the game industry, from console manufacturers to publishers and game titles. Of particular note is the fact that the focus remains at the studio level even as developers level up and improve as they remain with your company. The game developers themselves disappear into the background, functioning as yet another resource to be managed. And the game reinforces this perspective; the procedural rhetoric of the game marginalizes the labor of game developers, yet outside the console, game developers are the culture and creative collaborative community that makes the game industry function in *Game Dev Story*, rather than forgettable resources.[2]

Game Dev Story was originally designed for Windows-based computers and was ported more than a decade later to iOS and Android. The basic premise of the game was that you played as the CEO of a game studio who is responsible for managing the game's underlying resources of points and money. You then have 20 years to produce a successful game studio and rake in as much cash as possible. This, of course, seems to be the core goal of most resource management games: grab as much as you can as efficiently as you can. In *Game Dev Story* you develop games based on a handful of characteristics and you compose your team as you choose, each of which has effects on the games' underlying systems. This is done primarily through the selection of projects and the movement of "sliders" (see figure 23.1) or sliding controls that indicate how much effort will be put into any given aspect of your game. The more time spent on a given game aspect, that is, artificial intelligence or graphics, the more experience one gains in that skill. Like most resource management games, *Game Dev Story*'s "products" are often a collection of various properties that are then run through the game's underlying algorithmic structures. Thus, the player's "direction" of the fictional video game's development in *Game Dev Story* dictates what the product is at a very abstract level. When a game ships, it either attracts an audience, or it does not. The game softly lampoons the broader game industry and even identifies developers in ways that poke fun at industry luminaries.

In many respects, *Game Dev Story* misses a great deal in how it abstracts the process of game development, segmenting it in ways that make little sense in terms of how games are actually designed and developed.[3] Yet, despite the game's limited features, the title nevertheless hints at considerations that game development teams invariably tackle. The game communicates that there are various recipes or formulas that developers regularly invoke when thinking about the kinds of games that they make. A "Pirate" + "Puzzle" game or an "Action" + "Car" game becomes shorthand for the general shape a game might take and the kind of audience it seeks to attract.

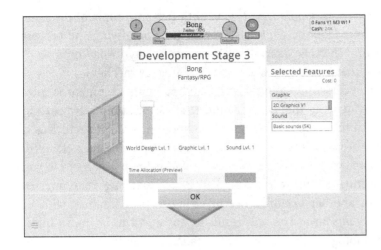

FIGURE 23.1
Managing game
development
resources in *Game
Dev Story*.

To be clear, some game developers may think about making games in the simplistic ways that *Game Dev Story* and *Game Dev Tycoon* model. But the process of game creation isn't as easy or straightforward as these titles suggest. Developers will use general categories of games and "game talk" as insider discourse to help communicate design features and goals to one another.[4] For instance, when I opened this chapter by referring to *Game Dev Tycoon* as a "resource management" game, I was doing something quite similar. The critical difference is that I was trying to describe a game, not to make one. This persistent disconnect between describing how games work and creating play mechanics remains a tension for any title interested in making a game about game development. After all, how much can one really describe a strangely iterative and technologically difficult task of making games without abstracting that process to the point of absurdity?

Not surprisingly, early criticisms of *Game Dev Tycoon* accused it of simply being a "clone" of *Game Dev Story*—a charge frequently leveled at games that closely resemble earlier titles in terms of their gameplay mechanics and/or visual design. Where is the line between inspiration, homage, and copying?[5] The basic premise of *Game Dev Story* was simply that there are magic recipes that developers happen on. And if the proverbial stars should align, the studio can leverage its assets to continue making games. Incorrectly managing one's resources, conversely, results in the eventual collapse of the studio. This volatile boom-and-bust production environment helps explain why so many studios tend to design from commercially established generic formulas rather than innovating and creating new, interesting game mechanics and narrative storylines.

Despite its similarities, *Game Dev Tycoon* is neither a clone nor an homage to *Game Dev Story*. Rather, it is an attempt to imagine what a game *about* game development might look like. *Game Dev Tycoon* both falls into some of the same reductive traps as its predecessor while also successfully gamifying the process of studio management. (There is, after all, little about the day-to-day minutia of software development that readily translates to fun gameplay mechanics.)

Game Dev Tycoon successfully conveys that good game development is integrally tied to the individuals in that organization. The various points awarded in the game correlate with the categories of design, technology, and research. This is presented in the form of various projects you and your team can undertake. Will time be spent developing a new engine or a new kind of game mechanic? Do you invest time in supporting a new console or device or improving your internal game technology? For another example, overinvesting in programmers without corresponding investments in artists will result in an organization more interested in pushing technological limits than with realizing a game's visual design. Game development is frequently imagined to be a direct corollary to software development—a point I have argued that results in a misunderstanding of game development that privileges software engineering over the other fields necessary for the successful creation of video games.[6]

Game Dev Tycoon explores the fraught terrain of precarious and contingent labor necessary to make ends meet after a project fails or to survive between longer-term gigs. In fact, the game gives players opportunities to take on "contract work" when their projects fail. Ironically, I never had to do that in my various playthroughs of *Game Dev Tycoon*, whereas I did take on unsatisfying contract jobs when I worked in the game industry. Why would I want to work on a learning management system or a content management system when there are games to be made? But these are very real decisions that aspiring and independent game developers face. One need only to look at the team of Greenheart Games to know that in all likelihood, these developers know the real pain of doing work made for hire while one's passion lies in creating a still-unrealized game.

Perhaps *Game Dev Tycoon* is too much of an insider's game. Having made video games for nearly 25 years and now having studied game development and the broader game industry for nearly a decade, I know the jokes. I have a sense of the genre recipes and formulas. Quite plainly, I don't come to *Game Dev Tycoon* in the same way as a player from outside the industry. The game is vocationally instructional but only to a point. It isn't going to actually make you a better game developer; rather, it is going to give you a sense of how most games are interesting configurations of old ideas.

Game Dev Tycoon isn't as adept at making an argument about labor politics as it is about outlining the general kinds of creative laborers needed to make games. The games' fictional studios don't hemorrhage employees in the same, life-altering ways as do real-world studios.[7] In many respects, the player's investment in team members in *Game Dev Tycoon* is more lasting and more pleasurably strategic. Their capacity to level up abilities over time mirrors the experience that game developers achieve as they work in the industry, learning the various "dark arts" of the process. This contributed to an ongoing source of anxiety and reticence in my personal playthroughs. I didn't want to hire anyone because what if I had to let them go? What if I was a management failure, thereby affecting their lives and livelihoods? The game communicates the value of investing in the employees' skills and in their futures; it does not, however, adequately model the personal and professional horrors that come with failure.

Perhaps *Game Dev Tycoon*'s greatest conceptual strength is in how represents a basic history of the game industry's structure. Things were different in the 1980s. Incessantly jumping from one console to another wasn't simply the whimsical meanderings of game development imagination but emerged from trying to make money. *Game Dev Tycoon* represents this and other structural facets of the industry that forces the player to ask questions about what kinds of games they desire to make and ultimately if there is a market for those games. What is it *precisely* that drives game developers to make games? The answer isn't always money, but that comes with a very specific cost as well. *Game Dev Tycoon* offers players a glimpse at a game industry that no longer exists. Some might argue there isn't really a kind of unified game industry as one found back in the 1980s and 1990s. The marketplace has fragmented and shifted in ways that force game developers to ask new kinds of questions. While developers continue to jump from console to console, they are now also jumping from app store to app store, from phone to tablet to browser and even to television. What seemed a kind of predictable uncertainty of the 1990s and 2000s has given way to a much more turbulent and fractured industry in the early twenty-first century.

Games are ultimately, at their core, systems of play.[8] As the game designer and game scholar Colleen Macklin has stated in a handful of presentations, "[i]f the real world is like a tiger, then games are like fluffy white kittens." Put another way, games allow us to play with complex systems that can tell us something about the all-too-real systems that we inhabit. They can never substitute for the worldly system, but we can learn about a host of issues, including labor, through these more playful "kittenlike" models. Indeed, I can run a game studio into the ground picking the strangest combinations of games in search of the one really odd one that ultimately tanks the company without any repercussions. I can begin to understand the relative design timidity that often grips the game industry and that leads to tired genres full of clichés. However, I cannot truly appreciate how complex and nerve-wracking those employment decisions really are for those running triple-A and indie studios. Although not all resource management games suffer from this degree of affective disconnect, they all remain abstractions of the real world. That is, although we might model social processes in game franchises such as *SimCity* or *Sid Meier's Civilization*, and although they can offer us insights into how those systems function, they are always already limited as simulations that come with their own sets of assumptions and biases (for more on this see Peter Krapp's contribution to this collection).

Game Dev Tycoon makes visible some structures of the game industry that might miss some players unfamiliar with the general contours of game production. The fact that players in the game have to pay licensing fees to gain access to new game development platforms is likely foreign to many but one that has consequences for the kinds of games that get made. Yet the game also neglects important aspects of this creative process as well. When moving to a new game platform, developers often have to port their entire engine to the new hardware. Thankfully in *Game Dev Tycoon* I could effortlessly move my game engine from platform to platform. As one who toiled on cross-platform game engine technologies before it was common practice, I can attest that this process is not so easy; platform selection came with real labor costs aside from licensing fees.

When one asks, "How *should* one play video games?" and uses *Game Dev Tycoon* as an interpretive lens, a legitimate response would be to consider the working lives of the developers, at least for a moment, whose labor often hides behind colorful fictional characters and immersive worlds. Yet in making a game of this professional pursuit, these titles necessarily reduce and abstract the creative process to easily manageable point systems—systems that necessarily elide the very real stresses affecting game development workers, their significant others, and their extended families. These human resources are more resource than human, having been transformed into units to be managed not creative laborers with whom we are asked to identify. I have remarked to my students that video games are "made of people," alluding to the quote made famous in the film *Soylent Green* (Richard Fleischer, 1973). (For those unfamiliar with the reference, Soylent Green is a "food" substance that was literally made from humans.) But the reality is that games *are* made of people in the same way that culture is made of people, technologies, economies, media, and so on. *Game Dev Story* and *Game Dev Tycoon* vitally acknowledge their presence in the process of game development.

Game Dev Tycoon is, at its foundations, a title that encourages the player to enjoy it both as a game to be played and as a self-conscious reflection of a challenging production process. It lampoons and leverages gamer culture throughout its various iterations over the years, and it recognizes games for what they are: a creative and commercial product of human work. This is *Game Dev Tycoon*'s real contribution, a playful (mostly) self-conscious reflection on where the industry has been and where its creative teams of workers might take it in the coming decades.

NOTES

1 Patrick Klug, "About Greenheart Games," *Greenheart Games*, accessed March 6, 2017, www.greenheartgames.com.

2 Casey O'Donnell, *Developer's Dilemma: The Secret World of Videogame Creators* (Cambridge, MA: MIT Press, 2014), 284.

3 Jason Schreier, "What's Right (and Wrong) with *Game Dev Story's* Addictive Simulation," *Wired*, December 3, 2010, accessed March 6, 2017, www.wired.com.

4 It even makes me wonder why "cloning" a game isn't part of the simulation in *Game Dev Tycoon* because the game does take very seriously issues such as piracy that also affect game developers. See O'Donnell, *Developer's Dilemma*, 43–44.

5 Casey O'Donnell, "Institutional Alzheimers: A Culture of Secrecy and the Opacity of #GAMEDEV Work," *Gamasutra*, February 20, 2014, accessed March 6, 2017, www.gamasutra.com.

6 Casey O'Donnell, "This Is Not a Software Industry," in *The Video Game Industry: Formation, Present State and Future*, ed. Peter Zackariasson and Timothy L. Wilson (New York: Routledge, 2012), 17–33.

7 Patrick Klug, "What Happens When Pirates Play a Game Development Simulator and then Go Bankrupt Because of Piracy?" *Greenheart Games Blog*, April 29, 2013, accessed March 6, 2017, www.greenheartgames.com.

8 Casey O'Donnell, "Getting Played: Gamification, Bullshit, and the Rise of Algorithmic Surveillance," *Surveillance & Society* 12, no. 3 (2014): 349–359.

FURTHER READING

Kazemi, Darius. *Jagged Alliance 2*. Vol. 5. Boss Fight Books. Los Angeles: Boss Fight Books, 2014.

Meadows, Donella H. *Thinking in Systems: A Primer*. White River Junction, VT: Chelsea Green Publishing, 2008.

Shaw, Adrienne. *Gaming at the Edge: Sexuality and Gender at the Margins of Gamer Culture*. Minneapolis: University of Minnesota Press, 2015.

24

Cookie Clicker

Gamification

SEBASTIAN DETERDING

Abstract: Incremental games like *Cookie Clicker* are a perfect exemplar of gamification, using progress mechanics and other game features to make a rote act like clicking compelling. Sebastian Deterding analyzes the game *Cookie Clicker* for its motivating features to illustrate the logic and limits of gamification.

As I type these words into my text editor, the open browser tab next to it informs me that I am currently baking 62,526 sextillion cookies per second. Since I began playing *Cookie Clicker* (Thiennot, 2013) in earnest, I have unlocked 233 of the game's 252 achievements, purchased 312 of its 319 upgrades, and baked 712,105 octillion cookies. All this has taken me—and this is particularly distressing—8,432 hours and counting. Granted, play time and cookies continue to accrue when I don't keep the game open in one of my many browser tabs. But still, counting the hours I did switch attention to the game tab every couple of minutes to click here and there, I have invested orders of magnitude more time in *Cookie Clicker* than any other video game in my life.

This was not meant to be. *Cookie Clicker* and similar so-called incremental games were never supposed to be played in earnest. They were intended as parodies.[1] In particular, they ridiculed online role-playing games like *EverQuest* (Sony Online Entertainment, 1999) and social network games like *FarmVille* (Zynga, 2009), which relied heavily on so-called *progress mechanics* pioneered by role-playing games.[2] By killing monsters or harvesting crops, players gain resources (experience points, gold) that they can spend on upgrades such as character attributes or equipment which increase their ability to kill more monsters, harvest more crops, and so on. A common view among game designers is that what makes games fun is a sense of skilled mastery arising from overcoming

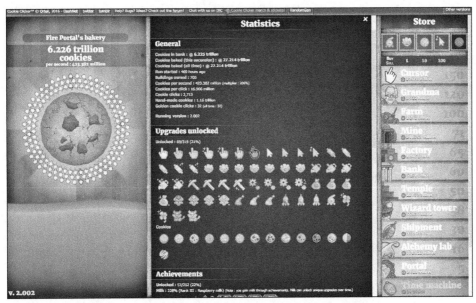

FIGURE 24.1 Counters, upgrades, achievements: Progress trackers make up most of *Cookie Clicker*'s interface.

challenges.[3] Yet progress mechanics involve no such challenge or skill, only time to churn one increasing number (damage per second) into another (experience points) and back in an ever-accelerating positive feedback loop. Starting with *Progress Quest* (Fredericksen, 2002), game designers therefore created numerous little parodies—proto-incremental games—that presented a *reductio ad absurdum* of progress mechanics to demonstrate how unengaging and un-game-like they were.

Cookie Clicker is a perfect case in point. Launched in 2013 as an "internet experiment" by French artist Julien Thiennot, this browser game presents the player with nothing but a big virtual chocolate chip cookie. Clicking this cookie produces a baked cookie in the bank.[4] The player can invest baked cookies into cursors that then *automatically* click the big cookie (see figure 24.1). As more cookies are produced, more expensive and powerful auto-cookie makers become available: grandmas who bake cookies, banks that generate cookies from interest, cookie factories, wizard towers, and spaceships, complete with productivity upgrades (steel-plated rolling pins) and exponentially rising numbers—tens, thousands, trillions, nonillions of cookies earned and spent. The self-deprecating silliness is apparent, as is the lack of challenge and skill. Indeed, early on, players can leave the game to play itself. *Cookie Clicker* is not just an *incremental game* where the goal is to increase a number but also an *idle game* that makes progress on its own, requiring no player input.[5] Beyond erasing any semblance of challenging gameplay, *Cookie Clicker* (like other incremental games) exemplifies the financial principle of compound interest and how returns on capital must in time outpace returns on labor. Even with all upgrades purchased, my cookie factories and banks outperform my manual clicking labor at a rate of at least 10 to 1. And while my mouse finger fatigues within seconds, my capital assets never sleep. All I need to do is reinvest overnight gains when I return to the computer in the morning.

Nevertheless, *Cookie Clicker* counts tens of thousands of dedicated players penning online confessions about their "addiction" to the game.[6] In an ironic twist of game history, incremental games have become a highly engaging game genre unto its own. On the online gaming platform Kongregate, which hosts over 120,000 free games, incremental games are the genre that retains and monetizes players better than any other.[7] This raises an obvious question: How? How does this "internet experiment" render the rote act of clicking so compelling? The answer: *Cookie Clicker* gamifies clicking.

Gamification is commonly defined as the use of game design elements in non-game contexts.[8] Emerging in the late 2000s as a strategy in interaction design and online marketing to increase user engagement, it has since solidified as a design practice across domains such as education, health, productivity, and civic engagement.[9] An early influential forerunner was the local recommendation app *Foursquare*. The app asked people to "check in" to places they visit, thereby creating a data log that would feed recommendation algorithms suggesting locations of likely interest. But why would people want to check in to begin with? Enter progress mechanics. Every check-in accrued points, and users could compete with friends on an in-app leaderboard to see who scores the most points in a week. Checking in to certain places would unlock achievements, such as the "Gym Rat badge," for 10 check-ins into gyms within one month. This trifecta of points, badges, and leaderboards became the blueprint for most gamified experiences. Launched in 2006, the *Nike+ FuelBand* activity tracker and app, for instance, tracked and translated fitness activity into "NikeFuel points" that would unlock achievements and could be used to compete with friends.

Gamification has been likened to incremental games from the outset, with the argument that both are "taking the thing that is least essential to games and representing it as the core of the experience."[10] Both rely almost exclusively on the same catalog of progress mechanics. And importantly for this book, both invite a particular *reading* of video games: they ask us to identify the "active ingredients" that make a game compelling. For gamification, incremental games and related genres manifest "pattern-based design."[11] Like prefabricated house parts, they aim to reduce the time, cost, risk, and required expertise of design by identifying and reusing *patterns*: reproducible solutions to reoccurring problems, like "door" or "wall." This pattern focus makes gamification akin to persuasive tropes in rhetoric.[12] At the same time, it foregrounds the limits of treating games (or texts) as isolatable, modular building blocks. Much like the appeal of a house depends on how all its parts fit together, its neighborhood, and the needs of its inhabitants, so, too, does the appeal of games and other designed experiences depend on the systemic whole of object, person, and social context.[13] Yet the common terms and underlying theories of gamification—game mechanics, design elements, design patterns—suggest a more straightforward and deterministic notion of media effects, namely, that the same pattern will produce the same effect in any user.[14]

To illustrate gamification as a way of "reading" games, in the following I analyze how *Cookie Clicker* gamifies the act of clicking. Motives and connected design elements are teased out, and the limitations of such an approach are illuminated. But before I begin, one caveat is in order: unlike rhetoric, gamification research is still in its infancy. It lacks established methods for identifying its "tropes" and empirical evidence. Instead, the literature is littered with post hoc fallacies of the form like the following: successful web app Slack lets users customize bots, which looks very much like customizing avatars in the popular game *World of Warcraft* (Blizzard Entertainment, 2004). *Therefore*, Slack is successful *because* it copied customization from *World of Warcraft* to engage its users.[15] Such stories are seductive. But they are almost always evidence-free speculations that *appear* plausible thanks to the cognitive catnip of analogy and correlation. So reader beware. Although the motives I reference in the following are grounded in literature, I have no evidence for their linkage to *Cookie Clicker*'s design beyond 8,432 hours of autoethnography.

In 2011, psychologist Teresa Amabile coined the "progress principle." Analyzing diaries of more than 12,000 hours of work life, she found that no single experience proved more motivating than "making meaningful progress."[16] In adult work life, progress is often protracted and elusive, tasks stuck in nested waiting loops, to-do lists growing longer by the day. Amabile argued that managers should therefore learn from video games how to organize work, as games are purpose-built to give constant, abundant, and clear progress feedback.[17] *Cookie Clicker* presents players with countless counters and visualizations of cookies baked, cookies baked per second, upgrades purchased, achievements unlocked, all of which know only one direction: upward. Every click increases some number, makes some measurable progress. The most common gamification features—points, badges, levels—all deliver such progress feedback.

Critics have called the resulting sense of progress "false" as it doesn't track actual skill growth.[18] "Real" games deliver a motivating sense of competence by presenting "real" challenges that require "real" skill to overcome; the progress mechanics of role-playing games or *Cookie Clicker* deliver only "virtual" skill increases through upgrades that require nothing but time to accumulate.[19] Yet this critique is doubly mistaken.

First, *progress*, the positive feeling of completing a book chapter or adding line by line of tiles to a wall, often but not necessarily coincides with *competence*, the experience of one's growing skill, such as laying an intricate tile mosaic without fail.[20] Researchers Yee and Duchenaut observed a similar distinction in gaming motivations between achievement (completion and growing power) and mastery (overcoming challenges) and found that incremental game players predominantly seek the former.[21]

Furthermore, a closer look into actual *Cookie Clicker* gameplay reveals that its community has framed its own *mastery challenges*. One is sheer tenacity. Keeping at a single "silly" pursuit for hundreds of hours is a real, self-regulatory skill. Additionally, players are actively analyzing and strategizing about how to *optimally* invest resources, playing the meta-game of min-maxing play time spent on resources gained.[22] Fan websites and wikis abound with speedrun league tables (who bakes a set amount of cookies fastest), mathematical formulas and tools to calculate the interacting compound rates of return of upgrades, and strategy guides to decide when to switch investments, all reverse-engineered from observing gameplay. This highly involved, quasi-scientific style of gameplay differs in no way from that of "power gamers" playing at the high-skill end of traditional video games.[23] Critics likewise often overlook the manifest joy and skill in strategically "gaming" (proto-) gamified systems like frequent-flier miles.[24]

Beyond progress and challenge, the progress mechanics of *Cookie Clicker* also serve as a form of *goal setting*. People work harder, are more focused, and are more persistent when they have clear, taxing-yet-attainable goals.[25] At any point of play, *Cookie Clicker*'s counters and collections always suggest a range of additional goals (e.g., buy seven more wizard towers to unlock the next wizard tower upgrade, save 10 trillion more cookies to buy the next cookie upgrade).

Importantly, for a new player, what upgrades and achievements exist is a mystery. *Cookie Clicker* milks the whimsy of a cookie-making world for maximum comic effect. The alchemy lab "turns gold into cookies," the septillion fingers cursor upgrade comes, literally, with "[cursory flavor text]". There are many Easter eggs triggered in obtuse ways, such as minimizing the browser window so that the milk animation touches the main cookie (unlocking the "Cookie-dunker" achievement). About 200 hours into an average first play session, players get to purchase the "Bingo center/Research facility," unlocking a range of extra upgrades that (spoiler alert) will unlock the "Grandmapocalypse," which turns grandmas into a fleshy, cthulhoid superorganism. This cornucopia of hidden content provides a steady flow of novelty and surprise, stoking *curiosity*[26] in the player.

Progress mechanics evoking steady feelings of accomplishment; a meta-game of min–maxing; achievements providing a continuous flow of goals; hidden and novel content fueling curiosity: these are some of the ways *Cookie Clicker* transforms clicking into a compelling experience. Just this compulsion has spurred critiques that progress mechanics "trick" players into playing and paying with user data, free labor, or micro-transactions to the players' detriment. App developers and web companies such as Facebook are beginning to be called out for using similar "dark patterns" to "addict" users and harness and resell their attention and data to advertisers. Urgent as this current ethical reckoning is, it easily slips into a false distinction between ethically "neutral" and "problematic": *any* design affords and constrains people's future acting and thinking, and as such, *any* design is persuasive. If anything, gamification and its siblings, persuasive technology, nudging, and design for behavior change, have the merit of clarity: carrying their persuasive intent on their sleeves, they cannot evade ethical deliberation.[27]

Finally, just as gamification and incremental games illustrate the power of design, they also remind us of its limitations. After all, in playing *Cookie Clicker* and other early incremental games continuously, passionately, and in the thousands, players did the opposite of what their original designers intended and expected.

Take the cautionary tale of game designer and critic Ian Bogost (who is included in this book) and his Facebook game *Cow Clicker*. Bogost published it in 2010 as "a satire with a short shelf life" to show "the worst abuses of social gaming in the clearest possible manner."[28] Players could click a cow every six hours, producing a "click" and Facebook post. Clicking on the cows and posts produced more clicks, which players could spend on premium cows. *Cow Clicker* had no progress loop: premium cows didn't earn more clicks than basic ones do. But to Bogost's own dismay, *Cow Clicker* became a viral hit with more than 50,000 players at its peak. What moved its players was often irony—being in on the joke. Other times, it was the social bonds formed over discussing the absurdity of clicking cows. Yet others played *Cow Clicker* in "cheeky protest." Even when the "Cowpocalypse" removed all the pixel cows, players could and would still click the void. As one user put it, "It is very interesting, clicking nothing."[29]

Although often outwardly fruitless or even counterproductive, such protest play can serve an important psychological need, namely, to reassert one's autonomy against a coercive environment. Autonomy is itself an important source of game enjoyment, leading us to a fundamental paradox. On one hand, compelling people into engagement through gamification can deplete the very source it tries to tap—the joy of autonomous play.[30] On the other, faced with games designed to coerce them, players can respond by playing *despite*—and therefore freely. Nothing gained, nothing learned, clicking nothing. "One must imagine Sisyphus happy."[31]

This is not to say that *all* people play *Cookie Clicker*, *Cow Clicker*, or any other incremental game out of enlightened existential spite. Most of my own 8,000-plus hours, I certainly didn't. But the fact that we *can* and occasionally *do* testifies that the appeal of games is not exhausted nor determined by their design. After designers put games and gamified experiences in the world that afford certain motives and behaviors, people find their own reasons and ways of engaging that designers can neither fully predict nor control.

NOTES

1 Sebastian Deterding, "Progress Wars: Idle Games and the Demarcation of 'Real' Games," in *DiGRA/FDG'16 Abstract Proceedings* (Dundee, Scotland: DiGRA, 2016), www.digra .com.

2 José P. Zagal and Roger Altizer, "Examining 'RPG Elements': Systems of Character Progression," in *Foundations of Digital Games 2014* (Fort Lauderdale, FL: SASDG, 2014).

3 Raph Koster, *A Theory of Fun for Game Design* (Scottsdale, AZ: Paraglyph Press, 2004).

4 *Cookie Clicker*, last modified July 24, 2016, http://orteil.dashnet.org.

5 Sultan A. Alharthi, Olaa Alsaedi, Zachary O. Toups, Joshua Tanenbaum, and Jessica Hammer, "Playing to Wait: A Taxonomy of Idle Games," in *Proceedings of the 2018 CHI Conference on Human Factors in Computing Systems (CHI '18)* (New York: ACM Press, 2018), Paper No. 621.

6 Kevin Ohanessian, "How Idle Clicking Games Took Over My Life," *KillScreen*, November 22, 2013, www.killscreen.com.

7 Anthony Pecorella, "Idle Chatter: What We All Can Learn from Self-Playing Games," *Slideshare*, March 18, 2016, www.slideshare.net.

8 Sebastian Deterding, Dan Dixon, Rilla Khaled, and Lennart E. Nacke, "From Game Design Elements to Gamefulness: Defining 'Gamification,'" in *MindTrek'11* (New York: ACM Press, 2011), 9–15.

9 Steffen P. Walz and Sebastian Deterding, "An Introduction to the Gameful World," in *The Gameful World: Approaches, Issues, Applications*, ed. Steffen P. Walz and Sebastian Deterding (Cambridge, MA: MIT Press, 2015), 1–13.

10 Margaret Robertson, "Can't Play, Won't Play," *Kotaku*, November 10, 2010, www.kotaku.com.

11 Ahmed Seffah and Mohamed Taleb, "Tracing the Evolution of HCI Patterns as an Interaction Design Tool," *Innovations in Systems and Software Engineering* 8 (2011): 93–109.

12 Edward P. J. Corbett, and Robert J. Connors, *Classical Rhetoric for the Modern Student*, 4th ed. (Oxford: Oxford University Press, 1989).

13 Marc Hassenzahl, *Experience Design: Technology for All the Right Reasons* (San Rafael, CA: Morgan & Claypool, 2010).

14 Katie Seaborn and Deborah I. Fels, "Gamification in Theory and Action: A Survey," *International Journal of Human-Computer Studies* 74 (2015): 14–31. For a more holistic conceptualization of games' active ingredients as motivational affordances, see Sebastian Deterding, "Eudaimonic Design, or: Six Invitations to Rethink Gamification," in *Rethinking Gamification*, ed. Mathias Fuchs, Sonia Fizek, Paolo Ruffino, and Niklas Schrape (Lüneburg, Germany: Meson Press, 2014), 305–331.

15 See, for example, Amy Jo Kim, "Bots, MODs & Multiplayer Co-Op: Why Slack Is Game-like—NOT Gamified," *Medium*, accessed September 22, 2015, https://medium .com/@amyjokim.

16 Teresa M. Amabile, *The Progress Principle: Using Small Wins to Ignite Joy, Engagement, and Creativity at Work* (Boston, MA: Harvard Business Review Press, 2011).

17 Amabile, *The Progress Principle*, 87.

18 Jonas Linderoth, "Why Gamers Don't Learn More: An Ecological Approach to Games as Learning Environments," *Journal of Gaming and Virtual Worlds* 4 (2012): 45–62.

19 Deterding, "Progress Wars."

20 Richard M. Ryan and Edward L. Deci, "Self-Determination Theory and the Facilitation of Intrinsic Motivation, Social Development, and Well-Being," *The American Psychologist* 55 (2000): 68–78.

21 Nick Yee, "The Surprising Profile of Idle Clicker Gamers," *Quantic Foundry*, July 6, 2016, http://quanticfoundry.com.

22 Sultan A. Alharthi, Zachary O. Toups, Olaa Alsaedi, Josh Tanenbaum, and Jessica Hammer, *The Pleasure of Playing Less: A Study of Incremental Games through the Lens of Kittens* (Pittsburgh, PA: ETC Press, 2017).

23 T. L. Taylor, *Play Between Worlds: Exploring Online Game Culture* (Cambridge, MA: MIT Press, 2006), 67–90.

24 Jason Margolis, "Obsessed with Your Frequent Flier Miles? You're not Alone," *PRI*, September 24, 2015, https://pri.org.

25 Peter M. Gollwitzer and Gabriele Oettingen, "Goal Pursuit," in *The Oxford Handbook of Human Motivation*, ed. Richard M. Ryan (Oxford: Oxford University Press, 2012), 208–231.

26 Paul J. Silvia, "Curiosity and Motivation," in *The Oxford Handbook of Human Motivation*, ed. Richard M. Ryan (Oxford: Oxford University Press, 2012), 157–67.

27 Deterding, "Eudaimonic Design."

28 Jason Tanz, "The Curse of Cow Clicker: How a Cheeky Satire Became a Videogame Hit," *Wired*, December 20, 2011, http://archive.wired.com.

29 Tanz, "Cow Clicker."

30 Sebastian Deterding, "Contextual Autonomy Support in Video Game Play," in *Proceedings of the 2016 CHI Conference on Human Factors in Computing Systems* (New York: ACM Press, 2016), 3931–43.

31 Albert Camus, *The Myth of Sisyphus and Other Essays* (New York: Alfred A. Knopf, 1955), 123.

FURTHER READING

Pedercini, Paolo. "Making Games in a Fucked Up World." *Molleindustria*, April 29, 2014. www.molleindustria.org.

Seaborn, Katie and Deborah I. Fels. "Gamification in Theory and Action: A Survey." *International Journal of Human-Computer Studies* 74 (2015): 14–31.

Walz, Steffen P. and Sebastian Deterding, eds. *The Gameful World: Approaches, Issues, Applications*. Cambridge, MA: MIT Press, 2015.

25

Ball-and-Paddle Games
Domesticity

MICHAEL Z. NEWMAN

Abstract: As the name *PONG* implies, the ball-and-paddle games of the 1970s are adaptations of familiar amusements: not just table tennis but also soccer, hockey, and other sports simulated on boards and tables. The emergence of video games in the home begins with ball-and-paddle games, which Michael Z. Newman argues, carry on a tradition of family leisure in the domestic sphere and transform the typically feminized space of the home into a playground for masculine competition and technological innovation.

A typical video game when video games were new was an electronic version of table tennis played on a television screen. The most famous was Atari's *PONG*, released as a coin-operated game in public places in 1972. Soon after, a version of *PONG* was marketed for consumers to buy and play at home using their television sets. The Magnavox Odyssey, the first video game sold to the public also in 1972, whose prototype had influenced Atari's more popular version (some would say rip-off), was a ball-and-paddle game. This was true too of dozens of *PONG* imitators including Coleco's Telstar and APF's TV Fun. Many of these used the same General Instruments (GI) AY-3-8500 integrated circuit, introduced in 1976, or one of many variations adding or subtracting games or offering color images. These chips contained versions of tennis, soccer, hockey, basketball, squash, rifle games, and tank and driving games for one or two players. Hundreds of different game consoles were brought to market built around the GI chips. Unlike the "programmable" games to emerge in the later 1970s and early 1980s—such as Atari's VCS, Mattel's Intellivision, and Coleco's ColecoVision—ball-and-paddle consoles did not accept cartridges. They were all hardware. Consoles that could play a wide variety of different games sold separately helped video games become a big business and a pop culture craze, but ball-and-paddle games came first.

The console's paddle was a knob turned clockwise or counterclockwise by the player's thumb and first two fingers to control a line or rectangle on the screen, moving it up and down or side to side. The paddle was the name for both this game controller and the image representing a ping PONG paddle (or hockey stick, etc.) making contact with an electronic spot of light—the ball—and hitting it back to the other side. These games were greeted as technological marvels: "space-age pinball machines," "new tricks your TV can do." But along with being a novelty, they were also familiar adaptations of amusements already found in the home: not only table tennis but also other sports played on boards and tables such as table soccer (aka foosball), table or air hockey, Electric Football, and Strat-O-Matic baseball. Ball-and-paddle games carried on a tradition of family play in domestic space, but they also transformed the typically feminized space of the home into a playground for masculine competition and technological innovation. It's tempting to see a new medium as a bold departure from business as usual, as a revolutionary break from the past, dividing time neatly into *before* and *after*. In reality, continuities over time can be just as important as changes, and new things are made familiar in relation to old commonplace ones.

About the ball and paddle games themselves there may not be all that much to analyze. They have no narrative qualities and they are audiovisually abstract in comparison to later sports games with more sophisticated computerized graphics and sound effects and more elaborate forms of player input. Their imagery was made up of lines and dots, and the first ball-and-paddle games were in black-and-white only. Odyssey was packaged with plastic overlay sheets that adhered to the television screen using its static electricity charge, and game imagery glowed under the translucent playfield. Odyssey's *Tennis* was played using a green tennis court overlay, and *Hockey* was played using a white sheet representing an ice rink. But as experiences of play, which helped establish an identity for the new medium, ball-and-paddle games have a special significance in the history of electronic games. They were perhaps more important as artifacts in the domestication of video games than they were as game texts for critical interpretation.

Domestication of technology is a term with several related meanings. When new products are introduced, they emerge as novel and often strange objects without clear or fixed meanings. Domestication is a process of familiarizing the unfamiliar, of taming wild things, similar to domestication in nature—the practice of making plants and animals safe and predictable for agriculture. Domesticating media technology means arriving at a broadly shared understanding of its functions: who uses it for what purposes? For instance, when radio was new, it was unclear if it would be a point-to-point or a broadcast technology. It has long been used for both, but in the 1920s, broadcasting became radio's dominant use for most people, and radio developed from that point on as a commercial mass medium. In popular imagination, radio came to be identified most strongly as broadcasts over the air that you tune in using a receiver set. Video games also could have been identified in various different ways and were domesticated as an object with particular associations and values in popular imagination.[1]

For many media technologies, including radio and video games, domestication also refers more literally to the integration of the novel object into the home, into domestic space. The home is more than just a physical shelter for its inhabitants. It is also a place full of meanings that shape and define the experiences of the people who dwell within its walls. These ideas concern distinctions between inside and outside, public and private, work and leisure, adult and child, and male and female. The domestication of media technologies also means fitting the new object into routines of domestic life. Who uses the technology and to what ends? Technologies are socially constructed in relation to their users. Ball-and-paddle TV games were integrated into domestic space, the space of the American home, in ways similar to existing amusements and technologies, drawing their significance from already-domesticated objects: rec room games like table tennis and media technologies like television.

We can read ball-and-paddle games in two ways: along the lines of the marketing discourses of the time (advertising and promotion), as a way to bring the family together in play, as well as against the grain of these cheerful messages, as a means for some members of the family to escape the confinement of the home and live out fantasies of competitive sporting achievement. The games themselves tell us some things about their meanings, but sources such as television commercials and popular press articles also offer evidence of how people encountered these new objects and how they were encouraged to consider them. We might not have access to people's thoughts and experiences from decades past, but we do have access to the things they watched and read.[2] And the messages in packaging, advertising, and other framing discourses offer ideas about how users might have interpreted these new media forms.

As devices to plug into a home television set, ball-and-paddle consoles were, first of all, a way to expand the potential of television. Television's reputation in the 1970s was on the whole pretty lousy. It was seen as a highly commercialized mass medium catering to a lowest common denominator, at best a waste of time and probably a cause of social problems. Television's various nicknames speak to its low cultural status: idiot box, boob tube, vast wasteland, plug-in drug. But television had also been idealized since the time of its introduction to consumers in the 1940s and 1950s as a force for family unity, a way to bring the members of the household together during their hours of leisure, a common experience for all to share together. In advertising, the television set was often represented as an "electronic hearth," the focal point of a family circle.[3] Marketing imagery for many domestic products would picture such a scene: gathering around a telephone in an AT&T ad or around a board game in a Parker Brothers catalog. Early video games would revive the notion of the family brought together by a high-tech appliance in the home. But they would also remediate the lowly television set, transforming it into a newly participatory technology affording user interaction.

Representations of video games in news stories and in advertisements for the first consoles sold to consumers typically portrayed a family brought together by futuristic technology, taking pleasure from playing games on a family television set. In its marketing messages, Magnavox, an electronics manufacturer as well as the company behind the Odyssey, presented families gathered around the television to play the new electronic game in a very similar scene to the ones that had been used to sell its televisions (see figure 25.1). The typical representation of TV games in ads and magazine pieces showed electronic play as a social activity. If not a whole family, the scene would be composed of players of different ages and sexes: a man and a woman, a father and a son. Solitary players were rarely pictured even if solo play was among the uses of the new medium. Video games were sold as ways of bringing people together in the home, just as they would have been brought together by playing a board game or a card game. In the pages of department store catalogs, the electronic TV games were pictured on pages facing pool, air hockey, shuffleboard, and soccer table games. Games were too expensive to be sold in toy stores and were out of reach of most children's allowance-saving budgets. Video game marketing messages were about establishing an innovative, cutting-edge technological upgrade of domestic amusement for adults as well as kids, and the message was also that the games would delight their users by bringing them closer together. If television had developed a reputation for being a brainless, harmful diversion, video games would be a new use for the TV set that would upgrade its status, transforming it into a playfield, encouraging the active participation of the user rather than the supposedly passive conditions of ordinary viewing of broadcasts over the air.

In Odyssey commercials from the time of its original release, a male voice-over announcer describes the console as "the electronic game of the future" and "a new dimension for your television" that will "create a closed-circuit electronic playground." Magnavox promises "eleven play and learning games for the entire family," picturing a man and a woman competing against one another at hockey, tennis, and other games. One commercial ends on a family together playing Odyssey while the voice-over describes "a total play and learning experience for all ages." Many newspaper accounts of the time make similar claims about the

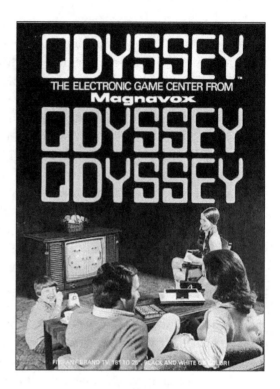

FIGURE 25.1
Advertisement for Odyssey by
Magnavox depicting family unity
around the game console.

Odyssey's potential to transform the TV set. A *New York Times* story in 1972
claims that the video game console "transfers television from passive to an active
medium."[4] A promotional film distributed to Magnavox dealers shows a family
playing together while the voice-over makes the sale: "People who want television
to do *their* thing entertain themselves with Odyssey." A Telstar commercial for
Coleco shows a man and woman playing against each other (hockey and tennis)
and concludes with the tagline "Hitch your TV to a Telstar." The standard appeal
of this period would be to show an ensemble of players in a family room using
the television set for a new and more legitimate and active purpose.

But at the same time that games were domesticated by being made to seem
like amusements for the leisure of family members united in electronic play, they
were also in many ways singled out as toys for boys. This didn't happen all at once.
Gendered appeals became more common later in the 1970s and into the 1980s after the period of the ball-and-paddle games' supremacy when it had become clear
to the industry that male teenagers were their most profitable market segment.

A good example of this development is the ball and paddle game *Breakout*
(Atari, 1976). *Breakout* was an Atari product developed by Steve Wozniak and
Steve Jobs before they founded Apple computers. It built on the premise of *PONG*

and other ball-and-paddle games but transformed them into a more challenging single-player experience. In *Breakout*, there is just one paddle, and it sits at the bottom of the screen and moves laterally. The player bounces the ball against a number of layers of bricks lined up at the top of the display. When struck by the ball, a brick disappears from the screen. The objective is to break through the lines of bricks and clear them all away, at which point a new level with a fresh set of layers appears. It is an addictive game, described by one of its players, along with other Atari titles, as "the ultimate adrenaline."[5]

Like many successful arcade games, *Breakout* was adapted for play on home consoles—on the Atari VCS. On the original arcade game, *Breakout* is narrativized through the depiction of a jailbreak scene of a brick wall being demolished both above the screen on the marquee, on either side of the screen, and on the sides of the cabinet. A cartoonish prisoner in jailhouse stripes wields a mallet for busting through the bricks on the marquee. Television advertising for Atari's home game cartridges in the later 1970s included a *Breakout* scene of a prisoner (played by well-known television comedy star Don Knotts) escaping confinement. The tagline in this advertising campaign was "Don't Watch TV Tonight. Play It!" This message affirmed the value of video games as a more participatory experience than television viewing, promising that the new technology would overcome some of the perceived flaws of a familiar medium.

When Atari released a technically improved new version called *Super Breakout* in 1978, the cartridge art and other promotional imagery now pictured a male astronaut competing in a racquet sport against an outer space backdrop (see figure 25.2). Interstellar adventure had become one of the most compelling themes of youth culture in the later 1970s, appealing, in particular, to boys (though also to all members of a mass audience). *Star Wars* and *Space Invaders* (Taito, 1978) were among the most popular texts of the late 1970s and early 1980s aimed at youth, fitting into a tradition of boy culture that stresses courageous daring, heroic struggle against a mortal foe, and aggressive and competitive action. Popular *Star Wars* toys such as character action figures gave children the opportunity to participate in fantasy role play within the narrative world of the space opera, and many video game cartridges were packaged with similar appeals to play as a way of enacting familiar dramatic scenarios. *Super Breakout* was narrativized not only via the product's packaging but also in *The Story of Super Breakout* (1982), an audiobook set (combination 33⅓ record and picture book) described on its cover as "an exciting read-along adventure based on your favorite Atari video games." According to this version of *Breakout*, the game represents a space shuttle transporting valuable ore from a moon of Jupiter to a space center called New California orbiting Venus. *Super Breakout*, as the book narrates, is about firing missiles

FIGURE 25.2
Box art for *Super Breakout* (1978)
by Atari, featuring sole male
astronaut protagonist.

against the colored layers of a force field obstructing the path of the shuttle. Upon the astronaut's success at penetrating the force field, "[h]e was doing it, breaking through, he had won! What a triumph for a son of earth, for Captain John Stewart Chang!" The young male player is being addressed here, invited to imagine a fantasy in which succeeding at challenging video games has the highest possible stakes.

The ideas presented in *The Story of Super Breakout* are similar to many of the images of play for boys represented in video game imagery of the time. Boys were often sold an ideal of electronic play as not only immersive, transformative, potentially dangerous but also exhilarating and empowering. These messages are a stark contrast against the earlier domestication of the ball-and-paddle console as a tool for harmonizing the family. We have come a long way from families passing time in the pleasure of one another's company while playing Odyssey *Tennis*. Rather than bringing together adults and children, male and female family members, the messages directed at boys and young men promoted the opposite experience: escape into a world of heroic masculine drama. The meanings of video games worked out in the medium's first decade established the new technology as an improvement on television that might fulfill some of its lost promise as a more participatory experience for families in the home, but they also promoted some players—boys—as the primary owners of the game console in the home. Ball-and-paddle games worked both ways, first as a means to renew and reinforce family ties through electronic leisure and then as a way for young, male players to escape from the home into microworlds of sporting and space adventure.

NOTES

1 Roger Silverstone and Leslie Haddon, "Design and the Domestication of Information and Communication Technologies: Technical Change and Everyday Life," in *Communication by Design: The Politics of Information and Communication Technologies*, ed. Robin Mansell and Roger Silverstone (Oxford, UK: Oxford University Press, 1996), 44–74.

2 Lynn Spigel, *Welcome to the Dreamhouse: Popular Media and Postwar Suburbs* (Durham, NC: Duke University Press, 2001), 11.

3 Lynn Spigel, *Make Room for TV: Television and the Family Ideal in Postwar America* (Chicago: University of Chicago Press, 1992); and Ceclila Tichi, *Electronic Hearth: Creating an American Television Culture* (New York: Oxford University Press, 1992).

4 "Magnavox Unveils TV Game Simulator," *New York Times*, May 11, 1972.

5 David Sudnow, *Pilgrim in the Microworld* (New York: Warner Books, 1983).

FURTHER READING

Flynn, Bernadette. "Geographies of the Digital Hearth." *Information Communication and Society* 6, no. 4 (2003): 551–576.

Herman, Leonard. "Ball and Paddle Consoles." In *Before the Crash: Early Video Game History*, edited by Mark J. P. Wolf, 30–52. Detroit, MI: Wayne State University Press, 2012.

Kirkpatrick, Graeme. "How Gaming Became Sexist: A Study of UK Gaming Magazines 1981–1995." *Media, Culture & Society* 39, no. 4 (2016): 453–468.

Newman, Michael Z. *Atari Age: The Emergence of Video Games in America*. Cambridge, MA: MIT Press, 2017.

26

Angry Birds
Mobile Gaming

GREGORY STEIRER AND JEREMY BARNES

Abstract: Through an examination of the reception, design, and distribution of the original *Angry Birds* mobile game, Gregory Steirer and Jeremy Barnes demonstrate how the mobile game as a genre represents a new mode of constructing and experiencing the act of play.

Although hard-core gamers will cringe at the claim, Rovio's *Angry Birds* might fairly be called the most successful video game of the twenty-first century. Released for Apple and Nokia smartphones in December of 2009 (with Android, BlackBerry, and other versions released the following year), *Angry Birds* quickly became the best-selling paid mobile app of all time, racking up as many as 1 million downloads a day during the 2010 holiday season.[1] A year after release, the game had been downloaded an unprecedented 50 million times, with total play time, according to Rovio, averaging 200 million minutes a day globally.[2] *TouchArcade* writer Eli Hodapp accordingly dubbed 2010 "The Year of 'Angry Birds,'" while journalists Paul Kendall and Erik Holthe Eriksen likened the property's long-term prospects to that of Disney's Mickey Mouse.[3] Even highbrow cultural critics felt the urge to weigh in on the game. *The New York Times Magazine*'s Sam Anderson, for example, proclaimed *Angry Birds* "the string of digital prayer beads that our entire culture can twiddle in moments of rapture or anxiety."[4] Although other video game properties have produced more revenue over the course of their lifetimes than *Angry Birds* has, few have been played or discussed by so many people so shortly after their debut.

In this chapter, we argue that *Angry Birds* epitomizes what was, in 2009, a relatively new form of video game: the mobile game. Although such a claim might at first seem obvious, even tautological, in what follows we reject the commonsense equation of mobility with portable hardware. What makes a mobile game a mobile game, we argue, is not simply the fact that the game is played on a phone or tablet; more important are the ways that play itself is constructed, not only via the code of the mobile application but also via the social interactions and industrial processes that surround it. The secret to *Angry Birds'* success lies in Rovio's early reconceptualization of how a mobile game should work. Indeed, *Angry Birds* exemplifies what we identify as the four core components of mobile gaming: gameplay accessibility, software accessibility, everyday ubiquity, and variable monetization.

Both the story and gameplay of *Angry Birds* are immediately accessible to both new and veteran game players. *Angry Birds'* story is explained in-game with a single scrolling screenshot and a few sound effects: a group of bird eggs have been stolen by pigs, and the birds must get them back. The game then jumps into the first level, wherein the player discovers that the pigs have holed themselves up in flimsy architectural structures while the birds, curiously unable to fly on their own, have produced an oversized slingshot with which to launch themselves at and bring down the structures—and thereby defeat the pigs. The main action of the game, flinging the birds at their porcine foes with the slingshot, is simple, satisfying, and intuitive. The player has only to touch and hold a finger to the primed bird, drag that finger (and with it the slingshot's cradle) back, aim, and then release the finger from the screen to send the bird flying (see figure 26.1). Many of the birds have special abilities that are activated by tapping the screen once airborne, and the player can use special items to increase the size of the birds or to better visualize the trajectory of the shots. These upgrades can help improve a player's score, but they are not necessary to complete any of the game's levels, all of which can be repeated ad infinitum without cost or penalty. The demands that *Angry Birds* makes on players' cognition and dexterity are extremely light: there are no complicated button combinations to remember, no stats or character attributes to manage, and no essential resources to acquire. To succeed at *Angry Birds*, all a player must remember is how to point and shoot.

Although the simple and intuitive approach to gameplay employed by *Angry Birds* and other mobile games is similar to that employed by console games aimed at so-called casual players, mobile games' deliberate minimization of the spatial and temporal constraints that normally accompany play partially distinguish them from the kind of games usually labeled casual. In his book *A Casual Revolution*, video game scholar Jesper Juul (whose work appears in this collection) defines casual games as "games that are easy to learn to play, fit well with a large number of players and work in many different situations."[5] He establishes two basic flavors of casual games, those with mimetic interfaces (games in which "the physical activity that the player performs mimics the game activity on the screen") and downloadable casual games, "which are purchased online, can be

FIGURE 26.1 *Angry Birds'* in-game screen is free of clutter and easy for both video game veterans and newcomers to understand.

played in short time bursts, and generally do not require an intimate knowledge of video game history in order to play."[6] *Angry Birds* might reasonably satisfy both sets of criteria, yet it stands apart from most examples from Juul's book for its ability to be played anywhere for virtually any length of time with little direct engagement or attention. *Wii Sports* (Nintendo, 2006), *Guitar Hero* (Harmonix, 2005), *Tetris* (Alexey Pajitnov, 1984), browser-based games, and other games typically labeled casual tend to require that players temporarily inhabit specific ludic spaces while playing. Although your grandmother, for example, might be more willing and able to play a round of tennis in *Wii Sports* than an execution match in a "hard-core" game such as *Gears of War* (Epic Games, 2006), both require that she play in a specific room and devote most of her attention while playing. *Angry Birds*, by contrast, imposes such few demands on the player's body and attention that it can be played while riding a train to work, sitting in class, going to the bathroom, in between emails, while watching TV, or during a late-night study session.

In addition to making few demands of players, *Angry Birds* makes few demands of players' technology. It exemplifies what we call *software accessibility*. Because of the game's initial release on the iPhone, a platform that tens of millions of people already owned, potential players required no additional hardware or accessories to play. Once it had expanded to Android, BlackBerry, and the Windows phone, its market included virtually everyone with a smartphone. So eager, in fact, was Rovio to make the software accessible to potential gamers that *Angry Birds* was released for the Nintendo DS, 3DS, PlayStation Portable, Wii, and PlayStation 3 (presumably to target children who did not have smartphones), as well as Apple's Macs, Windows-based PCs, streaming set-top boxes such as Roku, and even the social media platform Facebook. Such wide-scale availability resulted in more than 200 million active players a month at the height of the games' popularity in late 2012.[7] Everyone, in fact, seemed to be playing it, from celebrities such as Conan O'Brien and Justin Bieber to politicians such as Dick Cheney and David Cameron.[8] By 2016, thanks, in large part, to the game's wide availability, the original *Angry Birds* had been downloaded an incredible 3 *billion* times.[9] For comparison, *Wii Sports*, a "casual game" that benefited from being packaged with the Nintendo Wii (one of the all-time best-selling video game consoles), had sold 83 million units collectively (as a stand-alone unit and as part of a bundle) as of March 2017.[10]

Angry Birds, of course, is not the first game to have become a cultural sensation or to have been played by tens of millions of people. But few other games— even mega-hits like *Pac-Man* (Namco, 1980), *Tetris* (Alexey Pajitnov, 1984), and *World of Warcraft* (Blizzard Entertainment, 2004)—have been able to integrate themselves so seamlessly into the everyday lives of players. Indeed, *Angry Birds* and other mobile games deliberately resist the traditional construction of play as a unique mode of interaction separated off from nonplay activities; instead, *Angry Birds* suffuses play throughout the mundane and generally antiludic activities of everyday life. We call this characteristic of mobile games *everyday ubiquity*. Mobile games achieve such ubiquity in part thanks to their gameplay and software accessibility: the barriers to playing *Angry Birds* are so minimal that interaction with the game can occur throughout the day whether the player be at work, school, home, or on a commute.[11] One could even play the game while engaged in social interactions with non-players, who—thanks to the game's design—could at any moment be made *into* players. One might, for example, pass the phone to a friend at lunch, letting her take a shot at a particularly difficult level. Some mobile games—though not *Angry Birds*—attempt to mandate everyday ubiquity by utilizing gradually refilling energy gauges that limit how long a play session can last. Others employ sporadic push notifications to act as triggers, encouraging players to repeatedly reopen the gaming app.

Although the original *Angry Birds* uses such triggers sparingly, Rovio has achieved much the same effect via media extensions, licensing, and merchandising. In fact, within a few years of the game's initial release, *Angry Birds* had become just as much a mobile brand as it was a mobile game. There were (and, at the time of writing, still are) *Angry Birds* T-shirts, books, stuffed animals, action figures, toothbrushes, coffee cups, lamps, backpacks, cereal—even inner tubes for use in

FIGURE 26.2
A collection of
Angry Birds plush
toys, featuring
characters from
the games. Flickr
image credit:
Mike Mozart;
https://creative
commons.org
/licenses/by/2.0;
image unaltered.

pools (see figure 26.2). As part of the company's goal of becoming a twenty-first-century Disney, Rovio has also inked deals giving rise to an *Angry Birds* cartoon, a 2016 feature-length film, a series of amusement park attractions in the United Kingdom and Finland, and a number of branded retail stores in China.[12] By creating the possibility that players might interact with *Angry Birds* even when they are *not* playing the game, the products and media extensions help give rise to the game's remarkable ubiquity.[13] Indeed, Rovio even engaged in what we might call "reverse licensing"—acquiring the rights to utilize other popular media brands such as *Star Wars* and *Transformers* within its *Angry Birds* line of products (a practice that, as Derek Johnson explores elsewhere in this collection, is similar to The LEGO Group's licensing of multiple media brands for their LEGO toy sets). Such a move insinuates the *Angry Birds* brand into older, more established fandoms, thereby further broadening (at least in theory) the game's reach into the everyday lives of other media properties' fans.

So far, we have framed mobile gaming in terms of the dismantling of the various barriers to play typically associated with video games. Indeed, we have suggested that one might even understand mobility, in the context of gaming, as the dissolution of the concept of play as a discrete activity. Mobile games are also unique, however, for the reduced barriers to market entry they offer publishers and developers. Broadly speaking, game development is much easier and less expensive for a mobile platform than a traditional console or PC. Development for the PlayStation 4 or Nintendo 3DS typically requires the express permission of the platform owner (in this case Sony or Nintendo), the purchase of expensive development kits consisting of special hardware and software, the provision of detailed business plans, and the signing of various contracts enabling the platform owner to monitor and control the activities of the licensed developer. The PlayStation 4 dev kit, for example, was rumored to cost US$2,500 around the time of the platform's launch, whereas the 3DS dev kit was reportedly priced between US$3,000 and US$4,000.[14] With mobile development, by contrast, licensing costs are extremely low (Apple currently charges US$99 a year while Google charges a onetime fee of US$25), the dev kits require no special hardware, and the contractual regulations are much lighter. Accordingly, the cost of making a mobile game is often in the thousands rather than millions of dollars—and in some cases (such as that of the phenomenally successful *Flappy Bird* [dotGears, 2013]) scarcely more than the cost of the dev kit. *Angry Birds* cost approximately US$100,000 to make, a mere fraction of that of most console games (by way of comparison, Rockstar's *Grand Theft Auto V* [2013] cost an estimated US$137.5 million).[15]

Although the reduced barriers to entry have made mobile game development comparatively easy, they have also resulted in a retail market swamped with games. The sheer number of titles available on Apple's App Store or Google Play creates problems with what publishers call "search and discovery," the ability of consumers to find or encounter a publisher's game in an online retail environment. Although marketing can help solve such problems, most mobile game publishers do not have the budgets to undertake the expensive ad campaigns required to reach their target demographic. Even Rovio had little funding available for advertising *Angry Birds* at launch; instead, it relied almost entirely on the good fortune of being featured by Apple on its UK store and the subsequent free attention this brought.[16] If the lack of marketing budgets was not problem enough, mobile games also suffer from lacking the kind of specialized magazines and fan communities that play such a large part in traditional video game culture and that serve to lower marketing costs. Feature-length articles, reviews, or fan-made wikis—all of which provide added exposure for games—are virtually nonexistent for mobile games.

Faced with the challenge of acquiring customers without the use of traditional marketing, many mobile game publishers have developed profit models that enable them to give away their games for free. Pricing games at zero—as Rovio currently does with *Angry Birds* (the game cost $0.99 at launch)—in some ways ameliorates the difficulty of acquiring players as it significantly reduces the risk consumers face when buying a game they know little about. Such pricing, however, creates new monetization problems for publishers, who—deprived of the most common means of generating revenue—must construct their games so that they provide alternate methods of monetization. We call this aspect of mobile games *flexible monetization*. *Angry Birds*, for instance, generates revenue through in-game advertising, micro-transactions providing power-ups, and—as detailed previously—licensing and merchandising. The Mighty Eagle power-up, which allows players who purchase it to lay waste to previously completed levels, generated by itself nearly $2 million in revenue.[17] Other mobile games charge for in-game currency, access to levels, extended play time, additional characters, or cosmetic enhancements. PocApp Studio's *Castle Cats* (2017), for instance, offers units of in-game currency (starting at $1.99) and bundles of "common" and "rare" crafting resources (at US$2.99 and US$9.99 per bundle), whereas Bethesda's *Fallout Shelter* (2015) provides "lunch boxes," each containing a random assortment of weapons, pets, outfits, and other items, for US$0.99 a box. In some cases, in-game charges can be quite high. Racing game *Angry Birds Go!* (Rovio Entertainment, 2013), for example, offers its "Big Bang Special Edition Car" for US$99.99, and TinyCo's *Marvel Avengers Academy* (2016) charges as much as US$50 worth of in-game currency for access to new characters. Although most players balk at spending such amounts on a game (mobile or otherwise), publishers need only a small portion to do so to make a game profitable. These big spenders, called "whales" in industry parlance, effectively subsidize the cost of play for low or nonspenders, called "minnows." But they also ensure that mobile games are regularly constructed, as one *South Park* character explains in an episode devoted to the genre, "to be just barely fun. If the game was too fun, there would be no reason to micropay in order to make it more fun."[18]

Whether mobile games such as *Angry Birds* are fun to play or not is, of course, subjective. But we have suggested in this chapter that, when we play mobile games, fun may very well be beside the point. What makes mobile gaming distinctive is the way in which it reconceives play by dissolving the boundaries that typically define it. The increased accessibility and flexible monetization that characterize mobile games help give rise to a mode of play that, in its everyday ubiquity, blends into and resembles nonplay. As hard-core gamers would be quick to observe, there is something potentially sad or off-putting about the transformation of play in this fashion, but at the same time, we have hoped to suggest that there is also something exciting, even radical, in the way mobile games simultaneously hollow out and expand what it means to play a game.

NOTES

1 Tom Cheshire, "In Depth: How Rovio Made Angry Birds a Winner (And What's Next)," *Wired*, March 7, 2011, www.wired.co.uk.

2 Hillel Fuld, "Peter Vesterbacka, Maker of Angry Birds Talks About the Birds, Apple, Android, Nokia, and Palm/HP," *Tech n' Marketing*, December 27, 2010, http://technmarketing.com.

3 Paul Kendall, "Angry Birds: The Story Behind iPhone's Gaming Phenomenon," *The Telegraph*, February 7, 2011, www.telegraph.co.uk; and Erik Holthe Eriksen and Azamat Abdymomunov,

"Angry Birds Will Be Bigger than Mickey Mouse and Mario. Is There a Success Formula for Apps?" *MIT Entrepreneurship Review*, February 18, 2011, http://miter.mit.edu.

4 Sam Anderson, "Just One More Game . . . ," *The New York Times Magazine*, April 4, 2012, www.nytimes.com.

5 Jesper Juul, *A Casual Revolution: Reinventing Video Games and Their Players* (Cambridge, MA: MIT Press, 2012), 5.

6 Juul, *A Casual Revolution*, 5.

7 J. J. McCorvey, "Birds of Play," *Fast Company* (December 2012/January 2013): 103.

8 Jenna Wortham, "Angry Birds, Flocking to Cellphones Everywhere," *The New York Times*, December 11, 2010, www.nytimes.com; and Chesire, "In Depth."

9 Andy Robertson, "'Angry Birds 2' Arrives 6 Years and 3 Billion Downloads after the First Game," *Forbes*, July 16, 2015, www.forbes.com.

10 Nintendo, "Hardware and Software Sales Units: Total Unit Sales," *Nintendo.co.jp*, March 31, 2017, www.nintendo.co.jp.

11 Other scholars have characterized such a relationship to gaming as "ambient play" or "co-attentiveness." See Hjorth and Richardson, "Mobile Games and Ambient Play" in *Social, Casual, and Mobile Games: The Changing Gaming Landscape*, ed. Michelle Wilson and Tama Leaver (New York: Bloomsbury, 2016), 105–116; and Brendan Keogh, "Paying Attention to Angry Birds: Rearticulating Hybrid Worlds and Embodied Play through Casual iPhone Games," in *The Routledge Companion to Mobile Media*, ed. Gerard Goggin and Larissa Hjorth (New York: Routledge, 2014), 267–276.

12 McCrovey and Hennttonen, "Birds of Play," 128.

13 Tama Leaver thus provocatively characterizes *Angry Birds* as a "social network market." Leaver, "Angry Birds as a Social Network Market," in Wilson and Leaver, *Social, Casual, and Mobile Games*, 213–224.

14 Colin Campbell, "So How Much Does It Cost to Develop for PlayStation 4?" *Polygon*, July 24, 2013, https://www.polygon.com; and Peter D., "Price of 3DS Dev Kits Leaked, Cheaper than Expected," *3DS Buzz*, February 16, 2011, www.3dsbuzz.com.

15 McCrovey and Hennttonen, "Birds of Play," 107; and Brendan Sinclair, "GTA V Dev Costs over $137 Million, Says Analyst," *Gamesindustry.biz*, February 1, 2013, www.gamesindustry.biz.

16 Ryan Rigney, "The Origins of Angry Birds," *PCWorld*, October 2, 2010, www.pcworld.com.

17 Cheshire, "In Depth."

18 *South Park*, season 18 episode 6, "Freemium Isn't Free," directed and written by Trey Parker, aired November 5, 2014, on Comedy Central.

FURTHER READING

Evans, Elizabeth. "The Economics of Free: Freemium Games, Branding and the Impatience Economy." *Convergence* 22, no. 6 (2016): 563–580.

Feijoó, Claudio. "An Exploration of the Mobile Gaming Ecosystem from Developers' Perspective." In *The Video Game Industry: Formation, Present State and Future*, edited by Peter Zackariasson and Timothy Wilson, 76–98. New York: Routledge, 2012.

Leaver, Tom, and Michele Willson, eds. *Social, Casual and Mobile Games: The Changing Gaming Landscape*. New York: Bloomsbury, 2016.

27

LEGO Dimensions
Licensing

DEREK JOHNSON

Abstract: Giving players control over characters from many different media franchises, the toys-to-life game *LEGO Dimensions* marshaled a complex structure of co-branded relationships and licensing agreements across entertainment industries and modes of digital and material experiences. That industrial conjuncture, argues Derek Johnson, produced a game most centrally concerned with the mediating power of LEGO in entertainment licensing where the mechanics of interchangeable, articulated LEGO play provided the in-game means of transcending boundaries of intellectual property ownership.

Although the concept of building with LEGO blocks has long supported video gameplay in titles like *LEGO Star Wars: The Video Game* (Traveller's Tales, 2005) and *LEGO Universe* (NetDevil, 2010), this has relied on a virtual representation of those toys in game space until very recently. However, as part of the rise (and fall) of the "toys-to-life" genre that paired play in digital space with interactive collection and manipulation of plastic figures in the physical realm, *LEGO Dimensions* (Traveller's Tales, 2015) transformed the ubiquitous studded construction toy into a video game peripheral akin to a controller or input device. Players who purchased the console game acquired not only the software but also a pile of material LEGO bricks to be interacted with during the game—269 pieces, to be exact, in Starter Packs for Xbox One, PS4, and WiiU. Of those 269 pieces, several dozen enabled players to construct minifigure versions of the Batman, Gandalf, and Wyldstyle avatars (as well as a Batmobile) available in-game with this first purchase. Yet most of these pieces went toward building what was called the Vorton hub: a circular portal that, as represented onscreen in the game, led players to many different playable levels and sandbox areas. Vorton linked together narrative worlds drawn from many different sources of pop culture inspiration beyond DC Super Heroes, *Lord of the Rings*, and *The LEGO Movie* from which the three Starter Pack avatars hailed. Vorton offered gateways to many more universes across the history of games, film, television, and media entertainment. The number of pieces and time spent building the Vorton hub before starting digital play in earnest (perhaps 15 minutes or more, even for experienced builders) corresponded with its centrality to the core pleasures and conceits of a game focused on uniting different intellectual properties under the shared LEGO brand umbrella.

The Vorton hub, in other words, represented the power of LEGO toy products to marshal a complex structure of co-branded industry relationships and licensing agreements across many entertainment industries and modes of digital and material experience. *Dimensions* was a game most centrally concerned with entertainment licensing and the mediating power of LEGO, where the mechanics of interchangeable, articulated LEGO play provided the means of transcending boundaries of intellectual property ownership in-game. Although this term was not prevalent in the game itself, developers, press releases, critics, and players all discussed the Vorton hub as a means of gaining access to a multiplicity of popular entertainment "franchises."[1] In this sense, play in and through the hub went beyond jumping between and uniting characters from different media universes; the hub also produced play out of the industrial management of intellectual properties and the complex relationships shared among different media companies. LEGO's Vorton opened doors not just between spaces of gameplay but also between different franchise industry formations it brought into connection. By looking first at the web of partnerships and licensing agreements between LEGO, the game developers, and the many media companies that consented to co-brand their franchises as part of the game, we can uncover the industrial forces that gave shape to this product. Considering the experience of playing *Dimensions* itself, we can secondly understand how that industrial conjuncture produced a game out of the logics and mechanics of licensing to bring these many franchises together. Throughout these industrial and gameplay dynamics, LEGO—like Vorton itself—emerged as the focal point for industry play, both onscreen in the game world and in the physical space where players paired their digital and plastic playthings. Ultimately, *Dimensions* demanded that players engage with both industrial boundaries between different media franchises and the potential power of LEGO play to transcend them.

Before development of additional add-on packs ceased in 2017, *Dimensions* united at least 25 different media franchises, drawn from multiple media and across many different companies' intellectual property holdings. This scope demands careful consideration of what organizations had a stake in the game and which contributed what kinds of creative labor, authority, and permission to bring it to market.

Denmark-headquartered The LEGO Group was obviously most prominent in the merchandising and packaging of the game, designing and manufacturing the plastic blocks and character minifigures players had to buy to gain access to the virtual game space. Although some of these materials could be drawn from existing stock already produced for construction sets in the traditional toy market, *Dimensions* did require the company to manufacture new construction elements for pieces and characters unique to the game. Yet LEGO did not develop and publish the game software itself: that role fell to TT Games, a subsidiary studio of Warner Bros. Interactive Entertainment. This partnership between LEGO and UK-based TT Games emerged from the initial development of the *LEGO Star Wars* game in 2003. Originally, the LEGO Interactive division was to develop the game, extending its existing relationship with Lucasfilm from the construction toy market.[2] As the licensor of the *Star Wars* franchise, Lucasfilm granted to LEGO in 1998 the right to produce toys—and later games—based on its characters in exchange for a license fee and sales royalties.[3] By 2003, however, the Interactive division shuttered with its *Star Wars* game still in development. To sustain the project, several key Interactive managers founded Giant Interactive Entertainment to serve as publisher and exclusive game licensee for the LEGO brand while contracting with the independent studio Traveller's Tales to continue developing the game.[4] After the release of *LEGO Star Wars* in 2005, Traveller's Tales and Giant merged to become TT Games, and its ongoing relationship with LEGO meant sublicensing not only with Lucasfilm but soon companies like Warner Bros. as well to create similar games like *LEGO Batman: The Videogame* (Traveller's Tales, 2008) (following LEGO's lead in creating Batman construction sets). By 2007, Warner Bros. targeted TT Games for acquisition, seeking "a great match with our brnds as well as an opportunity to effectively leverage our existing global infrastructure"—or, translated from corporate-speak, a bigger piece of TT Games' successful partnership with LEGO.[5]

This partnership supported numerous other LEGO-meets-media-franchise titles, including *LEGO Harry Potter: Years 1-4* (2010) under the Warner Bros. corporate umbrella, as well as games like *LEGO Indiana Jones: The Original Adventures* (2008), *LEGO Jurassic World* (2015), and *LEGO Marvel Super Heroes* (2013) that depended on TT Games sublicensing LEGO's agreements with Lucasfilm, Universal, and Disney, respectively. The development of *Dimensions*, therefore, did not significantly depend on new kinds of licensing agreements across toys, games, and screen media but was instead notable for uniting such licenses in a single-play experience rather than across separately branded titles.

To be sure, *Dimensions* did rely more heavily on franchises under direct control of Warner Bros. or LEGO than on those controlled by companies without the same investment in the game or this long-term partnership. The 2017 *Dimensions* lineup included game avatars and physical toy products based on Warner Bros.

franchises, including *DC Super Heroes*, *Harry Potter/Fantastic Beasts*, *The Wizard of Oz*, *Scooby Doo*, *Adventure Time*, *The Powerpuff Girls*, *Gremlins*, *Goonies*, and *Beetlejuice*, as well as those based on LEGO product lines such as *Ninjago*, *Chima*, and *CITY Undercover*. Across both these categories sat products based on the Warner Bros. distributed LEGO production *The LEGO Movie*. The game also drew on the defunct Midway Games brand that Warner Bros. controlled since acquiring the game publisher in 2009. In these cases, TT Games could count on the interest LEGO and Warner Bros. shared in *Dimensions* to facilitate cooperation and support the game with valuable franchise content. Nevertheless, the decade-plus of success that LEGO (and less visibly, but no less importantly, TT Games) had demonstrated as a co-branding partner supported additional license agreements with other major media companies in film, television, and games. *Dimensions* exploited agreements with NBC-Universal for *Back to the Future*, *The A-Team*, *Jurassic World*, *ET*, and *Knight Rider*; with Paramount for *Mission Impossible*; with 20th Century Fox for *The Simpsons*; with Sony for *Ghostbusters*; and with BBC for *Doctor Who*. Competing game publishers also saw value in making their franchises available to LEGO and TT Games, with Valve licensing *Portal 2* for use in the game and its physical playsets and SEGA licensing *Sonic the Hedgehog*.

These agreements also revealed the two-way relationship between LEGO as toy licensee and TT Games as digital licensee responsible for game production. Game director James McLoughlin explained that some *Dimensions* licensing deals were driven by LEGO executives interested in generating toy product based on existing franchises, who subsequently turned to the TT team for "feedback" in bringing those franchises to the game, too; yet design director Arthur Parsons suggested that TT Games also pursued the franchises that its designers most wanted in the game, encouraging LEGO to newly acquire the rights to particular franchises.[6] So instead of a linear hierarchy of licenses, LEGO and TT Games participated in a licensing loop where each generated play product to support the other while looking outward toward other entertainment companies as sources of sustaining franchise material.

Glaringly missing from this expansive web of licensing agreements was the Walt Disney Company, which owns the *Star Wars* and *Marvel* brands licensed to LEGO for traditional construction sets yet did not allow their participation in *Dimensions*. Until 2016, Disney had offered its own toys-to-life game, *Disney Infinity* (Avalanche Software, 2013), and thus did not extend its existing agreements with LEGO and TT Games to this game category. Much like *Dimensions*, *Infinity* relied on a franchise-focused strategy that brought the Disney-owned Pixar, *Star Wars*, Marvel, and Princess brands under a single, proprietary gameplay umbrella. Although Disney's May 2016 decision to cease production of new *Infinity* content could have opened new license possibilities for *Dimensions*, many analysts speculated that the toys-to-life "trend seem[ed] to have crested" (with another leading toys-to-life game, *Skylanders*, scaling back in its own most recent release).[7] Having come late to the toys-to-life market, *Dimensions* was thus forced to weather this genre decline rather than expanding aggressively into Disney's abandoned franchise territory. Still, TT Games and The LEGO Group continued to invest in *Dimensions* well after Disney and others had abandoned the market, only finally announcing the end of new development in late October 2017.[8]

Although this cancellation came a year before the end of a planned three-year cycle, *Dimensions'* relative persistence in the fading and faddish toys-to-life market depended on the unique role of the LEGO brand as a mediating force in the marriage of franchised media entertainment, physical playthings, and video gaming. On the one hand, *Dimensions* could go beyond uniting disparate screen franchises to deploy the value-added co-branding of LEGO, which *Brand Finance* ranked as rivaling the entire Disney empire in terms of brand power (ranked first globally in 2015 and second only to Disney in 2016).[9] On the other hand, in terms of gameplay, LEGO's melding of multiple media franchises incorporated unique themes and dynamics based on an aesthetic of interchangeability and articulation drawn from its construction toy system. In other words, the collision of multiple media franchises in the game world built upon more than a decade of co-branding in which intellectual properties held by different companies had been organized by and through LEGO-related experiences. This included films such as *The LEGO Movie* that used different franchises as not only the building blocks from which to build comedic encounters but also, on a more mundane level, the co-habitation of LEGO versions of Darth Vader, Batman, and Harry Potter in the assorted boxes, bins, and containers in which consumers stored their LEGO pieces. Publisher TT Games, moreover, had firmly established an evergreen market for LEGO-based gameplay, meaning that the established design formula at the core of *Dimensions* granted the game additional accessibility, familiarity, and risk mitigation.

In playing *Dimensions*, therefore, consumers experienced this mélange of media franchises in different ways than offered by *Disney Infinity*. Although the latter allowed players to choose their characters in open exploration areas and even build their own play spaces from elements of different franchises, its predesigned missions and levels typically required players to use specific characters appropriate to the familiar narratives enacted. For example, the *Disney Infinity: Marvel Super Heroes* Avengers Playset (Avalanche, 2014) introduced Marvel characters to the game with a set of new missions pitting the included Iron Man, Captain America, and Black Widow avatars against Loki and the Frost Giants. Players who purchased additional Marvel figures, like Hulk, could swap them into play at any time, but bringing in non-Marvel *Disney Infinity* characters was prohibited.

In *Dimensions*, by contrast, those restrictions did not exist; players could use any character they owned to play through any mission. As director James McLoughlin promised, "In our game, any character can be in any situation at any time."[10] Thus, on a narrative level, the game followed an aesthetic of interaction and interchangeability across franchise lines organized by the idea of LEGO play and its recombination of compatible pieces.

Even if any character could tackle any situation, players still did not have full, equal access to all characters. Instead, the game encouraged players to make additional purchases beyond the Batman, Gandalf, and Wyldstyle minifigures of the Starter Pack. Ingeniously (from a marketing standpoint, at least), the game did possess a mechanism for making other characters *temporarily* available to players without additional retail purchase. In various places throughout the game's levels, players encountered obstacles that the three starter characters simply could not pass. In these instances, players could choose to "Hire-a-Hero," trading thousands of multicolored "studs" collected in the course of play for 30 seconds of access to a needed but unowned character. Effectively, this game mechanic allowed the player not to own but to rent, temporarily licensing the character from LEGO, in a way. Moreover, because that would-be license fee often grew with each use, it encouraged players enamored with hired characters to make that license permanent with subsequent retail purchase of the physical toy.

Although the Hire-a-Hero mechanic evoked licensing after a fashion, the design of the Vorton hub world made even clearer how the game both positioned players within the licensed logics of franchising and constructed LEGO consumption as the means of navigating those boundaries between franchises. The Vorton hub prompted players to choose between 14 scripted, sequentially unlocked mission levels included with the Starter Pack or free-play exploration of open sandbox spaces based on different media franchises. Players could freely wander the Vorton hub to see the doors to each of these sandboxes, but they could only enter one of these portals if they owned a franchise-appropriate character. Put another way, players with the Starter Pack could travel to the DC Comics Super Heroes, *Lord of the Rings*, and *LEGO Movie* franchise worlds to which Batman, Gandalf, and Wyldstyle belong (as characters and intellectual properties), but they needed to purchase the *Harry Potter* Team Pack, for example, to enter the gateway to an open-world Hogwarts School. In this way, the in-game design of Vorton respected boundaries between different media franchises and discrete claims of competing corporate ownership held over them, prompting players to recognize and engage with these boundaries in exploring the hub world (see figure 27.1).

Although *Dimensions* did offer an aesthetic of interchangeability, the Vorton hub nevertheless asked the player to consider each franchise as a separate industrial component. In doing so, the game positioned the LEGO brand and the

FIGURE 27.1 *LEGO Dimensions* prompted players to purchase numerous physical toys from different branded franchises to gain access to each gateway in the in-game Vorton hub.

experience of playing LEGO as the means of overcoming those boundaries: only by purchasing more physical bricks and minifigures could players freely operate across these clear lines of industry demarcation. In this way, *Dimensions* encouraged players to play with the entertainment industry, negotiating its terrains by embracing the seemingly unique power of LEGO to move across stark franchise structures. Most importantly, these licensing practices both preceded *Dimensions* and promised to outlive them even as the toys-to-life market collapsed. Even though Disney lost its proprietary gaming platform with the end of *Infinity*, the strategy of leveraging LEGO as a mediating gateway between multiple entertainment franchises would continue beyond *Dimensions*, as TT Games simply reverted to publishing individual, franchise-bounded game titles like The *LEGO Ninjago Movie Video Game* (TT Fusion, 2017) and *LEGO The Incredibles* (TT Fusion, 2018). Players could still move between different franchise realms through their successive, LEGO-branded game purchases. *Dimensions* did not survive, but LEGO and TT Games continued their practices of playful franchise mediation and intercompatibility, offering a licensing model that other developers might emulate in the future.

In 2013, The LEGO Group's brand relations director, Michael McNally, qualified suggestions by industry analysts that the corporation might be an "entertainment company," emphasizing instead its aim to engage children in building experiences.[11] Yet *LEGO Dimensions* suggests that the company *was* in the business of mediating the franchise worlds—and specifically, the industry relationships—of entertainment. While the licensing relationships that organize entertainment franchises and link them to industries like toy manufacturing help us understand *Dimensions* as a commodity, they also help us better comprehend the play patterns at the heart of the game. The *Dimensions* player did not merely take on the role of Batman, Gandalf, or Wyldstyle in a game space but also engaged with a restrictive system of intellectual property ownership claims that ostensibly only the interchangeable and articulated play of LEGO could transcend. Ironically, while the game lacked the more substantive free building and creative construction mechanics that distinguished *Disney Infinity*, the act of building and then stepping through the Vorton portal lent players the *industrial* power of LEGO to turn different media franchises into the building blocks of play experience.

NOTES

1 See, for example, "Franchises," *LEGO Dimensions Wiki*, http://lego-dimensions.wikia.com; Riley Little, "5 Franchises We Want to See in 'LEGO Dimensions,'" *GameRant*, 2015, https://gamerant.com; Andy Robertson, "'Lego Dimensions' Wave 6 Expands Features and Franchises," *Forbes*, June 15, 2016, www.forbes.com; and Roar Rude Trangbaek, "Warner Bros. Interactive Entertainemnt, TT Games, and The LEGO Group Announce LEGO Dimensions." LEGO.com, April 2015, www.lego.com.

2 Allstair Wallis, "Playing Catch Up: Traveller's Tales Jon Burton," *Gamasutra*, November 9, 2006, www.gamasutra.com.

3 "Lego in 'Star Wars' Deal with Lucasfilm," *Los Angeles Times*, May 1, 1998, http://articles.latimes.com.

4 Wallis, "Playing Catch Up."

5 "Warner Bros. Home Entertainment Group Agrees to Acquire Highly Successful UK Game Developer and Publisher TT Games," *Warner Bros.*, November 8, 2007, www.warnerbros.com.

6 Chris Baker, "The Ludicrously Lucrative Licensing Deals Behind 'Lego Dimensions,'" *Glixel*, November 15, 2016, www.glixel.com.

7 Baker; Matt Weinberger, "Disney Cancels Its Hit 'Disney Infinity' Video-Game Series and Take a $147 Million Charge," *Business Insider*, May 10, 2016, www.businessinsider.com.

8 Mitch Wallace, "'Lego Dimensions' Officially Cancelled," *Forbes*, October 23, 2017, www.forbes.com.

9 Will Heilpern, "These are the 10 Most Powerful Brands in the World," *Business Insider*, February 1, 2016, www.businessinsider.com.

10 Wallis, "Playing Catch Up."

11 Sam Thielman, "How Lego Became the Most Valuable Toy Company in the World," *Adweek*, April 15, 2013, www.adweek.com.

FURTHER READING

Bak, Meredith. "Building Blocks of the Imagination: Children, Creativity, and the Limits of *Disney Infinity." The Velvet Light Trap* 78 (2016): 53–64.

Elkington, Trevor. "Too Many Cooks: Media Convergence and Self-Defeating Adaptations." In *The Video Game Theory Reader 2*, edited by Mark J. P. Wolf and Bernard Perron, 213–235. London: Routledge, 2009.

Johnson, Derek. *Media Franchising: Creative License and Collaboration in the Culture Industries.* New York: NYU Press, 2013.

Wolf, Mark J. P., ed. *LEGO Studies: Examining the Building Blocks of a Transmedial Phenomenon.* London: Routledge, 2014.

28

Tomb Raider
Transmedia

JESSICA ALDRED

Abstract: Video games have been productively analyzed for their narrative and world-building possibilities as transmedia expansions of other cinematic or literary source material, yet decidedly less attention has been paid to what is at stake when games characters provide the "primary" source material for other media. Through a close examination *Tomb Raider's* Lara Croft, and the shifting relationship between Croft-as-game-character and Croft-as-film-character, Jessica Aldred contends that video game characters have never been more crucial to the successful translation of intellectual property across media.

In the years since her 1996 debut in *Tomb Raider* (Core Design), Lara Croft's evolution, translation, and transformation across a multiplicity of subsequent games and other media forms—including comic books, novels, animated series, and films—have made her a crucial case study in transmedia character construction. Henry Jenkins influentially defines transmedia storytelling as a process wherein "integral elements of a fiction get dispersed systematically across multiple delivery channels for the purpose of creating a unified and coordinated entertainment experience."[1] However, the figure of Lara Croft points out the ways in which characters—especially those who originate in the context of digital games—can challenge and complicate the unity and coordination of the best-laid transmedia plans. In this sense, Lara Croft and the *Tomb Raider* franchise can be more productively understood through the lens of transmedia play, which, as Matthew Thomas Payne and Derek Frank have argued, "refers less to adapting stories or characters for different mediums, and refers more to developing ways for users to interact with their intellectual property (or IP)—simultaneously and asynchronously—across multiple media devices in a variety of spaces."[2]

Although Lara Croft's corporate ownership has shifted over the course of her fictional lifetime, she has always been constructed as intellectual property that audiences could access, and interact with, in a multiplicity of ways that didn't necessarily adhere to the unified coherence of transmedia storytelling, with the many disjunctions in Lara's fictional identity often providing the greatest source of pleasure for her fans. By analyzing Croft for how her game and film incarnations represent different modes of "transmedia play," we can redress some of the narrative biases of transmedia storytelling and destabilize the remaining boundaries between "primary" and "secondary" media forms within most transmedia franchises. Although video games have been productively analyzed for their narrative and world-building possibilities as transmedia expansions of other cinematic or literary source material, decidedly less nuanced attention has been paid to what is at stake when digital games, and their characters, in particular, provide the primary source material for other media. By closely examining *Tomb Raider*'s Lara Croft, with a focus on the shifting relationship between Croft-as-game-character and Croft-as-film-character—wherein the gritty, emotional realism of Croft's latest in-game iteration actually prompted debates about which human star would be capable of "living up" to the digital Lara—we can see that video game characters have never been more crucial to the successful translation of intellectual property across media.

To understand the implications of this shift, we must first acknowledge how the relationship between films and digital games—and film and game characters—has always been a complicated one. While games have struggled historically with "cinema envy," aspiring to create digital spaces and characters that evoke the same emotional involvement and narrative immersion as film, so, too, has cinema become increasingly enamored with replicating certain "gamic" modes of visual grammar, narrative structure, and character construction. Games and films thus exemplify Jay David Bolter and Richard Grusin's definition of remediation as a dual logic wherein new media must always be understood in relation to how they emulate and repurpose existing media forms while, in turn, older media forms must respond, both formally and narratively, to the challenges posed by newer media.[3] Consider the eerily photorealistic motion-captured character performances in *L.A. Noire* (Team Bondi, 2011) for an example of the former, while the dizzying, often first-person explorations of digital spaces on display in recent blockbusters ranging from *The Hobbit: The Battle of the Five Armies* (Peter Jackson, 2014) to *Captain America: Civil War* (Anthony and Joe Russo, 2016) exemplify the latter. As Robert Alan Brookey points out, this complicated relationship of mutual influence and admiration has only become more fraught because of the ongoing push toward the technological convergence of films and games through common media storage formats and shared digital imaging software and hardware, often driven by the perceived need for a given piece of intellectual property to move across media from film to game or vice versa.[4]

Although cheaply and/or hastily produced movie-licensed tie-in games were once standard industry operating procedure, many media producers have realized what a crucial role games can play in expanding and enriching a franchise story world. The growing cultural prestige of such licensed game titles was nowhere more evident than at the 2015 GDC Awards, when two big-budget, high-profile games licensed from other media—*Middle-earth: Shadow of Mordor* (Monolith Productions, 2014) and *Alien: Isolation* (Creative Assembly, 2014)—were nominated for "Game of the Year" awards, with *Shadow of Mordor* taking home the top prize.[5] Such transmedia successes, however, do not simply rely on expanding a franchise storyline and story world; they must also provide a *different* kind of character alignment and engagement than their source material. In *Shadow of Mordor*, for example, players are freed from the moral obligations of Frodo et al. to wreak vengeful havoc on countless orcs as Talion, a ranger whose family has been murdered by Sauron. Meanwhile, in *Alien: Isolation*, players are subject to the terrifying claustrophobia (and insane difficulty) of navigating the Sevastopol space station as Amanda Ripley, Ellen's daughter, relying largely on stealth mechanics and evasion to uncover the truth about what happened to Ellen aboard the *Nostromo*. In these instances, transmedia play succeeds through intentional character differentiation—and a differential mode of playful engagement—rather than seamless cross-media translation from film to game, despite overhyped industry claims that their "converged" means of production will make the latter possible or even desirable.

While movies based on digital games have been decidedly slower to achieve critical and commercial legitimacy, a selection of recent titles with high-profile acting talent attached point to the ongoing industry push to playfully repurpose successful IP in different contexts, as well as what is at stake when media forms once considered "secondary" come to the fore as generative or "primary" source material. *Tomb Raider* provides an ideal franchise for exploring the affordances and limitations of transmedia play with digital games as a point of origin.

Since her debut, Lara Croft, with her multiplicity, has consistently defied the possibility of experiencing *Tomb Raider* as a "unified and coordinated entertainment experience," often to the delight and enthusiasm of her biggest fans. Even in her early days, Croft's backstory as fledgling aristocrat-turned-globe-trotting, dual-pistol-wielding archaeologist was constantly—and often inconsistently—reworked and retconned from one game to the next, prompting much debate and discussion amongst players about what, if anything, was Lara's "true" origin story.[6] (In this sense, Lara's fractured fictional identity can be most readily likened to those figures currently at the center of the most successful transmedia character-driven franchises: comic-book characters whose constant rebirths and reimaginings within their "primary" media form and across other media also eschew the binds of tidy, linear narrative storytelling.) Croft was killed off by exasperated Core developers—literally buried under a pile of rubble at the end of *Tomb Raider: The Last Revelation* (Core Design, 1999)—in the hopes of escaping the grind of churning out a new *Tomb Raider* game each year, only to be resurrected shortly thereafter at the publisher's insistence with little textual explanation as to how she'd survived her apparent doom.[7] Novels and comics intended to bridge the narrative gaps and character arcs between games add to this multiplicity, providing either self-contained vignettes of Croft's adventures or wholly contradictory character studies never to be addressed in subsequent games. Meanwhile, Lara's appearance didn't just morph according to the increasingly photorealistic capabilities of next-generation game consoles but was also repeatedly altered to suit the medium she was appearing in—magazine "photo shoots" and advertisements, for example, differed considerably from her lower-resolution image in the context of gameplay.

In this sense, transmedia play with Lara Croft necessitates negotiating an ever-varied and shifting selection of performances and personae; Lara Croft's in-game toughness and savvy might translate, albeit with considerable narrative inconsistency, into Lara Croft as the heroine of *Tomb Raider* novels and comics, but it contrasts harshly with the seductive, string-bikini-clad Lara who slinks out of the ocean to seduce a prospective buyer in a car commercial or the come-hither topless Lara posed seductively on the cover of *Loaded* magazine or the bevy of real-world models and actresses who portrayed Lara at game conferences and conventions. As Mary Flanagan suggests, Lara Croft is the first female "cyberstar" with wholly digital origins, and she began her journey through the gauntlet of transmedia play with little by way of precedent to follow.[8] Flanagan asserts that Lara's multiplicity derives from a kind of liberatory planned obsolescence, her always-changing formats allowing consumers to enjoy the process of her constant reinvention:

> Unlike a film star's eternal image on screen, electronic screen images show age within a year as technology outstrips itself. Though the body model can be refined through the years, remapped into the technology of the time, previous incarnations of stars' bodies will grow more and more obsolete. In the future, a star's repertoire will consist of a set of obsolete film formats and media. With the "experience" of a digital star taking place in a continuous present, the star's histories are erased as quickly as technology is updated.[9]

Therefore, to deride some of Lara Croft's incarnations as sexist or exploitative perhaps misses the larger point—that a wholly digital female star with no "authentic" self to serve could be many things to many people, and that navigating her various transformations and apparent inconsistencies might provide one of the greatest pleasures of this type of transmedia play.

With the 2001 release of the first *Tomb Raider* film, Lara Croft's digital mutability collided with the need for a "real" actress—not a convention circuit look-alike—to portray her. After much public and fan speculation as to who could successfully embody the world's first digital star, the casting of Angelina Jolie was, for the most part, quickly integrated into the fractured Croft canon as just one more playful transformation of Lara Croft-as-shape-shifter. Although Jolie's willingness to physically transform for her previous roles had been viewed through the lens of actorly commitment to physical and emotional authenticity, her casting as Croft reframed this dedication as one to Lara's willful disobedience of physical realism in terms of both appearance and action. This discourse was characterized by repeated discussions of whether Jolie could live up to the precedent set by Croft's near-impossible virtual acrobatics, with Jolie, director Simon West, and a range of stunt coordinators attesting in multiple press interviews, promotional materials, and DVD special features to Jolie's commitment to the physical training and modifications required to "become" Lara.[10] Jolie's insistence on approximating Lara's lean-but-muscular frame was exhaustively documented through repeated mention and description of a high-protein diet designed to help her gain 15 pounds of muscle mass, while television interviews and entertainment news features showcased the martial arts, riding, and weapons training Jolie supposedly received to do her own stunts.[11] Stunt coordinators, in particular (for both *Tomb Raider* and its 2003 sequel, *The Cradle of Life*), were quick to point out how readily Jolie didn't just master these tasks but also rapidly surpassed the knowledge and skill of her various teachers, unintentionally replicating the narrative of mastery players experience as they learn to navigate game space as Lara. Meanwhile, snide critical commentary about Jolie's noticeably padded bra, as well as speculation about whether she had her lips surgically enhanced to look more like Lara, points out the challenges not-digital female stars still face in terms of being expected to maintain some perception of their inherent authenticity.[12]

With the 2013 reboot of the *Tomb Raider* game, the reinvention of Lara Croft created a new set of challenges for a planned reboot of the *Tomb Raider* films. *Tomb Raider* (Crystal Dynamics, 2013) revisited Lara's origin story once again, this time to depict her beginnings as a naïve graduate student transformed by her quest to discover the secrets of the sacred island of Yamatai once investigated by her late father, evolving from vulnerable victim to skilled (if conflicted) killer. Although this revision of Lara's backstory doesn't seem to differ significantly from those countless revisions that preceded it, when paired with the gritty, emotional realism of Lara's in-game performance, it was viewed as nothing short of a wholesale reimagining of the franchise.

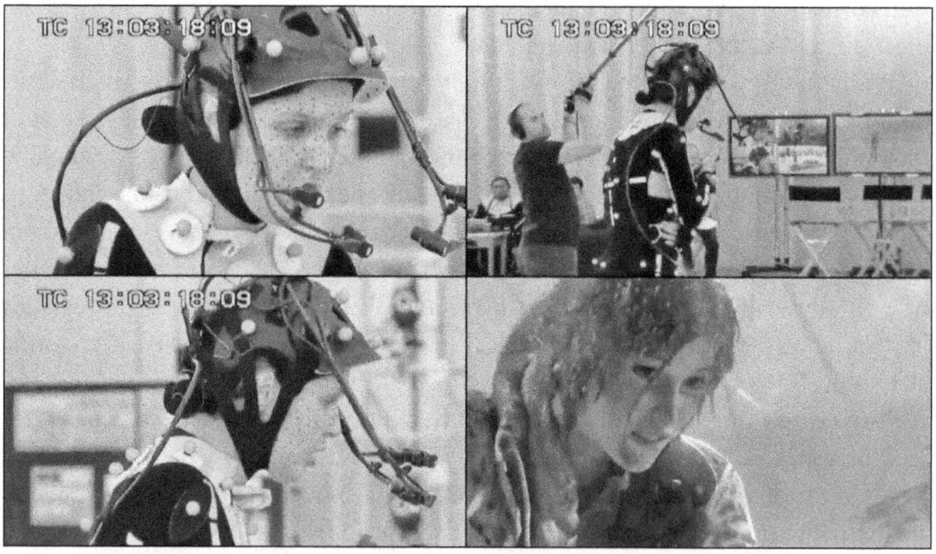

FIGURE 28.1 Screen capture from promotional footage of the making of *Rise of the Tomb Raider* (Crystal Dynamics, 2015) that highlights British actress Camilla Luddington's role in bringing the "new" Lara Croft to life.

In the years since Jolie played Croft on the big screen, Lara-as-wholly-digital star acquired a new layer of lived corporeality via the progressive addition of motion-captured performers and voice actors responsible for her creation; in *Tomb Raider: Underworld* (Crystal Dynamics, 2008), for example, many of Lara's movements were provided by Olympic gymnast Heidi Moneymaker, while her voice was provided by actress Keeley Hawes. However, the 2013 reboot was the first game to strongly link Lara with the unified performance of a recognizable actress—Camilla Luddington—who would provide her vocal, facial, and bodily performance and feature prominently in the game's promotional materials, including film stills and footage showing her live-action performance on the motion capture stage alongside Lara's final, fully rendered in-game scenes (see figure 28.1).[13]

While the majority of Luddington's vocal performance was recorded separately from Luddington's physical performance as Croft, this discursive attempt to unify the two strives to replicate the discourse of authentic actorly performance that has been used to elevate the cultural prestige of cinema. Similarly, games journalists consistently asked Luddington about her emotional commitment to the character of Lara Croft, crediting her with "breathing life into the role" at the same time as they minimize the work of the many animators and programmers who are also responsible for Lara's performance. In one "making-of" featurette that includes a lengthy clip of Luddington performing a particularly grueling scene as Lara, the actress confides to her interviewer that "this was some of the most emotionally and physically draining work I'd ever done."[14] Subsequent reviews of *Tomb Raider* and its 2015 sequel, *Rise of The Tomb Raider*, were quick to point to Luddington's "incredible performance"[15] as crucial to our belief in and alignment with this re-invented Lara: "Luddington *is* Lara Croft. She imbues the character with a sense of wonderment and determination like no other performer,"[16] raves one reviewer while another critic asserts that "Camilla Luddington's performance as Croft is im-pressively convincing, and throughout this adventure you'll really feel for Lara."[17]

With the perceived authenticity of Luddington's performance as a starting point, speculation over who could take on the role of Lara Croft in the rebooted films took on a drastically different character to that which surrounded Jolie's casting just a decade prior—fans and critics alike wondered what actress could live up to the realism of Luddington's portrayal of Lara.[18] With female stars rang-ing from Daisy Ridley (*Star Wars: The Force Awakens*) to Saoirse Ronan (*Brook-lyn, Lady Bird*) in the running, the eventual casting of Oscar-winner Alicia Vi-kander, known for nuanced, prestige roles in *The Danish Girl* and *Ex Machina*, suggests that the playful gap between Lara's film and game iterations could be coming to a close and that the *Tomb Raider* franchise could be reimagining Lara Croft as an ostensibly "unified and coherent" transmedia character known for her raw, emotional believability and consistency across media. Although the 2018 *Tomb Raider* film received middling reviews on release, film critics almost univer-sally praised Vikander's performance in similar terms to those mobilized by game critics in relation to Luddington's: she "balance[s] flinty charm with sympathetic humanism";[19] "emotionally, she's all there—achingly vulnerable . . . and fierce";[20] and in sharp contrast to Jolie, who "was halfway to a cartoon, as if Rambo had been gene-spliced with Jessica Rabbit . . . there is nothing luscious or overheated about the new-look Lara. She wants to be a fighter, not a fantasy, and her feminist credentials are impeccable."[21]

However, as Flanagan reminds us, the digital star's image has always been de-fined by its strategically planned obsolescence—the need for constant updating and upgrading, the necessity of moving from one format to the next, and the de-mands of meeting (and sometimes challenging) always-shifting consumer expec-tations. With this in mind, we can view Vikander's casting, and Lara's transmedia turn toward "realism" and "authenticity" more broadly, as just another shedding of her cyber skin, bound to conflict in some way with the versions that preceded her, and ultimately destined to be reframed and reworked in whatever other in-carnations may follow.

The *Tomb Raider* franchise and the figure of Lara Croft have historically ben-efited from a playful and often dissonant approach to transmedia character con-struction. Although the more recent incarnations of Croft may seem poised to close the gap between her gamic and cinematic self, we must remember the extent to which Lara's *true* origin story—not that of her aristocratic upbringing or her training as an adventurer but, rather, her techno-industrial origins as the world's first cyberstar—will always encourage a multiplicity of interpretations and possibilities. Ultimately, rather than being locked down or "fixed" into a unified, easily transmediated being, Lara provides a rare site where real and digital bodies—and, more broadly speaking, the often-conflicting mediums of games and cinema—can overlap in compelling and challenging ways.

NOTES

1 Henry Jenkins, *Convergence Culture: Where Old and New Media Collide* (New York: NYU Press, 2006), 95–96.

2 Matt Payne and Derek Frank, "Transmedia Play," *Proceedings of 2013 DiGRA International Conference*, Atlanta, Georgia, August 26–29, 2013, http://homes.lmc.gatech.edu.

3 Jay David Bolter and Richard Grusin, *Remediation: Understanding New Media* (Cambridge, MA: MIT Press, 1999), 5.

4 Robert Alan Brookey, *Hollywood Gamers: Digital Convergence in the Film and Video Game Industries* (Bloomington: Indiana University Press, 2010), 1–29.

5 Eddie Makuch, "Middle-earth: Shadow of Mordor Wins Game of the Year at GDC Awards," *Gamespot*, March 4, 2015, www.gamespot.com.

6 "Retconning" (the popular short form for retroactive continuity) refers to the revision of fans' established knowledge of a fictional universe or character through the addition of new, often seemingly contradictory information.

7 See Wesley Yin-Poole, "20 Years On, the Tomb Raider Story Told by the People who Were There," *Eurogamer*, October 30, 2016, www.eurogamer.net.

8 Mary Flanagan, "Digital Stars Are Here to Stay," *Convergence* 5, no. 2 (1999): 16–17.

9 Flanagan, "Digital Stars," 17–18.

10 See, for example, Prairie Miller, "Angelina Jolie on Filling Lara Croft's Shoes and D-Cups," *NY Rock*, June 2001, www.nyrock.com.

11 See, for example, "Angelina Jolie: Workout, Diet and Fitness Training for Tomb Raider," Celebrity Fitness Training, http://celebrityfitnesstraining.com.

12 See, for example, Stephen Hunter, "One Game Dame: Tomb Raider Is a Few Pixels Short of Two Dimensional," *Washington Post*, June 15, 2001.

13 GameNewsOfficial, "Tomb Raider Making Of: Episode One," YouTube video, 6:35, published July 10, 2012, https://www.youtube.com/watch?v=yf-WFePbH10.

14 GameNewsOfficial, "Tomb Raider Making Of."

15 Alessandro Barbosa, "Rise of the Tomb Raider Review: Master of Their Croft," *Lazygamer.net*, November 9, 2015, www.lazygamer.net.

16 Peter Paras, "Rise of The Tomb Raider Review," *Gamerevolution.com*, November 9, 2015, www.gamerevolution.com.

17 Keza Macdonald, "Tomb Raider Review," *IGN.com*, February 25, 2013, http://ca.ign.com.

18 Many advocated for Luddington's casting, but they were also realistic about her perceived lack of "star power" as a relatively successful television and video game actress who had yet to anchor a major motion picture.

19 David Sims, "*Tomb Raider* Is a Gritty Reboot of a Video-Game Classic," *The Atlantic*, March 15, 2018, www.theatlantic.com.

20 David Edelstein, "*Tomb Raider* is the Sort of Pulpy Action Fun That We Undervalue," *Vulture*, March 15, 2018, www.vulture.com.

21 Anthony Lane, "Tomb Raider and The Isle of Dogs Reviewed," *The New Yorker*, March 26, 2018, www.newyorker.com.

FURTHER READING

Aldred, Jessica. "I'm Beowulf! Now It's Your Turn: Playing with (and as) the Digital Convergence Character in the Transmedia Franchise." In *The Oxford Handbook of Sound and Image in Digital Media*, edited by Amy Herzog, John Richardson, and Carol Vernallis, 381–396. Oxford, UK, and New York: Oxford University Press, 2013.

Brooker, Will. *Hunting the Dark Knight: Twenty-First Century Batman*. London: I. B. Tauris, 2012.

Elkington, Trevor. "Too Many Cooks: Media Convergence and Self-Defeating Adaptations." In *The Video Game Theory Reader 2*, edited by Mark J. P. Wolf and Bernard Perron, 213–236. New York; London: Routledge, 2009.

29

Medal of Honor
Militarism

TANNER MIRRLEES

Abstract: This chapter analyzes the production history and representational elements of *Medal of Honor*, a best-selling military video game that illustrates multiple points of convergence between the United States Department of Defense and the digital games industry. Tanner Mirrlees demonstrates how this game furthers the militarization of American culture during the global war on terror.

The growth of the United States as a world superpower has long been tied to war—preparing for war, waging it, and glorifying it. Following the terrorist attacks of September 11, 2001 (9/11), the United States launched a global war on terror (GWOT), which—to date—has cost US citizens about $6 trillion and has killed half a million people around the world.[1] The GWOT knows no boundaries, territorial or temporal, as the US Department of Defense (DOD) is fighting battles seemingly without end in Afghanistan, Iraq, Pakistan, Somalia, Yemen, and Syria and is pivoting to East Asia to contain a rising China while also deploying resources to Belarus, Latvia, and Lithuania to surround Russia.

As the GWOT continues to play out around the world, the ideology of "militarism" works its way into the hearts and minds of American citizens. Militarism extols the state's use of coercion to achieve security interests in a world divided between a righteous "us" (i.e., the United States and its Western allies) and an evil and threatening "them" (i.e., potentially everyone else). Militarism permeates popular culture, encouraging American citizens—from the politicians who craft security policies to the soldiers who take up arms to civilians—to perceive martial violence as a righteous and noble solution to the geopolitical problems that vex the United States.

The media industries give shape to, and are, in turn, shaped by, the culture of militarism. Although this has certainly been true long before September 11, post-9/11 popular culture in the United States emerges in an era marked by a decade-plus of politically suspect invasions and occupations, extrajudicial raids, and drone strikes. Thus, military entertainment (or "militainment") is a particularly powerful means of communicating to citizens how they should think about the wars and conflicts conducted in their name. Militainment refers to the cultural goods co-produced by the military and media firms that carry stories and images that glorify the state at war by translating military violence "into an object of pleasurable consumption."[2] Examples of militainment include Hollywood blockbuster films such as Michael Bay's DOD-promoting *Transformers* franchise; commercial sporting events, such as the NFL games in which rival teams get paid by the DOD to "support the troops" with halftime shows featuring flyovers by F-22 Raptor fighter jets; and, of course, military-themed video games made by the US Army, such as *America's Army* (2002).

Because of their sophisticated technological design and because of their commercial popularity, military-themed video games, generally, and military "shooters," in particular (a subgenre of military games), are stationed on militarism's proverbial frontlines. Typically, shooters simulate combat on virtual battlefields—scenarios both fantastic and historical—by immersing players in the boots of average soldiers (usually from first- and third-person points of view). The symbiosis of war and play in digital games has been so successful, in fact, that it constitutes its own "DOD-digital games complex"—an idea that I develop in greater detail in my book *Hearts and Mines: The US Empire's Culture Industry*.[3] The global market for military training and simulation hardware and software is worth about $6 billion annually, and the United States accounts for about 68 percent of expenditure in this market.[4] Thanks to the DOD's considerable largesse and increasing outlays, high-tech firms routinely research and develop advanced modeling and simulation technologies in consultation with the government's security needs and then, by connecting to their largest constituency, sell versions of these games and technologies to consumers. War justifies the making of war games, and war games—in turn—legitimate dominant forms of warfighting.

As the mutually beneficial partnerships between the DOD and digital game firms multiply, the development and marketing of the military shooter *Medal of Honor* offers one such example of this alliance. To highlight the points of convergence between the DOD and the games industry and to show how a military-themed game contributes to the militarization of everyday life, this chapter analyzes the military shooter *Medal of Honor* (Danger Close Games and EA DICE, 2010). It is particularly interested in assessing how the game's producers advertise the military support they received in the game's production history through interviews and publicity materials, and also, how the gameplay's design of "realism" necessarily offers a limited experience of modern warfare.[5] *Medal of Honor* makes for an excellent case study of how militarism is expressed by a video game, for the ways in which its studios advertise its "authentic" production process and for the title's commitment to a militarized "realism" that celebrates certain combat truths over others. *Authenticity* and *realism* emerge as two production keywords central to the design and framing of this game and to similar military shooters.

Beginning in 2008, the Electronic Arts (EA) partnered with Los Angeles-based Danger Close Studio and Sweden-based Digital Illusions CE to develop a new *Medal of Honor* game in a decadelong series. To rebrand the aging World War II–centric *Medal of Honor* franchise for consumption during the GWOT, and to remain competitive with Activision's highly lucrative *Call of Duty* franchise, EA rebooted *Medal of Honor* with design assistance from Tier 1 operatives who fought Taliban forces in Afghanistan. Seeing an opportunity to put themselves before the public in a positive light, Tier 1 personnel helped the game studios design the game's simulated realities of war, so long as these simulations aligned with their point of view.

The EA–Tier 1 synergy underlying *Medal of Honor*'s development is highlighted by EA's publicity materials for the game, materials that underscore its rhetoric of authenticity. EA's website states that "the new *Medal of Honor* is inspired by and has been developed with Tier 1 operators from this elite community" and allows players to "step into the boots of these warriors and apply their unique skill sets to a new enemy in the most unforgiving and hostile battlefield conditions of present day Afghanistan."[6] It continues: "from story to dialogue to weaponry and technique, these elite operators guided the action on the screen to help best represent the action on today's battlefield."[7] In an "EA Showcase" interview, *Medal of Honor*'s executive producer Greg Goodrich describes the support EA received from the DOD, stating of the Tier 1 operators, "[T]hese guys . . . came into the studio and started interacting with the team" and that this collaboration helped "find the backbone of our narrative."[8] Goodrich says that Tier 1 operatives also assisted "not only in the storytelling, but also in terms of weapons systems, gear and just helping us keep it authentic."[9]

To further emphasize its collaboration with Tier 1 soldiers, EA launched a "*Medal of Honor:* Tier 1 Interview Series," which consisted of eight 2-minute online videos packaged as interviews with Tier 1 soldiers.[10] These videos are "promotional paratexts":[11] they whet players' appetites by hyping the game as something that will bring them close to "the real thing," pre-framing how gamers should understand the kind of virtual war available for play, and paying due deference to real-life military forces. Each video opens with an "ERSB Rating Mature 17+ for Blood, Strong Language and Violence" warning and is followed by the caption:

The elite operators of the US Special Operations community are tasked with only the most difficult and dangerous missions. The subject featured in the following interview operated within this community and acted as a consultant on the development of *Medal of Honor*. Their identity has been concealed for security purposes.

In the interviews, these soldiers discuss why they joined the military and what it takes to fight wars. These interviews are intercut with gameplay sequences and footage that seemingly depicts Tier 1 soldiers fighting the Taliban in Afghanistan. These videos all end with a "This is Tier 1" tagline, followed by the *Medal of Honor* game box cover, its October 12, 2010, release date, and an invitation to "learn more" on Facebook and Twitter.

In two videos ("Consulting" and "Authenticity"), Tier 1 soldiers talk about how they helped EA make the game. One soldier says he gave EA advice on how to create an authentic warfighting experience for players: "They asked me to watch some of the footage and comment on the weapons, comment on some of the tactics." Another says he helped EA's designers develop the game's avatars: "There are personality aspects which we injected into the game to give it a little more flavor, realistic flavor." The Tier 1 soldiers also talk about why they chose to assist EA. "Some people have got this Hollywood image of what an operator is" says one of the soldiers. "It's more than just: I'm a soldier. I knew some of the folks at EA were interested in working with a specific group of people. They wanted an authentic feel to what was going on in the game and how they were going to build the game." Another soldier implies that by working with EA on *Medal of Honor*, he was able to shape how the DOD and war get represented to the American public: "I thought it was important to get involved because this game was going to come out, one way or another. By me being a part of it, I at least have some say in the way the community gets represented." Others concur: "We have sacrificed so much of our lives to become what we are and [by helping EA make a game] we can help them understand what [war] is all about, what is going on over there." The soldiers even directly support EA's promotional effort to distinguish its brand from rivals: "The games that are currently out there, at least the ones that I've seen, nothing simulates being on a real [operation]. *Medal of Honor* is going to be different. It's the human side that they are bringing to the soldier and bringing back respect." By showing Tier 1 soldiers who fought in the Afghanistan war attesting to the authenticity of *Medal of Honor*'s simulated war play experience (as opposed to displaying quotes from the generals who planned and administered

FIGURE 29.1
Subjective realism
in *Medal of Honor*:
Playing 'Dusty,'
a Tier 1 opera-
tor. Promotional
image by Elec-
tronic Arts.

this war at a safe distance), these videos make the *Medal of Honor* promotional campaign seem less like a crass and manipulative exercise in creating hype for selling militainment and more like realistic war experiences borne of a credible creative process.

By co-producing *Medal of Honor* with Tier 1 support, EA was able to brand this game as "realistic." *Medal of Honor*, however, does not offer players a "realistic" experience of military service that re-creates the boredom of everyday life punctuated by moments of intense chaos. Instead, the game simulates socially acceptable "modalities of realism" that support the DOD's approved brand of war play. *Modalities of realism* are different sets of messages and communicative symbols that, when taken together, convey a sense of realism that connects to the real world, in this case, the DOD's approved vision of contemporary warfare. In the following, I discuss a few of these militarizing modalities of realism, including historical, subjective, and gameplay, among others, all of which work to convince gamers of *Medal of Honor*'s connection to reality.

Medal of Honor's historical referent is the post-9/11 GWOT, in general, and the war in Afghanistan, in particular, which began on October 7, 2001. The specific historical and geographical war referent simulated is "Operation Anaconda," or the March 2002 American and Allied battles at the Bagram Airfield and at Takur Ghar, the mountainous site of a deadly battle between Tier 1 operators and al Qaeda. US forces took the mountain, but seven soldiers were killed and many were injured.

Medal of Honor simulates subjective realism by constructing male warfighting characters who are members of the Joint Special Operations Command (JSOC), including a Naval Special Warfare Development Group agent, an Army Delta Force sniper, an Army Ranger, and a US Army Night Stalker helicopter gunner (see figure 29.1). While the post-9/11 invasion of Afghanistan was a large-scale assault and ground war, this battle strategy was accompanied by covert or "dirty" warfare tactics undertaken by the little-known JSOC. JSOC's existence and the covert operations it undertakes are cause for public deliberation,[12] but *Medal of Honor* encourages players to identify with "the most elite operators in the world" and "a new breed of warrior for a new breed of warfare." It renders the physically exhausting and intellectually challenging work of war as a simplified leisure and sanitizing play experience.

Medal of Honor's gameplay referent is the DOD's warfighting doctrine. *Medal of Honor* immerses players in how JSOC fights via a "procedural rhetoric"[13] that enables players to ritualistically reenact strategies and tactics comparable to the ones the DOD employed in Operation Anaconda. The DOD describes Operation Anaconda as a "new type of war" that mixed conventional territorial combat with deterritorialized and information age strategies and tactics.[14] This war was fought by soldiers on the ground, but it was also fought by soldiers using global positioning systems, lasers, and Predator drones to conduct attacks across Afghanistan from above. *Medal of Honor*'s functional realism simulates this "new type of war." *Medal of Honor*'s gameplay realism immerses players into a rules-bound and linear narrative of how JSOC fights dirty wars. Each level briefs players about their mission, instructs them to complete tasks, previews the weapons they will use, and highlights the enemy threats. For example, in level three ("Running with Wolves"), players must "infiltrate the rugged mountains surrounding the Shahikot Valley on stealthed-out ATVs" and, after encountering "enemy outposts and villages along the way," "rain down tactical airstrikes on enemy positions." Players fight in small and flexible groups that take remote orders from Pentagon commanders.

Medal of Honor's subjective and functional modalities of realism are enhanced by its audiovisual design. Indeed, *Medal of Honor* claims to give its consumers "Unparalleled Authenticity." It simulates sounds of battle (recorded from live training exercises in a mock Afghan village at Fort Irwin, California), the look of the landscapes of Afghanistan (mountains, fields, and urban locales), the appearances of actual Tier 1 soldiers (their bodies, clothing, and equipment), and the actual weapons used in combat (M9s, Glocks, M16s, SV-98s and GP-25s). *Medal of Honor* merges the player's first-person gaze with the mediated sights of new weapons technology, resulting in a "weaponized gaze."[15] Players virtually kill Afghani fighters, destroying them from behind weapon sights. *Medal of Honor*'s single-player campaign simulates many modalities of realism: historical, geographical, subjective, functional, and audiovisual. By doing so, this game enlists and immerses players in the rhetoric and logic of why, how, and who the DOD fought in the early stages of the GWOT.

Released about 9 years following Operation Anaconda and 11 years after the first *Medal of Honor* (1999) hit store shelves, *Medal of Honor* (2010) situates players in a "hyperreal war"[16] in a virtual Afghanistan that aims to foster a sense of national pride in war and civic deference to the DOD. *Medal of Honor*'s simulated war is partial, selective, and deceptive. When playing *Medal of Honor*, we don't learn anything about the war crimes perpetrated by US soldiers, the resistance to the DOD's presence by Afghan civilians, the autocratic governance of the US-backed Karzai regime, the mental anguish and hardship of American and Afghani war veterans, and the thousands of Americans and Afghans left injured and dead. For all its supposed authenticity and realism, *Medal of Honor* ignores this war's ugly history, offering in its place a glorifying and sanitizing substitute—one crafted to successfully execute combat tactics and evoke jingoistic patriotism.

When we play war in *Medal of Honor*, we bolster EA's profit margins and support the DOD's brand of militarism. *Medal of Honor* sells itself as a means of getting real, up close and personal with war. However, this game takes us far away—intellectually, politically and morally—from the war's actual horrors and sorrows, heroics and sacrifices.

NOTES

1 John Haltiwanger, "America's 'war on terror' has cost the US nearly $6 trillion and killed roughly half a million people, and there's no end in sight," *Business Insider*, November 14, 2018, accessed December 1, 2018, www.businessinsider.com.

2 Roger Stahl, *Militainment, Inc.* (New York: Routledge Press, 2010), 6.

3 Although the "military entertainment complex" is a useful heuristic device for identifying a range of symbiotic institutional relationships between military agencies and entertainment companies, it is too broad. The concept glosses over the national specificity of the military involved in the complex, the sectoral particularity of the entertainment firms partnering up with a military, and the distinct type of entertainment media resulting from the partnership between a military and an entertainment industry firm. The "DOD–digital games complex" is a more precise concept that names a specific national military (the US Department of Defense) and a specific sector of the entertainment industry (digital games–interactive entertainment) as the institutional sources of militarized and militarizing war games. Additionally, the DOD–digital games complex concept is indebted to Herbert I. Schiller's five-decade-old military-industrial-communication-complex concept and is attuned to the political economy of communications tradition's normative concerns pertaining to democracy, social justice, and equality. Furthermore, the concept contextualizes current symbiotic relationships between the DOD and US-based globalizing digital games firms and militarizing interactive entertainment products with regard to the long history of the US's rise as a world empire and the capitalist, geo-strategic, and cultural-ideological imperatives that underpin this empire's reliance on war as a way of business, politics, and life. The DOD–digital games complex highlights the significance of digital games to the overall growth and maintenance of the US empire, and the DOD's preparation for, promotion and waging of, and recovery from war.

4 Sandra Erwin, "Military Simulation Market to Remain Flat," *National Defense*, December 1, 2014, accessed January 15, 2017, www.nationaldefensemagazine.org.

5 Matthew Payne, *Playing War: Military Video Games After 9/11* (New York: NYU Press, 2016). Payne develops and demonstrates the analytical value of an approach to studying the practices of game design, marketing and play holistically, and calls this method a "critical gameplay analysis."

6 Electronic Arts, "*Medal of Honor* Website," accessed October 1, 2016, www.ea.com.

7 Electronic Arts, "*Medal of Honor* website."

8 medalofhonor, "*Medal of Honor*: Tier 1 Interview Series Part Four: Consulting," YouTube video, 3:43, August 19, 2010, http://www.youtube.com/watch?v=4-MYTrqZiDM.

9 medalofhonor, "*Medal of Honor*: Tier 1 Interview Series Part Four: Consulting."

10 medalofhonor, "*Medal of Honor*: Tier 1 Interview Series—Part One: The Wolfpack," YouTube video, 2:20, June 28, 2010, https://www.youtube.com/watch?v=JYHa1gD8h3E.

11 Jonathan Gray, *Show Sold Separately: Promos, Spoilers, and Other Media Paratexts* (New York: NYU Press, 2010).

12 Jeremy Scahill, "JSOC: The Black Ops Force That Took Down bin Laden," *The Nation*, May 2, 2011, accessed January 15, 2017, www.thenation.com.

13 Ian Bogost, *Persuasive Games: The Expressive Power of Video Games* (Cambridge, MA: The MIT Press, 2007).

14 Richard Kugler, *Operation Anaconda in Afghanistan: A Case Study of Adaptation in Battle* (Washington, DC: Office of the Deputy Assistant Secretary of Defense Forces Transformation and Resources, Center for Technology and National Security Policy, 2007).

15 Stahl, *Militainment, Inc.*, 110.

16 James Der Derian, *Virtuous War: Mapping the Military-Industrial-Media-Entertainment-Network* (New York: Routledge, 2009).

FURTHER READING

Crogan, Patrick. *Gameplay Mode: War, Simulation and Technoculture*. Minneapolis: University of Minnesota Press, 2011.

Dyer-Witheford, Nick, and Greig de Peuter. *Games of Empire: Global Capitalism and Video Games*. Minneapolis: University of Minnesota Press, 2009.

Huntemann, Nina B., and Matthew Thomas Payne, eds. *Joystick Soldiers: The Politics of Play in Military Video Games*. New York: Routledge, 2010.

Mirrlees, Tanner. *Hearts and Mines: The US Empire's Culture Industry*. Vancouver: University of British Columbia Press, 2016.

30

Pokémon Go
Globalization

RANDY NICHOLS

Abstract: Much of our thinking about video games focuses on immediate questions of design, play, and fun. Using the 2016 mobile game *Pokémon Go* as an example, Randy Nichols offers an analysis of gaming products—whether a software franchise or a hardware product—as emblematic of globalization, revealing insights about how video games are made and what that means for players.

Shortly after the 2016 launch of Niantic's mobile phone game *Pokémon Go*, complaints from a variety of real-world locations including the Holocaust Museum in Washington, D.C.; the Holy Kaaba and Grand Mosque in Mecca; the Auschwitz Memorial in Poland; and the September 11 Memorial in New York City began to come in.[1] Most of the concerns had to do with one of the game's central features—PokéStops, where players could restock items for their inventory and where Pokémon were more likely to be caught—disrespecting sacred and sacrosanct spaces. That the game, created by San Francisco developer Niantic, could place these stops in locations around the world is just one example of the game's reliance on globalization.

Globalization may be seen as part of the process of modernization, particularly in relation to the changing nature of business. Global trade in the sixteenth century is an early example; however, the growth of communication and information technologies in the nineteenth, twentieth, and twenty-first centuries has accelerated the process of globalization. Because it has a long history and is reliant on a range of social developments, the concept of globalization is complex, touching on economics, culture, and politics. Economically, globalization allows both the production and distribution of a product to be dispersed around the world. For example, rather than just selling the game in its home city of San Francisco or its home country the United States, Niantic's use of the app stores on Apple and Android devices allowed the game to be sold globally. By expanding to global audiences, the only limits on the game's penetration are based on players with access to a smartphone and locations with sufficient bandwidth to download and play the game.

Those economic constraints are deeply connected to the cultural questions raised by such a global product. Because much of video game software development globally is concentrated in just a few countries—the United States, Canada, a few European countries, and Japan—most game players engage with games that do not reflect their own culture but, rather, with games that are designed according to another culture's idea of how something should be globally entertaining. As such, it should not be surprising that there were a number of negative reactions to the game based on cultural differences. One such example is the renewal of a fatwa by Saudi Arabian clerics because Pokémon are seen as un-Islamic.[2] There is also a political dimension. Under globalization, power begins to shift away from the nation-state to transnational centers of power. Often these centers of power are transnational corporations, although they are not the only examples. As such, when the Holocaust Museum and the Auschwitz memorial wanted to have the PokéStops removed, they had to appeal not to their local or national governments but to the companies involved in the game's production.

Perhaps not surprisingly, Japan has been supportive of the franchise. One government official went on record, stating, "[The Japanese government] is glad that content from [Japan] is well-known overseas and will thoroughly support overseas expansion in the future."[3] Of course, not all governments have seen the game in such a favorable light. Political objections to the game have centered around two key issues: first, its use of public and private space for gameplay and, second, its imposition of one set of cultural values onto other cultures. South Korea forbids the use of Google Maps, fearing security concerns from North Korea, limiting the game's use there. Kuwait has banned playing the game near government sites, and Egyptian officials have called for a similar ban. Russia has warned against hunting Pokémon near the Kremlin and has been considering prison sentences for those found playing the game in churches. Perhaps most strikingly, Bosnia has issued cautionary warnings to players for fear that their explorations might result in players stepping on landmines left from the nation's recent conflicts.[4]

Pokémon Go is just one long-established globalized media franchise managed by the Pokémon Company, a consortium of three Japanese companies—Nintendo Co., Ltd.; Game Freak; and Creatures, Inc. Those companies have managed a wide range of Pokémon products, including video games across a range of platforms, trading card games, films, and television series, as well as associated merchandise and toys. The franchise even produced a music CD that sold more than a million units.[5]

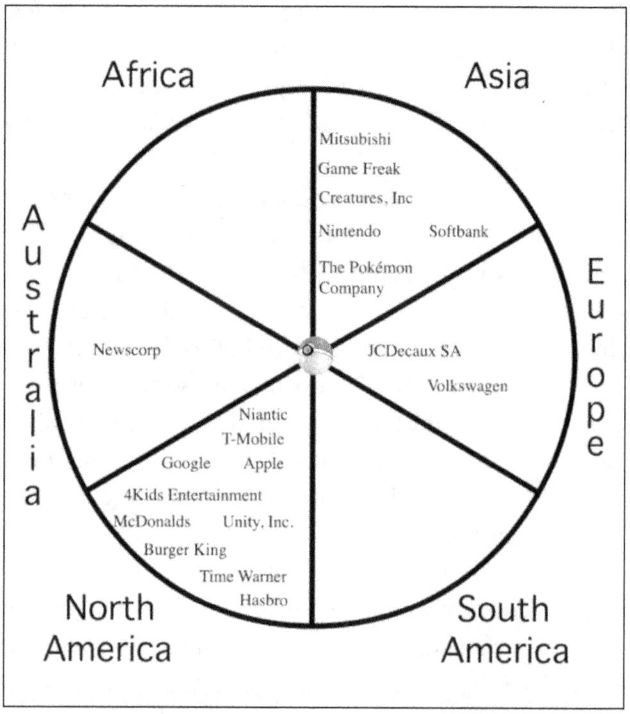

FIGURE 30.1
Global distribution of
corporate partners and
creators connected to
Pokémon Go and *Poké-
mon: The First Movie.*

Thinking about who owns and profits from Pokémon is another way to reveal
the complexities of globalization (see figure 30.1). A critical examination of the
Pokémon Go franchise allows us to look beyond rules, players, and representations
to better understand how production, distribution, and corporate relationships are
integral in crafting a profitable, long-term global media property. The origins of
the franchise provide evidence both of the extent of the product's global reach and
of the global network involved in the production and maintenance of the brand.
By 2016, Pokémon was clearly a global franchise, with an estimated 55 percent of
its sales happening outside of Japan.[6] The first Pokémon video game was released
in February 1996 in Japan, followed by a trading card game in July of the same
year. By April 1997, the franchise cartoon was released in Japan. Based on these
successes, the franchise was rolled out in other parts of the world, starting with
the United States.[7]

In the United States, Pokémon products also proved wildly successful, but the
company used a different strategy than the one deployed in Japan. Both the cartoon
and the video game were launched in September 1998, followed by trading cards in
January of 1999. Perhaps most impressively, within two months of the US launch,
more than 100 companies were already involved in making products for the US
market.[8] The game, which was released for the Nintendo GameBoy, set impressive

records, selling more than 200 million units in the United States in the first two weeks on the market, making it the fastest-selling game for portable devices to that point. In fact, the game sold at a rate roughly three times that of any game featuring Mario or Donkey Kong to that point and quickly exhausted the 400 million units produced in the initial production run.[9] By July 1999, the game sold 2.5 million units, which made it the best-selling software title in the 10-year history of the Nintendo GameBoy.[10] The game's impact was seen as broadening the market, as well. Dan DeMatteo, the president of software retailer Babbage's Etc., credited the game with "[bringing retailers] a whole new group of gamers, including girls."[11]

At least two of the company's US partners experienced dramatic benefit. 4Kids Entertainment, which was partnered at different times with Time Warner's The WB network and News Corp's Fox network, credited much of its early success to its ties to the Pokémon franchise. Between Christmas 1999 and early 2000, the franchise saw the launch of two movies, 52 new episodes of the television show, and multiple video games.[12] Another partner, Burger King, was brought in to promote *Pokémon: The First Movie* (1999) with its kids meals. The company undertook a fast-food promotional campaign larger than those for Disney's *The Lion King* (1994) or Nickelodeon's *The Rugrats Movie* (1998). Burger King's promotion created 57 toys at a rate of 8 per week, as well as 150 trading cards and 6 gold-plated cards made especially for the promotion. Some stores sold in excess of 1,200 toys a day, and many ran out of toys, prompting concern about the craze's effects on customers.[13]

Since the first Pokémon product's release in 1998 through to *Pokémon Go* in October 2016, another 210 games and related software applications have been released globally, totaling more than 250 million units sold worldwide.[14] The company has released 18 Pokémon films, which have grossed more than $149 million.[15,16] The television series, which began in Japan in 1997, moved to the US and other markets in 1998.[17] By 2016, the television show aired in almost a hundred countries and regions. The company's trading cards are available in eleven languages and are sold in more than 70 countries. Estimates suggest that more than 21 billion cards have been sold worldwide. In total, more than 400 companies globally are licensed to sell Pokémon products, with more than 5,000 related products being sold in Japan alone.[18] (For more on games and licensing, see Derek Johnson's chapter in this collection.)

Pokémon has continued to be a best-selling video game–based franchise in the world, second only to the Mario franchise, with more than 277 million units sold.[19] The franchise, which passed the $1 billion mark in 1999, achieved $2 billion in sales in 2014 alone.[20]

Because of the franchise's historic sales, it should come as no surprise that the most recent game, *Pokémon Go*, would do so well. In the game's first week, more than 7.5 million Americans downloaded it, registering more users than the social-networking platform Twitter.[21] The game was initially released in Australia, New Zealand, and the United States, followed by Japan and parts of Europe a week later.[22] In spite of this limited availability, by the end of the first week, the app had been downloaded more times than any other product in the history of Apple's App Store.[23] It was the fastest app to reach 50 million downloads, and by early August 2016—one month after its initial release—it hit 100 million downloads and $200 million in revenue.[24] It took mere days to dethrone the previous top free app, *Candy Crush Saga*.[25] By October 2016, the game was available in more than 110 countries.[26] Like *Candy Crush Saga*, *Pokémon Go* is a free app; its primary source of revenue is from in-game purchases.

The game's success wasn't just built on the power of the franchise, but also on the network of global companies it utilized. *Pokémon Go* was developed by Niantic, Inc., a US-based company that began in 2010 as a start-up subsidiary of Google, tasked with exploring the possibilities at the intersection of entertainment, geolocation, and mobile devices.[27] In 2015, when Google reorganized itself, Niantic became a separate, private company in hopes that the move would allow it to partner with companies who might hesitate to get involved with a company the size of Google.[28] The company is believed to employ between 50 and 100 people and has been valued by analysts at approximately $3 billion. The company's first project, a mobile app called *Field Trip*, was released in 2011. Its first game, *Ingress*, was released in 2013. Both products took advantage of the connection to Google Maps to build the databases vital to their functions. The game *Ingress*, which had been downloaded more than 15 million times by 2016, took this a step further, directly providing the backbone for *Pokémon Go*.[29] The game allowed players to submit pictures tied to locations that could be used in the game as portals, and the company also allowed local merchants to promote their businesses in the game as portals as well.[30] The portals from *Ingress* became the first Pokéstops in *Pokémon Go*, and Niantic has indicated that it expects to add sponsored Pokéstops to the game.[31] Businesses ranging from Cinnabon to New York's Strand Bookstore hope that the game will bring more people to their stores, and some estimates suggest that more than half the game's revenue will eventually come from in-game advertising.[32]

The influence of this complex relation has other, less obvious impacts. The release of *Pokémon Go* resulted in a surge to Nintendo's stock valuation, raising it more than 86 percent in the first 10 days of the game's release, only to see it tumble when investors realized Nintendo isn't the sole owner of the property. Instead, profits from the game were split between Niantic and the Pokémon Company, after Apple and Google each took their cuts, leaving Nintendo only an estimated 10 to 18 percent of the game's profits.[33] Even as estimates suggest the game could become worth $1 billion by 2017, Nintendo's portion remains small and wasn't enough to help the company's sluggish 2016 balance sheet.[34] Because one of the chief benefits of creating a mobile game is a lower cost of development and the ability to be easily updated, it isn't hard to imagine that the game could sit atop the download chart for years.[35] This accounts for some estimates that suggest the online game alone could become its own franchise worth more than $3 billion by 2019.[36]

By tracing the range of businesses that *Pokémon Go* and its designers were able to tap into, the network of global power Niantic could leverage from an amazing range of corporate conglomerates around the world is made visible. It also paints a clear picture of an unequal distribution of power, with most of the major partners sitting in either North America or Asia. Although the franchise is in more than 100 countries around the world, the profits are concentrated, providing critics of globalization some evidence for concerns over the one-way flow of capital.

The example of *Pokémon Go* also raises questions about how successful games are made. By emphasizing global accessibility and relying on global networks, making a game with hopes of similar success becomes particularly challenging. It may also impact the types of content in the games themselves. As the examples provided at the start of this chapter illustrate, for games to succeed in the broadest number of markets, they have to be mindful of a range of cultural norms and prohibitions. Thus, although *Pokémon Go* is a considerable financial success, there are markets it hasn't been able to penetrate because of fears of cultural imposition. It also raises the question of how games that don't have the extensive network of corporate alliances will be able to compete in an increasingly globalized marketplace.

NOTES

1 Allana Akhtar, "Holocaust, Auschwitz Museums Say No to Pokémon Go," *USA Today*, July 13, 2016; "Pokémon Mania Near Holy Kaaba Slammed," *Arab News*, July 28, 2016; and Karen Zraick, "Nations of the World Confront the Pokémon Menace," *New York Times*, July 20, 2016.

2 Zraick, "Nations of the World."

3 "Japan Gov't Kicks Off Safety Campaign for Pending Pokémon Go Launch," *Kyodo News Service*, July 21, 2016.

4 Zraick, "Nations of the World."

5 David Bloom, "Will Pokemon Be Godzilla of Holiday Gift Season?" *Sun Sentinel*, September 19, 1998, 12D.

6 *Pokémon in Figures*, last modified October 2, 2016, www.pokemon.co.jp.

7 "The Fabulous History of Pokemon," *The Salt Lake Tribune*, October 10, 1999, J1.

8 "The Fabulous History of Pokemon."

9 Business/Technology Editors, "Nintendo Pokemon Game Sets Sales Record; Fastest Selling Handheld Game in U.S. History," *Business Wire*, October 14, 1998, 1.

10 Gordon Johnson, "Attack of the Pokemaniacs through Game Cartridges, Trading Cards, TV Shows and the Internet, Nintendo's Pokémon Characters Are a Monster Hit with Inland Area Youth. And More Goodies Are on the Way," *The Press—Enterprise*, April 18, 1999.

11 Business Editors, "Babbages Predicts Record Holiday Sales for Gaming Industry," *Business Wire*, September 15, 1999, 1.

12 Business and Entertainment Editors, "4Kids Entertainment Announces Record Revenues and Net Income for Fiscal Year 2000; Net Cash Rises to Record $91.9 Million, New Contracts, Properties Slated for 2001," *Business Wire*, March 29, 2001.

13 "Toying with the Customers, Pokémon Craze Providing Royal for Burger King," *Daily Press*, November 13, 1999, C7.

14 "Franchise Report: Pokémon," last updated October 8, 2016, www.BoxOfficeMojo.com; and "Pokémon Global Sales (in millions of units) per Game," last updated October 8, 2016, www.VGChartz.com.

15 "Franchise Report: Pokémon"; and Aaron Zheng, "I Still Choose You, Pokémon: Real-Life Trainer Aaron Zheng on 20 Years of Catching 'Em All," *The Daily Beast*, February 28, 2016.

16 All figures in US dollars unless otherwise noted.

17 "The Fabulous History."

18 *"Pokémon in Figures,"* last updated October 2, 2016, www.pokemon.co.jp.

19 Zheng, "I Still Choose You."

20 Zheng, "I Still Choose You"; and Greg Hernandez, "Pokémon Fever Turns Into a Headache at Burger King; Promotion: Frantic Demand for Popular Toys Exhausts Supply, Leading to Children's Tears and Parents' Anger," *Los Angeles Times*, November 12, 1999, 1-A, 1, 5.

21 Mark C. Anderson, "Pokémon Go . . . Mad," *Monterey County Weekly*, July 14–July 20, 2016, 22.

22 Allegra Frank, "Is *Pokémon Go* Available in Your Country?," *Polygon*, July 15, 2006, www.polygon.com.

23 Romain Dillet, "Apple Says Pokémon Go Is the Most Downloaded App in its First Week Ever," *TechCrunch*, July 22, 2016, http://social.techcrunch.com.

24 Paresh Dave, "Technology; 'Pokémon Go' Maker's CEO Expects Big Future," *Los Angeles Times*, August 4, 2016.

25 Bobbi Booker, "Social Media Phenom 'Pokémon Go' Is Here," *Philadelphia Tribune*, July 22, 2016.

26 Alina Bradford, "Here Are All the Countries Where Pokémon Go Is Available," *CNET*, October 20, 2016, https://www.cnet.com.

27 Tim Bradshaw, "Man behind Google Earth Puts Pokémon Go on World Map," *Irish Times*, July 16, 2016, 17.

28 Michael Liedtke, "Pokémon Go: From Prank to Sensation," *Charleston Gazette Mail*, July 23, 2016.

29 "Pokémon Hunt Leads to Glory for Google-Born Niantic," *Daily Nation*, August 15, 2016.

30 Paresh, "Technology; 'Pokemon Go' Maker's CEO."

31 Damon Van Der Linde, "Can Nintendo Replicate Pokémon Go Success?; Company Isn't Making Much Money on Game, but Investors Are Buying," *The Vancouver Sun*, July 18, 2016.

32 James Covert, "Pokémon Go Wild TV Show, Movie, $3B Value in 3 Yrs.: Forecasts," *New York Post*, July 13, 2016, 27.

33 Van Der Linde, "Can Nintendo Replicate."

34 Covert, "Pokémon Go Wild."

35 Van Der Linde, "Can Nintendo replicate."

36 Covert, "Pokémon Go Wild."

FURTHER READING

Dyer-Witheford, Nick, and Greig de Peuter. *Games of Empire: Global Capitalism and Video Games*. Minneapolis: University of Minnesota Press, 2009.

Gray, Jonathan. *Show Sold Separately: Promos, Spoilers, and Other Media Paratexts*. New York: NYU Press, 2010.

Kerr, Aphra. *Global Games: Production, Circulation and Policy in the Networked Era*. New York: Routledge, 2017.

Nichols, Randall J. *The Video Game Business*. New York: Palgrave Macmillan on behalf of the British Film Institute, 2014.

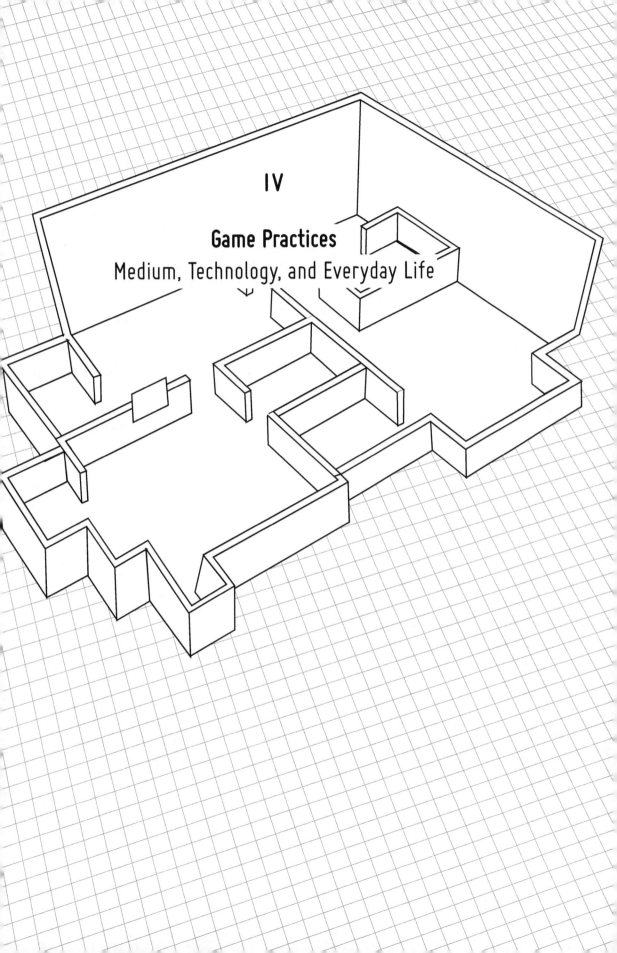

IV

Game Practices
Medium, Technology, and Everyday Life

31

Pelé's Soccer
Platform

IAN BOGOST

Abstract: The *platform* is the particular configuration of hardware and software that underlies a computer program like a video game. In this chapter, Ian Bogost argues that understanding how a platform influences the game built atop it can make the difference between appreciating that game for what it is and passing it over for what it is not.

Pelé's Soccer (Atari, 1980) is a terrible game. It is terrible today as I write this in 2017, and it was terrible in 1980 when it was first released. It was terrible a year or two later, when I first played it on the Atari Video Computer System (VCS), sitting cross-legged on the floor of my neighbor's bedroom, mouth open, hands cramped, brain confused. Whatever it was I was playing, it wasn't soccer. It was only years later that I would realize that the game was indeed soccer, but soccer as uniquely seen through the platform of the Atari VCS (see figure 31.1).

Pelé's Soccer starts on a green pitch, at center field. A white ball waits for the match to commence. Above and below center pitch, the teams line up. If you can even call them "teams"—three players each, represented as oval blobs of color, arranged in a triangular pattern. A press of the joystick button kicks off the ball— and, to the player's likely surprise, the entire triangle of players moves as a unit across the field, like a synchronized swimming team or a dance performance troupe. It's like no soccer I've ever seen or played.

To move the ball down the field, any of the three player-blobs can be piloted toward it. Upon making contact, the teammate in question takes control of the ball, dribbling it every few steps. Pressing the single, red button on the Atari joystick passes or shoots, the ball. But such description understates the difficulty of actually playing *Pelé's Soccer*. When a player-blob takes control of the ball, it

FIGURE 31.1
Pelé's Soccer on an
original Atari VCS and
vintage cathode-ray-
tube display.

doesn't automatically maintain control but merely kicks it a touch in the direction
the player-blob faces. Shooting and passing follow suit, requiring that the human
player steer the blob around the ball so as to make it pass in the correct direction.

Passing becomes an exercise in futility anyway because the three players all
move together; one cannot target an advancing forward for an approach on goal.
And because the opposing team (playable by another human player or by the
computer) is subject to the same conditions, the resulting match bears little similarity to the sport it supposedly simulates. If the player can get the ball to the
goal, successful shooting is hampered by the placement of the goalie—inside the
goal line, such that even a ball that passes the line can be saved successfully by
the goaltender.

How is this soccer? And what's more, how did Atari get away with making it?
And even further still, how did they get Pelé, known as the greatest player of all
time, to endorse it?

Pelé was already a bit of an anachronism in 1980. His international career was
over by the early 1970s, and his professional career as a member of the now-
defunct North American Soccer League ended by 1977, the year the Atari VCS
(later known as the Atari 2600) was released. That same year, a documentary film
about the footballer's life was released; Pelé transformed from superstar athlete to
athletic legend, a role that continues to this day.

Amidst the olive-green pile of my neighbor's carpet, I had very little idea who
Pelé was. This was the heyday of American Youth Soccer Organization league
play, and the sport was hardly unknown to kids even despite its unpopularity in
the United States. But the complexities of international play were lost on me, not
to mention its personalities of the near past. What wasn't lost on me—or on Pelé,

it would seem—was the unlikelihood of playing computer soccer on a television in the first place.

Sports were among the first video games—and among the first commercially successful ones, too. In 1958, an engineer at the Brookhaven National Laboratory, named Willy Higinbotham, had wired up an analog computer, an oscilloscope, and a set of makeshift controllers to play a game somewhat resembling tennis. By 1967, Ralph Baer had designed the "brown box" prototype for Sanders Associates, the first electronic game to connect to a conventional television. It was later commercialized as the Magnavox Odyssey and played versions of sports like tennis and hockey. And then there was *PONG*, Atari's successful 1972 coin-op table-tennis game, which ushered in the era of the electronic arcade. Precedents such as these set the stage for games like *Pelé's Soccer*, and all of them have something in common, something that helps explain why the latter game wouldn't have embarrassed Atari—or Pelé—as a take on the Beautiful Game circa 1980.

That thing is *abstraction*. These games all simplify, abridge, condense, and extract aspects of the sports that are their subjects. Today, thanks to games like EA's *FIFA* and *Madden* series, sports games are measured by realism and complexity. But even those games, with their visual realism, updated rosters, and real-world arenas, are also simplifications. The onscreen players move when the player presses a controller's analog stick and pass at the press of a button. These choices simplify the movement of physical bodies, real or simulated. They'd have to do so; otherwise, there would be no difference between a simulation and the world.

In the early days of computing, the hardware itself imposed more constraints on how creators could represent—which is just to say how they could simplify—a subject like tennis into a game like *PONG*. Atari's game used custom-designed digital circuits to interface with a standard, raster-scan television display. The paddles in *PONG* remain situated at the edges of the court, partly thanks to the combination of hardware cost, space for digital circuits in the cabinet, and so on. In fact, that *PONG* is considered a table-tennis game, rather than a simulation of tennis like Higinbotham's *Tennis for Two*, is largely an accident of the fixed location of the paddles and the evocative title, which plays off the name Ping-Pong.

For Atari 2600 home console owners circa 1980, sports would have been of great interest and appeal—but of limited access as home computer games. Home versions of *PONG* had been created in the mid-1970s, and Odyssey had offered takes on tennis, squash, and other ball sports. But the popular sports—soccer, American football, basketball, baseball—remained rare in video game form.

Pelé's Soccer actually had been released earlier that year, without the celebrity endorsement, as *Championship Soccer*. The game looked and played identically; the later edition changed only the name and packaging, adding Pelé's name and image to the box and cartridge. Pelé's willingness to lend his name and likeness to such a seemingly terrible rendition of the world's favorite sport, the one to which he'd dedicated his life, makes more sense in the context of the era. The very fact that a somewhat credible version of soccer was made playable on a home television, via an Atari console, was enough of a miracle to warrant the nod of the world's greatest player.

Pelé's Soccer looks and plays the way it does because the Atari VCS hardware platform is profoundly limited. Designed in the mid-1970s, the system followed-up on Atari's successful marketing of one-off Home Pong hardware, which had allowed people to play variants of their coin-op hit on home televisions. But after a family had bought one Home Pong unit, there was no need to purchase another, posing a serious business problem as Atari's expanded from arcade cabinets to consumer electronics. The answer was a home system that could play many games via interchangeable cartridges. The Atari VCS wasn't the first such idea—Fairchild had released a competitor, the Channel F, in 1976—but the VCS was the first to gain real traction in the marketplace.

When Atari's engineers set out to design the system, reducing cost and complexity was one of their foremost concerns. A home system had to be affordable enough that consumers would buy it but not so cheap that Atari wouldn't be able to cover the costs of manufacturing it. It needed to be able to play a variety of games, but at the time nobody knew what such a variety might mean or how long such a device might remain viable.

Atari's engineers looked to the successful coin-op titles they had already released as a model. *PONG* was popular, of course, as was a head-to-head tank battle game called *Tank* (1974), made by an Atari subsidiary called Kee Games. The VCS, it was determined, would be designed to play versions of those two games, and a few other, similar games. Atari had no idea that the system they would ship in 1977 would remain in production, in some form, until 1992 or that the programmers who worked on it would find so many new ways to use the limited capacities of its original hardware.

Those capacities followed directly from the two model games, *PONG* and *Tank*. Both assume two human players, facing each other head-to-head. In both games, each player occupies one side of a screen, standing side by side operating controls corresponding with that half of the screen. Each player has some kind of cursor to control in the game—a paddle or tank. A ball game like *PONG* assumes a ball for the paddles to deflect, and a combat game like *Tank* assumes projectiles for each player to fire.

Every computer contains a central processing unit, or CPU, which performs the operations and calculations to operate the rest of the computer—reading and writing its memory, its controls, and its display. In 1975, MOS Technology released a new, 8-bit microprocessor called the 6502, which cost about a tenth of what other processors sold for at the time. (The 6502 would also be used in the Apple II, the Commodore 64, the Nintendo Entertainment System, and many other early computers.) But to display images and create sounds on the television, the Atari would need a way to interface between the cartridge read-only memory (ROM), the 6502 processor, a profoundly modest amount—128 bytes—of random access memory (RAM), and the television. For this, Atari designed a custom chip, which its creators appropriately named the Television Interface Adapter (TIA). The TIA itself contained electronics to manage the different visual and sonic elements that the Atari could send to the television. To make a game work, programmers would store data in and send instructions to the TIA, which it would, in turn, configure on the television display.

The CPU is sometimes called the brain of a computer, but for a video game system, the graphics and sound system are its soul. In the Atari's case, that soul was designed to accommodate the features of games assumed from *PONG* and *Tank*. Specifically, the TIA supported two player sprites, each with a corresponding missile, a ball, a backdrop, and a playfield background, formed in blocks across the screen. Everything about the TIA was designed to limit the amount of silicon it used. The player graphics, for example, are 8 bits in size, allowing a single, eight-chunk pattern to be stored for a character at a given time. The missiles and ball are dots whose size could be adjusted. And the playfield, which is 40 "chunks" wide, is stored as 20 values, which are simply copied or mirrored from one side of the screen to the other.

The TIA implements assumptions about what video games could and should do. The idea of two players, for example, is represented by the two sprites, one for each player. The idea that games are probably about sport (ball) or combat (missile) is likewise implemented directly in the machine's hardware—not just in the cultural assumptions creators and players bring to the medium. The idea that the two players are probably human operators, sitting or standing side by side as they face the screen and compete, is made material in the way the playfield is created—as two identical sets of borders or boundaries, one each on the right and left sides of the screen.

Finally, the Atari had very limited memory—only 128 bytes of RAM. That means that it couldn't store and display a full screen's worth of image, like most modern computer graphics systems can do. Instead, the programmer had to understand something about how a cathode-ray-tube television operates. Modern displays show their images by addressing all the pixels on screen at once. But an old-style television is a raster display—an electron gun scans horizontally across the picture in consecutive rows (called scan lines), making a phosphorescent screen glow in patterns corresponding to the desired image. The Atari programmer had to manage the TIA's settings as each of the 192 scan lines of the visible picture were rendered by the television.

The TIA designers implemented several features to squeeze more flexibility out of the chip. Among them were a set of number and size registers, which could produce two or three copies of the single sprite for each player, positioned near or far apart. These settings, along with the need to manage the raster-scan display directly, begin to explain the unique take on soccer found in *Pelé's Soccer*. The triangle of field players is not really a triangle, but two sets of player sprites. The tip of the triangle is a single sprite. Then, on a subsequent scan line, the set of two is created by using the number size register to create two copies of the sprite and repositioning them to form the base of the triangle. When the player moves the joystick, all three (really "both") sprites are moved with a single gesture.

Understanding something about the material constraints of the Atari suddenly makes *Pelé's Soccer* more comprehensible, not to mention intriguing. It's not so much a terrible rendition of soccer, as it is a unique and curious implementation of soccer on a piece of equipment that wasn't intended to make soccer possible in the first place. One analogy for the game is the table game foosball, a version of soccer in which players control wood or rubber athletes hung from bars by turning those bars. It would be absurd to call foosball a "bad" implementation of soccer when really it's just a materially idiosyncratic one. The difference, of course, is that the players can see the physical constraints at work in foosball whereas those of the Atari are hidden inside the electronics.

That the game took great license with the sport on account of its technical constraints was not lost on Atari. The company went to great lengths to contextualize—and silently apologize for—the abstractions in *Championship Soccer* (and its endorsed follow-up). At the time, games relied on packaging and manuals to explain what the title was about and how to play it. *Pelé's Soccer's* manual reads like a much more complex, nuanced, and even dramatic game than it feels like to play. Each of the four players (including the goalie) get names and personalities: "Crash" Morgan (so named because he is "forever slamming into the goal posts"), Nick Danger ("mean and nasty"), "Lumpy" Duran ("the clumsiest player in the world of soccer"), and Alexie Putsnowski ("a real ladies' man").

Few players would be duped by the setup—but some might be inspired by it. Given that the players are mere blobs, rather than intricate renderings of real-world athletes, the player is free to project any background or personality atop them. Lumpy and Crash might seem silly, but they offer examples of the way players can read into the abstract graphics and gameplay of *Pelé's Soccer*, specifying and personalizing them.

FIGURE 31.2
The *Pelé's Soccer*
cartridge. The realism
of the label contrasts
with the abstraction of
the game.

Atari used the same approach to overspecifying their simplistic, abstract game-play on box and cartridge art. Early games featured intricate, realistic paintings that depicted the titles' subjects—*Pelé's Soccer* sports a handsome head-and-shoulders portrait of Pelé himself, along with an on-the-field rendering of the famous player in action (see figure 31.2). Some Atari players might have scoffed at the profound difference between the box art and game's appearance, but Atari's technique helped show that there was an enormous gap between the real world and the video game's interpretation of that world. The game's struggle to conform to the actual nature of soccer was made a part of the experience of play itself.

The unlikely mapping of the game to the sport even became a selling point for the title itself. In a catalog for Atari games, *Pelé's Soccer* enjoys this surprisingly honest pitch: "It takes a lot of practice to play a winning game of soccer. And what is true on the field is true on your ATARI® Video Computer System™ game. PELÉ'S SOCCER™ challenges you every inch of the way."

Eventually, the standards for popular sports games changed and evolved. The Mattel Intellivision, a competing console released in 1979, had an entirely different hardware design that better supported more realistic representations of sports; this capability became an important part of Mattel's marketing for the system. And by 1983, Atari VCS programmers had amassed enough experience with the system to make the limited hardware perform new tricks. That year, Atari released a series of sports games under the banner "Realsports," which offered more realistic depictions of popular sports like baseball, basketball, football, and soccer. By this time, cartridge ROM was also cheaper, allowing games to take up more space and thereby to store more instructions, images, and sound.

To see *Pelé's Soccer* as little more than a false start in the early evolution of sports video games is tempting. Constrained by hardware and inexperience, it was the best that could be done in the late 1970s. But such an attitude presumes that video game sports can only mirror the play of traditional, professional sport rather than offering a distinctive abstraction of sports unique to the hardware on which and era in which they were made. *Pelé's Soccer* can still charm and confuse, just as foosball still can. The trick to enjoying the game is in treating it for the successful curiosity it is, on the specific platform for which it was custom-designed, rather than as a failure to recreate the general idea of soccer. When seen as an expression of the Atari platform circa 1980, even an ugly game such as this can embody the beauty that Pelé himself found in the Beautiful Game.

FURTHER READING

Altice, Nathan. *I Am Error: The Nintendo Family Computer / Entertainment System Platform.* Cambridge, MA: MIT Press, 2015.

Lapetino, Tim. *Art of Atari.* Runnemede, NJ: Dynamite Entertainment, 2006.

Montfort, Nick and Ian Bogost. *Racing the Beam: The Atari Video Computer System.* Cambridge, MA: MIT Press, 2009.

Newman, Michael. *Atari Age: The Emergence of Video Games in America.* Cambridge, MA: MIT Press, 2017.

32

NES D-pad
Interface

DAVID O'GRADY

Abstract: Video game controllers shape, enhance, and constrain the relationship between the virtuality of digital games and the physical agency and meaningful actions of the player. David O'Grady's examination of perhaps the most significant video game controller ever developed—the Nintendo Entertainment System Directional Pad (D-pad)—traces the material history of a game interface, and analyzes how controller design and use profoundly influence the aesthetic experience of video games as played, interactive art forms.

In a nod to the evolutionary history of video game controllers, *Game Informer* magazine ranked in 2016 what it considered the best console-bundled controllers of all time. But the article began by acknowledging the debt owed by nearly all contemporary controllers to one in particular: Nintendo's iconic Directional Pad, or D-pad. Nintendo simply called it the "PLUS" button when it debuted in a handheld version of *Donkey Kong* (1982), and it was a key feature of the "+Control Pad" for the company's groundbreaking video game console, the Famicom, in 1983—better known as its North American incarnation, the Nintendo Entertainment System, or NES (see figure 32.1). As *Game Informer* observed, "Nintendo did not invent the controller, but with the release of the NES in 1985, it established what we consider to be the modern controller archetype: movement on the left, actions on the right, and menu-related buttons in the middle."[1]

This recognition only begins to explicate the D-pad's contribution to video game history and culture, and the larger role interfaces play in tracing an archeological history—both material and virtual—of what game manufacturers, designers, artists, and players desire to achieve with gameplay. The interface or controller serves as a metonym of the video game's fundamental aesthetic quality—player action—and it presents a fascinating locus for examination; it is the site where the physical and digital come together—where screen-based, audiovisual actions and biomechanical agency are mutually translated. Exploring the origins and limits of history's most indebted controller configuration—the D-pad's organization of screen movement in four or eight directions at the press of a thumb—can tell us much about video games as an interactive medium and about what we want from gaming as an emotional and aesthetic experience. This chapter highlights some of the technological and practical considerations Nintendo faced in developing the D-pad for handheld and console gaming while also beginning to outline the aesthetic contributions the D-pad has made to 8-bit gaming—and beyond.

Video game controllers are the tactile, in-hand hardware component of an interface, which in computing combines hardware and software with audiovisual representations to establish an interactive relationship between humans and machines. The typewriter-derived keyboard, for example, implements interaction as a linguistic and symbol-making activity, while the mouse utilizes graphical user interfaces that exploit spatial representations and movement metaphors onscreen (e.g., point and click). Computer interfaces have become the "contact surface," as Brenda Laurel described them, for most cultural activities, whether work or play.[2] As humanly constructed—and therefore culturally tinted—lenses for mediated experiences, interfaces facilitate a two-part relationship for human–computer interaction: first, between the interface or controller's configuration for afforded actions (its buttons, levers, knobs, etc.) and the screen elements presented for use (avatars, objects, symbols, etc.) and, second, between the controller and the person using it to convert decisions into screen input. Whatever qualities we ascribe to the play of video games flow from the controller's dual relationship with screens and players.

Although the goals of "good" interface design defy easy description, many interfaces exhibit what interaction designers call the principles of direct manipulation.[3] Direct manipulation comes in a variety of flavors, from controllers that rely on metaphor and "natural mapping" (e.g., moving a joystick to the right to move to the right onscreen) to devices that support more literal or gestural input, as found with touchscreens and styluses. Regardless of implementation, direct manipulation interfaces pursue intuitive use, avoid translational "noise," and collapse the gap between human action and computer reaction (and vice versa). Graphical user interface pioneers Alan Kay and Adele Goldberg likened controller and interface use to playing a musical instrument; with practice and mastery, the keys and strings of an instrument "disappear" and become an expressive, artistic extension of the brain and body of the musician.[4] Most any mainstream interface, including video game controllers, can be thought of as an expressive instrument designed to recede or disappear with use.[5]

Interfaces not only disappear into the body; they also transmute, chameleon-like, into screenic representations and actions: the video game controller "becomes" a gun, pressing X "becomes" jumping, and so on. As controller functionality and player familiarity fuse and develop into virtuosity, these transmutations become automatic and seamless. Arcade machines achieve this with dedicated interfaces, but console controllers must support a *variety* of play experiences with a single configuration (although button-mapping conventions have emerged that predictably facilitate actions repeated from game to game, such as jumping, firing, crouching, and running). In short, controllers are more than just a fluid and elusive *means* of attaining a play experience; they also serve a necessary, constitutive part of the aesthetics of gameplay itself, as the following analysis will investigate in relation to the NES D-pad controller.

In the late 1970s, Nintendo president Hiroshi Yamauchi tapped engineer Gunpei Yokoi to help the company expand its presence in electronic gaming. Yokoi had developed a variety of mechanical and electronic toys, and he aided Nintendo's entry into the game console market in Japan by creating early consoles derived from systems such as the Magnavox Odyssey and Atari Home Pong. In 1979, Yokoi stumbled onto the idea of developing handheld video games for Nintendo when he noticed a commuter on the train playing idly with a pocket calculator. Yokoi realized calculators could be cheaply retooled and turned into a platform for playing handheld games, giving birth to Nintendo's popular Game & Watch series. Such an insight would come to epitomize Yokoi's—and Nintendo's—overall approach to game interfaces: eschew expensive, cutting-edge technology and instead find new, playful uses for old hardware. Yokoi would later describe Nintendo's philosophy as "lateral thinking with withered technology," a phrase that some have read as more akin to "weathered" or "well-worn" technology.[6]

This philosophy was put to the test when adapting Nintendo's runaway arcade hit, *Donkey Kong* (Nintendo R&D1, 1981), to a Game & Watch handheld. Designed by Shigeru Miyamoto (see Jennifer deWinter's chapter in this collection), *Donkey Kong* famously requires navigating a platform-and-ladder environment in four directions and jumping through the air. Confronted by this combination of actions, Yokoi realized that regular navigational movements should be collected into a single configuration and separated from the jump action. As a result, Yokoi and his team devised a simple but elegant plus-sign or cross-shaped button that could take the place of four discrete buttons (the four X and Y switches underneath are concealed inside). The plus button was easy to manufacture, and it appeared to replicate the fast, precise control afforded by arcade joysticks. With the plus sign placed under the left thumb and a jump button placed on the right, the portable version of *Donkey Kong* (Nintendo, 1982) introduced a new approach to gaming interface design.

FIGURE 32.1

The D-pad controller (pictured here in its 1985 NES iteration) unified handheld and console interface design, and the plus button came to dominate the 8-bit era of video gaming. Photo credit: Evan Amos.

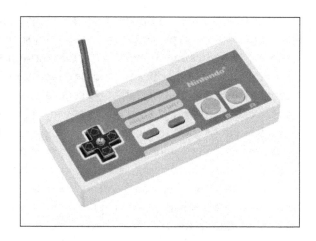

The success of *Donkey Kong* in the arcades and the Game & Watch line in Japan spurred Nintendo's development of a new home gaming console, despite the video game market crash of 1983. Masayuki Uemura, manager of the team developing the console, sought an alternative to the common joystick interface, which posed a number of manufacturing, design, and even child safety concerns.[7] Another Nintendo employee, Takao Sawano, head programmer for the Game & Watch series, intuited a solution: replace the joystick with Yokoi's plus button from the handheld games. Despite initial reservations by the development team, Sawano connected a plus-button handheld to the prototype console, and the ensuing demonstration proved that the plus button could bridge the gap between handheld and console controller design.[8] The new plus button debuted on Nintendo's Family Computer, or Famicom, in 1983, which was retooled and rebranded by Nintendo of America as the Nintendo Entertainment System for release in 1985. By the late 1980s, the "+Control Pad"—colloquially, the D-pad—had become the default controller configuration for 8-bit gaming worldwide.

The D-pad's streamlined design and highly responsive gameplay proved more effective and relatable than the complex, button-laden configurations offered by Mattel Intellivision (1979), Atari 5200 (1982), ColecoVision (1982), and others in the 8-bit or second generation of consoles. But the D-pad's simplicity obscures how cleverly it solves at least two practical challenges in designing for hand-based, human–computer interaction. First, the D-pad intuits the ability of the thumb to serve as our primary mode of interface manipulation. Although the thumb is not unique to us, the human thumb's unusual saddle joint, relatively long length, and extensive supporting musculature enable it to move with precision across a wide range of motion not found in our other digits.[9] The NES controller's horizontal layout and form factor position its primary action buttons (D-pad under the left thumb, A and B buttons under the right) in a way that allows the player to cradle the controller with the fingers, placing the wrists in a fairly neutral position. This creates a stable, symmetrical platform on which the thumbs can go to work. Thanks in no small part to the D-pad's orientation and its underlying cradle grip, "thumbing" has now become the interaction success story—and repetitive use injury—of our digital age as almost every interface (texting, gaming, mobile touchscreens, remotes) addresses the thumbs.

In addition to exploiting the thumb's unique biomechanical features, the D-pad solves a second problem confronting interface design: "finding" the hand in space when not looking directly at it. Cognitive scientists note how the human body situates our hands for use primarily within our field of view, cultivating strong correlations between sight and touch. Hands out of sight become hands out of mind as our sense of hand position deteriorates rapidly without visual monitoring.[10] Whereas handhelds, touchscreens, and arcade machines largely avoid the problem of hand-centered space by placing the controls and screen in the same visual field, console-based gaming typically decouples controllers and screens. Nintendo engineers, aware of the hand-centered space problem when developing the NES controller, initially rejected the plus button, in part, because they thought it required visual supervision of the thumb—until Sawano proved otherwise.[11] The plus button presents a tactile surface for legible feedback about the thumb's position and its relative distance from the center of the input space. Thumbs also can intuit diagonal movements by feeling the contours of adjacent x- and y-axes and can depress them simultaneously. With a D-pad, the thumb can slide, roll, or circumnavigate and receive precise feedback for position and action with minimal effort; no visual monitoring or correction is required.

These observations offer a pragmatic account of the D-pad's particular genius as a direct manipulation interface. However, an examination of the aesthetics of video games—and the central role of the controller in shaping the experience of play—extends beyond a controller's utility. Deducing the controller's "share" of gameplay's aesthetic aspirations defies reduction to a singular explanation, but we can examine how game designers and game scholars approach the art of interaction with the interface in mind. Game designer Steve Swink, for example, advises a comprehensive approach to making games based on what he calls "game feel."[12] Swink encourages game makers to design from the controller up; only after its features, tolerances, and limitations are understood can the designer begin to elaborate on core mechanics. Swink's method, in other words, echoes the concept of "human engineering" espoused by Miyamoto: "The first and most important part of creating a game should be creating the interface. A good game has to be fun to play."[13]

Fun would appear to be the final aesthetic arbiter of mainstream video games and their interfaces, but game design and controller use suggest much deeper, complex, and more diverse psychological and emotional responses to gameplay than just "playing with power," as Nintendo advertised in the 1980s. For example, scholar David Sudnow's "field notes" of playing video games in the late 1970s capture the visceral thrill of using hands to navigate playspaces: "Seated upright on behinds made just for that, our hands dangle near the lap at their most relaxed point of balance, while these fingers, capable of such marvelous interdigitation, have a territory for action whose potentials and richness are electronically enhanced beyond the wildest dream."[14] Propelling Mario forward in *Super Mario Bros.* (Nintendo R&D4, 1985) with a D-pad press and hitting the jump button to land on Goombas and Koopa Troopas certainly delivers spectacular engagement with space and objects.

But the particular genius of Nintendo's controller-centric game design also ensnares us on another level, as Mario's fortunes are soon overtaken by our personal investment; it's not Mario who rescues Princess Toadstool but, rather, the player who says, "*I* beat the game." Scholar Bob Rehak has investigated how avatar and interface often collapse into a human–computer relationship that is as much ideological, discursive, and psychological as it is pleasurable: "Part of what users seek from computers is continual response to their own actions—a *reflection* of personal agency made available onscreen for reclamation as surplus pleasure."[15] The controller, then, not only has the potential to recede experientially into screen objects and actions during video gameplay but also to forge a level of identification that turns the avatar into a heightened, even superpowered, extension of the self (see Harrison Gish's chapter in this collection for an analysis of avatars).

Designer Brenda Laurel described the identification achieved through interface action as "first-personness," a constructive way to theorize gameplay as an aesthetic form that sidesteps popular but ambiguous notions of presence and immersion.[16] More important than high-fidelity modeling of "real-world" actions is the sense of consequential ownership that even abstract but well-designed interfaces can deliver as a dramatic, enactive experience—as both heightened, pleasurable agency ("this is me doing this") and as the recipient of an interaction ("this is being done to me"). Although mainstream video games and their corresponding interfaces contour and constrain first-person agency for compelling experiences of mastery or accomplishment, many independent designers and artists are exploring new aesthetic terrain by creating video games that engage the personal, the political, and the polemical. New, noncommercial interfaces are emerging, too, as declining barriers to hardware customization allow artists to consider novel controller designs as an integral part of game-making. It is difficult to imagine the diversity of video gaming today without the success of the D-pad in revealing video gameplay as a richly complex, responsive, emotional, and even artistic cultural activity.

Because of its functional qualities and aesthetic possibilities for gameplay, the D-pad collapsed the divide between console and handheld controllers and standardized the layout and scale of video game interfaces outside of the arcade. The D-pad's unrivaled success catapulted it from the 8-bit to the 16-bit era of consoles, where it appeared on every mainstream controller with only slight modification. Despite this dominance, Nintendo continued to experiment with controllers that would ultimately anticipate the arrival of thumbsticks, virtual reality, gestural motion, console-handheld combinations, and other interface modalities. While dual-analog thumbsticks came to replace the D-pad for three-dimensional navigation, Yokoi's plus button still occupies crucial real estate on many controllers, and for Nintendo it remains a brand signifier (despite its absence from Nintendo's latest console, the Switch). Given the D-pad's unparalleled influence in video game interface history, it was formally recognized in the United States with a Technology & Engineering Emmy in 2007—some 25 years after its debut. Although the NES was discontinued in 1995 after selling about 62 million units worldwide, the enduring legacy of the D-pad it popularized remains literally under our thumbs—the "digital" interface we use, perhaps now more than ever, to make sense of our physical and virtual worlds.

NOTES

1 Kyle Hilliard, "Ranking the First-Party Controllers," *Game Informer* (November 2016): 92.

2 Brenda Laurel, "Introduction," *The Art of Human-Computer Interface Design*, ed. Brenda Laurel (Reading, MA: Addison-Wesley, 1990), xii.

3 Ben Shneiderman, Catherine Plaissant, Maxine Cohen, and Steve M. Jacobs, *Designing the User Interface: Strategies for Effective Human-Computer Interaction*, 5th ed. (New York: Pearson Education, 2010), 214.

4 Alan Kay and Adele Goldberg, "Personal Dynamic Media," *The New Media Reader*, ed. Noah Wardrip-Fruin and Nick Montfort (Cambridge, MA: MIT Press, 2003), 393–404, originally published in *Computer* 10, no. 3 (March 1977): 31–41.

5 This theorization accounts for the mainstream design and use of interfaces for computing and video games. However, indie and art gaming practices often use interface as an opportunity to disturb or disrupt the interactive relationship of gameplay to achieve other aesthetic effects. Contrarily, then, interfaces may reannounce their presence when users, players, and artists defy interaction conventions and devise new applications, interfaces, and ways to use them.

6 Adam Ghahramani, "Nintendo's Little-Known Product Philosophy: Lateral Thinking with Withered ("Weathered") Technology," *Medium*, September 2, 2015, https://www.medium.com.

7 Ghahramani, "Nintendo's Little-Known Product Philosophy."

8 Ghahramani, "Nintendo's Little-Known Product Philosophy."

9 Research by primatologists and anthropologists into evolutionary tool use reveals that hand positions where the thumb is placed on top of the tool—and the rest of the hand

wrapped underneath for support—encourage more precise manipulation. See John Napier, *Hands* (Princeton, NJ: Princeton University Press, 1980); and Mary W. Marzke, "Evolutionary Development of the Human Thumb," *Hand Clinics* 8, no. 1 (February 1992): 1–8.

10 See Nicholas P. Holmes, "Hand-Centered Space, Hand-Centered Attention, and the Control of Movement," in *The Hand, an Organ of the Mind: What the Manual Tells the Mental*, ed. Zdravko Radman (Cambridge, MA: MIT Press 2013), 61.

11 Masaharu Takano, "How the Famicom Was Born—Part 8: A System Synonymous with the Domestic Game Console," *Nikkei Electronics*, October 6, 2008, originally published January 16, 1995, trans. Aria Tanner, *GlitterBerri's Game Translations*.

12 Steve Swink, *Game Feel: A Game Designer's Guide to Virtual Sensation* (Burlington, MA: Morgan Kaufman Publishers, 2009).

13 Chris Kohler, *Power-Up: How Japanese Video Games Gave the World an Extra Life* (New York: Dover Publications, 2016), 258.

14 David Sudnow, *Pilgrim in the Microworld* (New York: Warner Books, 1983), 25.

15 Bob Rehak, "Playing at Being," in *The Video Game Theory Reader*, ed. Bernard Perron and Mark J. P. Wolf (New York: Routledge, 2003), 111, emphasis included.

16 Howard Rheingold, *Tools for Thought: The History and Future of Mind-Expanding Technology* (Cambridge, MA: MIT Press, 2000), 267.

FURTHER READING

Gallagher, Shaun and Dan Zahavi. *The Phenomenological Mind*, 2nd ed. New York: Routledge, 2012.

Keogh, Brendan. *A Play of Bodies: How We Perceive Videogames*. Cambridge, MA: MIT Press, 2018.

Kirkpatrick, Graeme. "Controller, Hand, Screen: Aesthetic Form in the Computer Game." *Games and Culture* 4, no. 2 (April 2009): 127–143.

Reynolds, Daniel. "The Vitruvian Thumb: Embodied Branding and Lateral Thinking with the Nintendo Game Boy." *Game Studies: The International Journal of Computer Game Research* 16, no. 1 (October 2016). http://gamestudies.org.

33

Minecraft
User-Generated Content

JAMES NEWMAN

Abstract: This chapter examines the many ways in which *Minecraft* serves as a platform and engine for wide-ranging user-generated content. James Newman argues that to understand *Minecraft* means appreciating how playing and making are indivisible acts, and that user creativity manifests both as in-game goods and as extratextual content shared to social media, activities that grow the community and trouble what it means to be a "game."

One of the great challenges in writing about *Minecraft* (Mojang, 2011) is defining exactly what it is. This might seem an unlikely problem because, on the surface, it should be a straightforward proposition. As Mojang's website notes, "*Minecraft* is a game about placing blocks and going on adventures."[1] However, as we read on, we soon uncover additional strata of complexity and mutability as different game modes shift the potential focus between solo play or collaboration, creation or destruction.

"Explore randomly generated worlds and build amazing things from the simplest of homes to the grandest of castles. Play in Creative Mode with unlimited resources or mine deep in Survival Mode, crafting weapons and armor to fend off dangerous mobs. Do all this alone or with friends."[2]

Minecraft's mutability as a game means that, experientially, it is almost entirely contingent on the actions and creativity of its players. Simply put, *Minecraft* is what its players make it. The grandest castles or the simplest shelters are the direct results of players' creativity, ambition, and labor. Of course, there are many other games which can be modified and extended by players; *Minecraft* is not the first title to build itself around player creativity. Indeed, as Hector Postigo and others have noted, user-generated content (UGC)—in-game material and resources created by players rather than developers—has long been a part of video gaming.[3] Popular titles such as *Team Fortress* (Valve, 1999) and *Counter-Strike* (Valve, 2000) grew out of so-called user mods (modifications) to existing games[4] while titles such as *Racing Destruction Set* (Rick Koenig, 1985) offered level design tools for players to augment the tracks created by the developers. So, although *Minecraft* is far from the first game to allow players to remake, remix, and remodel its ludic building blocks, it is—perhaps more than any other title—a video game predicated on, and whose success is owed to, a rich assortment of UGC. *Minecraft* is not so much modified by UGC as it is constituted through user creativity. To play *Minecraft* is to be a content generator.

Moreover, *Minecraft*'s UGC is not limited to creations made within its pixelated game world. Countless online video channels offer advanced building tutorials, tours, and explanations of expert creations. Meanwhile, other video series forgo discussions of construction technique in favor of using *Minecraft* as a virtual stage for the performance of ongoing stories. Such is the centrality of UGC to *Minecraft*'s very existence that it might be more accurate to think of it not as a game about "placing blocks" but as a platform for storytelling and game-making (albeit a highly contingent and unstable one).

Minecraft's "instability" is crucial to its status as a platform and as an object of study.[5] Although initially released on PC, *Minecraft* now exists across multiple platforms including television-connected consoles, mobile phones, tablets, and virtual reality. Each incarnation of *Minecraft* has its own specific set of capabilities, and each platform brings distinctive affordances and variations in interface and control methods. With multiple versions offering materially different ludic potential, *Minecraft* is perhaps the perfect example of what Federico Giordano has called the "extreme fragmentation" of video games.[6] Given the number of ports and updates available since its initial release, we might argue that *Minecraft* is best approached not as a single game but as a web of interrelated titles that unfold over time.

Developed by Markus "Notch" Persson, and initially released on May 17, 2009, on the TIGSource forums, *Minecraft* was updated numerous times before entering what became known as its "alpha" stage on June 28, 2010, and "beta" on December 20, 2010. (Typically, the alpha and beta phases of development are conducted within the development studio, with a public beta sometimes being released to players toward the end of a development cycle for playtesting.) However, *Minecraft*'s development has been far more public throughout and even after the "official release" on November 18, 2011 and has continued even after its acquisition by Microsoft in 2014 for $2.5 billion.

The ongoing updates, renewal, and expansion have changed *Minecraft* in meaningful and far-reaching ways that go beyond the big fixes or downloadable extras that contemporary gamers have become familiar with. New features and modes of play extend core gameplay by adding layers of creative complexity. In some cases, updates fundamentally alter what *Minecraft* is—or perhaps more accurately— expand the horizons of what *Minecraft* can be.

In its first incarnation, *Minecraft* was limited to its Creative mode; the Survival and Adventure modes, were added later (in fact, Creative mode was temporarily eliminated before it was reinstated in Beta version 1.8). In Creative mode (as it exists at the time of writing and as it was in the first release), resources are un- limited and players have unrestricted access to all block types from the outset— much like being in possession of the world's most extensive LEGO set. Although enemies still appear in Creative mode, they do not attack the player (even if pro- voked). Even the mighty Ender Dragon—so feared in the other game modes—is harmless in Creative mode. By removing the jeopardy that comes from the diur- nal cycle of enemies and presenting a fully unlocked inventory, Creative mode explicitly equates sandbox-style "play" with "content generation."

Defining *exactly* the point at which "game development" and "gameplay" over- lap is sometimes difficult. Certainly, *Minecraft* might call to mind games such as *LittleBigPlanet* (Media Molecule, 2008) or *Super Mario Maker* (Nintendo EAD, 2015) that offer robust design tools and that conspicuously operate at the inter- section between playing and making and between play and labor. But there are some important differences between these games. Both *Super Mario Maker* and *LittleBigPlanet* shipped with premade stages and challenges, and—importantly— they can be enjoyed without engaging in any original content creation. Similarly, whereas *Super Mario Maker* and *LittleBigPlanet* closely link their making and playing modes, *Minecraft* does not distinguish between them. *Minecraft* is not a tool for level design. It is a game where, without the creative labor of making, there is nothing to play. Playing *is* making. Playing *is* content generation.

Some creations are notable for their scale and ambition while others impress with their inventiveness, precision, and innovative use of the functionality of blocks and in-game behaviors. The building team members of WesterosCraft have set themselves the inestimable task of re-creating George R. R. Martin's *Game of Thrones* universe to provide a setting for themed role-playing while ohmganesha and Cody Littley created a 16-bit computer and a fully functioning hard drive, re- spectively. Commenting on the computer, ohmganesha explains, "It has 32 bytes of RAM and 256 bytes of ROM. It runs on a variable speed clock, 28 ticks for a data instructions, 45 ticks for calculations. That's about 250 millihertz on average (1 instruction every 4 seconds)."[7] Such is the breadth of the building work that has been undertaken in *Minecraft* that it is perhaps small wonder that in 2012, Cody Sumpter of Massachusetts Institute of Technology's Media Lab insightfully, if playfully, noted, "Notch hasn't just built a game. He's tricked 40 million people into learning to use a CAD program."[8]

FIGURE 33.1
Players build Link,
Cucco, and Navi
from *The Legend
of Zelda* series
inside *Minecraft*.
Image credit:
iShadowCat

Of course, although it is comparatively easy to find lists of the best, biggest, or just downright coolest creations by trawling online news sites and *Minecraft* forums, the extravagance of these constructions should not overshadow the myriad everyday acts of creation, building, and collaboration. These occur each time players build a shelter to survive the first night, work together to tend to a garden, create pixel art based on *The Legend of Zelda* (Nintendo R&D4, 1986) (see figure 33.1), or make an obstacle course for a parkour challenge that tests the inventiveness of the creator and the dexterity of the virtual free-runner.

While these smaller-scale builds often take place in ad hoc play sessions with players working alone or together, they are also often structured by new game modes created and more formally curated by the community of "Minecrafters." Servers such as Hypixel and Mineplex are among the many that frame player creativity and turn UGC into a demonstrable—and winnable—gameplay mechanic. Hypixel's "Build Battle" game is a case in point. Built within *Minecraft*, it challenges players to create an original construction in response to a set theme within a strict time limit.

Here, then, building prowess is not merely instrumental to the game; it is also an absolutely integral part of the gameplay that proceeds from the response to a creative challenge (who can build the best structure using the available blocks in five minutes). Other games offer different challenges. Hypixel's "Crazy Walls" invites four teams of four players to mine, trade, and strategize to maximize their offensive and defensive capabilities before the titular walls separating them drop and a 16-player melee ensues. Mineplex's "Dragon Escape" focuses more on the mastery of performance and control by reconstructing *Minecraft* as a three-dimensional platform game in which the player races through the complex environment while evading the eponymous dragon.

User-generated modifications—or "mods"—further add to the functionality of *Minecraft*'s core gameplay and the challenge of pinpointing the "game." Flan's Mod, for instance, adds guns, tanks, and grenades to facilitate combat while Pixelmon mixes in creatures and gameplay mechanics from Nintendo's *Pokémon* franchise (unofficially borrowed, of course). Here, as Sue Morris notes in relation to first-person-shooter games, the extent of UGC and fan labor at work in *Minecraft* goes beyond the manifest creativity of *Game of Thrones* environments and computer peripherals with tools to launch mods and enhance the game's user interface similarly created and shared by users.[9]

Looking for examples of creative, UGC "inside" *Minecraft*'s digital space is almost certainly the most obvious strategy, and in addition to forums and user group discussions, YouTube certainly makes the discovery of such material easier to locate for scholars and players alike. However, there is considerably more to *Minecraft*'s appearance on YouTube than the showcasing of in-game technique, and it is important to recognize the use of *Minecraft* as a virtual space within which new forms of narratives and celebrity may be performed and cultivated.

Perhaps the most well-known form of gaming video production is the "Let's Play" genre. Dating back to the mid-2000s when they appeared on the forums of the "Something Awful" website, Let's Plays predate *Minecraft*. At their simplest, these videos feature recorded gameplay narrated by the player with his or her voice-over merged with the game's music and sound effects.[10] In some cases, Let's Players appear onscreen in an overlaid picture-in-picture window so that the player-narrator, his or her in-game avatar, and gameplay performance are rendered indivisible.

Although their impact on games sales and even game design has been documented,[11] Let's Plays are not typically game reviews. Instead, they can function both as guides to gameplay functionality and, perhaps more interestingly, as sites of original narrative production. In this latter case, *Minecraft* is reconstituted as a virtual film lot with stage and props constructed from blocks and players both voicing and controlling characters. The use of game engines for narrative production is not unique to *Minecraft*. Rooster Teeth's *Red vs Blue* series is perhaps the best-known example of machinima (a portmanteau of *machine* and *cinema*).[12] However, where *Red vs Blue* makes imaginative, creative, and often subversive use of the character models and environments provided by the *Halo* franchise, *Minecraft*'s malleability encourages a far greater degree of set design and avatar customization. Accordingly, using the performative and communicative affordances of *Minecraft*, YouTube and other social media platforms to create "consumable personas,"[13] Stampylongnose, iBallisticsquid, DanTDM et al. are microcelebrities writ large.[14]

Let's Players such as these are also notable for performing their authenticity through conspicuously "amateur" production techniques (identifying themselves as enthusiastic bedroom producers, for instance).[15] The barely contained excitement in Stampy's videos, for instance, speaks to the "passionate" nature of the labor that negotiates financial and personal rewards and professional independence.[16] Importantly, the presence and popularity of these players' channels serve also to legitimize the idea of UGC not just as a way of playing but also as a route to paid content production work.

We might be tempted to view these serial and episodic videos as part of the paratextual world of *Minecraft* that supports and sustains it. However, it is just as likely that much of the pleasure of "playing" *Minecraft* derives from watching others. Indeed, *Minecraft* directly supports this idea by including a Spectator mode. This allows the player to effortlessly glide around viewing the contents of the world and the action of other players. Thus, *Minecraft* not only encourages the generation of content but also the scrutiny of players' creations—elevating these pieces of digital handiwork to the status of consumable spectacle, setting the stage for the popular Let's Play videos that follow.

The sheer variety of platforms, game modes, and modifications ensures that *Minecraft* is difficult to categorize. Moreover, the ongoing development adds new functions and features that continually reshape the experiential potential by opening up new ways to play and new sets of rules and affordances to play with. Perhaps the most important characteristic of *Minecraft*, however, is the volume and diversity of UGC that conjures the game into existence and reconfigures our understanding of it in significant and often unexpected ways.

This combination of play and labor, or "playbour" as Julian Küchlich[17] has called it, can be viewed in different ways. Although many players view their creativity as an extension of play, as there is clear value to game makers, publishers, and developers with newly-made levels and add-ons enhancing player loyalty, driving innovation, and generating new sales, it may be tempting to consider UGC creators as an exploited source of free labor. However, as Sotamaa[18] and others have noted, many creators voluntarily, and even strategically, operate in such contexts where they identify sufficient personal benefit, such as the lure of being discovered as a developer or becoming the next YouTube celebrity.

However we view it, it is essential that we recognize that the breadth and depth of UGC created and consumed by communities of Minecrafters includes the digital brickwork of the virtual world *and* recorded material that is distributed on social media and video-streaming sites such as YouTube. In this way, complex, serial meta-narratives are performed, and *Minecraft* is cast as a flexible toolkit, highly customizable virtual stage, and deeply connected communication platform. Once we consider the diversity of content created by users and consumed, annotated and built on through in-game play and cross-media interaction, this "game" about placing blocks is revealed as a sandbox-style, community-driven, multimedia-content-generation platform.

NOTES

1 Mojang, "Games," Mojang Official Website, https://mojang.com.

2 Mojang, "Games."

3 Hector Postigo, "Of Mods and Modders: Chasing down the Value of Fan-Based Digital Game Modifications," *Games and Culture* 2, no. 4 (2007): 300–313.

4 John Dovey and Helen W. Kennedy, *Game Cultures: Computer Games as New Media* (Maidenhead: Open University Press, 2006).

5 James Newman, *Best Before: Videogames, Supersession and Obsolescence* (Abingdon, UK: Routledge, 2012).

6 The reference to Survival and Creative play modes in the official website text shown earlier accurately describes *Minecraft* at the time of writing, but it is important to note that these modes were not always present. The iterative development process is a distinctive feature of *Minecraft* and has material implications on its emergence as a creative platform for UGC. Bruce Sterling, "Dead Media Beat: Federico Giordano: Almost the Same Game," *Wired*, April, 21, 2011, www.wired.com.

7 ohmganesha, "My ALU/CPU/Computer Progress Thread (+ Video and Worldsave)," Minecraft Forum, July 16, 2011, https://www.minecraftforum.net.

8 Tom Cheshire, "Want to Learn Computer-Aided Design (CAD)? Play Minecraft," *Wired* November 22, 2012, www.wired.co.uk.

9 Sue Morris, "WADs, Bots and Mods: Multiplayer: FPS Games as Co-creative Media," in *DiGRA '03—Proceedings of the 2003 DiGRA International Conference: Level Up*, 2003, vol. 2, University of Utrecht, the Netherlands, www.digra.org.

10 Patrick Klepek, "Who Invented Let's Play Videos?," *Kotaku*, May 6, 2015, https://kotaku.com.

11 Chris Kohler, "Nintendo's YouTube Ad-Grab Is Playing with Fire," *Wired*, May 16, 2013, www.wired.com; Emanuel Maiberg, "Why Horror Games Are More Fun to Watch than Play," *Motherboard*, May 30, 2015, https://motherboard.vice.com; and Brendan Sinclair, "Play Matters More than Video Games—Octodad Dev.," *GamesIndustry.biz*, March 27, 2014, www.gamesindustry.biz.

12 Henry Lowood and Michael Nitsche, eds., *The Machinima Reader* (Cambridge, MA: MIT Press, 2011).

13 Alice Marwick and dana boyd, "To See and be Seen: Celebrity Practice on Twitter," *Convergence: The International Journal of Research into New Media Technologies*, 17, no. 2 (2011): 139–158.

14 Theresa Senft, *Camgirls: Celebrity and Community in the Age of Social Networks* (New York: Peter Lang, 2008).

15 Alice Marwick, *Status Update: Celebrity, Publicity, and Branding in the Social Media Age* (New Haven, CT: Yale University Press, 2013).

16 Hector Postigo, "Playing for Work: Independence as Promise in Gameplay Commentary on YouTube," in *Media Independence: Working with Freedom or Working for Free?*, ed. J. Bennett and N. Strange (Abingdon, UK: Routledge, 2015), 202–220.

17 Julian Küchlich, "Precarious Playbour: Modders and the Digital Games Industry," *The Fibreculture Journal* 5, no. 25 (2005), http://five.fibreculturejournal.org.

18 Olli Sotamaa, "On Modder Labour, Commodification of Play, and Mod Competitions," *First Monday* 12, no. 9 (2007), http://firstmonday.org.

FURTHER READING

Garrelts, Nate, ed. *Understanding Minecraft: Essays on Play, Community and Possibilities*. Jefferson, NC: McFarland, 2014.

Jones, Steven E. *The Meaning of Video Games: Gaming and Textual Strategies*. New York: Routledge, 2008.

Newman, James. *Playing with Videogames*. Abingdon, UK: Routledge, 2008.

34

Quake
Movies

HENRY LOWOOD

Abstract: How to watch video games? Henry Lowood asks this question through the historical perspective of "*Quake* movies," the term commonly used for game-based videos before the term *machinima* was coined. *Quake* movies showed not only how games could be watched, but also how game technologies could be repurposed creatively, thus bolstering the claim that games can be about something more than play.

If the present volume about playing games owes something to Thompson and Mittell's *How to Watch Television*, it is perhaps an essay on watching games. This is it. Perhaps it is obvious that machinima—game-based moviemaking—involves putting down the game controller and *watching*. Linear and interactive media engage us in different ways, but instead of contrasting the watcher and the player, this chapter focuses on players who adopted games as a platform for doing something besides "just" playing. Specifically, I am referring to the historical moment when a game, *Quake* (id Software, 1996), became a platform for making movies. This repurposing of *Quake*, unanticipated by its developers, yielded a new relationship between watching and playing, or viewing and doing, that has since burrowed into player cultures.

A second underlying theme of this brief account of *Quake* movies is the value of historical studies of games. Historical interactions among game technology, game development, and player culture deserve more attention from game studies than they have thus far received. The historical target for this chapter is the new approach to game software pioneered by the team at id Software that developed *Quake*, led by John Carmack and John Romero. Their technology was the "game engine," which id had announced to the world with the release of its previous game, *DOOM*, near the end of 1993. A game engine is not just a particular kind of software; it also defines a general structure for assembling game software that separates execution of core functionality by the game engine itself from the "assets" (maps, audio, models, etc.) that define the play space or "content" of a game title. In a news release issued at the beginning of 1993, id predicted that the "*DOOM* engine" would "push back the boundaries of what was thought possible" and produce a new kind of "open game."[1] *DOOM*'s spectacular success in achieving these goals altered the marketplace for computer games and marked a defining moment for game technology.

During the six years from id's founding to the *Quake* launch on June 22, 1996, Carmack, as lead programmer, had presided over a series of technical achievements that transformed computer game design and play. These changes led from horizontal scrolling on the personal computer (the breakthrough that led to the company's founding) through the incremental development of three-dimensional (3D) graphical representation. *Quake* completed id's delivery of the first-person shooter as a new game genre built on the foundation of its technical innovations. As it developed *Quake*, id's team took account of how players had eagerly altered and added to their previous games, surprising Carmack and Romero by using *Wolfenstein 3D* (id Software, 1992) and, especially, *DOOM* as a kind of software platform. Players modified assets, such as character appearances ("skins") or game maps, and untangled intricacies of the software, such as Carmack's data compression scheme, in ways that impressed id's lead designers. Players were as keen to tinker with games as they were to play them. Romero remarked later, "[W]e never thought that people would be modifying our game. We never modified anyone else's game, why would we think that people would modify ours?"[2] Carmack and Romero expected players to look under *Quake*'s hood, figure out the workings of the game engine, and use that knowledge. They decided to encourage these activities by easing access to the game's assets and providing tools to change them. *Quake* would not just be a game. It would also become a set of packaged game technologies that players exploited for their own purposes. id thus changed what players would and could do with a computer game.

Despite their efforts to encourage modifications, Carmack and Romero did not foresee every creative option that *Quake* offered to players. Using this game—its environments, gameplay, and rendering capabilities—to make animated movies was an application of the game engine that players invented. The Rangers' "Diary of a Camper," the first *Quake* movie, revealed and demonstrated *Quake*'s moviemaking potential.

These Rangers were a *Quake* clan. Clans were organized groups of affiliated players that began to appear after id provided access to the "Qtest" version of *Quake* in February 1996. Although intended only as a technology test or demonstration, players eagerly downloaded and played this preview build while they waited for the completed game. Qtest could only be played in a multiplayer "death-match" mode, so naturally it brought players together online. One improvement in *Quake* over *DOOM* was its built-in client-server architecture, so multiplayer games could be played more easily over the internet. Players who played online together stayed online together. It is difficult to determine exactly when groups of players began to self-organize and call themselves "clans," but clans were in place before *Quake* was published and were thus poised to form the backbone of *Quake*'s online community. With names like The Ruthless Bastards, Evil Geniuses, or The Muppet Clan, clans achieved reputations as much for their websites as for their members' playing skills. These websites provided information about *Quake* technology and were places to share modifications and tools for modifying the game.

The Rangers did all these things, but they differed from other clans active in 1996 by distinguishing themselves as moviemakers. "Diary of a Camper" was not just any kind of movie but a *Quake* movie as well. The Rangers did not produce "Diary of a Camper" as a sequence of still images. Nor did they capture computer-generated screen output, edit video footage, or distribute the final cut as a video file. This *Quake* movie would not be distributed on a website such as YouTube, and it could not be streamed by a video player application such as today's VideoLan VLC viewer. These various options had little to do with computer game technology and, in any case, generally did not exist yet. Network bandwidth and speeds, streaming technologies and unlimited enthusiasm for online video had not yet come together to produce them. "Diary of a Camper" was produced in *Quake* and viewed in *Quake*.

The Rangers' movie existed in the form of a small data file, called a "demo." id had developed a demo format for *DOOM*. Recorded gameplay captured in this simple replay format loaded automatically when the game software launched. The demo then provided a *demonstration* of gameplay. (The recorded player was John Romero.) On one hand, the *DOOM* demo was an asset activated and executed by id's engine. On the other, it functioned like arcade "attract mode" sequences by showing how to play and inviting the player to jump in. Demo recording therefore connected id's new game technology with an established technique for firing up potential players. For some *DOOM* and *Quake* players, this "intro" sequence would have called to mind the "cracktros" (crack intros, sometimes called "loaders") that had been inserted by hackers into cracked game software since the late 1970s. Originally simple introductory screens, by the early 1990s cracktros presented busy multimedia sequences that attested to the coding skill and reputation of the hacker named in this opening credit animation. As standalone demo programs or "demos," these audiovisual performances fueled an international "demoscene" that included computer game players.

Id's separation of the game engine from assets such as a *DOOM* or *Quake* demo file made it relatively easy for players to replace the developer-produced replay recording with a player-created movie. The switch required that players learn how to produce and edit their "movies" and save them in the demo format, at which point other players could load and execute the demo using their own copy of the game. "Diary of a Camper" introduced the idea of moving beyond replay by using the demo movie format to tell a simple story. The Rangers were not the only players to exploit id's computer game technology, but they "led the way" (the clan's motto) by reimagining what that achievement could do for them.

Quake movies were a player-driven innovation. The game engine architecture stimulated game culture by making it possible for players to easily modify games. Carmack and Romero understood that the company that made the game engine could succeed spectacularly without controlling the assets. These assets could be created or changed on top of the engine without hacking essential engine code. Players did just that. Once they understood how the game engine worked in concert with the assets built on top of the engine, it was easier than ever before to exchange these assets to run on another player's copy of the same game engine. Many players made character skins or a new map; the Rangers used *Quake* as their platform for movie production and playback. *Quake* movies became an innovative use of id's technology and a form of player participation in the cultural economy of the game.

But why use a game to make a *movie*? *DOOM* established the sharing of demo recordings as a method for documenting gameplay achievements and learning skills from other players. The *DOOM* demo format constructed these replays by saving information about controller input captured at specified intervals of time, then converting these inputs into a sequence of primitive commands. Like a player-piano roll, when the demo file's data and metadata were loaded into *DOOM,* the game engine faithfully reexecuted the same sequence of actions as in the original game session, resulting in playback of that session on the screen. A *DOOM* demo was *not* a video recording. It was a script that reactivated a game system and produced a perfectly rendered reperformance by the machine of captured human performance. Despite or perhaps because of the simplicity of this format, the demo method of replay proved to be quite robust. It was legible (quite literally because the sequence of commands could be displayed in text format), it activated the game engine to produce exact, version-specific replay sequences, and it produced small files that could easily be exchanged regardless of available bandwidth.

DOOM established a viewing culture around replays. Carmack and Romero had responded to players' enthusiasm for modifying game assets in earlier games by designing the *DOOM* engine to accommodate such changes more easily. As the id team members geared up for the development of *Quake*, they realized that players wanted even more access to their game technology. id produced documentation and tools to serve this purpose, as well as opened up access to some of *Quake*'s computer code. The existing replay culture benefited from *Quake*'s technical improvements, as well. For example, id developed a new format for demo recording. Appropriately named .dem files (for "demo") used this format to capture significantly more information than *DOOM*'s relatively simple .lmp ("lumps" of data) files.

There is no evidence that id improved the demo format as an invitation to make movies. Nonetheless, the new format served the enthusiasm *DOOM* players had shown for replays of competitive matches and other player-invented modes of play such as speedruns. *DOOM* replay recordings had become an important part of player culture. With the new recording format, the door between sharing replays and making movies was open. Players walked through it. Thanks to id's openness, these players were able to explore the new demo format in detail. Uwe Girlich, for example, had produced *DOOM* demos and became the leading expert on the .lmp format, authoring a set of specifications for it. He dived into the *Quake* format and produced the first version of his "Unofficial DEM format description" in early July, just two weeks after the game was released. Girlich realized that "[f]or people with too much spare-time *Quake* can replace a full 3D modelling system for cartoons or the like."[3] They could make movies, in other words. The exploration by players such as Girlich of id's game technology while *Quake* was still under development, coupled with their inclinations to learn, tinker, and share, is reminiscent of Eric Von Hippel's characterization of the "lead users" of a technology. A lead user is someone whose use of a novel product or technology presents "strong needs" that *later* "become general in a market-place." Lead users not only provide "need-forecasting" but also often fill the need they experience by providing "new concept and design data, as well."[4] Girlich exemplified *Quake*'s lead users.

DOOM and *Quake* players were users of id's game technology in a sense that has received little attention in game studies: as "enthusiasts." Technological enthusiasm has a long history, particularly in the United States. Steve Waksman, writing on "tinkering" in the development of the electric guitar, argues that enthusiasm for technology leads "individuals not only to use technology, but also to take pleasure in it, and to apply themselves to it as a form of recreation."[5] During *Quake*'s long gestation period, anticipation and marketing whipped up enthusiasm. By the early 1990s, fandoms had begun to form around the prereleases, previews, and development status reports that accompanied technology development, particularly with respect to computer- and internet-related product releases. *Quake* was id technology as much as id game design, and the boundless attention of its players to every shred of information about id tech resembled that of consumers in other realms of technology for the latest thing. *Quake* enthusiasts applied themselves to understanding and tinkering with a new form of entertainment technology: game software. This became a "form of recreation" parallel to their enjoyment of the game itself. Girlich, the Rangers, and others took pleasure in their tinkering with the demo format.

Back to "Diary of a Camper." Just as *Quake* was constructed from the ground up to support client-server networking and enable competitive play over the internet, players also congregated online, visiting clan websites or game-oriented news sites such as *Blue's News* that focused on id's games. A player visiting one of these sites at the end of October 1996, about two months after GT Interactive published the full retail version of *Quake*, would have found a demo file called CAMPER3.DEM. After downloading the folder containing this file to his or her computer, that player probably read a text file included in the folder, dated October 30, 1996 (two days after CAMPER3.DEM) that identified the production team as "United Rangers Films," a spin-off from the well-known Rangers clan. The short text explained how to load and run the demo in *Quake* "for viewing pleasure in the highest video mode your computer can handle." It probably was not surprising that playing back the demo produced an animated movie that resembled replays, with short bursts of frantic action typical of id's first-person shooters. Yet, "Diary of a Camper" broke with *DOOM*'s demo replays in two important ways. First, the spectator's view was not that of any player/actor in the game. Girlich had discovered that in the new demo format, "player coordinates and the camera positions may be different." In other words, camera views could be "edited" to change the viewpoint in replay demos. This was the discovery that led him to comment on the potential for *Quake* moviemaking. The Rangers had captured gameplay data in *Quake*'s demo format and, as with *DOOM* demos, those data were played back by the game engine to produce the movie. However, an affordance of the new format was that an independent camera view could frame the action, replacing the expected first-person perspective of the shooter. "Diary of a Camper" had been "recammed." The Rangers (as well as some speedrunners) had figured out how to move cameras in *Quake* and made their own tools to do this, thus demonstrating coding skills alongside gameplay. Recamming was an innovation resulting from the players' skills, *Quake*'s robust technology, and the guidance of lead users such as Girlich (see figure 34.1).

"Diary of a Camper" was not a replay. Unlike any previous *DOOM* or *Quake* demo, the visual action followed a simple narrative arc, not a game session. With spare visual reference to the *Quake* storyline, the script was little more than a brief sequence of inside jokes—the Rangers take revenge on a "camper" (a player who gains game advantage by occupying a prime location). A headshot literally reduces this camper to a head that reveals the camper to be none other than John

FIGURE 34.1
Quake speedrun from
a "recammed" view.
"*Quake* Done Quick"
(1997).

Romero. The star of *DOOM*'s launch demo is taken down by the players in the first *Quake* movie.

"Diary of a Camper" was a modest bit of moviemaking, yet *Quake* players were inspired by it. It piqued the curiosity of a few players with experience in television or film production about the potential for animation produced by game technology. One such player was Paul Marino. Marino and a group of friends—some with backgrounds in television or improvisational comedy—were among the *Quake* players who saw "Diary of a Camper" in 1996.[6] They formed the Ill Clan. Along with other individuals and teams who had cut their teeth on *Quake* movies, the Ill Clan expanded game-based moviemaking beyond *Quake* and demos to encompass a more diverse set of techniques for making animated movies using game environments and technologies. A few years later, Hugh Hancock and Anthony Bailey, also veterans of *Quake* movies, coined the term "machinima"—a portmanteau for *machine cinema*—for this more general concept of game-based moviemaking. Machinima continues today as a vital component of digital games cultures.

Describing the activities that led to the making of *Quake* movies simply as "watching *Quake*" is misleading. Watching a *Quake* movie involved something more than consumption or spectatorship. From knowing how to operate *Quake* to play back a demo to understanding the tricks of play in the Rangers' performance and the in-jokes in their modest script, watching presumed mastery of the game that produced it. The use of *Quake* technology to produce short animated movies emerged out of a mix of technological enthusiasm and gameplay, leavened with the inclination of some players to share their performances with other players.

Gameplay plus game technology plus performance can be a powerful, productive elixir. Indeed, each of these activities includes spectatorship in one form or another. Watching games turns out to be a lot more than watching, and playing with a game is more than just gameplay.

NOTES

1 id Software Press Release, "Id Software to Unleash DOOM on the PC" (Dallas, TX: id Software, 1993).

2 John A. Romero, *Oral History of Alfonso John Romero* (Mountain View, CA: Computer History Museum, 2012), part ii, 43.

3 Uwe Girlich, "The Unofficial DEM Format Description" Version 1.02 (30 July 1996): 3.2 and 3.4, www.gamers.org.

4 Eric von Hippel, "Lead Users: A Source of Novel Product Concepts," *Management Science* 32 (1986): 791–806.

5 Steve Waksman, "California Noise: Tinkering with Hardcore and Heavy Metal in Southern California," *Social Studies of Science* 34 (October 2004): 675–670.

6 Adam Penenberg, "Deus ex machinima," *Economist*, April 4, 2004.

FURTHER READING

Lowood, Henry. "Found Technology: Players as Innovators in the Making of Machinima. In *Digital Youth, Innovation, and the Unexpected*, ed. Tara McPherson, 165–196. Cambridge, MA: MIT Press, 2007.

Lowood, Henry, and Michael Nitsche, eds. *The Machinima Reader*. Cambridge, MA: MIT Press, 2011.

Marino, Paul. *3D Game-based Filmmaking: The Art of Machinima*. Scottsdale, AZ: Paraglyph Press, 2004.

Ng, Jenna. *Understanding Machinima: Essays on Filmmaking in Virtual Worlds*. New York: Bloomsbury Academic, 2013.

35

Counter-Strike
Spectatorship

EMMA WITKOWSKI

Abstract: *Counter-Strike*'s status as an established and mature esport highlights the critical role of player-spectators, networked broadcasting, media sports packaging, and celebrity in transforming competitive gaming into a spectator sport. In this chapter, Emma Witkowski examines the rich socio-technical systems advancing the state of esports as media sports entertainment in *Counter-Strike*.

It's 2005. A Dallas hotel convention hall fills with teams ready to compete in Valve Corporation's popular computer game *Counter-Strike* (*CS*). Multiple versions make up *CS*'s franchise history. Starting as a player modification in 1999, the original release (*CS* 1.0) to the most recent version, *Counter-Strike: Global Offensive* (Hidden Path Entertainment, 2012), all iterate on basic gameplay: players join "Terrorists" or "Counter-Terrorists" teams and compete to eliminate the opposition or to win a time-based objective (such as detonating/defusing a bomb). *CS*'s global reach was on show as teams filtered into the Dallas hotel, with participants hailing from Brazil, the United States, and South Korea representing esports franchises still active today. In all, 21 teams competed in Dallas for a piece of the US$60,000 prize pool in the leading North American tournament—the Cyber Professional League (CPL). *SK Gaming* (founded in 1997) won the championship match in front of approximately 100 player-spectators, but the esports (electronic sports) industry also claimed a victory that day. Thousands of people watched the in-game broadcast, indicating that competitive computer gaming had the potential audience to organize as a spectator sport.[1]

CS scenes across Europe were also evolving. Low-cost internet made playing online games one of the most affordable team-based activities in Denmark. Esports tournaments thrived, as organized competitions took place both online and as regular LAN (local area network) events. In Central Europe, expert *CS* scenes were fostered within net-cafés in the Polish cities of Warsaw and Kielce. For a low price (2½ złoty/hour), local establishments afforded players with powerful CPUs, maximum internet speed, LAN usage, and skillful locals, offering the necessary infrastructure to incubate expert practice. Michał "Carmac" Blicharz, Electronic Sports League vice-president of pro-gaming, recalls how Polish net-café communities revolved around hanging out, supporting locals, and watching the best "clans" compete against cross-town rivals. The cafés functioned as "hatcheries for talent," and skilled players enjoyed audience power.[2] That is, players could attract new viewers to watch them compete for cash prizes, gain modest sponsorships, and harness their growing "gaming capital" by sharing their expertise and gaming knowledge (see Consalvo's chapter in this collection for more on gaming capital).[3] These regional practices indicate the rich socio-material foundations on which Pro/Am[4] *CS* cultures have developed from localized gaming communities into international, professionalized spectator sports.

Although definitions for *esports* are evolving, the term commonly refers to institutionalized and regulated elite-level competitive digital game tournaments. In this chapter, esports growth as a commercially viable spectator sport is explored through the lens of socio-technical practices. As an industry still undergoing professionalization, zooming in and out on the conventions, systems, and human/technical relationships fleshes out how esports are shaped and maintained as live media spectacles. In the following, particular attention is paid to the role of player-spectators, esports broadcasting conventions, and player celebrity as generated through *Counter-Strike*'s considerable fanfare.

Organized competitive computer gaming events have existed on a small scale since the 1970s. Arcade games such as *Atari Football* (Atari, 1978) were promoted in the November 1978 Atari *Coin Connection* newsletter as tournament-ready games. As touted on *Coin Connection*'s front page, "[a]nyone who enjoys football as a player or spectator will love to play ATARI FOOTBALL." Drawing together player-spectator sports markets, old and new, is a historic practice within the games industry. While the esports player-spectator—an active participant who switches between playing and watching—finds historical precedent in the arcade, beta versions of *CS* brought networked design thinking to the role of the player-spectator, with options for spectator-view and, later, in-game broadcasting functions. Forty years on, online esports broadcasts and seasonal mega-events represent the increased complexity and convergences between communication technologies, gaming communities, and diverse media industries—a far cry from the stand-alone, nonnetworked local arcade tournament. Modern esports are cultivated from these historic and complex practices, with spectatorship revealed as always already a part of competitive play.

Perhaps the most noteworthy capacity to engage consistently with a considerable esports audience came in 2011 with the launch of the live-streaming platform Twitch.tv (now Twitch). Twitch brought together content producers, or "streamers," and spectators into a space dedicated to sharing and archiving video gameplay. With 45 million viewers per month by 2013 and more than 1.7 million users streaming by 2016,[5] the scale of viewership and content production signals significant socio-technical changes to how people engage with games. Live esports spectatorship gained significant popularity alongside Twitch's development as a networked platform. Twitch spectators don't just watch, they are encouraged to engage with their favorite streamers by participating on the integrated stream-chat window. Viewers can "follow," "subscribe," or donate money directly to streamers, constituting various levels of commitment and support.[6]

Counter-Strike's growth as a media sport is owed to many actors, technical and social, amateur and professional. For instance, Valve's intellectual property agreement permits third-party player/organizers to monetize *CS* game broadcasts. YouTube user profiles are used as a repository of past recorded events for players and organizations. Tweets muster up attention pre–live stream, and Facebook/Instagram posts perform asynchronous community engagement and profile-building, highlighting just some of the cross-platform labor and systems involved in building and maintaining an audience. Developing the "self-as-brand" is everyday networked labor in esports, strengthened and monetized through community engagement, underpinned by industry relationships and central to understanding *Counter-Strike*'s trajectory as a spectator sport.[7]

Players have galvanized *CS*'s profile as a high visibility, mainstream esport by producing player-spectator communities across multiple platforms. Valve has also responded to the game's popularity and developed a supportive framework, which includes industry professionalization through various financial commitments (including US$1 million prize pools to all major tournaments in 2016), as well as through software modifications to increase esports appeal and prominence among current and would-be player-spectators. Furthermore, Valve's creation of cosmetic virtual items (known as "stickers") for in-game purchase and display on in-game weapons is just one of these approaches.[8] Players purchase these stickers for US$1. As in-game micro-transactions, they pay to express their allegiances and fandom. This initiative proved to be a valuable new revenue stream for Valve as well as for major *CS* esports teams (who acquire a 50–50 split on sticker sales). To wit, over a single tournament weekend in 2015, Valve made US$4.2 million in sticker sales.[9] Thus, if we want to understand *Counter-Strike*'s popularity, it is imperative that we attend to its design as a game *and* its construction as a media production that fuses community-supported gameplay and corporate design practices.

Traditional sports mega-events have influenced the structure and delivery of spectator-oriented esports. North American leagues such as the CPL or, more recently, the ELEAGUE—a cable TV *CS* tournament—draw readily, somewhat uncritically, from North American professional sports production models. Traditional media sports such as the National Basketball Association have been used as blueprints for commercial viability for many esports industries: where the existence of the mega-event relies on profit maximization from traditional media investments such as broadcast rights and top-tier sponsorships.[10] Although, as T. L. Taylor rightly recognizes, esports mega-events are shifting from their sports-focused market strategy and are expanding as "media entertainment products"—utilizing audience engagement techniques drawn from music festivals, live performances, and technology conventions.[11]

While broadening entertainment opportunities, major esports leagues are simultaneously tightening their audiencing techniques. Nicholas Taylor's exploration of Major League Gaming, North America's largest esports league, details how spectators have been oriented into specific consumer subject positions through strategic "marketing strategies, data collection methods, public relations, and technological media."[12] Where player-spectators once mingled with esports competitors, major events now separate competitors from fans—through autograph booths, raised stages, and personalized equipment—emphasizing the distinction between spectator/consumers and star/commodities. It's a more formalized, celebrity-oriented, presentational format that delivers a traditional event entertainment–driven experience, an event tailor-made for screen delivery.

Cultural studies luminary Raymond Williams's commentary on televised sports from 1989 deeply resonates with the current shift in esports productions. He notes, "Television is so good when it presents real events that it gains a power which it then abuses: nominally, to set up an anteroom, beside everything that is happening—a budget, a cup final, an election, a horse-race—but actually making the anteroom the arena, the reaction to the event, and the commentators the real agents."[13] The esports anteroom includes many of the props from traditional media sports, from glossy stage to professional production crew. The comprehensive backstage esports crew involves professional game observers (selecting in-camera shots for spectator view), hosts (player interviewers), and shoutcasters (live technical analysts and color commentators) deploying sports broadcasting conventions complete with bravado and emotion-whipping accounts expressing the dynamism of gameplay.[14] Enhanced screen displays and increasing professionalism in shoutcasting and observer work[15] contribute to online audience uptake, with individual event viewer numbers rivaling legacy sports spectacles (see figure 35.1).[16]

But not everyone is happy with the attention on the anteroom. Venting frustration about this particular evolutionary stage of esports as a live sports production,

FIGURE 35.1
Over the years,
Counter-Strike has
developed into the
dominant specta-
tor esport.

Carmac tweeted, "[Shout]casters are bigger stars than players."[17] The complaint
hints at the changing valuation of participants under rapid professionalization of
established grassroots esports scenes. For esports industries and players alike, the
struggle for a desirable and sustainable model for *CS* as an esport is an ongoing
battle. But perhaps one of the more complex discussions around esports sustain-
ability and influence sits with the state of esports celebrity and how fandom is
made and maintained across "networked publics."[18]

For esports live-streamers, becoming a Twitch "partner" is an indispensable
foundation for monetizing and maintaining a sustainable esports career. A platform partnership is a means toward esports' longevity and, for the few, microcelebrity.[19] For players, the readily accessible, deep socio-technical networks surrounding their game are well suited to the making of esports stars: as Teresa
Senft reminds us, microcelebrity is enabled through "a new style of online performance that involves people 'amping up' their popularity over the Web using
technologies like video, blogs, and social networking sites."[20] A Twitch partnership unlocks new ways to configure fandom in esports, from the management of
communication (visual and text) to audience engagement and, ultimately, monetization by way of a suite of embedded payment options. A triweekly Twitch
broadcast is a regular practice for many esports star players, but esports microcelebrity often involves consistent cross-platform performances evolving a
player's popular, manufactured media image.[21] As such, esports microcelebrity
is formed within the assemblage of major tournaments, independent broadcasts,
team branding, Twitter personalities, follow buttons, and expert practices.[22] As
esports live-streamers continue to accept four- and even five-figure donations
(direct monetary donations transferred to players through third-party sites), to

silo the action and influence to one game, one team, or to one social media plat-form is clearly unwise.

Professional gamer Jarosław "pashaBiceps" Jarząbkowski is an exemplar of microcelebrity in esports. He brings in diverse earnings and wage points—from traditional team contracts (from Virtus.pro, a Russian esports franchise founded in 2003) to technology sponsorships and dividends from sticker purchases (as one of the most purchased player stickers in the game). But pashaBiceps also draws a more consistent and self-managed wage from his independent Twitch stream. Fan-to-player donations on Twitch are mostly nominal amounts. But this income, built on top of a robust subscriber base and solid viewership numbers across multiple platforms (which produce advertising revenue) equates to a regu-lar paycheck for the practice of playful self-branding.[23] Even as his playing power declines (visualized through deteriorating in-game statistics), his lucrative net-worked microcelebrity makes him an essential team member for his esports orga-nization. Playing to win is deeply complicated by individual networked stardom in a growing sports industry. The circuits of performance and support around esports microcelebrity are integral to how people engage in esports as player/fans—from mimicking Virtus.pro game tactics in their own sessions to amplify-ing celebrity through sticker purchases and acquiring other pieces of physical and virtual merchandise. pashaBiceps's multitiered career suggest that esports have numerous new pillars of provision for spectatorship and fan engagement. Think-ing of media sports as entertainment products, sociologist Larry Wenner offers a great contribution to the current state of esports: the "new" we are seeing is not the expertise on show, not the virtuoso plays but, rather, the production of the play as spectacle.[24] Player celebrity is produced and entangled across networked esports brands, and a career as a current or former esports star is made possible through the work of many, not the least of which being fan labor.

Writing of his time spent on the North American *CS* esports scene in 2005, Michael Kane observed, "*Counter-Strike* is already a specialized spectator sport, one whose reach extends through cyberspace far beyond the walls of this hotel. Someone out there is watching. Who knows how many hundreds of thousands around the world?"[25] Today, we have a better sense of those watching, and it's in the millions. Player and fan uptake of the live broadcast and esports events has shifted *CS* into a period of intensified networked visibility, with deep integration across media platforms. But this media sports positioning also sees *CS* shifting as a game culture, with expertise being consciously performed and constructed toward the networked crowd rather than the local one. As a media sports produc-tion, esports spectatorship includes the fans as a key part of the mega-spectacle. Indeed, the crowd pays for their own commodification. But this is not a one-sided affair. Those watching also gain something deeply personal—they are reminded of their own embodied passions in play, their best team comebacks and failures in the game, and the multiple pleasures produced in their gaming leisure. As a game, an esport, and, more recently, as a deeply networked marketplace, the historical shifts in *CS* reveal how networked play, participation, capital, and spectatorship have transformed how we engage with expert play in games.

NOTES

1 Michael Kane, *Game Boys* (New York: Viking, 2008), 6–17.

2 Michał Blicharz, "The Paradox of Polish eSports" (paper presented at the 2008 eSports Europe Conference, Köln, Germany, May 28, 2008).

3 Mia Consalvo, *Cheating: Gaining Advantage in Videogames* (Cambridge, MA: MIT Press, 2007), 18.

4 Events involving both professionals and amateurs in the practice.

5 YouTube (a Google-owned streaming platform) refined its platform to include games' specific branding with YouTube Gaming in 2015. By this time, Twitch had secured games live-streamers and spectator communities, with 1.7 million games streams broadcast every month. See Twitch Retrospective, www.twitch.tv/year/2015.

6 Followers are those who add a channel to their own Twitch profile catalog of favorite streams. Subscribers sign up to pay a monthly fee to the partnered Twitch streamer (proceeds are split between the streamer and Twitch). Donations are direct contributions to a streamer through a third-party account.

7 Theresa Senft, *Camgirls: Celebrity and Community in the Age of Social Networks* (New York: Peter Lang, 2008).

8 As virtual items, stickers represent different esports teams and can be attached to the purchaser's own in-game weapon in *CS*.

9 Counter-Strike Blog, "Milestones," August 25, 2015, http://blog.counter-strike.net.

10 Jo Maguire, Grant Jarvie, Louise Mansfield, and Joe Bradley, *Sport Worlds: A Sociological Perspective* (Champaign, IL: Human Kinetics, 2002), 52–55.

11 Brett Hutchins, "T.L. Taylor: The Rise and Significance of Esports," *The Media Sport Podcast Series*, October 31, 2016, https://soundcloud.com.

12 Nicholas Taylor, "Now You're Playing with Audience Power: The Work of Watching Games," *Critical Studies in Media Communication*, published ahead of print, July 18, 2016, https://doi.org/10.1080/15295036.2016.1215481.

13 Raymond Williams, *Raymond Williams on Television: Selected Writings* (New York: Routledge, 1989), 97.

14 Henry Stenhouse, "What It Takes to Be a *Counter-Strike: Global Offensive* Observer," *PC Gamer*, February 8, 2017, www.pcgamer.com.

15 Gameplay visualization has seen ongoing media sports fine-tuning. By continually improving the spectator heads-up display (HUD), such as adding an x-ray glow around all onscreen players and health bars on avatars, HUD improvements have not only enhanced the live and online spectator view but also brought more at-hand information for shoutcaster narration while increasing the readability of the game-to-screen observer camerawork—collectively working toward professionalizing esports as a media sport.

16 Deloitte Report, "Technology, Media, and Telecommunications Predictions 2016," www
.deloitte.com.

17 Michał Blicharz (@mbCARMAC), "SC2 as a spectator spoort [*sic*] is too focused on commentators. Casters are bigger stars than players," Twitter post, November 5, 2011, https://
twitter.com/mbCARMAC/status/132835802261618689?s=19.

18 danah boyd, "Social Network Sites as Networked Publics: Affordances, Dynamics and Implications," in *A Networked Self: Identity, Community and Culture on Social Network Sites*,
ed. Zizi Papacharissi (New York: Routledge, 2010), 50.

19 Twitch, "Twitch Partner Program," 2017, https://www.twitch.tv.

20 Senft, *Camgirls*, 25.

21 Ellis Cashmore and Andrew Parker, "One David Beckham? Celebrity, Masculinity, and the
Soccerati," *Sociology of Sport Journal* 20, no. 3 (2003): 214–231.

22 Esports microcelebrity includes the accumulation of a large online following, and engagement with followers/fans across multiple online/off-line spaces while monetizing their
following through the integration of commercial products in their platform/performance.
See Crystal Abidin, "#InstagLam: Instagram as a Repository of Taste, a Brimming Marketplace, a War of Eyeballs," in *Mobile Media Making in the Age of Smartphones*, ed. Mar-
sha Berry and Max Schleser (New York: Palgrave Pivot, 2014), 119–128.

23 Jay Egger, "How Exactly Do Twitch Streamers Make a Living? Destiny Breaks it Down,"
Dot Esports, April 21, 2015, https://dotesports.com.

24 Lawrence Wenner, "On the Limits of the New and the Lasting Power of the Mediasport
Interpellation," *Television & New Media* 15, no. 8 (2014): 732–740.

25 Kane, *Game Boys*, 17.

FURTHER READING

Jin, Dal Young. *Korea's Online Gaming Empire*. Cambridge, MA: MIT Press, 2010.

Kane, Michael. *Game Boys*. New York: Viking, 2008.

Taylor, T. L. *Raising the Stakes: The Professionalization of Computer Gaming*. Cambridge, MA:
MIT Press, 2012.

Taylor, T. L. *Watch Me Play: Twitch and the Rise of Game Live Streaming*. Princeton, NJ:
Princeton University Press, 2018.

36

EVE Online
Cheating

KELLY BERGSTROM

Abstract: Cheating—the act of gaining an unfair advantage—has always gone hand in hand with analog and digital gameplay. Using *EVE Online* as a case study, Kelly Bergstrom illustrates how definitions of cheating are contingent on a game's player community, and that actions deemed to be illicit by some will be seen by others as being an integral element of that gaming experience.

Dictionaries tend to define *cheating* as an action through which one gains an unfair advantage over others. However, it is rare to agree about what specific actions make up this "unfair advantage" when playing video games. When game scholar Mia Consalvo, whose work appears in this collection, interviewed players about what they defined as cheating, she found her informants often disagreed about what constitutes unethical practices within a game, be it played online or off-line, or be it a single-player or multiplayer experience.[1] Consalvo's work is an important reminder that labeling specific actions as cheating in video games is difficult because making such a determination is highly contextual. Complicating matters, gaming actions may be contested even within a single gaming community, with some players disagreeing about the degree of a perceived infraction. Has the rule been bent? Or has it been broken?

This chapter does not forward a universal definition of cheating in video games; instead, it illustrates the difficulty of arriving at any singular understanding. Despite these difficulties, I argue that acts of cheating offer a means to investigate how norms and expected behaviors within particular communities are continually evolving. I begin by surveying activities that are frequently labeled as cheating in off-line games (e.g., cheat codes, third-party hardware, and walkthroughs), offering a brief description of how these practices provide an unfair advantage. This is followed by a discussion of how developer rules and community norms influence what is considered cheating in online multiplayer games. These examples of cheating are of interest because they offer the opportunity to observe players participating in "unethical" behavior that violates the magic circle but typically does not result in "real world" harm. Finally, this chapter concludes with a discussion of *EVE Online* (CCP Games, 2003), or *EVE*, a space-themed massively multiplayer online game (MMOG) that hosts a player community that pushes boundaries for what might be considered cheating and complicating the idea that cheating is merely a violation of the magic circle. Taken together, these discussions, especially the example of *EVE*, provide an opportunity to observe players engaged in actions at the edge of acceptability.

Obtaining an advantage in an off-line digital game may take the form of entering a "cheat code"—a sequence of letters, numbers, or button presses that unlock some in-game benefit, such as unlimited character lives or unlimited ammunition. These sequences are programmed into the software and exist as remnants of development processes or are purposefully hidden to reward particularly industrious players—objects known as "Easter eggs."

The most famous cheat code is arguably the "Konami Code," the name given to the following sequence: ↑↑↓↓←→←→BA. This 10-character sequence first appeared in *Gradius* (Konami, 1986) for the Nintendo Entertainment System (NES). When asked about the origin of this code, Kazuhisa Hashimoto, a game developer at Konami, explained that he had been tasked with making a version of his popular arcade game for the NES, but he found his game difficult to finish. This made play testing a real challenge. To make his job easier, he added the code to power up his character.[2] This code was left behind in the game software, and after being discovered by players, news of this cheat code quickly spread. The Konami Code has since appeared in numerous games and has evolved into a larger cultural phenomenon appearing as an interactive feature on various websites.[3] The Konami Code's popularity has perhaps reduced the stigma associated with cheat codes as contributing to unethical play practices. However, because entering in a code (Konami or otherwise) provides the player with extra lives or power-ups that they didn't earn, the use of such codes is typically considered a minor form of cheating.

Another way players may gain an advantage is by purchasing third-party hardware such as the Game Genie or GameShark. Unlike cheat codes that are hidden away in the software, these tools temporarily overwrite the game code to grant the user custom modifications. That is, while cheat codes are either implicitly or explicitly endorsed by the developer by virtue of their inclusion in the game, developers have worked to block third-party products from reaching consumers. For instance, in 1992 Nintendo sued Lewis Galoob Toys, the maker of the Game

Genie cartridge.[4] In this lawsuit, Nintendo claimed the Game Genie used proprietary information and therefore had engaged in copyright infringement. The courts ultimately sided with Galoob, and the Game Genie was released to moderate commercial success.

Third-party cheating tools have continued to evolve alongside video games. For example, Marcus Carter and Staffan Bjork interviewed players who used a software program to bypass the need to pay for power-ups and extra lives in the mobile game *Candy Crush Saga* (King, 2012).[5] It is interesting to note that for some of their informants actually paying for power-ups, which is a core monetization design component, was viewed as a form of cheating (i.e., "paying to win") while using the ad hoc software was not. And yet, tools like the *Candy Crush Saga* software or the Game Genie are more frequently viewed as cheating because of how they break with the perceived producer–consumer social contact.

Fan-produced "walkthroughs" occupy an even murkier area of what is thought to be proper gameplay for the way these aids offer step-by-step instructions for successfully completing games. For some players, walkthroughs are a form of cheating because they obviate the need to discover things for oneself, resulting in unearned victories. For others, walkthroughs are a part of a game's greater ecosystem and the act of creating a walkthrough is simply another way to promote community building and to grow their own social capital (see Mia Consalvo's chapter in this collection).[6]

In the examples discussed thus far, cheating is primarily a means for creating a shortcut to the end of the game or decreasing the difficulty of playing a game. The "advantage" gained is rarely more than ill-gotten bragging rights or an artificially inflated score on the leaderboard in single-player or off-line games. In contrast, cheating in an online, multiplayer game tends not to be associated with third-party cartridges or cheat codes. Instead, what is or is not considered cheating is usually measured against the rules set by the game's developer or how player actions violate community norms. Typically, these behavioral expectations are set by a developer in a code of conduct or terms of service agreement and players who violate these terms will be temporarily or permanently banned. It is also common for players to endlessly debate these boundaries via in-game chat channels or in discussion forums outside the game world.

As an example of how opinions about cheating differ between developers and players, and how views across a player community are far from uniform, I briefly turn my attention to the use of gameplay aids for MMOG titles. Some MMOG developers allow players to create their own additions for the game client—materials colloquially known as "mods" or "add-ons." These assets can be tools to help parse large amounts of data in easier-to-read formats, such as the "damage meters" in *World of Warcraft* (Blizzard Entertainment, 2004) that quantify the effectiveness of a player's damage or healing output by creating a visual ranking of players in the same area, allowing easy comparison among party or raid members. Other mods are more akin to the walkthroughs discussed previously, providing a visual overlay indicating where to go or what to do next to complete a quest. A more extreme example is the "Glider" add-on, which automates an avatar's movement, allowing players to complete tedious tasks such as collecting raw materials or killing monsters for experience points without having to be present at the computer.[7] Community forums play host to lively debates about which add-ons are essential to particular in-game activities (e.g., damage meters being necessary for all members of an end-game raiding guild), but some players maintain a hardline stance that the use of *any* mod—even those like damage meters that merely repackage existing information into an easier-to-read format—provide an unfair advantage over those who play an unmodified version of the game.[8]

Community criticisms about using damage meters or walkthrough mods typically consider them to be playing the MMOG "on easy mode," yet the use of automation mods is generally seen as cheating as it removes the human act of gameplay, crossing firmly into unethical play when the items collected by automated avatars are sold to other players. Real Money Trading (RMT)—in-game currency or in-game items being bought or sold for real-world currency—is generally seen as providing an unfair advantage to those players who wish to "pay to win." This is a similar critique leveled at *Candy Crush Saga* players. Here, the concern is about items that are purchased from gray- or black-market vendors who may be exploiting poorly paid workers who spend their days "goldfarming." But what does cheating look like in an MMOG that includes RMT as part of the developer-sanctioned economy? To explore this question, I turn my attention to *EVE Online*, an MMOG that not only provides a means for players to participate in RMT but one that is also notorious for its unforgiving play mechanics and ruthless player community.[9]

At its peak, *EVE* enjoyed 500,000 subscribers—a number that has since decreased at the time of this writing.[10] This is a game that is infamous for its steep learning curve, its hostility to newcomers, and for its complex user interface (see figure 36.1).[11] *EVE* is often described as an outlier among MMOGs for the ways it breaks from key genre conventions. First, players do not interact with one another via humanoid avatars but instead play as ships that change depending on the player's goals. Second, death brings harsh consequences. Unlike other MMOGs where death is an annoyance (e.g., returning to your corpse in *World of Warcraft*), ships and their cargo can be permanently destroyed. As *EVE* includes RMT, this means that any in-game items destroyed represent a loss of both time and money. Because of the RMT instituted by CCP Games, it is possible to calculate the conversion between in-game currency-to-US-dollar, which provides

FIGURE 36.1 *EVE Online*'s interface isn't revealed step-by-step via a tutorial system, adding to the game's notoriously difficult learning curve.

an exact means of calculating the "real world" value of lost goods. Particularly vicious battles can result in net losses in the tens of thousands of US dollars. Finally, CCP Games remains *remarkably* hands-off when it comes to regulating play. The firm will rarely intervene in player activities except in the most extreme cases, such as attempts to modify the game's code. Unlike most MMOGs, CCP permits scamming and "griefing" among its players. If, for instance, another player double-crosses you and steals your in-game items or currency, CCP will not return your lost goods. Similarly, CCP will not prevent players from repeatedly destroying others' ships and escape pods or otherwise engaging in behaviors that prevent others from having fun by pursuing their own gameplay goals.

As a sandbox-style game, *EVE* is marketed as an MMOG where players are free to forge their own paths. Players can choose to mine raw materials, manufacture and sell items to other players, or build an empire to amass a fortune of ISK, the in-game currency. There is also the ability to engage in player-versus-player (PVP) combat. With death carrying such high consequences, entering into battle is a particularly fraught endeavor. *EVE*'s universe of New Eden is divided into zones where players are offered varying degrees of protection from PVP consequences. In "high-sec," the non-player character space police, called "CONCORD," will intervene should someone find themselves under attack by another player. At the other end of the spectrum is "null-sec," a lawless space where no one except possible human allies will come to your defense.

For much of *EVE*'s early history, high-sec was a safe place for miners or any-one else wishing to avoid PVP combat. This changed in 2009 with the player-run in-game event, "Hulkageddon," a coordinated attack on miners in high-sec. This group was not operating on behalf of a particular corporation or alliance; instead, it was an opt-in event, at least on the part of the attackers. Their victims, the pilots operating Hulks (the most efficient mining vessel in the game at the time), were decidedly less enthused about the unprovoked attacks on their ships. Hulks were targeted because not only were they efficient, they were also the preferred ship of players who would set their ship to automatically mine while away from their computers—a practice known as "afk mining."[12] Prior to Hulkageddon, afk mining was a safe activity because if anyone attacked their ship while they were away from their computer, the *EVE* server-controlled CONCORD would step in and destroy the attacker(s). Although afk mining is not against CCP's terms of service, a group of players decided it was against the spirit of the game. Players participating in Hulkageddon would attack unattended mining vessels. And because the high-sec zone was intended to be without PVP threats, players would rarely equip their Hulks with much in the way of defense, optimizing their ships for mining-related tasks. These underdefended ships and their precious cargo would be quickly de-stroyed before CONCORD could rescue them. But, because the attackers did not attempt to evade CONCORD, allowing their own ships to be destroyed ("suicide ganking"), their aggressive actions did not violate CCP's rules. Moreover, the de-veloper did nothing to prevent future Hulkageddons. Suicide ganking was not an activity that CCP anticipated. Rather, it is one example of emergent gameplay that the company sees as being a hallmark of their MMOG.

During another notable event known as "Burn Jita," players engaged in a block-ade of one of the game's largest trading hubs, preventing others from selling their wares. This particular event earned praise on the Official CCP blog: "as developers we watched in awe at another amazing thing our players brought to the universe we created."[13] Such statements carry with them an endorsement that blocking large segments of players from the PVE elements of the game (e.g., mining, trading, etc.) through hostile acts is decidedly *not* cheating in the eyes of the developer.

CCP does not officially endorse suspect player activities like suicide ganks, but these practices are also not against their world's rules, and CCP celebrates such actions as the "emergent behavior" they hope to foster in their sandbox game. Re-turning to the dictionary definition of cheating—gaining an unfair advantage—and applying it to the *EVE* examples, does CCP's hands-off approach result in an unfair advantage being given to the most aggressive PVPers? This question does not have an easy answer. Indeed, there may be no single answer because it only begets additional questions concerning the connection between rules and moral-ity and the fuzzy line separating fair play from cheating.

What such questions make clear, however, is the importance of recognizing that game communities are not homogeneous in their shared mores concerning fairness and justice. Even within a single MMOG such as *EVE* where the majority of players share similar demographic profiles—*EVE* players tend to be self-identifying straight white men in their 30s and 40s[14]—players will never approach the game from a unified perspective. What constitutes "cheating" for a player interested in steadily mining for resources may differ considerably from a player who cruises New Eden looking for easy PVP targets. Cheating in *EVE*, as in all games, is ultimately context-dependent, and its assessment cannot be divorced from extant community norms. Like the other approaches to video games discussed throughout this anthology, cheating illustrates the importance of paying close attention to play's circumstances so we can better assess why gamers play the way they do and how they justify their actions.

NOTES

1 Mia Consalvo, "There Is No Magic Circle," *Games and Culture* 4, no. 4 (2009): 409–410.

2 Laura Hudson, "Unlocking the Gaming Magic of the Konami Code," *Wired*, January 31, 2012, www.wired.com.

3 A history of the Konami Code and a comprehensive list of games that use the code are currently maintained on Wikipedia: https://en.wikipedia.org/wiki/Konami_Code. A list of websites that use the Konami Code to unlock an Easter egg is maintained on http://konamicodesites.com.

4 See *Lewis Galoob Toys, Inc. v. Nintendo of America, Inc.* (9th circuit 1992), law.justica.com.

5 Marcus Carter and Staffan Björk, "Cheating in Candy Crush Saga," in *Social, Casual and Mobile Games: The Changing Gaming Landscape*, ed. Michele Wilson and Tana Leaver (New York: Bloomsbury, 2016), 261–274.

6 Mia Consalvo, "Zelda 64 and Video Game Fans: A Walkthrough of Games, Intertextuality, and Narrative," *Television & New Media* 4, no. 3 (2003): 321–334.

7 Consalvo, "There Is No Magic Circle," 412.

8 Mark Chen, *Leet Noobs: The Life and Death of an Expert Player Group in World of Warcraft* (New York: Peter Lang, 2011).

9 Marcus Carter, "Treacherous Play in EVE Online" (PhD diss., University of Melbourne, 2015).

10 Bree Royce, "CCP's 2015 Finances Included Year-over-Year Revenue Decline for *EVE Online*," *Massively Overpowered*, April 12, 2016.

11 Christopher Paul, "Don't Play Me: *EVE Online*, New Players and Rhetoric," in *Proceedings of the 6th International Conference on Foundations of Digital Games* (New York: ACM Press, 2011), 262–264.

12 "Afk mining" takes its name from the acronym for "away from keyboard." That is, players are not present at the computer and instead leave their ship to mine unattended for extended periods, returning only to empty a full cargo hold.

13 CCP Explorer, "Observing the 'Burn Jita' Player Event," *EVE Community*, May 2, 2012, www.eveonline.com.

14 Kelly Bergstrom, "Imagined Capsuleers: Reframing Discussion about Gender and *EVE Online*," in *Internet Spaceships Are Serious Business: An EVE Online Reader*, ed. Marcus Carter, Kelly Bergstrom, and Darryl Woodford (Minneapolis: University of Minnesota Press, 2016), 148–163.

FURTHER READING

Carter, Marcus, Kelly Bergstrom, and Darryl Woodford, eds. *Internet Spaceships Are Serious Business: An EVE Online Reader*. Minneapolis: University of Minnesota Press, 2016.

Consalvo, Mia. *Cheating: Gaining Advantage in Videogames*. Cambridge, MA: MIT Press, 2009.

Kücklich, Julian. "Homo Deludens: Cheating as a Methodological Tool in Digital Games Research." *Convergence* 13, no. 4 (2007): 355–367.

37

Night Trap
Moral Panic

CARLY A. KOCUREK

Abstract: Various kinds of cultural watchdogs—parents' groups, nonprofit organizations, religious and political leaders, and others—often decry the violence of video games, but these reactions frequently rest on severing so-called violent games from their wider cultural context. By contextualizing *Night Trap*—historically, politically, and culturally—Carly A. Kocurek shows the ways in which the response to this game treats it as an anomaly rather than a reflection of widespread trends.

Violence has long been a key lens through which video games have been considered and evaluated. In the United States, gaming moral panics dating to the release of *Death Race* (Exidy) in 1976 have rested, in large part, on publicly expressed disgust with in-game violence. In these performances of distaste, critics often provide voluptuous descriptions of onscreen transgressions. Opinion writers pen lurid accounts of pixelated cars striking pedestrians in *Death Race*, of finely muscled combatants beating one another to a pulp in *Mortal Kombat* (Midway Games, 1992), or of the experience of mowing down humanoid extraterrestrials in *DOOM* (id Software, 1993). Outraged moral guardians appear in television interviews to decry the insidious personal and cultural impact of allowing players to hire and then kill in-game sex workers as in *Grand Theft Auto V* (Rockstar North, 2013) or to watch cutscenes ripe with piled bodies, slit throats, and copious drugs as in *Mad Max* (Avalanche Studios, 2015). Violent games attract significant media attention, in part, because they are controversial, and this intense scrutiny raises visibility and often sales figures. The tendency to hold up games for censure has complicated effects with sometimes contradictory results. Shouting "Look at this! Isn't it awful?" may indeed mark something as awful, but this kind of statement simultaneously draws the public's attention to the "awful" thing, potentially generating press coverage and consumer dollars. The overwhelming majority of commercial games rated by the Entertainment Software Review Board (ESRB) in recent years have been rated "E for Everyone."[1] Nonetheless, the top-selling pantheon of games remain populated by titles that grab headlines by including content that features graphic violence, drug use, and sexually mature subject matter.[2]

Public discourse around violent games often seems to luxuriate in the descriptions of objectionable themes and representations. Yet critics and key players often fail to offer concrete definitions of violence or to bother distinguishing between how violence is rendered or integrated into the game or how it might be justified narratively. Significant research over past decades has shown that on-screen violence, including that in video games, has negligible to no effect on most players.[3] Research has also suggested that the context of these actions is meaningful. For example, racialized violence in which white protagonists are pitted against enemies of another race has been shown to reinforce players' racist beliefs; additionally, players who are exposed to games in which violence is justified and rewarded are more seduced by an acceptance of violence as a valid means of addressing problems. These findings do not suggest violent games are fundamentally harmful but, rather, suggest that careful attention to context is essential to understanding the relative potential for harm, even when research has shown the overall potential is relatively low. However, the industry's current ratings system and public discourse about gaming violence both frequently shy away from such subtleties.

The Entertainment Software Association (ESA) first established the ESRB in the early 1990s as a response to yet another wave of moral panic. (Today the ESRB is an independent self-regulating body of the games industry.) Unlike previous incidents, this one gained significant attention from national policymakers and culminated with a hearing by the US Senate Governmental Affairs and Judiciary Subcommittees on December 9, 1993. These hearings included testimony from a variety of video game industry professionals and experts from diverse fields who spoke about issues related to gaming violence, and, ostensibly, sexual content, although little testimony focused on the latter. As the testimony unfolded, video games were introduced via recordings of play; those present watched the game unfold as video, and few, if any, of the senators played the games themselves. The hearings covered several games, including the previously mentioned *Mortal Kombat* and *DOOM*, both of which launched long-running series with new titles still being produced more than 20 years later. The hearing also helped create the infamous lore around *Night Trap* (Digital Pictures, 1992), a game that occupies a strange position historically and is a particularly useful title through which to consider the lack of complexity in the cultural discourse surrounding violent games.

Unlike the other games at the center of the Senate hearings, *Night Trap* did not go on to secure a visible position as an influential title in the development of video games; rather, it has spent the intervening decades cloaked in a strange blend of infamy and obscurity, often invoked but rarely played. The realities of inconsistencies and difficulties in preserving games mean that *Night Trap* is not alone in this fate; *Death Race* today is an extremely rare cabinet game, and fewer than a handful are available for public access; *Custer's Revenge* (Mystique, 1982), while frequently written about, is similarly difficult to access. A game's infamy is not enough to preserve it, and so these games linger more as specters than substance, their alleged salacious details recounted like ghost stories.

In the hearings, *Night Trap* is introduced by Senator Joseph Lieberman as "a game set in a sorority house where the object is to keep hooded men from hanging the young women from a hook or drilling their necks with a tool designed to drain their blood."[4] The particular technologies used for the game doubtless contributed to the reaction from policymakers. As Lieberman went on to point out, "*Night Trap* uses actual actors and achieves an unprecedented level of realism." Lieberman, who was one of the original sponsors of the Violence Against Women Act of 1994, stressed his particular disgust with the game's depiction of sexualized violence against women.

Although *Night Trap* can and should be understood in the context of the federal hearings and accompanying testimony, the game should be placed in its historical and cultural context. Beginning in the mid-1980s and into the early 1990s new media technologies, including the laser disc and CD-ROM, greatly increased the potential size of games, and game companies saw significant potential in interactive movies. The interactive movie format became popular among developers after the success of Cinematronics's *Dragon's Lair* in 1983. As the form evolved from the animated arcade game, a number of high-budget interactive movie projects deliberately mirrored the look and feel of Hollywood productions. *Night Trap* was part of this short-lived wave of interactive movies and full-motion video (FMV) live-action games that used film conventions and live casts.[5]

Although *Night Trap* was ultimately released in 1992, the footage for the game was first shot in 1987 as part of the development of a VHS-based video game system for Hasbro. The development of the system ultimately called Control-Vision was carried out by Isix. Isix was a new company that Atari founder Nolan Bushnell established after Hasbro approached his current business, Axalon, about developing the VHS game system. When Hasbro shelved the project, several team members from Isix, including Tom Zito, who founded Digital Pictures in 1991,

FIGURE 37.1
The camera frames the houseguests in the house's kitchen before the trouble begins. Plato is second from the right.

purchased the software assets from the sidelined project. That purchase included the footage for *Night Trap* and *Sewer Shark* (Digital Pictures, 1992). *Night Trap*'s commercial release for the Sega CD and other platforms is fundamentally a port of the earlier, shelved game that had been titled *Scene of the Crime*.

The timeline of the game's production is an important factor when considering its controversial content. Moral guardians and policymakers blanched at the game's depictions of violence and its B-movie erotics. However, these thematic and stylistic choices make sense when the game is understood as an homage to the teen slasher movies of the 1980s and 1990s—in fact, *Night Trap* can usefully be considered one. And, as the game unfolds, its debt to movies such as *Prom Night* (Paul Lynch, 1980), *The Slumber Party Massacre* (Amy Holden Jones, 1982), and *Sleepaway Camp* (Robert Hiltzik, 1983) is obvious.

The player views the home through a control panel that allows them to move between cameras that show views of the house (see figure 37.1). The game opens in an upper-middle-class home as a pair of sinister figures enter through the front door. The player can control trap doors throughout the house. These doors, when opened, trap the intruders who are pulled in amid a cloud of steam. The fundamental mechanics of the game include the operation of the traps and the navigation of the house through a map that moves play between rooms. The game's mechanics and, in particular, the player's perspective, which is functionally that of someone monitoring a security camera, both place the player directly in the game and force the player to operate at a physical remove. The player is not in the house, literally or figuratively, and their engagement is limited to the remote operation of traps and the choice of which camera to view. Narratively, the game follows a slumber party at the house, which belongs to a Mr. and Mrs. Martin.

While the Martins, along with their two children Sarah and Jeff, are ostensibly a normal family, strange things have been happening, and most ominously, five girls who had previously stayed at the house disappeared.

The player, as a member of the "Sega Control Attack Team," is tasked with collaborating with undercover team member Kelly (played by Dana Plato, best known as a child star of the television series *Diff'rent Strokes*) to protect Sarah Martin's new guests and investigate the previous incidents. The addition of the player may be novel, but the horror film that unfolds amid a gaggle of teen girls is a standard trope. At various points, girls are clad in crop tops and satin nightgowns. The footage shows them primping and gossiping in early scenes. They act like iconic scream queens, pursued by the vampiric villains, double-crossed by hosts, and picked off one by one in sometimes grisly fashion. Characters plummet to their deaths through traps or are bitten by vampires or have their blood removed by a drill-based device; onscreen blood is extremely minimal, but the implied gore is, at times, enough to make the player's skin crawl.

The game exists at an intersection of historical, technical, and cultural contexts. In this context, it is not some kind of horrifying aberration. The shelved games for the Control-Vision seem to make clear that Hasbro and Isix intended the system to attract an audience of young adults, and at the time, a slasher game would have been an obvious choice. Throughout the 1980s and into the present, teen horror films have remained reliable moneymakers. The game's mechanics and play pull from genre conventions and allude to the notion of a haunted house riddled through with secret passages and trapdoors. For the player who has taken control of the house's elaborate security system, the trap doors are themselves a defensive weapon. Viewed in retrospect, the trapping mechanic seems a clever means of allowing the player to intervene without implicating the player in anything particularly violent.

Importantly, however, *Night Trap* looks less like a game and more like a movie. That a game framed as an interactive movie, first intended to be played using a novel video technology, would borrow heavily from Hollywood conventions makes sense. Interactive movies were a leap forward for games in graphical representation but the limitations on player input (despite *Night Trap*'s creative solutions within the interactive movie genre) meant that developers needed to look for inspiration from outside of video games.

Although *Night Trap* makes sense within its immediate historical context, so, too, does the 1993 congressional hearing that addressed it. First, the United States culturally associates games and play largely with childhood. Games targeted for censure by moral guardians are often not intended for children, and this is likely true of *Night Trap* as well. The characters in the game are in their teens and 20s, and the plot and theme are clearly tailored for an audience of similarly aged consumers. However, in backlash all games somehow become dangers to children, ignoring or erasing the possibility of teen or adult viewers. This is true in the 1993 hearing. When broadcasting the event, CSPAN summarized the proceedings as being about "video game violence and its impact on kids."[6] And, of course, games were widely distributed through channels meant to appeal to children, regardless of the intended audience. Circulars for retailers like Toys "R" Us and KB Toys regularly featured games, including titles such as *Mortal Kombat* and others cited in the hearings. Rhetorically, in a moral panic, violent games like *Night Trap* or *Mortal Kombat* become a stand-in for all games; this, the testimony, and the evidence presented in the hearings are what games are: a series of decontextualized, televised violent threats.

Second, the hearings came amid a number of high-profile crimes. In particular, Lieberman invoked the kidnapping and murder of Polly Klaas in his opening remarks; Klaas was abducted at knifepoint during a slumber party at her mother's home. The details of the crime eerily mirrored the setting of many teen horror films and, of course, *Night Trap*. Violence and violent images, Lieberman suggested, had come to permeate the broader culture, and parents had requested the line be drawn at violent video games. The early 1990s saw a peak in violent crime in the United States with the highest date being placed between 1991 and 1993, depending on the measure.[7] Lieberman's comments imply some causal relationship between violent games and violent acts. Although the effort to curtail youth access to violent games seems as though it would do little to prevent adult-on-youth crime like the murder of Polly Klaas, violence onscreen, and, especially, violence easily blamed on a handful of bad media objects, surely seemed easier to address than the tide of murders and other violent crimes taking place across the United States and the complex sociological issues at play.

Third, the Motion Picture Association of America (MPAA) had first introduced its voluntary ratings system in 1968. Under this system, completed films are submitted for review and rating. Although this system can be problematic, it allowed the industry to retain control of its own ratings system and to remain free of direct government intervention. The Parents Music Resource Center had advocated for a similar ratings system for popular music releases in the mid-1980s, a public discussion that culminated in a hearing of the US Senate Committee on Commerce, Science, and Transportation. The debate was resolved with a compromise by which affected audio recordings were labeled "Explicit Lyrics: Parental Advisory" or sold with lyrics on the back of their packaging. This Recording Industry Association of America system, first standardized in 1990, was even less nuanced than the MPAA system but was and is similarly industry controlled (as of 2002, some record companies have begun including more detailed information about the reason for warning labels specific to individual records). These industry-led efforts set a clear precedent for ratings and labeling regimens led by industry.

Night Trap needs to be understood in this context as well: one in which violent crime is at or near a peak nationally, a time when children seem vulnerable and unprotected and a point where other forms of media are clearly labeled in industry-led efforts to provide information to parents. The US cultural association between toys and games and childhood is important, so, too, is the proliferation of teen slasher movies and the failed attempt by Hasbro to develop an interactive video system. The games such as *Night Trap* invoked in national debates about game violence are often singled out as evidence of games' moral depravity and negative influence, but these games make true sense only in carefully considered context including the broader cultural, historical, social, economic, and political landscape. In this, as in many panic situations, lawmakers sought a simple, clear-cut solution to a complex problem and, in doing so, transformed a single game into a cultural bogeyman.

In the hearings at which policymakers and game industry leaders weighed the significance of video games as a violent form, much is at stake for the games industry. Regulation (or the lack thereof) can shape production and distribution practices in profound ways; for decades, for example, most major theatre chains refused to carry films rated NC-17, effectively ensuring that films receiving that rating would be difficult to distribute and very hard to profit from, a practice that has been mirrored in games with few retailers willing to carry titles rated AO, for Adults Only. However, as those leading the hearings would want us to know, much is also at stake for the broader society: for how we understand and misunderstand our own complicity in a culture of violence and for where and to whom we assign and misassign blame for social breakdowns. *Night Trap* became a key text of a critical moment in the history of the video game industry, and the Senate subcommittee hearing that ensured the game's infamy also precipitated the current ESA regimen of ESRB ratings ubiquitous across major game releases. These are inarguably significant events, and *Night Trap* is inarguably an important game—both for that unprecedented level of realism that made policymakers so uncomfortable and for the pivotal role it played in the establishment of contemporary regulatory practices.

NOTES

1 The ESRB today is a self-regulatory organization that assigns ratings to video games. It was initially established by the Entertainment Software Association (ESA, previously the Interactive Digital Software Association) in response to the hearings discussed in this chapter.

2 For example, in 2015, the 10 top-selling physical games listed by Gamespot included *Call of Duty: Black Ops III* (Treyarch, 2015), *Madden NFL 16* (EA Sports, 2015), *Fallout 4* (Bethesda Game Studios, 2015), *Star Wars Battlefront* (EA DICE, 2015), *Grand Theft Auto V* (Rockstar North, 2013), *NBA 2K16* (Visual Concepts, 2015), *Minecraft* (Mojang, 2011), *Mortal Kombat X* (NetherRealm Studios, 2015), *FIFA 16* (EA Sports, 2015), and *Call of Duty: Advanced Warfare* (Sledgehammer Games, 2014). Of these, five, or 50 percent (*Call of Duty: Black Ops III*, *Fallout 4*, *Grand Theft Auto V*, *Mortal Kombat X*, and *Call of Duty: Advanced Warfare*), are all rated M for Mature. Additionally, although *Star Wars Battlefront* is rated T for Teen and *Minecraft* is rated E for Everyone, both of these games allow for online play in a larger community, and community regulation has proved a sticky problem for the games industry; while the content of *Minecraft* might be fine for an 8-year-old, the developers have, at best, limited control of what players say in in-game chat and how they behave, which means there are some unknowns in terms of what children might be exposed to in-game. See Gamespot, "Top Ten Best-Selling US Games of 2015 and December Revealed," *Gamespot*, January, 14, 2016, https://www.gamestop.com.

3 Although a number of individual studies have suggested ties between violent games and violent behavior, meta-analysis frequently shows null results, and critics have argued that many of the individual studies are flawed and results are difficult or impossible to reproduce.

4 US Senate Governmental Affairs and Judiciary Subcommittees, "Video Game Violence," C-SPAN video, 2:49:41, December 9, 1993.

5 These games could be expensive to produce. In the case of the FMV game *The Beast Within: A Gabriel Knight Mystery* (Sierra On-Line, 1995), the production costs were so tight that the director would only rarely allow for more than two takes of a scene.

6 US Senate Governmental Affairs and Judiciary Subcommittees, "Video Game Violence," C-SPAN video, 2:49:41, December 9, 1993.

7 D'Vera Cohn, Paul Taylor, Mark Hugo Lopez, Catherine A. Gallagher, Kim Parker, and Kevin T. Maas, "Gun Homicide Rate Down 49% Since 1993 Peak; Public Unaware," Pew Research Center Social and Demographic Trends, May 7, 2013; and Federal Bureau of Investigation, "Uniform Crime Reporting Statistics," Lauren-Brooke "L.B." Eisen and Oliver Roeder, "America's Fault Perception of Crime Rate," Brennan Center for Justice, March 16, 2015.

FURTHER READING

Bowman, Nicholas D. "The Rise (and Refinement) of Moral Panic," in *The Video Game Debate: Unraveling the Physical, Social, and Psychological Effects of Digital Games*, ed. Rachel Kowert and Thorsten Quandt, Thorsten, 22–38. London: Routledge, 2016.

Kocurek, Carly A., "The Agony and the Exidy: A History of Video Game Violence and the Legacy of Death Race." *Game Studies* 12, no. 1 (September 2012), http://gamestudies.org.

38

Shovel Knight
Nostalgia

JOHN VANDERHOEF

Abstract: The place of nostalgia in video game producing and consuming cultures
has been explored from a variety of critical perspectives, particularly the way the industry and fan communities struggle for control over gaming's collective past; however, little attention has been paid to nostalgia's functions in indie game production
contexts. Through an examination of the design, aesthetics, and intertextual allusions
of the indie game *Shovel Knight*, John Vanderhoef argues that the game becomes a
pastiche that celebrates the technological limitations of the past while also challenging the hegemony of the technological sublime that animates the mainstream video
game industry today.

Because of its intimate connection with our cultural experience, media have historically been linked to strong feelings of nostalgia.[1] This is particularly true for
gaming communities, whose adult members started playing games early in life
and now romantically associate particular eras of gaming with the pleasures of
childhood. Although nostalgia's Greek origins define the concept as a deep longing
to return to a place of home, for game players this return usually involves returning not to a specific place in the world but instead to a particular array of situated
technological limitations that *represent* a specific place and time—limitations that
manifest in distinct visual styles, gameplay mechanics, and level designs. Together,
these elements define each generation of video game technology for players and
often trigger strong feelings of nostalgia.

Retrogaming refers to the player practice of habitually returning to older video
games rather than playing newer titles. Engaging in these practices, players become retrogamers, a group defined by their preference for video games from
earlier PC and game console generations, such as the 8- and 16-bit eras. James

Newman—whose work appears in this anthology—has called retrogaming one of the significant gaming trends of our time, and Jaakko Suominen suggests that the growth of digital culture, including video games, has resulted in the simultaneous growth of nostalgic media cultures such as retrogamers.[2] In 2017, retrogamers consist predominantly of the so-called Nintendo Generation, people who grew up with the Nintendo Entertainment System (NES) as their first memorable gaming experience in the mid- to late 1980s.[3]

Recognizing an obvious opportunity for profit, the video game industry embraces the collective nostalgia of game players for commercial purposes. The industry targets the nostalgia of gaming culture through a number of strategies, including direct homage in big-budget blockbuster games, the remaking and remastering of canonical older games, and the actual resale of these canonical games through virtual storefronts or in "plug-and-play" facsimile console packages meant to resemble classic late-1980s and early-1990s hardware.

In opposition to the dominant industry, subcultures like the MAME (Multiple-Arcade Machine Emulator) community[4] and retro homebrew developers[5] have emerged to challenge the top-down, hierarchical control over the canonization, distribution, and archiving of older games. MAME communities actively produce alternative gaming archives while retro homebrew developers create original 8-bit titles like *Battle Kid: Fortress of Peril* (Sivak, 2010), designed from the ground up to work on the original NES hardware. Yet in between the dominant industry and the alternative shadow economy of homebrew retro games, the commercial independent games sector has risen to equally embrace nostalgia, incorporating gaming culture's collective memory into their aesthetics, game designs, and marketing schemes.

The Nintendo Generation reached maturity at the same time as widespread broadband internet access, the emergence of digital distribution in video game markets, and the ubiquitous rollout of free or cheap professional game development engines such as Unity. This confluence of cultural and technological forces resulted in an explosion of small, independent game creators by the end of the first decade of the twenty-first century. Free from the mandate of photorealism and bombastic presentations that drive the dominant game industry, many indie developers have turned to the games of their childhood as inspiration for their own development efforts. Indie games like *Cave Story* (Studio Pixel, 2004), *Braid* (Number None, 2008), and *Super Meat Boy* (Team Meat, 2010) draw from the structures, perspective, artistry, and mechanics of 8-bit video games.[6] Moreover, each game is layered with allusions to NES classics like *Super Mario Bros.* (Nintendo R&D4, 1985) and *Castlevania* (Konami, 1986). Yet one indie game in particular, 2014's *Shovel Knight* from Yacht Club Games, provides a prime example of the strategic deployment of nostalgia in the cultural economy of video games.

Kline et al. offer what they call "the three circuits of interactivity" model to evaluate digital play in a complex globalized landscape where concerns of technology, economy, and culture dynamically overlap.[7] Using this model as a lens through which to view *Shovel Knight* and its relationship to nostalgia—or "NEStalgia" as the case may be—illuminates the rationale behind Yacht Club Games' choice to adhere to decades-old technological limitations, antiquated textual and design influences, and a dedicated marketing campaign that emphasized *Shovel Knight*'s intimate connection with canonical titles in the NES game catalog. The three circuits of technology, text, and marketing combine to make *Shovel Knight* a uniquely nostalgic pastiche, one that celebrates the minimalism and limitations of the past while, more significantly, challenging the hegemony of the technological sublime characteristic of the photorealistic triple-A game genre that animates the mainstream video game industry.

Svetlana Boym identifies two competing forms of nostalgia that serve different purposes.[8] *Restorative nostalgia* wishes to recover the lost paradise of the past and reconstruct it in the present. In its zealous efforts, restorative nostalgia is uncritical of past mistakes or failures and instead relies on romanticizing and recreating, brick by brick, the monuments and moments lost to time. In contrast to this heavy-handed approach, *reflective nostalgia* does not seek to reconstruct the past in the present; instead, it is a nostalgia consumed with the act of longing itself, a nostalgia that wallows in the irrecoverable ruins of the past, ruminating on them to reveal lessons that can be taken forward into the present and the future. *Shovel Knight* encompasses both forms of nostalgia, at once reconstructing the textual and mechanical specifics of the past while also being aware of the impossibility (and frustration) of ever attempting to return to it.

From its earliest prototypes, Yacht Club Games positioned *Shovel Knight* as a spiritual successor to a slew of beloved NES games like *DuckTales* (Capcom, 1989), *Mega Man* (Capcom, 1987), and *Zelda II: The Adventure of Link* (Nintendo R&D4, 1987). In accordance with the tastes and dominant genres of the NES era, *Shovel Knight* inhabits the two-dimensional action-platformer genre, a type of game defined by an iconic hero character that must jump and fight his or her way through multiple side-scrolling levels. As the titular *Shovel Knight*, armed primarily with a shovel, players must navigate increasingly complex two-dimensional stages, battle enemies, avoid traps and pitfalls, collect loot, purchase skill upgrades, and ultimately defeat several rival knights on the way to rescuing a friend and potential love interest and saving the land from evil.

Promising familiar conventions and an instantly recognizable retro visual style, Yacht Club Games asked for the support of the retrogaming community in a crowdfunding campaign on Kickstarter in order to fund the development of *Shovel Knight*. After raising more than US$300,000, Yacht Club released *Shovel Knight* on the PC and Wii U in 2014, later porting the game to the PlayStation 4, Xbox One, and Nintendo Switch. *Shovel Knight*'s release on the Wii U, a console that failed to reach a mass audience, is particularly noteworthy. Despite the Wii U's troubles, the *Shovel Knight* developers were committed to offering their NES homage on a Nintendo home console, no doubt to lend more authenticity to the nostalgic experience they sought to (re-)create. Upon its release, critics praised the game for its "classic," "old school," "retro" appeal, acknowledging *Shovel Knight*'s uncanny likeness to many popular titles of the NES era.

However, *Shovel Knight* does not merely gesture toward retrograde, pixelated visuals and design elements. Instead, Yacht Club Games went out of its way to observe the original hardware limitations of the NES. This superfluous diligence identifies the development of *Shovel Knight* as an exercise in restorative nostalgia. While many indie games mimic the pixelated graphics of 8-bit games, Yacht Club Games forced itself, at least in spirit, to use the limitations of the NES hardware as a guiding philosophy, shaping character sprite sizes, color choices, and music composition. In many ways, *Shovel Knight* succeeds at this. The medieval-inspired characters are recognizably chunky and pixelated, and the environments are smattered with repeated bitmapped background sprites. Unfortunately, with its 8-bit microprocessor, the NES was a very limited console. It was only capable of producing 54 colors, only allowed 8 sprites per line without flickering, and had a maximum resolution of 256 × 240 pixels. Fortunately for Yacht Club Games, the graphical prowess of any given NES game depended on when it was released and what particular chipset was used for its game cartridge. Games released later in the NES life cycle offered developers more robust options in terms of visual and aural fidelity.

When developing *Shovel Knight*, Yacht Club Games imagined a scenario where NES cartridge chipsets continued to advance, allowing the indie developer to deviate slightly from the restrictions of the NES when necessary. Unlike NES games, *Shovel Knight* features a widescreen display, parallax scrolling, the elimination of sprite flickering, and the addition of colors beyond the NES's 54-color limit.[9] These technological flourishes challenge the argument that *Shovel Knight* represents a purely restorative nostalgic experience. Instead, despite its uncanny similarity to the graphical presentation of NES games, *Shovel Knight* offers a reflective retro experience, one that illustrates its developers have reflected on the conventions of the past and found them, in this modern era, slightly wanting.

Shovel Knight borrows core design principles and mechanics from prominent titles in the NES library. For instance, as the chunky blue Shovel Knight, players can thrust their shovel downward while falling, allowing them to both attack and bounce off of enemies, similar to how a pogo stick works. Yacht Club Games plucked this mechanic directly from fan-favorite *DuckTales*, in which players perform a similar move with a cane as Scrooge McDuck (see figure 38.1).

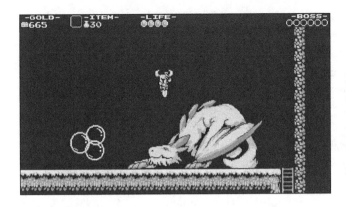

FIGURE 38.1
Shovel Knight illustrates the game's direct homage to the cane-bouncing mechanic found in *DuckTales*.

This conscious homage extends to the design of *Shovel Knight*'s levels, town areas, and world map. *Shovel Knight*'s levels resemble *Mega Man* stages, with underwater- or icy mountain–themed locations, each broken into short sections and ending in a climactic boss encounter with an opponent whose name and appearance situate him or her as a foil to the protagonist. Whereas Mega Man might have battled Heat Man, Shovel Knight must confront Polar Knight. Similarly, the game owes its world map design to *Super Mario Bros. 3* (Nintendo R&D4, 1988), in which players can move along predetermined lines on a large map between levels. Even *Shovel Knight*'s town areas, where players can purchase upgrades and explore, pay respect to the villages in *Zelda II*, with random townsfolk spouting irreverent knowledge and opinions. Through these bricolage design choices, *Shovel Knight* provides not just one particular nostalgic NES moment but a compilation of moments that together refer more to the collective memory of NES games than to how they actually operated individually at any given moment. Here again the tensions between *Shovel Knight*'s restorative and reflective nostalgic properties emerge.

Restorative nostalgia operates best when left unchallenged by the realities of the past. An actual return to the past destroys the fantasy of restorative nostalgia, revealing instead the sometimes painful truth that the nostalgic process ameliorates. Restorative nostalgia actively works to avoid this pain. In contrast, reflective nostalgia embraces it, recognizing in the discomfort a kind of wisdom gained. Although *Shovel Knight* goes further than most indie games in remaining true to NES restrictions, it stops short of troubling players with the shortcomings of older games. For instance, inspired by arcade cabinets of the 1980s designed to suck quarters from the pockets of players, many NES games featured "life" systems whereby players only had a certain number of attempts to finish the game before having to start over. Some players appreciate this kind of challenge, but most find the arbitrary system more frustrating than rewarding. *Shovel Knight* joins most other modern games that almost entirely avoid using this concept altogether. Instead, in *Shovel Knight*, players have unlimited attempts to overcome challenges. *Shovel Knight* also offers ample checkpoints where the game returns players if they do die, a feature that eliminates the needless and mundane replaying of early parts of levels. These modern features are subtly implemented, allowing players instead to focus on the nostalgic elements borrowed from the NES library of games.

Despite its complex relationship with either slavishly restoring the past or critically reflecting on its specificities and failures, *Shovel Knight* also represents the powerful place of nostalgia in the gaming industry's cultural economy. For all the warm feelings it may evoke, and regardless of its indie origins, *Shovel Knight* also operates as a cultural product within the nostalgia industry, in general, and the retrogaming industry, in particular. After securing a loyal audience of players with its nostalgic appeal, even before the game's release, Yacht Club Games wasted no time in leveraging its brand through several marketing strategies increasingly used by indie studios, including partnerships with platforms holders like Nintendo, cross-promotion between indie titles, and merchandising.

As part of its indie outreach program, Nintendo partnered with Yacht Club Games during *Shovel Knight*'s development. This is no doubt because Nintendo recognized the synergies between the two companies' intellectual property and brands. *Shovel Knight* is, after all, nothing if not a love letter to Nintendo's 8-bit NES console. Through this strategic partnership, Yacht Club Games received development and marketing support from Nintendo. This included sponsorship and promotion at events such as the IndieCade festival, where *Shovel Knight* was available to play in Nintendo's tent. Both companies gained productive exposure through this deal. *Shovel Knight* garnered more momentum and attention leading up to its launch in 2014, and Nintendo was able to promote its "Nindies" program with a hotly anticipated game that referenced classic Nintendo games the company still uses as a foundation for its cultural image today.

Merchandising has become another important revenue source for indie game developers. Extending its partnership with Nintendo, Yacht Club Games became the first developer outside of Nintendo to manufacture and distribute an amiibo figurine, small toys that interact with Nintendo platforms via near field communication technology. Even as its Wii U console failed financially, Nintendo launched its lucrative amiibo line of toys in 2014, each fashioned after a classic Nintendo character. Although many fans and critics bemoaned the actual functionality of the amiibo, they sold out frequently in their first year of release, bolstered by the nostalgic draw of owning small statues of iconic characters. It is noteworthy that Nintendo approved the release of a Shovel Knight amiibo, which can now sit next to characters like Mario and Link on retail displays and in the homes of retrogamers.

This illustrates the success of Yacht Club Games' strategic use of nostalgia in establishing a contemporary icon that also operates comfortably among icons of the past. Through all these efforts, Yacht Club Games has managed to sell over 1.5 million units of *Shovel Knight*, not only a landmark success for an indie developer but also a success that shows the benefits of producing a game that so seamlessly fits into the healthy nostalgia economy of retrogaming.

Nostalgia need not always be a restorative exercise in reversion. Rather, reflective nostalgia can be a powerful challenge to dominant political and economic structures in society. *Shovel Knight* sits uncomfortably between these two expressions of nostalgia. Certainly, the game celebrates the aesthetic limitations of the NES and directly quotes the design principles of canonical titles of that era. Yacht Club Games expressly leveraged the nostalgic appeal of these features in order to sell the game as precisely a journey into the Nintendo Generation's collective past, making use of the almost-instant iconic status of its character to build a successful business around their property. These factors cannot be ignored, nor can the game's prominent place within the nostalgic economy of retrogaming. Yet in an era where US$100 million games, such as *Grand Theft Auto V* (Rockstar North, 2013), push graphical fidelity to its limits, and virtual reality promises to transport us to ever-more realistic landscapes, there is something inherently challenging about continuing to produce and value visual and gameplay principles that were established on decades-old consoles. Retro video games like *Shovel Knight*, increasingly a central genre within indie game development, ask us to continually evaluate our individual and collective relationship to the past, interrogate personal and industrial forms of nostalgia, and meditate on the place of both within the complex and dynamic cultural economy of video game development and consumption.

NOTES

1 Katharina Neimeyer, ed., *Media and Nostalgia: Yearning for the Past, Present and Future* (New York: Palgrave, 2014).

2 James Newman, *Videogames* (New York: Routledge, 2004); and Jakko Suominen, "The Past as the Future? Nostalgia and Retrogaming in Digital Culture," *Fibreculture* 1, no. 11 (2008), http://eleven.fibreculturejournal.org.

3 Stephen Kline, Nick Dyer-Witheford, and Greig de Peuter, *Digital Play: The Interaction of Technology, Culture, and Marketing* (Montréal: McGill-Queen's University Press, 2003).

4 Matthew Thomas Payne, "Playing the Déjà-New: 'Plug it in and Play TV Games' and the Cultural Politics of Classic Gaming," in *Playing the Past: History and Nostalgia in Video Games*, edited by Zach Whalen and Laurie N. Taylor (Nashville: TN: Vanderbilt University Press, 2008), 51–68.

5 John Vanderhoef, "NES Homebrew and the Margins of the Retrogaming Industry," in *Fans and Videogames: Histories, Fandom, Archives*, ed. Melanie Swelwall, Angela Ndalianis, and Helen Stuckey (New York: Routledge, 2017), 111–127.

6 Jesper Juul, "High-Tech Low-Tech Authenticity: The Creation of Independent Style at the Independent Games Festival," in *Proceedings of the 9th International Conference on the Foundations of Digital Games*, ed. Tiffany Barnes and Ian Bogost (Santa Cruz, CA: Society for the Advancement of the Science of Digital Games, 2014).

7 Kline et al., *Digital Play*, 2003

8 Svetlana Boym, *The Future of Nostalgia* (New York: Basic Books, 2001).

9 D. D'Angelo, "Breaking the NES for Shovel Knight," *Gamasutra*, June 25, 2014, www.gamasutra.com.

FURTHER READING

Altice, Nathan. *I Am Error: The Nintendo Family Computer/Entertainment System Platform.* Cambridge, MA: MIT Press, 2015.

Heineman, D. S. "Public Memory and Gamer Identity: Retrogaming as Nostalgia." *Journal of Games Criticism* 1, no. 1 (2014), http://gamescriticism.org.

Lizardi, Ryan. *Mediated Nostalgia: Individual Memory and Contemporary Mass Media.* Lanham, MD: Lexington Books, 2015.

Whalen, Zach, and Laurie N. Taylor, eds. *Playing the Past: History and Nostalgia in Video Games.* Nashville, TN: Vanderbilt University Press, 2008.

39

Tempest
Archive

JUDD ETHAN RUGGILL AND KEN S. MCALLISTER

Abstract: Video games are often studied as "texts" that tell stories and as interactive technologies for play, but they can also be studied as artifacts using the archival method. In this chapter, Judd Ethan Ruggill and Ken S. McAllister outline the archival method for game analysis, drawing specifically on the 1981 Atari arcade classic *Tempest* to show how a game is more than the sum of its individual components; it is the sum of the many cultures, aesthetics, and industry practices that drive the game development process.

There are many approaches to studying video games, to thinking playfully and purposively about the medium and its cultures. One can, for example, consider how games invite players to receive—and help tell—stories. Even a simple game asks players to make decisions and perform actions in service of advancing its storytelling objective. Gameplay—and the stories it enables—is a kind of conversation between a player and a game's various elements: its rules, level design, aesthetic, and so on.

For a game like *Missile Command* (Atari, 1980), this conversation is straightforward: *Missile Command*'s Ready-to-Play Mode, which the arcade machine enters after the appropriate play token has been inserted, instructs players to "DEFEND CITIES." There is no other option for play, no other response to the game's invitation (except perhaps to walk away). The game's principal objective—and thus its fundamental premise—is unequivocal: help tell the story of *Missile Command* by trying to defend its cities.

Not all game objectives are conveyed so directly. *The Walking Dead* (Telltale Games, 2012–2018), for instance, presents players with choices that are unclear or that have unintended consequences later in the game. Moreover, *The Walking Dead* provides ambiguous feedback in response to players' selections (e.g., when the game responds to a player's decision with the text "Clementine will remember that"). In the case of young Clementine—the deuteragonist of the game's first season—it is unclear how *exactly* she will remember a given decision. Will she recall the player's choice fondly? With anger, disgust, or disappointment? The player can only wait until the narrative further unfolds to discover the consequences of those past actions. In contrast to *Missile Command*, then, *The Walking Dead* is deliberately vague in its communications, a design decision that drives player investment in the game world. This, in turn, drives deeper story-making.

Regardless of whether a game's objectives are clear or ambiguous, simple or complex, exploring how games persuade players to make decisions and thereby help unspool narratives can reveal a great deal about why games tell their stories the ways they do (see Salter's chapter about narrative and *King's Quest* and Russworm's chapter about race and *NBA 2K16* in this collection). From this perspective, games are storytelling artifacts with multiple voices: the prominent, interactive stories the games themselves present to players and the stories that the game's development tells scholars about the milieu in which the game was created.

This latter mode of storytelling is at least as interactive as the one in which players are directly immersed. In addition to being entertaining, games are industrial products, the results of developers' labor and publishers' monetary investment. Examining the conditions of a game's production can illuminate important reasons for why it looks, sounds, and plays the way it does. Such examination can also explain a game's performance in the marketplace. *L.A. Noire* (Team Bondi, 2011), for example, was in development for seven years, a long time even for top-tier titles. With such a lengthy development period—and therefore the opportunity to iterate and polish the game—that *L.A. Noire* was critically and commercially successful is no surprise.[1] At the same time, the working conditions at developer Team Bondi were reportedly quite challenging, and the studio closed a few months after *L.A. Noire* was released.[2] Thus, even though the market conditions seemed ideal for expanding the *L.A. Noire* story, the conditions for production were not, and a sequel was never made. *L.A. Noire*, then, like all games, is as much an artifact of its production as of its play. Stories like this—tales *about* the game—deserve to be told, but fashioning them requires a kind of research that sees games not as discrete objects but as complex cultural artifacts that are always already entangled in the world that gives them meaning.

This idea of game as "artifact" impels game archivists. Literally speaking, "artifacts" are skillfully made things (*arte* meaning "by skill" and *factum* meaning "something made"), objects crafted with care and purpose. Video games come by their artifactual status through many routes: their stories and industrial production processes are clearly skill-driven and are among games' most commonly studied miens. Some scholars, however, think of games as artifacts that emerge from convoluted legal arrangements. Others study them as artifacts designed to reproduce dominant sociocultural ideas involving gender, race, and sexuality. Still others view video games as artifacts that signify human beings' changing relationship to play. These different approaches to understanding the game as "artifact" converge in the *archival method.*

Generally, the archival method of game study facilitates many other kinds of game study: narratological, industrial, artistic, technical, and so forth. Video games are understood as connected to all other games (digital and otherwise), as well as to the variety of materials that support the video game medium. In other words, the archival method holds that all games are unique yet interconnected with all other games, as well as to past styles and histories of gameplay. The archival method also includes in its semiotic network the universe of game-related "paratexts," video game–based materials that are not games themselves: fan art, peripherals, Local Area Network (or LAN) equipment, syllabi from university courses on game history, blockbuster films, game-themed food and clothing, and so on. These materials, as much as the games from which they originate, merit study because they too contribute to how games mean; they, too, are game artifacts.

The archival method insists that it is through careful attention to the composition of actual artifacts (including digital ones) that researchers can enhance their understandings of individual games, game paratexts, and particular game artifact groupings (e.g., Japanese tennis games, Nintendo merchandise, *Atari Force* comics). The archival method aims to provide more historically situated, more geographically diffuse, more ideologically nuanced knowledge of games and their cultures by recognizing their means of production and their linkages to other artifacts. In this sense, the archival method recalls the arguments of actor-network theory, which considers objects as integral to social relations. The archival method also evokes structuration theory, which holds that structures and agents are mutually constitutive and inflective. In short, the archival method values the act of connection over that which is connected.

In the remainder of this chapter, we outline the archival method of game analysis. To illustrate how this approach can be deployed for different critical outcomes, we reference the 1981 Atari arcade classic *Tempest.* One of the strengths of the archival method is that it reveals how games are always the incalculable sum of the many cultures, aesthetics, and industry practices that drive their development process and embodiment in play. Arguably, such a wideband understanding of games and game culture is only possible through the archival method. The archival method of video game studies depends on three interconnected assumptions: games are networked phenomena, games are but one of many nodes in their networks, and studying game networks requires the preservation of those networks.

Video games are networked phenomena. They are part of many and vast systems connecting materials, people, ideas, and processes, all of which together constitute what games are and how they mean. Although it is possible (and sometimes desirable) in certain situations to examine a game as a discrete meaning-making object, the archival method holds that such disaggregation of games from their networks often produces misleading conclusions. A game studied in isolation appears quite different than when studied in a wider context. Depending on the claims made about the artifact under study, such differences can result in understandings ranging from simplistic—the artifact is understood but one's comprehension lacks definition and nuance—to flat-out wrong (imagine trying to describe a building to someone when only the front door is visible).

A case in point: on its surface, *Tempest* is a geometric, three-dimensional, space-themed shooter in which the player must destroy waves of enemies that emerge onto a fixed playfield (see figure 39.1). Once a level's enemies have been dispatched, the player moves on to a different playfield with a new set of enemies. Importantly, however, *Tempest* was inspired by designer Dave Theurer's nightmares of monsters crawling out of a hole in the ground, an origin story that appears in a variety of interviews and publications associated with the game (i.e., other archival artifacts). To apprehend *Tempest* as space-themed, therefore, is inaccurate (or at least notably incomplete); the game has terrestrial as well as extraterrestrial overtones, overtones that only become apparent after making the conceptual move from viewing *Tempest* as a game to viewing it as an artifact in a network of events, agents, and other artifacts.

Again, games are complex phenomena, and the archival method seeks to highlight and embrace this complexity to more fully analyze artifacts' influences and implications. The implications of *Tempest*'s origins are clear: the game is as much a horror story about pursuit and subterranean terrors close to home as it is an intergalactic shoot-'em-up. Without the archival method, without recognizing *Tempest* as an artifact connected to other artifacts—in this case, the multiple origin stories found within other artifacts connected to the game—the game's earthbound essence would remain hidden. Consequently, so, too, would an important piece of *Tempest*'s development history, thematic componentry, and other interpretive toeholds.

Even though games are often the most visible nodes in their networks, they are not always the best avenue for understanding a particular phenomenon. Consider *Tempest*'s unusual graphics, for instance. The game itself offers very little explanation about why it looks the way it does, why its design features geometric forms and substantial negative space instead of something more representational. The

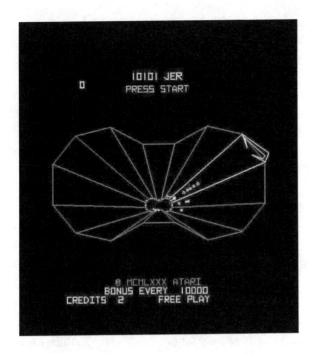

FIGURE 39.1
The colorful but abstract vector graphics playfield of *Tempest*.

game is meant to be looked at, not explained, or at least not explained in ways beyond those that directly assist with play. *Tempest*'s service manuals, by contrast, were developed specifically to explain how the game's technologies work, as well as how to troubleshoot those technologies should they break.[3] In other words, whereas the game's purpose is to be played, the service manuals' purpose is to enable, clarify, and empiricize that play.

The manuals do this work in numerous ways, from revealing marketplace assumptions to describing mechanical options. The *Tempest Operation, Maintenance and Service Manual*, for example, describes the game's enemies—something the game software itself does not—and explains the Skill-Step play system and its attendant point bonuses. Moreover, the manual describes how to alter the machine so that it can accept different international currencies, and reveals how to modify its settings to incentivize customer play. The end result is that the game's manuals provide a richer and more precise look into *Tempest*'s aesthetics and mechanics than does the game itself and thus are a more valuable node for understanding and analyzing the game's play options and other features than could be derived from actually playing the game. Put another way, the manuals are interconnected archival nodes that answer questions about *Tempest* that the game itself cannot.

Using the archival method as an approach to game study benefits scholars interested in understanding the complexity of how games create meaning. But the archival method's utility for game study extends beyond its set of analytical tools. It also defines a set of research and collection practices that involve the husbanding and sharing of resources for future use by oneself and others. To draw on and describe the materials and processes that constitute games as networked and nodal phenomena is also to bring them to light; it is to gift to other researchers otherwise lost, forgotten, or overlooked details that they can use in their own work. The archival method, by design, obliges its users to publicize their findings, thereby contributing to the archive itself. In this way, the archival method contributes to the general fund of game-related knowledge by adding new material and information.

This kind of intentional sharing is what differentiates archives—which tend to create, publicize, and preserve knowledge for the public good—from collections— which are often personal or maintained for enjoyment. Such collaborations result in the creation of knowledge *about* games as well as knowledge *of* games. This difference is mirrored in the archival method; in emphasizing the connections among objects, ideas, and practices, the archival method produces new knowledge, new opportunities for study, and new presentations of that knowledge to the world.

An email exchange between Atari engineer Jed Margolin and Ken McAllister is a good example.[4] Margolin has been credited in several sources with having originally developed *Tempest*'s mathbox microcode, the program that drives the game's vector graphics. In an email to McAllister, however, Margolin corrected that attribution, noting that Mike Albaugh, another Atari engineer, did that work. In fact, Margolin claims to have had nothing to do with *Tempest*, despite a number of corporately authorized assertions to the contrary. By noting Margolin's disavowal in this chapter and elsewhere,[5] we have entered it into the bank of public knowledge and consequently reshaped *Tempest*'s network. The game no longer has the same articulations it once did; a part of its authorship has changed, and therefore, so has its network of meanings and their implications. The archival method has transformed this object of study, and that object is now open for new intellectual excursions.

In game studies, such contributions are particularly important because the field's artifacts are often salvaged from the sale bin and the garbage dump. Unlike official documents, fine first editions, and other recognized collectibles, games and their ancillary materials are rarely expected to be preserved, not even by the people and companies who produce them. When researchers rely on the archival method, then, they automatically situate themselves within a preservational paradigm that not only contributes new scholarship to the archive but also newly discovered material objects that have been located in the course of study. An archival project that aims to study *Tempest*'s cabinet art, for example, might discover— and add to the archive—a promotional flyer found in an old issue of *Play Meter* magazine or a bill of lading from Atari's first warehouse.

A game's meaning is thus the compounding sum of everything from its code to the current events that shaped its design. Given the breadth of this analytical landscape, researchers who use the archival method cannot escape the knowledge that, for example, (a) all information about *Tempest* is always partial (and therefore so, too, are any conclusions drawn from such information) and (b) archives themselves are always incomplete and idiosyncratic. In practice, then, the archival method requires scholars to define their projects as crisply as possible because they know that even the sharpest project will conjoin an infinite number of other nodes that, although they are in the game's network of meanings, must be disregarded.

It is worth noting that a downstream research opportunity emerges as a result of attending to video games as interconnected artifacts, namely, the need for *meta-studies*. While not exclusive to the archival method, meta-studies—the study of how something is studied—are common in fields where scholars draw heavily on archival research. When scholars focus on, for instance, how their colleagues tend to analyze game narratives, they are doing meta-narrative studies. When they focus on how scholars analyze player behavior, they are doing meta-player studies. Such projects can be exceptionally revealing about the biases of research itself. To read two analyses of, say, *Tempest*'s visual aesthetic, could be instructive in terms of how two researchers think differently about the game's look and feel. But a meta-study of *Tempest*'s visual aesthetic would consider how *numerous* scholars had analyzed this aspect of the game, reporting on the analytical tendencies of the people who had studied it. Game meta-research thus reveals trends among analysts more than among developers, marketers, or players and, as a result, can open important new avenues of research.

One of the challenges of studying video games is selecting the appropriate analytical tools for the job. It bears noting that, connectional as it is, the archival method is unsuited for critically monovalent analyses such as those focused on, for instance, identifying the narratival logic of *Icarus Proudbottom & The Curse of the Chocolate Fountain* (Holy Wow Studios, 2010) or performing sales analyses for the Russian handheld Cybiko computer. The archival method can also prove unhelpful when the aim of an inquiry is primarily quantitative; the archival method is largely qualitative, interested in interpretations of how cultures unfold over time, how styles vary by region, how advertising comes to reflect social values, and so on. Quantitative data in the form of corporate records, industrial analytics, and manufacturing timetables (among others) may well be found in archives and be usefully studied for a range of analytical projects, but the archival method would mandate that such records and data be connected to other materials in the archival record: diaries, concept art, design histories, and other related ephemera. The archival method is thus more a hermeneutics than a data model and is most at home amid ambiguity.

The video game medium and the cultures that flow from and surround it are diverse, incorporating technologies, ideologies, and ways of doing from across history, geography, and intellectual traditions. As a result, even the most robust critical methods fall short in sounding the depths of a game's complexity. The archival method offers a good first step in recognizing and beginning to account for this complexity. It provides an opportunity to survey the artifactual landscape prior to developing specific analyses of it, such as the ones we gloss in our introduction. In so doing, the archival method enriches the analytical potential of researchers' projects and, perhaps more important, highlights the fact that games are a lively and confoundingly entangled component of the human condition.

NOTES

1 A prolonged production cycle—referred to as "development hell" in the industry—is no guarantee of quality, of course. *Aliens: Colonial Marines* (Gearbox Software, 2013) and *Duke Nukem Forever* (3D Realms/Triptych Games/Gearbox Software/Piranha Games, 2011) were each in development for more than 10 years and were widely panned on release.

2 Adam Rosenberg, "L.A. Noire Developer Team Bondi Officially Closing Down," *G4TV. com*, October 5, 2011, www.g4tv.com.

3 Atari, *Tempest Operation, Maintenance and Service Manual* (Sunnyvale, CA: Atari, 1981); Atari, *Wells-Gardner Color X-Y Monitor: Service Manual* (Sunnyvale, CA: Atari, 1981); and Atari, *Drawing Package Supplement to Tempest: Operation, Maintenance and Service Manual* (Sunnyvale, CA: Atari, 1981).

4 Jed Margolin, email message to Ken McAllister, August 11, 2012.

5 Judd Ethan Ruggill and Ken S. McAllister, *Tempest: Geometries of Play* (Ann Arbor: University of Michigan Press, 2015).

FURTHER READING

Gaillet, Lynee Lewis, Helen Diana Eidson, and Don Gammill Jr., eds. *Landmark Essays on Archival Research.* New York: Routledge, 2015.

Guins, Raiford. *Game After: A Cultural Study of Video Game Afterlife.* Cambridge, MA: MIT Press, 2014.

Newman, James. *Best Before: Videogames, Supersession and Obsolescence.* New York: Routledge, 2012.

Swalwell, Melanie. "Moving On from the Original Experience: Games History, Preservation and Presentation." In *Proceedings of DiGRA 2013: DeFragging Game Studies*, vol. 7 (Aug. 2014), Atlanta, GA. www.digra.com.

40

Walden, a game
Reflection

TRACY FULLERTON

Abstract: Games as an aesthetic form are typically understood as a medium of action, characterized by interactivity and stereotyped in the types of interactivity that they generally comprise. Here, game designer Tracy Fullerton speaks to the design of experimental games that are reflective in nature, taking on subject matter that requires emotional introspection and a sophisticated interplay between player and game to achieve their design goals.

To say that games are systems, in which players submit to a set of voluntary constraints, is both a description of their formal composition, and, perhaps inadvertently, an equally accurate description of their standard rhetorical boundaries. "Playing within the rules" might just as well refer to the adherence of designers to stereotyped situations and characters as it might refer to players remaining within the prescribed procedures and activities of the game. In the commercial games space as it exists today, we see this adherence to familiar boundaries in the narrowness of genres of play and within those genres to the style, tone, and overall experience design of games. Specifically, we find a predominance of games that focus on direct, violent conflict in fast-paced situations that allow for no room to question the meaning of such conflict but only to respond to it within the activities allowed by the mechanics. The tone of such experiences also suppresses critical interpretation of the activities of play, moving the player through the experience at a surface level of fight or flight emotions and disallowing deeper cognitive efforts through the sheer pace of play.

For more than a decade, however, I have been exploring ideas of play that stand in direct contradiction to this predominant format for games. Perhaps it is because I am naturally introverted, attentive to my own evolving internal thought process, and fascinated by the effects of the media I engage with on that unfolding personal narrative. But, after years of discussing and engaging with what I have elsewhere defined as "play-centric design" of game *systems*, I was led, naturally, I think, to consider the need for even greater emphasis on the experience of *players* in both the activities and inner life of their play—what we might call instead "player-centric design" of game *experiences*.[1] This exploration of the reflective possibilities of play led me to become interested in play that allows for, and even depends on, an internal and emotional process on the part of players and to the design of systems that were slower in pace than one might find in a majority of game systems.

This interest in slow-paced play is not because slowness itself is equivalent to meaningfulness but, rather, because the process of making meaning through reflection does take time at a human pace and takes cycles of response, interpretation, and unpacking of experience. So, it might be said that slowness is one of the affordances for reflective experiences. In projects that I have worked on such as *Walden, a game* (2017), or *The Night Journey* (Bill Viola and the Game Innovation Lab, 2007)—a game developed as a collaboration with media artist Bill Viola—I offer examples of this novel aesthetic approach to games: the idea that designing for slowness, or a human pace of thought, are critical to the development of digital games that afford reflection on the part of players.

This is not to say that there is not an internal process occurring in players of traditional game systems but, rather, that the design of these systems recognizes player "input" only so much as that input influenced the operation of the system. Players are considered as rats in the proverbial Skinner box, pushing at levers until they get the win, the reward, the prize, the pellet. As game designers, we "prove" the success of a great design when the rats are incentivized to keep pushing the lever, to keep going after the prize.[2] But the experience of the rat is only understood as measured by the delivery of that prize, not in terms of the interpretation, the emotions, the meaning of the push, the anticipation, the wait, or the wonder of the interaction.

In contrast, and as an example of what I mean by the idea of reflective or slow play, I offer my project *Walden, a game*, which is a translation of Henry David Thoreau's *Walden* into a playable experience. The game allows players to take on Thoreau's experiment in living in a first-person game simulation of that experiment. The game begins in the summer of 1845 in the woods of Walden Pond, where players must find a way to fulfill their "necessities of life" as Thoreau described them: food, fuel, shelter, and clothing. Caretaking these necessities takes time and energy, and players may find themselves grinding away at these basic needs and falling into a kind of mundane existence unless they also take time to seek out the beauties and inspirations of the woods—the sublime that Thoreau was looking for. Finding balance between these two—the mean and the sublime—was the goal of his experiment. And allowing players to explore their own sense of where this balance might lie, and to reflect on how the choices we make with regard to that balance affect the quality of our lives, is the goal of the game.

Thoreau's experiment might be said to be the original call for "slow living." To understand our basic needs and to live only to sustain them and then to spend the rest of our time not building greater houses or eating more elaborate meals but, rather, to seek inspiration in nature. We have seen the idea of "slowness" rise as a virtue in our modern life. Slow food, slow travel, slow cities—at the core of these movements is the belief that the very pace of our experiences with meals, with travel, with living, with the absorption of ideas through reading slowly can improve the effect of such experience on our lives, individually and collectively. When culinary activist and author Alice Waters speaks about slow food, I am always struck by the similarities in the way she discusses the values of sustainable eating and my own thoughts about play. "We eat the values that come along with our food," she says.[3] By this she means the values of the food's production, distribution, sale, preparation, and consumption and not just its own nutritional values, although these things all contribute to that, of course, and I could make the same distinction about play.

In 2007, I wrote an article with the Ludica Collective about our interest in the New Games Movement, in the concept of making and playing games that imbued values such as cooperation or generosity as opposed to pure competition and self-interest.[4] I was fascinated with the idea at the core of this movement that how we play signifies our way of being in the world. But even more than that, I think we might also go so far as to say how we make our play, in what social and commercial structures it is embedded, and, yes, how we engage with it, how we reflect on it and allow it to define us, more than signify that they are part of our existence in the world.

Stewart Brand, one of the primary thinkers at the heart of the New Games Movement, said, "[Y]ou can't change a game by winning it, losing it, or refereeing it, but rather by starting a new game."[5] A decade ago, when I was first thinking about how New Games might relate to our digital games, it felt then like we needed to heed this advice. And we have, to a certain extent, with the rise of the independent game community. However, I still feel that we're rushing to that new place, that we're not fully considering the means of production, distribution, and sale of making games as aspects of games that make up their "nutritional value." We still need to go someplace new today, to make our new, new games, slow games that are good for our bodies, our souls, and our society in the way that slow food endeavors to feed our bodies in ways that are good for us as individuals and for the world we live in.

FIGURE 40.1
"The forest has never so good a setting, nor is so distinctly beauti- ful, as when seen from the middle of a small lake."—Scene from *Walden, a game.*

When one starts out to design for reflective play, beginning with an experience goal that will afford players that opportunity is critical. For *Walden, a game*, the experience goal was to embody Thoreau's experiment in living, that is, to reduce life to its lowest terms and see if it is "mean" or "sublime." In designing a system to meet this experience goal, it was important to emphasize, as already described, the emotional experience of the player and not just the inputs and outputs of the system itself. And so, we needed equal emphasis on the game rules and activities balanced with the world development and simulation of nature.

If the challenge presented to the player was to engage in Thoreau's experiment in living simply while being tempted by both the beauties of the natural world as well as the luxuries and the responsibilities of society, these aspects of the game needed to hold equal weight in the design. Additionally, because the goal was not simply to present, de facto, Thoreau's solution to his quest but, rather, to allow players to reflect and come to their own understandings of these questions, the design needed to have a large enough possibility space for players to push against Thoreau's answers to find their own. And so, from the start, it was clear that the design needed to have these elements: (1) a rich, dynamic world in which to ex- plore the theme, (2) a system of activities that allowed for experimentation with and against the theme, and (3) a pace of play that allowed players to reflect on their activities and—if desired—change their approach to the game over time without strong penalties.

The design team used Thoreau's own writings to define the rich, dynamic world in which players can explore his ideas. Through a close reading of the text, we cre- ated an index of the plants, animals, and objects that made up Thoreau's descrip- tion of his world. And then, using this index as a guide, we developed a virtual Walden made up of those things, living and otherwise, that Thoreau felt most con- nected to. Our trees are those he writes about—the pitch and white pines, black birch, red maple, and more—and our plants and animals are the ones he had long relations with, such as the bean plants he painstakingly cared for or the hares and squirrels that busied themselves near his cabin. Our pond takes it shores directly from his survey, and the world we created has as its boundaries the Fitchburg Railroad to the west, the Concord Road to the East, and imagined property lines to the north and south that created a playable area of approximately 70 acres of woods.

Just as there are natural aspects of the world to investigate—the animals, trees, and plants of the woods—there are also societal aspects like the people and historical issues that surrounded Thoreau. So players can follow relationships with family, such as sister Sophia; friends, such as mentor Emerson; professional connections, such as editor Horace Greeley and naturalist Professor Louis Agassiz; or issues, such as the antislavery movement and the Underground Railroad.

This entire world is experienced over the course of eight "seasons" of play. The game begins in the early summer when the living is simple and food and fuel can be foraged easily from the woods, and shelter and clothes are not as critical in the warm New England weather. These basic needs, so easily fulfilled in the early days of the game, become more challenging as the fall, and then the winter, sets in.

To understand the importance of time and reflection to this system, it's important to dig a bit more deeply into the design of the system of activities that underlies it. This is, as described earlier, a simulation designed to allow for experimentation with and against the theme of the piece and, as such, a simulation that affords reflection on that theme.

Thoreau felt that at our core we had a kind of energy he called "the vital heat" that we needed to maintain to live. Food, fuel, shelter, and clothing help sustain that vital heat, but the very effort we put into maintaining these needs drains that energy as well. In the game, players maintain these basic needs by finding, growing, or buying resources to maintain them. If they let these needs fall by the wayside, their absence will cause a drain on their energy. On the other hand, Thoreau was not just interested in survival. He was also interested in seeking the sublime through activities like reading, listening to the sounds of the woods and civilization over the horizon, solitude, and interactions with his "neighbors" in the woods, the animals and some visitors whom he occasioned to meet.

Balancing these two sets of needs—the basic and the sublime—is the core of our gameplay, with time as both the energizer and oppressor at the heart of the experience. If we work too hard at our basic needs, we need to take time to rest and restore ourselves. On the other hand, time fades our brief moments of inspiration, so we need to keep attending to them as well. Achieving balance once is not a "win scenario" because time presses on, and we must stay mindful of that balance even as we pursue other interests. We might be lured to take jobs in town to make our lives easier, but the money we might use on necessities also attracts us to luxuries like bigger houses and fancy tools. And we may be attracted to activities beyond a simple life in the woods—pursuing a writing career, becoming an activist and helping slaves along the Underground Railroad, or working as a naturalist or surveyor. All these are ways that we can spend our time in the game, each with its own rewards and implications for achieving that elusive sense of balance that we seek.

And so, because of the scope of the first two affordances, the rich and dynamic game world and the system of activities within which to explore the theme, the final affordance necessary for the design of a reflective game is to provide a pace at which these two interrelated aspects can be properly explored. The relatively slow pace of *Walden, a game* allows for such exploration and reflection. Players seeking ideas about how Thoreau solved the questions he posed can find them throughout the woods in the form of "arrowheads," which are the relics, in this case, not of former inhabitants but of Thoreau himself.

Each arrowhead found is a thought or moment from *Walden* that fills our own player journal, building a procedural narrative of our own virtual experiment. This journal is offered for review at the end of every day cycle in the game so that players can reflect on the ideas they have found and the path they have taken through the experiment. One might think of the in-game journal as an opportunity for a kind of guided reflection offered throughout the gameplay.

The meaning that players may glean from playing a game lies between what they must do and what they can do, what they desire and what they discover. In *Walden, a game*, this dialectic fashions the potential for an emergent narrative to form from the collision of a player's own thoughts on their experience of the questions, insights, and reflections on the words we hear and read from Thoreau. This interplay allows players to find their own answers to Thoreau's questions, their own relationships to his themes.

We have recently passed the 200th anniversary of Thoreau's birth, and the questions that he raised seem ever more important to reexamine in a format that brings them to life for today's public: How much do we really need to live? Why and how do we work? What is the essence of progress? What can we learn of life by looking at the examples in nature? And, finally, how best shall we live, together and alone?

We live in a world that has sacrificed simplicity and self-reliance for interconnectivity and convenience. The speeding up of life that Thoreau identified as "railroad time" might now be just as well thought of as "internet time." It seems appropriate in such a time that both designers and players might desire a pace of play that embodies the antithesis of this lifestyle. *Walden, a game*, with its affordances for reflective play, offers such a chance for players, young and old, from all walks of life, to go to the woods, virtually; to live and play deliberately; to engage with Thoreau's questions about life, nature, and society; and to discover their own best answers to his enduring questions.

Looking beyond the design of *Walden, a game* over the past decade that I have worked on the game, I have seen other harbingers of the desire for slow, reflective play. There exists now a genre of game commonly called "walking simulators," exploratory games based on contemplation and environmental narrative. (*The Night Journey*, first released in 2007, was one of the original walking simulators.) There has also been a rebirth of interest in text-based games, largely because of the availability of Twine as a low-barrier entry tool for creating such games. And there have been critically acclaimed games, such as *Journey* (Thatgamecompany, 2012) and *What Remains of Edith Finch* (Giant Sparrow, 2017) that focus on delivering emotional gameplay over action. The appearance, and indeed success, of such games in the larger landscape of play, points to a significant shift in our expectations of the aesthetic form as a whole. It is my hope as a designer that games such as *Walden* will become part of an expanded territory for designers and players, one that includes a deeper emotional palette and opportunity for meaningful reflection.

NOTES

1 Tracy Fullerton, *Game Design Workshop: A Playcentric Approach to Creating Innovative Games*, 3rd ed. (Boca Raton: CRC Press/Taylor & Francis, 2014).

2 Nick Yee, *The Proteus Paradox: How Online Games and Virtual Worlds Change Us—and How They Don't* (New Haven, CT: Yale University Press, 2014).

3 Alice Waters, "Farming the Earth, Cultivating Humanity." Panel, Human / Ties: NEH@50, Charlottesville, VA, September 16, 2016.

4 Celia Pearce, T. Fullerton, J. Fron, and J. F. Morie. "Sustainable Play: Toward a New Games Movement for the Digital Age." *Games and Culture* 2, no. 3 (July 1, 2007): 261–278, doi:10.1177/1555412007304420.

5 New Games Foundation, and Andrew Fluegelman, eds., *The New Games Book* (Garden City, NY: Dolphin Books, 1976).

FURTHER READING

DeKoven, Bernie. *The Well-Played Game: A Player's Philosophy*. Cambridge, MA: MIT Press, 2013.

Flanagan, Mary. *Critical Play: Radical Game Design*. Cambridge, MA: MIT Press, 2009.

Suits, Bernard. *The Grasshopper: Games, Life, and Utopia*. Toronto: University of Toronto Press, 1978.

Thoreau, Henry David. *Walden, or, Life in the Woods*. New York: Knopf: Distributed by Random House, 1992.

Acknowledgments

Although we've edited anthologies before—both together and with other collaborators—we've never attempted anything quite this ambitious. Our appreciation that you are now reading this begins with our many contributors. Not only is their careful work on display throughout this collection, but they have each also demonstrated throughout the multiround editorial process, a steadfast commitment to improving their work for the book's intended readership: students. *How to Play Video Games* may feature 40 chapters on a variety of games and keywords, but they are all written by committed teacher-scholars. As editors, we found this collective desire and willingness to write for students to be one of the book's foremost strengths.

We also want to thank Eric Zinner, Alicia Nadkarni, Dolma Ombadykow, Martin Coleman, and the rest of the NYU Press team for their dedication to this project, as well as the constructive feedback provided by anonymous readers. Finally, we owe a debt of gratitude to Ethan Thompson and Jason Mittell, the co-editors of *How to Watch Television* (NYU Press, 2013), for their permission to iterate on their TV studies collection for game studies. Their collection provided the structural blueprint for our work. We thank them, too, for authoring this book's Foreword.

We want to thank Morgan Blue for her keen indexing work. The index was made possible, in part, by support from the Institute for Scholarship in the Liberal Arts, College of Arts and Letters, University of Notre Dame.

MATTHEW

I'm so incredibly grateful that Nina agreed to collaborate on yet another project with me. Her support—as a co-editor and as a friend—has been invaluable and incalculable. From the project's earliest beginnings as a "what-if" idea during a postconference conversation to the final stages of proofing years later, I'm consistently impressed by Nina's tireless work ethic and positive spirit. Thanks also to my colleagues in the Department of Film, Television, and Theatre at the University of Notre Dame for their encouragement on this project.

Finally, a special thanks to my partner, Joanna Jefferson, for her unending support on this as with all other academic things and to our kids, Sophie and

Jackson. Although our kids don't always help us with our work, they always teach us something about play.

NINA

Academia is often a single-player game, rewarding individual achievement over teamwork. And yet, for over a decade, Matthew has been a committed, encouraging, supportive, and enthusiastic co-player. Working alongside him has made me a stronger and sharper thinker, writer, and editor. I am deeply grateful for our long collaboration and friendship and am very proud of the projects we have created together, none more so than this one.

My participation in this collection was made possible by the love and support of my partner, Joshua Green. As always, he took such good and loving care of me and our family during the late nights, early mornings, and weekends that I devoted to this endeavor. Thank you.

Appendix
Video Games Discussed in this Volume

We have used the following format for the games in this list:

Game title. Designer. Publisher, Year. Platform.

The platform designations include *mobile* (for games originally released for two or more mobile phone/tablet operating systems, such as Apple iOS and Android), *multiplatform* (games originally released for two or more different platforms, e.g., Xbox and PlayStation), and *personal computer* (games originally released for two or more personal computer operating systems, e.g., macOS and Microsoft Windows).

20,000 Leagues Under the Sea: Captain Nemo. Mzone Studio. Anuman Interactive SA, 2009. Personal computer.

Advanced Dungeons & Dragons. Gary Gygax, Dave Arneson. TSR, Wizards of the Coast, 1977. Tabletop.

Age of Empires. Ensemble Studios. Microsoft, 1997. Personal computer.

Age of Empires II. Ensemble Studios. Microsoft, 1999. Personal computer.

Age of Empires III. Ensemble Studios. Microsoft Game Studios, 2005. Personal computer.

Alien: Isolation. Creative Assembly. Sega, 2014. Multiplatform.

Aliens: Colonial Marines. Gearbox Software. Sega, 2013. Multiplatform.

American Truck Simulator. SCS Software. SCS Software, 2016. Personal computer.

America's Army. United States Army. United States Army, 2002. Personal computer.

Angry Birds. Rovio Mobile. Chillingo, 2009. Apple iOS.

Angry Birds Go! Rovio Entertainment. Rovio Entertainment, 2013. Multiplatform.

Antarctic Adventure. Konami. Konami, 1983. MSX.

Atari Football. Atari, Inc. Atari, Inc., 1978. Coin-operated.

Baldur's Gate. BioWare. Interplay Entertainment, 1998. Personal computer.

Batman: The Telltale Series. Telltale Games. Telltale Games, 2016. Personal computer.

Battle Kid: Fortress of Peril. Sivak Games. Retrozone, 2010. Nintendo Entertainment System.

The Beast Within: A Gabriel Knight Mystery. Sierra On-Line. Sierra On-Line, 1995. Personal computer.

Beat Sneak Bandit. Simogo. Simogo, 2012. Apple iOS.

BioShock. 2K Boston. 2K Games, 2007. Multiplatform.

BioShock Infinite. Irrational Games. 2K Games, 2013. Multiplatform.

Borderlands. Gearbox Software. 2K Games, 2009. Multiplatform.

Borderlands 2. Gearbox Software. 2K Games, 2012. Multiplatform.

Borderlands: The Pre-Sequel. 2K Australia. 2K Games, 2014. Multiplatform.

Braid. Number None. Microsoft Game Studios, 2008. Multiplatform.

Breakout. Atari, Inc. Atari, Inc, 1976. Coin-operated.

Call of Duty: Advanced Warfare. Sledgehammer Games. Activision, 2014. Multiplatform.

Call of Duty: Black Ops III. Treyarch. Activision, 2015. Multiplatform.

Candy Crush Saga. King. King, 2012. Mobile.

Castle Cats. PocApp Studios AB. PocApp Studios AB, 2017. Mobile.

Castlevania. Konami. Konami, 1986. Nintendo Entertainment System.

Cave Story. Studio Pixel. Studio Pixel, 2004. Multiplatform.

Championship Soccer. Atari, Inc. Atari, Inc., 1980. Atari VCS/2600.

Civilization: Call to Power. Activision. Activision, 1999. Personal computer.

Clash of Clans. Supercell. Supercell, 2012. Apple iOS.

Clash Royale. Supercell. Supercell, 2016. Mobile.

Command & Conquer. Westwood Studios. Virgin Interactive, 1995. Multiplatform.

Cookie Clicker. Julien Thiennot. Julien Thiennot. 2013. Personal computer.

Counter-Strike. Valve Corporation. Valve Corporation, 2000. Microsoft Windows.

Counter-Strike: Global Offensive. Hidden Path Entertainment. Valve Corporation, 2012. Multiplatform.

Cow Clicker. Ian Bogost. Ian Bogost, 2010. Personal computer.

Crossy Road. Hipster Whale. Hipster Whale, 2014. Mobile.

Custer's Revenge. Mystique. Mystique, 1982. Atari VCS/2600.

Death Race. Exidy. Exidy, 1976. Coin-operated.

Defense of the Ancients 2. Valve Corporation. Valve Corporation, 2013. Personal computer.

Diner Dash. Gamelab. PlayFirst, 2004. Personal computer.

Disney Infinity. Avalanche Software. Disney Interactive Studios, 2013. Multiplatform.

Disney Infinity: Marvel Super Heroes (2.0 Edition). Avalanche Software. Disney Interactive Studios, 2014. Multiplatform.

Donkey Kong. Nintendo R&D1. Nintendo, 1981. Coin-operated.

Donkey Kong (Game & Watch). Nintendo. Nintendo, 1982. Handheld.

Don't Starve. Klei Entertainment. 505 Games, 2013. Personal computer.

DOOM. id Software. GT Interactive, 1993. MS-DOS.

Dragon's Lair. Rick Dyer and Don Bluth. Cinematronics, 1983. Laserdisc.

DuckTales. Capcom. Capcom, 1989. Nintendo Entertainment System.

Duke Nukem Forever. 3D Realms, Triptych Games, Gearbox Software, Piranha Games. 2K Games, 2011. Multiplatform.

Dungeons & Dragons. Gary Gygax, Dave Arneson. TSR, Wizards of the Coast, 1974. Tabletop.

Dys4ia. Anna Anthropy. Newgrounds, 2012. Personal computer.

The Elder Scrolls V: Skyrim. Bethesda Game Studios. Bethesda Softworks, 2011. Multiplatform.

Empire. Walter Bright. Walter Bright, 1977. Personal computer.

EVE Online. CCP Games. Simon & Schuster, 2003. Personal computer.

EverQuest. Sony Online Entertainment. Sony Online Entertainment, 1999. Personal computer.

Fable. Lionhead Studios Microsoft Studios, 2004. Xbox.

Fallout. Black Isle Studios. Interplay Entertainment, 1997. Personal computer.

Fallout 4. Bethesda Game Studios. Bethesda Softworks, 2015. Multiplatform.

Fallout Shelter. Bethesda Game Studios. Bethesda Softworks, 2015. Multiplatform.

Farming Simulator 2016. Giants Software. Focus Home Interactive, 2016. Multiplatform.

FarmVille. Zynga. Zynga, 2009. Mobile.

FEZ. Polytron Corporation. Trapdoor, 2012. Xbox 360.

FIFA. Extended Play Productions. EA Sports, 1993. Multiplatform.

FIFA 16. EA Canada. EA Sports, 2015. Multiplatform.

Flappy Bird. dotGears. dotGears, 2013. Mobile.

Fortnite. Epic Games. Epic Games, 2017. Multiplatform.

Game Dev Story. Kairsoft. Kairsoft, 1997. Mobile.

Game Dev Tycoon. Greenheart Games. Greenheart Games, 2012. Mobile; Personal computer.

Game of Thrones. Telltale Games. Telltale Games, 2014. Multiplatform.

Gears of War. Epic Games. Microsoft Studios, 2006. Xbox 360.

Goat Simulator. Coffee Stain Studios. Coffee Stain Studios, 2014. Personal computer.

Gradius. Konami. Konami, 1986. Nintendo Entertainment System.

Grand Theft Auto IV. Rockstar North. Rockstar Games, 2008. Multiplatform.

Grand Theft Auto V. Rockstar North. Rockstar Games, 2013. Xbox 360; Xbox One.

Grand Theft Auto: San Andreas. Rockstar North. Rockstar Games, 2004. PlayStation 2.

Guitar Hero. Harmonix. RedOctane, 2005. PlayStation 2.

Halo. Bungie. Microsoft Studios, 2001. Xbox.

Hockey. Magnavox. Magnavox, 1972. Odyssey.

Icarus Proudbottom & The Curse of the Chocolate Fountain. Holy Wow Studios. Holy Wow Studios, 2010. Personal computer.

Ice Core Quest (a *Neverwinter Nights* modification). Carleton University (Ottawa, Ontario). NP, ND. Personal computer.

Ingress. Niantic. Niantic, 2013. Android.

Jagged Alliance 2. Sir-Tech Canada. TalonSoft, 1999. Personal computer.

Jet Set Willy. Software Projects. Software Projects, 1984. ZX Spectrum.

Journey. Thatgamecompany. Sony Computer Entertainment, 2012. PlayStation 3.

Killbox. Joseph DeLappe and Biome Collective. Joseph DeLappe and Biome Collective, 2016. Personal computer.

Kim Kardashian: Hollywood. Glu Mobile. Glu Mobile, 2014. Mobile.

King's Quest. Sierra On-Line. Sierra On-Line, 1984. Personal computer.

King's Quest: Mask of Eternity. Sierra On-Line. Sierra On-Line, 1998. Personal computer.

King's Quest: Quest for the Crown. Sierra On-Line. IBM, Sierra On-Line, 1987. Personal computer.

King's Quest Chapter 1: A Knight to Remember. The Odd Gentlemen. Activision, 2015. Multiplatform.

King's Quest Chapter 2: Rubble Without a Cause. The Odd Gentlemen. Activision, 2015. Multiplatform.

King's Quest VI: Heir Today, Gone Tomorrow. Sierra On-Line. Sierra On-Line, 1992. Personal computer.

L.A. Noire. Team Bondi. Rockstar Games, 2011. Multiplatform.

The Last of Us. Naughty Dog. Sony Computer Entertainment, 2013. PlayStation 3.

The Last of Us Remastered. Naughty Dog. Sony Computer Entertainment, 2014. PlayStation 4.

League of Legends. Riot Games. Riot Games, 2009. Personal computer.

Leather Goddesses of Phobos. Infocom. Infocom, 1986. Personal computer.

The Legend of Zelda. Nintendo R&D4. Nintendo, 1986. Nintendo Entertainment System.

The Legend of Zelda: Ocarina of Time. Nintendo EAD. Nintendo, 1998. Nintendo 64.

The Legend of Zelda: Twilight Princess. Nintendo EAD. Nintendo, 2006. Nintendo GameCube.

LEGO Batman: The Videogame. Traveller's Tales. Warner Bros. Interactive Entertainment, 2008. Multiplatform.

LEGO Dimensions. Traveller's Tales. Warner Bros. Interactive Entertainment, 2015. Multiplatform.

LEGO Harry Potter: Years 1–4. Traveller's Tales. Warner Bros. Interactive Entertainment, 2010. Multiplatform.

LEGO Indiana Jones: The Original Adventures. Traveller's Tales. Warner Bros. Interactive Entertainment, 2008. Multiplatform.

LEGO Jurassic World. TT Fusion. Warner Bros. Interactive Entertainment, 2015. Multiplatform.

LEGO Marvel Super Heroes. Traveller's Tales. Warner Bros. Interactive Entertainment, 2013. Multiplatform.

The LEGO Ninjago Movie Video Game. TT Fusion. Warner Bros. Interactive Entertainment, 2017. Multiplatform

LEGO Star Wars: The Video Game. Traveller's Tales. Eidos Interactive, 2005. Multiplatform.

LEGO The Incredibles. TT Fusion. Warner Bros. Interactive Entertainment, 2018. Multiplatform.

LEGO Universe. NetDevil. The LEGO Group, 2010. Personal computer.

Leisure Suit Larry in the Land of the Lounge Lizards. Sierra On-Line. Sierra On-Line, 1987. Personal computer.

Leisure Suit Larry: Box Office Bust. Team17. Funsta, 2009. Multiplatform.

Leisure Suit Larry: Magna Cum Laude. High Voltage Software. Vivendi Universal Games, 2004. Multiplatform.

Leisure Suit Larry 5: Passionate Patti Does a Little Undercover Work. Sierra On-Line. Sierra On-Line, 1991. Personal computer.

Leisure Suit Larry 6: Shape Up or Slip Out! Sierra On-Line. Sierra On-Line, 1993. Personal computer.

Limbo. Playdead. Microsoft Game Studios, 2010. Xbox 360.

LittleBigPlanet. Media Molecule. Sony Computer Entertainment, 2008. PlayStation 3.

Madden NFL 16. EA Tiburon. EA Sports, 2015. Multiplatform.

Mafia III. Hangar 13. 2K Games, 2016. Multiplatform.

Manic Miner. Matthew Smith. Bug-Byte, 1983. ZX Spectrum.

Mario Adventure. See *The Legend of Zelda*.

Mario Kart 8. Nintendo EAD. Nintendo, 2014. Nintendo Wii U.

Marvel Avengers Academy. TinyCo. TinyCo, 2016. Mobile.

Mass Effect. BioWare. Microsoft Game Studios, 2007. Xbox 360.

Max Payne. Remedy Entertainment. Gathering of Developers, 2001. Microsoft Windows.

Medal of Honor. Danger Close Games and EA DICE. Electronic Arts, 2010. Multiplatform.

Mega Man. Capcom. Capcom, 1987. Nintendo Entertainment System.

Metal Gear. Konami. Konami, 1987. MSX2.

Metal Gear Solid. Konami. Konami, 1998. PlayStation.

Middle-earth: Shadow of Mordor. Monolith Productions. Warner Bros. Interactive Entertainment, 2014. Multiplatform.

Minecraft. Mojang. Mojang, 2011. Personal computer.

Missile Command. Atari, Inc. Atari, Inc., 1980. Coin-operated.

Mortal Kombat. Midway Games. Midway Games, 1992. Coin-operated.

Mortal Kombat (reboot). NetherRealm Studios. Warner Bros. Interactive Entertainment, 2011. Multiplatform.

Mortal Kombat X. NetherRealm Studios. Warner Bros. Interactive Entertainment, 2015. Multiplatform.

NBA 2K16. Visual Concepts. 2K Sports, 2015. Multiplatform.

Neverwinter Nights. BioWare. Infogrames, 2002. Personal computer.

The Night Journey. Bill Viola and the Game Innovation Lab. USC Games, 2007. Multiplatform.

Night Trap. Digital Pictures. Sega, 1992. Sega CD.

Nintendogs. Nintendo EAD. Nintendo, 2005. Nintendo DS.

Out Run. Sega AM2. Sega, 1986. Coin-operated.

Pac-Man. Namco. Midway, 1980. Coin-operated.

Papers, Please. 3909 LLC. 3909 LLC, 2013. Personal computer.

PaRappa the Rapper. NanaOn-Sha. Sony Computer Entertainment, 1996. PlayStation.

Pelé's Soccer. Atari, Inc. Atari, Inc., 1980. Atari VCS/2600.

Penguin Adventure. Konami. Konami, 1986. MSX.

Pikmin. Nintendo EAD. Nintendo, 2001. Nintendo GameCube.

Planescape. David "Zeb" Cook. TSR, Inc. and Wizards of the Coast, 1994. Tabletop.

Planescape: Torment. Black Isle Studios. Interplay Entertainment, 1999. Personal computer.

PlayerUnknown's Battlegrounds. PUBG Corporation. PUBG Corporation, 2017. Microsoft Windows.

Pokémon Go. Niantic. Niantic, 2016. Mobile.

PONG. Atari, Inc. Atari, Inc., 1972. Coin-operated.

Portal 2. Valve Corporation. Valve Corporation, 2011. Multiplatform.

Pro Evolution Soccer. Konami. Konami, 2001. PlayStation.

Progress Quest. Eric Fredricksen. NP, 2002. Personal computer.

Quake. id Software. GT Interactive, 1996. Personal computer.

Racing Destruction Set. Rick Koenig. Ariolasoft, 1985. Commodore 64.

Radar Scope. Nintendo R&D1. Nintendo, 1979. Coin-operated.

Rage. id Software. Bethesda Softworks, 2010. Multiplatform.

Railroad Tycoon. MicroProse. MicroProse, 1990. Personal computer.

Red Dead Redemption. Rockstar San Diego. Rockstar Games, 2010. Multiplatform.

Resident Evil. Capcom. Capcom, 1996. Multiplatform.

Rhythm Heaven. Nintendo SPD. Nintendo, 2008. Nintendo DS.

Rise of the Tomb Raider. Crystal Dynamics. Square Enix, 2015. Multiplatform.

Rock Band. Harmonix. MTV Games, 2007. Multiplatform.

Rogue. Michael Toy, Glen Wichman, and Ken Arnold. Epyx, 1980. Personal computer.

Roller Coaster Tycoon. Chris Sawyer Productions. Hasbro Interactive, 1999. Personal computer.

Samurai Shodown 64. SNK. SNK, 1997. Coin-operated.

The Secret of Monkey Island. Lucasfilm Games. Lucasfilm Games, 1990. Personal computer.

Sewer Shark. Digital Pictures. Sony Imagesoft, 1992. Sega CD.

Shovel Knight. Yacht Club Games. Yacht Club Games, 2014. Multiplatform.

Sid Meier's Civilization. MPS Labs. Microprose, 1991. Personal computer.

Sid Meier's Civilization: Beyond Earth. Firaxis Games. 2K Games, 2014. Personal computer.

Sid Meier's Civilization II. Microprose. Microprose, 1996. Personal computer.

Sid Meier's Civilization III. Firaxis Games. Infogrames, 2001. Personal computer.

Sid Meier's Civilization IV. Firaxis Games. 2K Games, 2005. Personal computer.

Sid Meier's Civilization V. Firaxis Games. 2K Games, 2010. Personal computer.

Sid Meier's Civilization VI. Firaxis Games. 2K Games, 2016. Personal computer.

Sid Meier's Colonization. MicroProse. MicroProse, 1994. Personal computer.

Silent Hill. Konami. Konami, 1999. PlayStation.

SimCity. Maxis. Maxis, 1989. Personal computer.

The Sims. Maxis. Electronic Arts, 2000. Personal computer.

Skylanders: Spyro's Adventure. Toys For Bob. Activision, 2011. Multiplatform.

Sniper Elite III. Rebellion Developments. 505 Games, 2014. Multiplatform.

Sniper Elite 4. Rebellion Developments. Sold Out, 2017. Multiplatform.

Sniper Elite V2. Rebellion Developments. 505 Games, 2012. Multiplatform.

Softporn Adventure. Blue Sky Software. On-Line Systems, 1981. Personal computer.

Sonic the Hedgehog. Sonic Team. Sega, 1991. Sega Genesis.

Space Invaders. Taito. Midway, 1978. Coin-operated.

Spore. Maxis. Electronic Arts, 2008. Personal computer.

Stair Dismount. Jetro Lauha. tAAt, 2002. Personal computer.

Star Wars Battlefront. EA DICE. Electronic Arts, 2015. Multiplatform.

Star Wars: Knights of the Old Republic II: The Sith Lords. Obsidian Entertainment. LucasArts, 2004. Multiplatform.

Stardom: The A-List. Blammo Games. Glu Mobile, 2011. Mobile.

Super Breakout. Atari, Inc. Atari, Inc., 1978. Atari VCS/2600.

Super Mario Bros. Nintendo R&D4. Nintendo, 1985. Nintendo Entertainment System.

Super Mario Bros. 3. Nintendo R&D4. Nintendo, 1988. Nintendo Entertainment System.

Super Mario Maker. Nintendo EAD. Nintendo, 2015. Nintendo Wii U.

Super Meat Boy. Team Meat. Team Meat, 2010. Multiplatform.

Super Smash Bros. HAL Laboratory. Nintendo, 1999. Nintendo 64.

Tales from the Borderlands. Telltale Games. Telltale Games, 2014. Multiplatform.

Tank. Kee Games. Kee Games, 1974. Coin-operated.

Team Fortress. Valve. Valve Corporation, 1999. Personal computer.

Tempest. Atari, Inc. Atari, Inc., 1981. Coin-operated.

Tennis. Magnavox. Magnavox, 1972. Odyssey.

Tennis for Two. William Higinbotham. Brookhaven National Laboratory, 1958. Donner Model 30.

Tetris. Alexey Pajitnov. Soviet Academy of Sciences at Computer Center in Moscow, 1984. Electronika 60 (mainframe computer).

There is No Pause Button! Scott Cawthon. Scott Cawthon, 2014. Mobile.

Time Crisis. Namco. Namco, 1995. Coin-operated.

Tomb Raider. Core Design. Eidos Interactive, 1996. Multiplatform.

Tomb Raider (reboot). Crystal Dynamics. Square Enix, 2013. Multiplatform.

Tomb Raider: The Last Revelation. Core Design. Eidos Interactive, 1999. Multiplatform.

Tomb Raider: Underworld. Crystal Dynamics. Eidos Interactive, 2008. Multiplatform.

Ultima IV: Quest of the Avatar. Origin Systems. Origin Systems, 1985. Personal computer.

Uncharted: Drake's Fortune. Naughty Dog. Sony Computer Entertainment, 2007. PlayStation 3.

Undertale. Toby Fox. Toby Fox, 2015. Personal computer.

VVVVVV. Terry Cavanaugh. Nicalis, 2010. Personal computer.

Walden, a game. USC Game Innovation Lab. USC Games, 2017. Personal computer.

Watch Dogs. Ubisoft Montreal. Ubisoft, 2014. Multiplatform.

Watch Dogs 2. Ubisoft Montreal. Ubisoft, 2016. Multiplatform.

What Remains of Edith Finch. Giant Sparrow. Annapurna Interactive, 2017. Multiplatform.

The Wolf Among Us. Telltale Games. Telltale Games, 2013. Multiplatform.

Wolfenstein 3D. id Software. Apogee Software, 1992. Personal computer.

World Game (or *World Peace Game*). Buckminster Fuller. NP, 1961. World Game Institute, 1972; OS Earth, 2001. Personal computer.

World of Warcraft. Blizzard Entertainment. Blizzard Entertainment, 2004. Personal computer.

Zelda II: The Adventure of Link. Nintendo R&D4. Nintendo, 1987. Nintendo Entertainment System.

Zork Nemesis: The Forbidden Lands. Zombie Studios. Activision, 1996. Personal computer.

Contributors

Jessica Aldred is an independent scholar, writer, and media producer. Her work on cinema and digital games has been published in *Animation, An Interdisciplinary Journal*; *Games and Culture*; *The Oxford Handbook for Sound and Image in Digital Media*; and *The Globe and Mail*. Jessica is the co-editor (with Felan Parker) of *Beyond the Sea: Navigating Bioshock*.

Jeremy Barnes received his BA in English in 2015 from Dickinson College, where he also completed a thesis on the morality of violence in military shooter video games. He is especially interested in the relationship between video game narrative and gameplay and is concerned about his own relationship with *DJ Hero*.

Kelly Bergstrom is an assistant professor of communication at University of Hawai'i at Mānoa. Her research examines drop-out and disengagement from digital cultures, with a focus on digital games. She is co-editor of *Internet Spaceships are Serious Business: An EVE Online Reader*. Previously she was a postdoctoral fellow at York University's Institute for Research on Digital Learning and a MITACS postdoctoral researcher at Big Viking Games.

Ian Bogost is the Ivan Allen College Distinguished Chair in media studies and a professor of interactive computing at the Georgia Institute of Technology, a contributing editor at *The Atlantic*, and a founding partner at Persuasive Games. His latest book is *Play Anything*.

Shira Chess is an assistant professor of entertainment and media studies at the University of Georgia. Her work on women and video games has been published in several journals and most recently in her book *Ready Player Two: Women Gamers and Designed Identity*.

Mia Consalvo is a professor of communication studies and Canada Research Chair in Game Studies and Design at Concordia University. She has most recently published the book *Atari to Zelda: Japan's Videogames in Global Context*, about Japan's influence on the video game industry and game culture. She is also the co-author of *Players and their Pets*, co-editor of *Sports Videogames*, and author of *Cheating: Gaining Advantage in Videogames*.

Steven Conway is course director of the games and interactivity degrees at Swinburne University of Technology. His research interests focus on the philosophy and aesthetics of play, games, and sport. Steven has published broadly on these topics in journals such as *Sport, Ethics and Philosophy*, the *Journal of Gaming & Virtual Worlds*, and *Eludamos*. Steven is also co-author of the first book on policy and digital games, *Video Game Policy: Production, Distribution and Consumption*.

Sebastian Deterding is a designer and researcher working on playful, gameful, and motivational design for human flourishing. He is a reader at the Digital Creativity Labs at the University of York in the UK, and founder of the design agency coding conduct. He is the organizer of the Gamification Research Network, and co-editor of *The Gameful World*, a book about the ludification of culture. He lives online at http://codingconduct.cc.

Jennifer deWinter is an associate professor of rhetoric and director of the Interactive Media and Game Development program at Worcester Polytechnic Institute. She has written about Japanese computer games, game policy, and games and technical communication. She is the co-editor of the Influential Game Designer series for which she wrote *Shigeru Miyamoto*.

Michael Fleisch is a managing member of Dpict, a member of The Value Web, a designer, a filmmaker, and a writer. He provides graphic facilitation and collaboration design services to clients all over the world, including the World Economic Forum and the Global Environment Facility, and has increasingly focused on supporting a movement to safeguard the Global Commons. In 2010, he founded Chase Public in Cincinnati, Ohio. He has co-authored several papers on video games and remains a cultural contributor to Hilobrow.com. Mike is a graduate of the University of Notre Dame and wishes his wife and three sons could travel with him.

Tracy Fullerton is a game designer and professor at the University of Southern California School of Cinematic Arts where she directs the Game Innovation Lab, a research center for games and play. She is also the author of *Game Design Workshop: A Playcentric Approach to Creating Innovative Games*.

Harrison Gish is a doctoral candidate in UCLA's Cinema and Media Studies program. His work appears in *eLudamos*, *Mediascape*, the *Encyclopedia of Video Games*, and *CineAction*. He is a member of the Society for Cinema and Media Studies Video

Game Studies Scholarly Interest Group, of which he was the co-chair from 2014 to 2017.

Dan Golding is a lecturer in media and communications at Swinburne University and an award-winning writer with more than 200 journalistic publications. He co-wrote *Game Changers*, made the soundtrack to *Push Me Pull You*, and from 2014 to 2017 was director of the Freeplay Independent Games Festival, Australia's oldest independent games event.

Christopher Hanson is an associate professor in the English Department at Syracuse University, where he teaches courses in game studies, digital media, television, and film. His book *Game Time: Understanding Temporality in Video Games* was published in 2018, and he is currently working on a book about video game designer Roberta Williams. His work has appeared in the *Quarterly Review of Film and Video*, *Film Quarterly*, *The Routledge Companion to Video Game Studies*, and *LEGO Studies: Examining the Building Blocks of a Transmedial Phenomenon*.

Nina B. Huntemann is the senior director of academics and research at edX. Prior to joining edX, Nina was an associate professor of media studies at Suffolk University. She is the co-editor of the anthologies *Joystick Soldiers: The Politics of Play in Military Video Games* and *Gaming Globally: Production, Play and Place*.

Katherine Isbister is a full professor in the University of California, Santa Cruz's Department of Computational Media, where she is the director of the Center for Games and Playable Media. Her research focuses on designing games and other interactive experiences that heighten social and emotional connections, toward innovating design theory and technological practice. Isbister's most recent book is *How Games Move Us: Emotion by Design*. Her research has been covered in *Wired*, *Scientific American*, and many other venues. She was a recipient of MIT Technology Review's Young Innovator Award, as well as a Humboldt Foundation Experienced Researcher fellowship.

Derek Johnson is an associate professor of media and cultural studies at the University of Wisconsin–Madison. He is the author of *Media Franchising: Creative License and Collaboration in the Culture Industries*, the editor of *From Networks to Netflix: A Guide to Changing Channels*, and the co-editor of *A Companion to Media Authorship* and *Making Media Work: Cultures of Management in the Entertainment Industries*.

Jesper Juul has been working with video game research since the late 1990s. He is an associate professor at the Royal Danish Academy of Fine Arts—School of Design.

His publications include *Half-Real, A Casual Revolution,* and *The Art of Failure.* He is also a co-editor of the Playful Thinking Series. He maintains the blog *The Ludologist* on "video games and other important things" at www.jesperjuul.net.

Carly A. Kocurek is an associate professor of digital humanities and media studies at the Illinois Institute of Technology. She is the author of two books, *Coin-Operated Americans: Rebooting Boyhood at the Video Game Arcade* and *Brenda Laurel: Pioneering Games for Girls.*

Peter Krapp is a professor of Film & Media Studies at the University of California, Irvine, where he is also a member of the Department of Informatics and helped found a Computer Game Science degree. He is the author of *Deja Vu: Aberrations of Cultural Memory* and of *Noise Channels: Glitch and Error in Digital Culture,* as well as an editor of the *Handbook Language-Culture-Communication* and *Medium Cool.*

Henry Lowood is the curator for the History of Science & Technology and the Film & Media Collections at Stanford University. He is the co-editor (with Raiford Guins) of the book series *Game Histories* and of a collection of essays in the series, *Debugging Game History: A Critical Lexicon.*

Ken S. McAllister is a professor of Public and Applied Humanities and associate dean of research and program innovation for the College of Humanities at the University of Arizona. A co-founder and co-director of the Learning Games Initiative, McAllister is the author or co-author of numerous books and articles on topics ranging from game preservation to critical technology studies.

Tanner Mirrlees is an associate professor in the Communication and Digital Media Studies Program at the University of Ontario Institute of Technology. He is author of *Hearts and Mines: The US Empire's Culture Industry* and *Global Entertainment Media: Between Cultural Imperialism and Cultural Globalization,* and is co-editor of *The Television Reader.*

Jason Mittell is a professor of Film & Media Culture and American Studies at Middlebury College. He is the author of *Genre & Television: From Cop Shows to Cartoons in American Culture, Television & American Culture,* and *Complex TV: The Poetics of Contemporary Television Storytelling,* and co-editor of *How to Watch Television.*

Souvik Mukherjee is assistant professor of English at Presidency University, Kolkata, India. He is the author of *Videogames and Storytelling: Reading Games and Playing Books* and *Videogames and Postcolonialism: Empire Plays Back.*

Soraya Murray is an interdisciplinary visual studies scholar, with particular interest in cultural studies, art, film, and video games. Murray is an associate professor in the Film + Digital Media Department at the University of California, Santa Cruz, and author of *On Video Games: The Visual Politics of Race, Gender and Space.*

James Newman is a professor of digital media at Bath Spa University. He is the author of numerous books on videogames and gaming cultures including *Videogames, Playing with Videogames, Best Before: Videogames, Supersession and Obsolescence, 100 Videogames,* and *Teaching Videogames.* James is a co-founder of the UK's National Videogame Archive, which is a partnership with the Science Museum, and a curator at The National Videogame Arcade.

Michael Z. Newman is professor and chair of the Department of Journalism, Advertising, and Media Studies at the University of Wisconsin–Milwaukee. He is the author of *Indie: An American Film Culture, Video Revolutions: On the History of a Medium,* and *Atari Age: The Emergence of Video Games in America.* With Elana Levine, he is the co-author of *Legitimating Television: Media Convergence and Cultural Status.*

Randy Nichols is an assistant professor in the School of Interdisciplinary Arts and Sciences at the University of Washington Tacoma. He is the author of *The Video Game Business,* co-author of *Inside the Video Game Business* and has written numerous chapters and articles on the political economy of the video game industry.

Rolf F. Nohr is a professor of media aesthetics and media culture at the University of Arts, Braunschweig. He is author of *Die Natürlichkeit des Spielens* (*The Naturalness of Play*), *Nützliche Bilder: Bild, Diskurs, Evidenz* (*Useful Images: Picture, Discourse, Evidence*) and *Die Auftritte des Krieges sinnlich machen* (*Making the Appearances of the War Sensual*). He is also a co-editor of the anthologies *The Cake is a Lie! Polyperspektivische Betrachtungen des Computerspiels am Beispiel von ›Portal‹* (*The Cake is a Lie! Polyperspectival Considerations of Computer Games Using Portal as an Example*), and *Strategie Spielen* (*Playing Strategy*).

Casey O'Donnell is an associate professor in the Department of Media and Information at Michigan State University. His research examines the creative collaborative work of video game design and development. His first book, *Developer's Dilemma,* was published in 2014. His work has been funded by the National Science Foundation and the National Institutes of Health.

David O'Grady is a doctoral candidate in the Cinema and Media Studies program at the University of California, Los Angeles. He has written about visual media for the *Encyclopedia of Video Games: The Culture, Technology, and Art of Gaming, The Game Culture Reader*, and the *New Review of Film and Television Studies*. He is also a researcher at the UCLA Game Lab and an instructor at California State University, Long Beach.

Matthew Thomas Payne is an associate professor in the Department of Film, Television, & Theatre at the University of Notre Dame. He is author of *Playing War: Military Video Games after 9/11* and is a co-editor of the anthologies *Flow TV: Television in the Age of Media Convergence* and *Joystick Soldiers: The Politics of Play in Military Video Games*.

Amanda Phillips is an assistant professor of English at Georgetown University. She writes about race, queerness, and social justice in video games and the digital humanities. You can find her work in *Games and Culture, Digital Creativity*, and *Debates in the Digital Humanities*.

Bonnie Ruberg is an assistant professor of digital media and games in the Department of Informatics at the University of California, Irvine. They are the author of *Video Games Have Always Been Queer*, the co-editor of *Queer Game Studies*, and co-lead organizer of the annual Queerness and Games Conference.

Judd Ethan Ruggill is an associate professor and head of the Department of Public and Applied Humanities at the University of Arizona. He is also co-founder and co-director of the Learning Games Initiative. He researches video game technologies, play, and cultures and has published a variety of books and articles on these subjects.

TreaAndrea M. Russworm is an associate professor of English at the University of Massachusetts, Amherst, where she teaches classes on video games, digital cultural studies, and African American popular culture. She is a co-editor of *Gaming Representation: Race, Gender, and Sexuality in Video Games*, the author of *Blackness is Burning: Civil Rights Popular Culture, and the Problem of Recognition*, and co-editor of *From Madea to Media Mogul: Theorizing Tyler Perry*.

Anastasia Salter is an associate professor of Games and Interactive Media at the University of Central Florida. She is the author of *What is Your Quest? From Adventure Games to Interactive Books* and *Jane Jensen: Gabriel Knight, Adventure Games, Hidden Objects*, and co-author of *Toxic Geek Masculinity in Media* and *Flash: Building the Interactive Web*.

Adrienne Shaw is an associate professor in the Department of Media Studies and Production at Temple University. She is the author of *Gaming at the Edge: Sexuality and Gender at the Margins of Gamer Culture* and the co-editor of the anthologies *Queer Game Studies, Queer Technologies* and *Interventions: Communication Research and Practice.*

Miguel Sicart is an associate professor at the IT University of Copenhagen. He is the author of *The Ethics of Computer Games, Beyond Choices: The Design of Ethical Gameplay* and *Play Matters.*

Gregory Steirer is an assistant professor of English at Dickinson College. His work on media industries, digital culture, and aesthetics has appeared in a variety of journals and anthologies, including *Television & New Media, The Journal of Graphic Novels & Comics, Convergence,* and *Postmodern Culture.* His book on the American comic book industry and Hollywood, co-authored with Alisa Perren, will be published by BFI/Bloomsbury in 2019.

Ethan Thompson is professor of Media Arts at Texas A&M University–Corpus Christi. He is the director of the documentary *TV Family,* author of *Parody and Taste in Postwar American Television Culture,* and co-editor of books including *How to Watch Television* and *Satire TV: Politics and Comedy in the Post-Network Era.*

Evan Torner is an assistant professor of German Studies and Film & Media Studies at the University of Cincinnati. He co-edited *Immersive Gameplay,* co-edits *Analog Game Studies,* and is an active role-playing games scholar.

John Vanderhoef is an assistant professor of emerging media at California State University Dominguez Hills. His research explores amateur and indie digital game production, media industries, residual media, and discourses around gender, sexuality, and race in media producing and consuming cultures. He has published work in *Television and New Media, Ada, Production Studies the Sequel,* and *The Routledge Companion to Video Game Studies.*

Emma Witkowski is a senior lecturer at RMIT University. Her research explores esports, media sports, and socio-phenomenological expressions of high-performance team play. She is a board member of the Australian Esports Association.

Mark J. P. Wolf is a professor in the Communication Department at Concordia University Wisconsin. He has written extensively about video games, publishing over a dozen books. His recent works on video games include *The Routledge Companion to Video Game Studies*, *LEGO Studies*, *Video Games Around the World*, the four-volume *Video Games and Gaming Culture*, and *Video Games FAQ*.

Index